P. 67

Metaphor is integral to _____
of thinking. The mind and everything
it does are in some way fictitious.

Blankets is the vehicle which is going
to be used to describe the way is
lying on the earth. Lying in the tenor
                          metaphied (metaphrat)
I think what Jaynes leaves out is the
part played by feeling.

"Kuijsten's fourth edited book on Jaynes is a marvel of collective scholarship across multiple disciplines. This book offers many perspectives on a proverbial elephant, Julian Jaynes's 1976 theory that a transition occurred around 1200 B.C. from gods speaking to us to humans speaking and thinking for themselves. Kuijsten has assembled 22 conversations with scholars about their ongoing inquiries into evidence for Jaynes theory: hearing voices, clinical hypnosis, the Bible as written record, cave art, mentality in ancient Tibet, evolution of Greek language in 'Homeric' authors, and consciousness in children. Jaynes had a gift for combining classics, psychology, psychiatry, religion, archeology, and anthropology. He smashes disciplinary silos and prompts dialogue in new areas of cognitive linguistics and rhetoric. One author broaches an anthropological theory of mind, wherein the more people accept that the mind is porous, 'the more voices and visions they reported.' Another chapter extends the work of I. A. Richards in exploring the use of language as metaphor to get things done. In this book, you will hear the voices of the most open-minded scholars of our generation."

— WILLIAM R. WOODWARD, Professor of Psychology,
University of New Hampshire, and author of
Hermann Lotze: An Intellectual Biography

"The word 'conscious' has become value-laden, making it harder to accept the limits of human consciousness. It's helpful to know that our brain is designed to do much of its work outside of conscious awareness. The better we understand this, the better we can allocate the scarce resource that consciousness is. *Conversations on Consciousness and the Bicameral Mind* helps us understand humanity's development of consciousness over millennia, as well as how we learn it in our first years of life."

— LORETTA GRAZIANO BREUNING, PH.D., author of
Habits of a Happy Brain, The Science of Positivity, and *Status Games*

Also from the Julian Jaynes Society

Gods, Voices, and the Bicameral Mind: The Theories of Julian Jaynes
edited by Marcel Kuijsten

The Julian Jaynes Collection
edited by Marcel Kuijsten

Reflections on the Dawn of Consciousness:
Julian Jaynes's Bicameral Mind Theory Revisited
edited by Marcel Kuijsten

The Minds of the Bible:
Speculations on the Cultural Evolution of Human Consciousness
by Rabbi James Cohn

Conversations on Consciousness and the Bicameral Mind

CONVERSATIONS ON CONSCIOUSNESS AND THE BICAMERAL MIND

INTERVIEWS WITH LEADING THINKERS ON JULIAN JAYNES'S THEORY

Edited by

Marcel Kuijsten

Julian Jaynes Society

First Julian Jaynes Society Hardcover Edition 2022

Library of Congress Cataloging-in-Publication Data

Kuijsten, Marcel
Conversations on Consciousness and the Bicameral Mind: Interviews with Leading Thinkers on Julian Jaynes's Theory
1. Consciousness. 2. Consciousness—History. 3. Psychology.
ISBN: 978-1-7373055-3-8 (hardcover)

Cover and interior design by Marcel Kuijsten

Julian Jaynes Society
Henderson, NV
julianjaynes.org

Printed in the United States of America and internationally

JJSSHD051822

Contents

Introduction: Julian Jaynes's Four Hypotheses on the Origin of Mind,
    Marcel Kuijsten   1
1. Julian Jaynes, the Bicameral Mind, and the Origin of Consciousness,   23
    Marcel Kuijsten

Hypothesis I:
Consciousness Based on Language

2. Consciousness and Language, *Marcel Kuijsten*   43
3. Julian Jaynes and the Features of Consciousness, *Brian J. McVeigh*   50
4. Metaphor and the Rhetorical Structuring of Consciousness, *Ted Remington*   60
5. The Development of Consciousness in Children, *Bill Rowe*   80
6. Julian Jaynes and Contemporary Philosophy of Mind, *Jan Sleutels*   90

Hypothesis II:
Bicameral Mentality

7. The Bicameral Mind Explained, *Marcel Kuijsten*   105
8. Vestiges of Bicameral Mentality, *Brian J. McVeigh*   120
9. Hearing Voices, Sensed Presences, and Imagined "Others," *Tanya Luhrmann*   130
10. Making Sense of Voices, *Marius Romme, Sandra Escher & Dirk Corstens*   153
11. Living with Voices, *Michel Knols*   163
12. A Vestige of the Bicameral Mind in the Modern World, *Elisabeth Bell Carroll*   169
13. Authorizing Clinical Hypnosis: From Bicameral Mentality to Autonomy,   178
    Laurence I. Sugarman
14. Consciousness, Hypnosis, and Free Will, *Edoardo Casiglia*   200
15. Hypnosis, Bicameral Mentality, and the Theory of Mind, *John F. Kihlstrom*   217

Hypothesis III:
Dating the Transition from Bicameral Mentality to Consciousness

16. Consciousness, Cave Art, and Dreams, *Marcel Kuijsten*   253
17. The Bible as a Written Record of the Dawn of Consciousness,   260
    Rabbi James Cohn
18. Evidence for Bicameral Mentality in the Bible, *Brian J. McVeigh*   274
19. Evidence for Bicameral Mentality in Ancient Tibet, *Todd Gibson*   291
20. The Evolution of Mental Language in the *Iliad* and the *Odyssey*,   297
    Boban Dedović

Hypothesis IV:
Jaynes's Neurological Model for Bicameral Mentality

21. New Evidence for Jaynes's Neurological Model, *Marcel Kuijsten*   317
22. Auditory Hallucinations and the Right Hemisphere,
    Iris E.C. Sommer & Sanne Brederoo   327
Epilogue   337
Appendix: Additional Discussion   341
Acknowledgments   363

Introduction:
Julian Jaynes's Four Hypotheses
on the Origin of Mind

Marcel Kuijsten

THE HISTORY OF IDEAS teaches us that new, paradigm-shifting theories typically face an uphill battle. Often they are initially rejected, then only gradually appreciated, with many details misunderstood. The concepts of plate tectonics and seafloor spreading were rejected (and often ridiculed) for decades. Glacial theory and the germ theory of disease were similarly dismissed. Many initially rejected Darwin's theory of the origin of species by natural selection, and a widespread misunderstanding of the details of this theory continues to this day. Serious applications of Darwin's theory to understanding human nature (beyond Darwin's own early efforts) took nearly 100 years to get underway — but eventually inspired entire new fields of study such as evolutionary psychology and human evolutionary biology.

This pattern of initial rejection, slow appreciation, and continual misunderstanding certainly applies to Julian Jaynes's theory of the origin of consciousness and a previous mentality he called the bicameral mind. In *The Origin of Consciousness in the Breakdown of the Bicameral Mind*, Jaynes, a psychologist who taught at Princeton for more than 25 years and served as the first Master of that university's Woodrow Wilson College, argued that consciousness, as we experience it today, is not an innate feature of the human mental apparatus but developed only relatively recently, emerging around the first millennium BCE in Greece, and somewhat earlier or later in other cultures. Prior to that, non-habitual behavior was guided by auditory hallucinations that were interpreted as the voices of leaders, dead ancestors, or the gods. Only later, through the development of metaphorical language and writing, did humans develop an inner mind-space that facilitated introspection and an inner dialogue.

The proposal was, to say the least, controversial. John Updike, reviewing the book in *The New Yorker*, wrote that "When Julian Jaynes...speculates that until late in the second millennium B.C. men had no consciousness but were automatically obeying the voices of gods, we are astounded but compelled to follow this remarkable thesis through all the corroborative evidence…" On the other hand, Ned Block, in the *Boston Globe*, asserted that "These claims, of course, are preposterous." Perhaps the most measured response came from Ernest Hilgard, a leading American psychologist:

> The bold hypothesis of the bicameral mind is an intellectual shock to the reader, but whether or not he ultimately accepts it he is forced to entertain it as a possibility. Even if he marshals arguments against it, he has to think about matters he has never thought of before, or, if he has thought of them, he must think about them in contexts and relationships that are strikingly new.

Now nearly half a century later, many consider Jaynes's theory to be one of the most important of the twentieth century — or the most important theory since Darwin's.[1] Others reject it, but often in a knee-jerk fashion without bothering to understand the details, or based on misconceptions rather than an accurate understanding of Jaynes's arguments.

The Importance of Jaynes's Theory

The tremendous importance of Jaynes's theory is easily defended. The Jaynesian paradigm attempts to provide a more accurate understanding of human history and the human condition, and people who understand the theory often come to see humanity in a completely different way. Author James Morriss proclaimed that Jaynesian psychology "could alter our view of consciousness, revise our conception of the history of mankind, and lay bare the human dilemma in all its existential wonder."[2]

Jaynes's discussion of the nature of consciousness brings tremendous clarity to the subject. Philosopher and consciousness theorist Daniel Dennett called it "one of the clearest and most perspicuous defenses of the top-down approach [to consciousness] that I have ever come across."[3] The psychologist and neuroscientist Michael Persinger noted that "Julian Jaynes's theories for

---

1. For example, John Gliedman noted, "If Jaynes's theories are right, he could become the Darwin of the mind" ("Julian Jaynes and the Ancient Mind-Gods," *Science Digest*, January 1982). Don Wooten wrote that Jaynes's theory "is the most important bit of theorizing since *The Origin of Species*." (*Quad-City Times*, Davenport, Iowa, July 1, 1990). For more reviews of Julian Jaynes's theory, see the Julian Jaynes Society website: julianjaynes.org.
2. James E. Morriss, "Reflections on Julian Jaynes's *The Origin of Consciousness in the Breakdown of the Bicameral Mind*: An Essay Review," *ETC: A Review of General Semantics*, 1978, 35, 3.
3. Daniel Dennett, *Brainchildren: Essays on Designing Minds* (MIT Press, 1998).

the nature of self-awareness, introspection, and consciousness have replaced the assumption of their almost ethereal uniqueness with explanations that could initiate the next change in paradigm for human thought."[4]

Jaynes's insight that consciousness — as he carefully defines it — is learned (and not biologically innate) raises exciting research questions. What is the exact process by which metaphorical language creates our inner mind-space? How can we explore developmental stages and cross-cultural differences in the linguistic development of consciousness? What are the precise differences between linguistic and non-linguistic thought? The trajectory of Jaynes's thesis leads to better ways to expand our capacity for conscious thought and to teach the features of consciousness more effectively to future generations.

Jaynes's theory provides explanations for a wide range of otherwise inexplicable historical and modern phenomena. For example, the proliferation of gods and idols throughout the ancient world; the emergence of oracles, prophets, omens, and divination; and the pyramids in Egypt and similar structures elsewhere. Hypnosis, hallucinations, "spirit possession," sensed presences, and children's imaginary companions are all informed by an understanding of Jaynesian psychology. Many of the strange psychological phenomena that have traditionally been ignored — or explained in a manner that is wholly unsatisfactory — suddenly begin to make sense when looked at through the lens of Jaynes's theory.

Jaynes did not set out to explain the origin of religion, but his bicameral mind theory offers perhaps the most convincing explanation for the origin of the belief in gods and religion — one of the great mysteries of human civilization. Jaynes theorized that prior to the development of subjective consciousness people had a bicameral mentality in which they heard voices guiding their behavior that they attributed to their leaders or to gods. As subjective consciousness developed and the voices were suppressed, the world's great religions took form from the anguish and nostalgia for the lost direct communication of the gods.[5] Whereas previous ideas on the subject have generally failed to account for all of the different aspects of both ancient and modern spirituality, Jaynes's theory offers a compelling

---

4. Michael Persinger, "Foreword," in M. Kuijsten (ed.), *Reflections on the Dawn of Consciousness* (Julian Jaynes Society, 2006).

5. The theory is recognized as possibly the best explanation for the origin of religion by the evolutionary biologist Richard Dawkins in *The God Delusion* (Mariner Books, 2006) and the late philosopher David Stove in "The Oracles and Their Cessation: A Tribute to Julian Jaynes" (*Encounter*, 1989, 72; reprinted in *Reflections on the Dawn of Consciousness*). See also Tanya Luhrmann's "Knowing God" (*The Cambridge Journal of Anthropology*, 2017, 35, 2) and her interview in this volume, "Hearing Voices, Sensed Presences, and Imagined 'Others'."

explanation for the origin of god beliefs that fits well with all of the socio-logical, archaeological, and neurological data.

Jaynes's theory renewed the modern study of hearing voices in otherwise normal populations.[6] Prior to Jaynes's book, the prevailing view was that auditory hallucinations were found only in the mentally ill. Yet hundreds of studies conducted over the past 40 years now show that hallucinations are found on a spectrum throughout societies worldwide. The theory offers a historical context for hearing voices — providing us with a radical new way of understanding mental illness from a socio-historical perspective. Jaynes's theory and the understanding that many more people hear voices than was previously known provided inspiration for the founding of the Hearing Voices Network, a support group for voice hearers that teaches coping strategies and works to destigmatize the voice hearing experience.[7]

Jaynes also proposed a neurological model for hearing voices — his ideas for what might be happening in the brain during auditory verbal hallucinations — that helped to inform future investigations.[8] Jaynes's ear-ly speculations have now been confirmed by numerous brain imaging and other studies, and the findings of right and left hemisphere language area involvement during auditory hallucinations are now being used to develop future non-pharmaceutical treatments for those with persistent, debilitat-ing voices that don't respond to medication.

Thomas Kuhn used "paradigm" to mean "universally recognized scien-tific achievements that, for a time, provide model problems and solutions for a community of practitioners."[9] It is hard to overemphasize the im-portance of Jaynes's theory, and his insights into the origin and nature of consciousness drive a paradigm shift that is often underappreciated, even among those who claim to understand it. The precise reasons for this are unclear, but likely involve some combination of personality characteristics

---

6. Jaynes's theory inspired the first influential modern investigation into hearing voices in a non-clini-cal population, "Auditory Hallucinations of Hearing Voices in 375 Normal Subjects," by the psycholo-gist Thomas Posey and then graduate student Mary E. Losch (*Imagination, Cognition and Personality*, 1983, 3, 2). Also inspired by Jaynes, the psychiatrist John Hamilton published "Auditory Hallucina-tions in Nonverbal Quadriplegics (*Psychiatry*, 1985, 48, 4). The claim that many individuals with no diagnosis of mental illness hear voices was provocative, and a flood of research investigating auditory hallucinations in a wide variety of non-clinical populations soon followed.

7. For more on the Hearing Voices Network and Jaynes's influence, see Marius Romme, Sandra Escher, and Dirk Corsten's interview in this volume, "Making Sense of Voices."

8. I.E.C. Sommer, *Language Lateralization in Schizophrenia* (Doctoral dissertation, University of Utrecht, 2004); K. Diederen and I.E.C. Sommer, "Auditory Verbal Hallucinations and Language Lat-eralization," in I.E.C. Sommer and R.S. Kahn (eds.), *Language Lateralization and Psychosis* (Cambridge University Press, 2009).

9. Thomas Kuhn, *The Structure of Scientific Revolutions* (University of Chicago Press, 1962/1996).

(such as openness to new ideas), a lack of understanding of one or more of Jaynes's arguments, waiting for other "experts" to weigh in before forming an opinion, and having previously formed beliefs that are challenged by Jaynes's theory. The ongoing significance of the theory to different fields of study and many aspects of modern life will be a point of emphasis in the interviews throughout this book.

Critiques & Misconceptions

Science progresses by rigorously evaluating new claims. Open-mindedness balanced with a healthy skepticism of new ideas is desirable. Judgment of new ideas ideally is withheld while evidence is accumulated, tested, and evaluated. When new discoveries build directly upon existing knowledge, the process generally works very well. The open-minded but critical evaluation of new ideas can delay the widespread acceptance of theories that are correct, but also serves the important function of guarding against the acceptance of false claims.

However, the process of evaluating new ideas is not always as rational as is generally believed. When it comes to truly original ideas that challenge long-held beliefs, reactions can more often be characterized as close-minded indignation. As noted by the British surgeon and philosopher Wilfred Trotter, "the human mind likes a strange idea as little as the body likes a strange protein and resists it with a similar energy."[10]

Objections to Jaynes's theory involve a number of factors. Jaynes's theory challenges conventional wisdom, and his insights result in part by connecting a seemingly unrelated pattern of evidence from a wide variety of fields. Holding all of the different pieces of the puzzle in mind can at times be difficult, especially after only one reading. When narrowly focused on one piece of evidence or another, Jaynes's theory may seem unconvincing. Similar to Darwin's theory of evolution, one must view the theory in the context of the overall pattern of evidence. The fact that the theory covers a range of topics that many people have little or no previous exposure to can also be a source of confusion. The unquestioned assumption that past cultures that looked similar to ours also shared our psychology presents another obstacle. Finally, historical evidence is often seen as speculative or open to interpretation, thus less convincing.

Although some critiques of Jaynes's theory have raised thoughtful issues, it can be stated confidently that the majority of objections are based

---

10. Quoted in William Beveridge, *The Art of Scientific Investigation* (W.W. Norton & Co., 1950).

on misconceptions or misrepresentations of Jaynes's arguments.[11] Primary among these is the failure to understand Jaynes's definition of consciousness. Jaynes's profound insights into the narrow scope of consciousness challenge our everyday assumption that consciousness is involved in all mentality. Thus readers often substitute their own (often erroneous) intuitions about consciousness for Jaynes's very precise definition, often without realizing it — an issue which I will address in more detail below. Misunderstandings or mischaracterizations of bicameral mentality are also not uncommon. These will be clarified in several of the interviews.

This is not to say that every aspect of Jaynes's theory has been resolved. Jaynes provided a foundation, but recognized that much more work would be required to build upon and further illuminate the many different aspects of his theory. A growing body of additional evidence has accumulated since the theory was first published, much of which will be described in the interviews that follow, but much more work is still necessary. All theories go through modifications over time, and vigorous debate based on facts is an essential part of the scientific process that helps theories evolve.

While the extent of the misconceptions surrounding Jaynes's theory may seem unusual, in reality, controversy and confusion over the details of most complex topics is common. There are many reasons for this and a full discussion is beyond the scope of this introduction.[12] Perhaps difficulties with the comprehension of new material are more widespread than is generally known. A cognitive bias known as the Dunning-Kruger Effect may also be involved: people are predisposed to believe that they have a deeper and wider understanding of topics than they actually do. Further, those new to a subject can fall prey to the problem that their perceived "facts" about a subject are actually based on falsehoods or incomplete information. It is difficult to know what one doesn't know, and understanding the limits of one's own knowledge is a skill that has to be developed and practiced.[13]

Outside of one's job, field of study, or area of expertise, there generally are no outside pressures — no tests, graded papers, performance reviews, input from peers, or consequences in general — to incentivize the accurate

---

11. Some of the most common misconceptions will be addressed in several of the interviews that follow. I have addressed many others on the Julian Jaynes Society website in the "Critiques & Responses" and "Myths vs. Facts" sections, where interested readers can evaluate them for themselves.

12. See Sara Dellantonio and Luigi Pastore, "Ignorance, Misconceptions and Critical Thinking," *Synthese*, 2021, 198 and Nils J. Nilsson *Understanding Beliefs* (MIT Press, 2014) for interesting ideas.

13. Jaynes makes a similar point about the limits of our ability to evaluate our own consciousness using an analogy of a flashlight in a dark room. Everywhere the flashlight turns, the room is brightly lit, so it remains unaware of the surrounding darkness. Similarly, because we cannot be conscious of things outside of our consciousness, we erroneously conclude that consciousness is involved in all mentality.

understanding of new material. So whether it is scholarly topics such as Darwin's theory of evolution or Jaynes's theory of the origin of consciousness, or more practical "everyday" subjects like what constitutes a healthy diet or an intelligent way to invest, seemingly endless misconceptions and non-evidence-based beliefs abound.

We have the illusion of arriving at our decisions and beliefs through thoughtful, conscious deliberation, yet experimental evidence suggests that they are often formed outside of consciousness[14] and subject to complex genetic predispositions.[15] Complicating things further, the beliefs we internalize are also often outside of our awareness — and thus can influence our thoughts and perceptions nonconsciously.[16] These nonconscious beliefs, often formed with little or no conscious consideration of evidence, can be powerful obstacles to understanding and accepting new ideas. Beliefs that are internalized in childhood and adolescence — either through our family, education, or the culture in which we are embedded — can be particularly difficult to both recognize and overcome.

So while we are often unaware of or unable to fully articulate our internalized beliefs, we can nonetheless be resistant to evidence that contradicts them. When confronted with new information, we are predisposed to defend our original conclusions and seek new information that confirms them, rather than modify our existing views.[17] In light of these significant challenges to the evaluation of new ideas, optimal reasoning requires a relentless focus on evidence as well as an ongoing effort to identify, analyze, and potentially modify our personal biases and long-held assumptions. Those formed early in life or those that are shared by the culture at large (but that are nonetheless flawed, irrational, unethical, or lacking in evidence) are of particular importance.[18]

---

14. Jonathan Evans and Keith Frankish, *In Two Minds: Dual Processes and Beyond* (Oxford University Press, 2009); Roy F. Baumeister, E.J. Masicampo, and Kathleen D. Vohs, "Do Conscious Thoughts Cause Behavior?" *Annual Review of Psychology*, 2011, 62.

15. L.J. Eaves, H.J. Eysenck, and N.G. Martin, *Genes, Culture, and Personality: An Empirical Approach* (Academic Press, 1989); Steven Pinker, *The Blank Slate: The Modern Denial of Human Nature* (Penguin, 2002).

16. See Joseph Weiss, "Unconscious Mental Functioning," *Scientific American*, 1990, 262, 3; Tim Crane, "Unconscious Belief and Conscious Thought," in U. Kriegel (ed.), *Phenomenal Intentionality* (Oxford University Press, 2013).

17. A cognitive bias known as the "confirmation bias." See Raymond S. Nickerson, "Confirmation Bias: A Ubiquitous Phenomenon in Many Guises," *Review of General Psychology*, 1998, 2, 2. For an excellent discussion of a wide range of nonconscious cognitive biases, see Daniel Kahneman, *Thinking Fast and Slow* (Penguin, 2011), which could have been titled "Thinking Nonconsciously and Consciously." Mercier and Sperber's *The Enigma of Reason* (Harvard University Press, 2017) and Sloman and Fernbach's *The Knowledge Illusion* (Riverhead Books, 2017) look at the problem of cognitive biases from the perspective of evolutionary psychology.

18. This exercise was first proposed by Francis Bacon, the "father of inductive reasoning," in his 1620

Critical thinking can further be enhanced by (1) developing the discipline to postpone judgment until such time as one has the opportunity to properly seek and evaluate a range of evidence from reliable, non-biased sources (rather than quickly jumping to conclusions or feeling compelled to offer an opinion on a topic one is unfamiliar with);[19] (2) remaining open to but impartial regarding topics that lack conclusive evidence (and not simply believing things that we would like to be true); (3) regularly exposing oneself to counterpoints or contradictory arguments; (4) maintaining the mental flexibility to revise one's views as new evidence becomes available; and (5) developing an awareness of the innate tribal instincts that nonconsciously compel us to identify strongly with one group or idea or another. Possessing above average intelligence may be helpful but is certainly not sufficient: many highly intelligent individuals display poor critical thinking skills, have difficulty integrating new information, and are surprisingly susceptible to irrational or non-evidence based ideas.

The ongoing objections to and misconceptions about Jaynes's theory serve as two of the inspirations for this book. It struck me that presenting ideas about Jaynes's theory in a conversational format may prove more accessible to many readers, and thus help facilitate a greater understanding of the theory. The Chicago-based filmmaker and Jaynes enthusiast Brendan Leahy conducted some of the interviews that follow (including interviews with me) for a potential documentary on the subject, which may still appear in some form. I conducted the remainder of the interviews over the course of the past year.

As noted by Michael Persinger, "the reflexive rejection of novel concepts is the antithesis of discovery."[20] The more that new ideas challenge existing beliefs, the greater the resistance they encounter, and thus the greater the evidence that is required. Jaynes's theory challenges a number of beliefs that are

---

book *Novum Organum Scientiarum* [New Instrument of Science]. Because of the largely unacknowledged role of underlying (and often nonconscious) premises and beliefs in opinion formation, intellectual discussion and debate is often unproductive when focused solely on facts and evidence. Underlying premises and beliefs must first be identified and addressed.

19. Just learning to identify reliable sources can initially be challenging. Whenever financial incentives come into play, deliberate deception becomes an additional source of confusion. For example, industry-funded "studies" should generally be treated as suspect until proven otherwise. One would similarly want to avoid making decisions relying solely on information from those who stand to profit from your decision, such as anyone in sales — including salespeople masquerading as "financial advisors." Apart from the corrupting influence of financial incentives, biases can also develop based simply on reputation or defending past work. This type of bias is often seen among academics, who rarely change their views on theories or ideologies that they are already heavily invested in, even in light of new evidence. Hence Max Planck's often quoted observation that "science progresses one funeral at a time."

20. Michael Persinger, "Foreword," in *Reflections on the Dawn of Consciousness*.

practically implicit in Western culture, such as that consciousness is involved in all mentality and that hearing voices is a relatively modern phenomenon, a symptom of mental illness, and limited to individuals with brain pathology. Groundbreaking theories such as Jaynes's require us to dispassionately reevaluate existing beliefs in light of new evidence — rather than have an emotionally-based reaction to things we perhaps don't yet fully understand. While this may sound like common sense, it is anything but common.

Consciousness Confusion

Most of the misconceptions about Jaynes's theory arise from confusion over how Jaynes defines consciousness, often substituting broad, vague definitions for Jaynes's narrow, more precise definition. Several interviews in this book discuss in detail Jaynes's definition of consciousness, but it is worth taking a moment here to address this topic.

Problems over precisely how to define consciousness are as old as consciousness itself. For example, Aristotle's discussion of the topic contains parallels to the modern debate over how to define it.[21] Jaynes defines consciousness in the manner following a long tradition of scholars, as "the contents of introspection":

> The basic connotative definition of consciousness is thus an analog 'I' narratizing in a functional mind-space. The denotative definition is, as it was for Descartes, Locke, and Hume, what is introspectable.[22]

The nineteenth-century philosopher and psychologist William James held similar views. He explores concepts such as the relationship of consciousness to the self and our ability to spatialize time, describing consciousness as a process that allows us to "consider the past, present, and future and to plan ahead in order to adapt our behavior to the current circumstances."[23]

While this was the predominately accepted view during the eighteenth and nineteenth centuries, confusion over the definition of consciousness was greatly exacerbated in the latter half of the twentieth century, as interest in consciousness grew and different groups and theorists began using the term in increasingly different — and often ill-defined — ways. Those

---

21. Victor Caston, "Aristotle on Consciousness," *Mind*, 2002, 111, 444.
22. Jaynes, *The Origin of Consciousness in the Breakdown of the Bicameral Mind*, p. 450. See also, Julian Jaynes, "McMaster-Bauer Symposium on Consciousness: Response to Discussants," *Canadian Psychology*, 1986, 27, 2; reprinted in M. Kuijsten (ed.), *The Julian Jaynes Collection* (Julian Jaynes Society, 2012).
23. William James, *The Principles of Psychology* (Henry Holt and Company, 1890); Morton Hunt, *The Story of Psychology* (Anchor Books, 1993).

in the medical field often define consciousness as simply a waking state, or not being unresponsive, fully anesthetized, or in a coma — the distinction that is most relevant to their profession. Many neuroscientists use consciousness in a similar manner, publishing articles claiming to measure or locate the "neurological correlates of consciousness" in the brain, while in reality typically only addressing areas involved in reactivity, attention, or a waking state. Talk of being "knocked unconscious" in sports like boxing furthers the perception among the general public that consciousness merely describes a waking state.

The popularization of Darwin's theory of evolution likely contributed to the widespread (but false) assumption that, much like gradual changes to the heritable characteristics of populations over generations, consciousness too is a biologically innate characteristic that evolved through the process of natural selection.[24] Adding to the confusion, many scholars who speak and write about consciousness fail to offer a precise definition, leaving their audience to read between the lines as to how they are using the term.

In recent decades, there has been a trend toward equating consciousness with vision and basic sense perception — the "experience of pain," for example — which are things we share with all non-human animals.[25] Prominent theorists write articles proclaiming that "consciousness doesn't depend on language" — then go on to suggest that consciousness is the experience of sense perception, a definition that is entirely different from the one used by those arguing for the necessity of language for consciousness.

Furthering our understanding of how the brain processes sensory information is foundational, but it is not investigating consciousness, unless we broaden the term so widely as to lose all useful meaning. As Jaynes points out, even white blood cells can respond and react to their environment. Do the proponents of a sensory perception view of consciousness really mean to imply that we have between 5 and 25 billion conscious beings circulating through our body at any given moment? Regardless of the answer, this has nothing to do with how Jaynes defines consciousness.

Centuries old and more esoteric definitions of consciousness have also been revived, with suggestions that consciousness is a "basic property of the universe," and that "everything is conscious" — a view known as

---

24. Christopher U. M. Smith, "Charles Darwin, the Origin of Consciousness, and Panpsychism," *Journal of the History of Biology*, 1978, 11, 2.
25. Jaynes points out that the British mathematician and philosopher Bertrand Russell was an early proponent of this misconception (*Origin*, p. 448). For a more recent example, see Francis Crick, *The Astonishing Hypothesis: The Scientific Search for the Soul* (Scribner, 1995). Crick seems to equate consciousness with visual perception, which we share with nearly all non-human animals.

panpsychism. The most we can say is that, again, these ideas simply have nothing to do with Jaynes's definition of consciousness. More critical evaluations suggest that these speculations descend into a form of neo-mysticism or non-scientific thinking.

Other uses of the word appear to be modern attempts to revive the concept of the soul using the more scientific-sounding "consciousness," packaged with vague references to higher dimensions and quantum mechanics that do more to obscure the subject than to clarify it.[26]

Still other scholars use consciousness to mean "the modern mind." This is, broadly speaking, similar to Jaynes's definition, but they often suggest that consciousness is much older, emerging sometime between 50,000 to 100,000 years ago. This dating is often the result of at least three assumptions: (1) that consciousness is biological (rather than learned), (2) that as human brains evolved over the millennia, consciousness simply "emerged" biologically at some point (without explanation), and (3) that consciousness is necessary for nearly every human behavior. Scholars point to tool use or cave art as signposts of the emergence of the modern mind. But the idea that consciousness in the Jaynesian sense is necessary for these behaviors is easily refuted.[27] More will be said about these topics in the interviews to follow.

One does not arbitrarily change the definitions of ingredients (freely substituting one for another) and then expect a recipe to have a successful outcome. Similarly, one cannot substitute a vague definition of consciousness for Jaynes's meticulous one, then hope to understand his arguments. Functions that are frequently assigned to consciousness by very broad definitions are more accurately relegated by Jaynes to reactivity (being awake and responsive to one's environment, but not conscious), sense perception, learning, and cognition. More recently, the term "phenomenal awareness" is sometimes used to describe the experience of sense perception, which helps to distinguish it from "conscious thought."

Understanding the importance of these distinctions is crucial to understanding Jaynes's theory.[28] Indeed, the entire field of consciousness studies

---

26. For more on this see Marcel Kuijsten, "Close-Mindedness and Mysticism in Science: Commentary on John Smythies's Review of *Reflections on the Dawn of Consciousness*," *The Jaynesian*, 2009, 3, 2.

27. Regarding cave art, see Julian Jaynes, "Paleolithic Cave Paintings As Eidetic Images," *Behavioral and Brain Sciences*, 1979, 2, 605-607 (reprinted in *The Julian Jaynes Collection*) and Nicholas Humphrey, "Cave Art, Autism, and the Evolution of the Human Mind," *Cambridge Archaeological Journal*, 1998, 8, 2. The mistaken assumption that consciousness emerged biologically sometime in human evolution also presents an obstacle to understanding Jaynes's arguments for bicameral mentality: if consciousness is 50,000 to 100,000 years old, then there is no need to take into account a different human mentality prior to consciousness.

28. Because Jaynes's insights are counterintuitive to the common assumption that consciousness is involved in all mentality — which is an illusion based on our everyday experience — I strongly encourage

is unlikely to make significant progress until the differences in conscious and nonconscious mental processes are more widely recognized, the use of more precise terminology for nonconscious processes (such as sense perception, learning, and nonconscious problem-solving) is widely adopted, and theorists no longer routinely use the term "consciousness" in vague and wildly different ways.[29] By way of analogy, the current state of affairs in the field of consciousness studies could be compared to the state of confusion that would arise if cooking courses and recipes referred to all of the various fruits and vegetables simply as "produce."

Finally, consciousness is best understood as a set of distinct features. In his chapter on consciousness, Jaynes describes six of these features: *spatialization, excerption, the analog 'I', the metaphor 'me', narratization*, and *conciliation*. In his Afterword, Jaynes describes two additional features: *concentration* and *suppression*. Jaynesian scholar Brian McVeigh has further clarified and added to this list.[30] These distinct features likely emerged over an extended period of time, at different times in different places, and with individual differences. Similarly, differences in the features of consciousness can still be observed in different individuals and cultures.

Given the conceptual and terminological confusion, scholars have suggested alternate terms for describing consciousness in the sense intended by Jaynes. These include "introspective consciousness," "subjective consciousness," "meta-consciousness," "self-awareness," "self-consciousness," and "conscious interiority," but widespread agreement is lacking. Different "types" and "levels" of consciousness have also been proposed. Based only on publication density, perhaps the leading contender is "self-consciousness," yet it faces the linguistic challenge of associations with social anxiety. Throughout this book, "Jaynesian consciousness," "subjective consciousness," and "interiority" can be considered synonymous with Jaynes's use of consciousness.

For those who adopt very broad (or vague) definitions — often lumping all mental activity under the umbrella term of "consciousness" — human mentality is generally viewed as being more or less unchanged for tens of

---

those interested in the theory to read the first two chapters and the Afterword of Jaynes's *The Origin of Consciousness in the Breakdown of the Bicameral Mind* several times, in order to gain a solid understanding of his discussion of this topic. Reading the discussions in *The Julian Jaynes Collection* will also greatly enhance one's understanding of the theory.

29. The field of chemistry underwent a similar much needed process of normalizing terminology and conventions during the nineteenth century. In *A Short History of Nearly Everything* (Broadway Books, 2003), Bill Bryson notes that prior to this, "there was hardly a molecule that was universally rendered everywhere."

30. See Brian J. McVeigh, *The 'Other' Psychology of Julian Jaynes: Ancient Languages, Sacred Visions, and Forgotten Mentalities* (Imprint Academic, 2018) and his interview in Part I of this volume.

thousands of years. For those who hold this view, more recent, profound changes in human psychology are generally minimized or ignored, and the fascinating psychological transition in recent human history that Jaynes identifies (along with all of its modern implications) remains an unexplored mystery. Proponents of broad definitions generally also overlook the variations of consciousness found in modern people — for example, cross-cultural differences in subjective consciousness; mental differences between linguistic and non-linguistic individuals, including infants and children prior to learning language; elderly individuals with advanced dementia; those in a vegetative state who nonetheless exhibit detectable signs of consciousness; and during altered states of consciousness such as hypnosis, "spirit possession," somnambulism, and those resulting from sensory deprivation or the ingestion of psychoactive substances. To put it another way, if consciousness is biologically innate and emerged between 50,000 to 100,000 years ago, what accounts for its ongoing variability and plasticity?

Understanding Jaynes's Theory: Four Hypotheses

Both before and after the publication of *The Origin of Consciousness in the Breakdown of the Bicameral Mind*, Julian Jaynes gave frequent lectures on his theory. In an effort to present his ideas in a format that would be easier to understand, in lectures as early as 1979 he began presenting his theory as four distinct hypotheses, each of which he claimed could stand or fall on its own.[31] Jaynes preferred presenting his ideas as a series of three to four lectures over the course of a week, often including separate sessions for group discussion, recognizing that his theory was too broad to convey in a single, one-hour lecture.[32]

In discussing Jaynes's theory over many years, I have also found it helpful to present the theory as four hypotheses. People new to the theory often have predictable initial objections that are usually articulated in the form of vague discomfort and often evidence confusion. Differentiating Jaynes's four main hypotheses helps bring the conversation into sharper focus, and, in some cases, helps people to realize that perhaps they misunderstand key points of Jaynes's theory.

---

31. See Julian Jaynes, "Four Hypotheses On The Origin of Mind," *Proceedings of the 9th International Wittgenstein Symposium*, 1985, 135-142 (reprinted in *The Julian Jaynes Collection*). Jaynes also describes his four hypotheses in the Afterword to his book, which appears in the 1990 and later editions.
32. Paul Grondahl, "A Pleasant Talk with Julian Jaynes," *The Trail* [Newsletter of the University of Puget Sound], March 26, 1980, 2, 18.

The present volume is also organized around Jaynes's four hypotheses. Four sections, corresponding to each of Jaynes's hypotheses, contain in-depth interviews that both expand upon and detail the latest thinking and research in support of each hypothesis. I will briefly introduce each of Jaynes's four hypotheses here, and will explain the relevance of the interviews in each section to Jaynes's hypotheses. While not all of the interviews correspond neatly with one hypothesis or another — some address multiple hypotheses — they each have a general, overriding theme that allowed for this type of organization. For those new to Jaynes's theory (or anyone who needs a refresher), the first interview provides an overview and explanation of the theory.

Hypothesis I: Consciousness Based on Language

Jaynes's first hypothesis is that consciousness, as he carefully defines it, developed through metaphorical language. Jaynes explains why consciousness is not biologically innate — why it does not simply arise from a certain level of brain complexity. Subjective consciousness, meaning our ability to introspect, or what Jaynes describes as "an analog 'I' narratizing in a mind-space" — is learned, and can only be learned when language develops to the point where metaphors of the physical world create an inner mental "space."

Jaynes was not the first to identify language as critical to higher forms of thought — ancient Greeks such as Aristotle explored these ideas, and in the modern era, the Russian psychologist Lev Vygotsky published *Thought and Language* in 1934, I.A. Richards stressed the importance of metaphor in *The Philosophy of Rhetoric* in 1936, and the Austrian-British philosopher Ludwig Wittgenstein wrote on consciousness and language in his 1953 *Philosophical Investigations*.[33] In the late 1970s, Jaynes not only revived this topic, he brilliantly elucidated the critical role of metaphorical language in developing key aspects of our inner mental life.

In the decades since Jaynes's book was published, the relationship between consciousness and language has been further explored in more general terms by a number of different philosophers, psychologists, and linguists. Cognitive scientist and linguist George Lakoff and philosopher Mark Johnson explored the importance of metaphor for thought in their popular 1980 book *Metaphors We Live By*.[34] Daniel Dennett, who spoke

---

33. For a comparison of the ideas of Jaynes and Wittgenstein, see Ralf Funke's lecture, "The Dangerous Metaphor: Wittgenstein and Jaynes and the Rise of Neobehaviorism" (Julian Jaynes Society, 2013).
34. For a comparison of Jaynes's ideas with those of Lakoff and Johnson, see Stanley A. Mulaik, "The Metaphoric Origins of Objectivity, Subjectivity, and Consciousness in the Direct Perception of Reality," *Philosophy of Science*, 1995, 62, 2 and Ted Remington's interview in this volume.

at a conference dedicated to Jaynes's theory, noted that "acquiring a human language (an oral or sign language) is a necessary precondition for consciousness."[35] The philosopher José Luis Bermúdez argues that "many cognitive abilities that have traditionally taken to be uniquely human are indeed unique to language-using humans."[36] The philosopher Peter Carruthers explores this topic in his 1996 book *Language, Thought, and Consciousness*. Psychologist Steven Pinker has written on the relationship between metaphorical language and thought for a popular audience in *The Stuff of Thought*, and the psychologists John Limber and Stanley Mulaik have both explored Jaynes's ideas in this area and compared his ideas to those of other theorists.[37]

In the first interview in this section, I elaborate on Jaynes's first hypothesis, explaining why language is essential for the development of Jaynesian consciousness, with discussion of children who don't learn language during the critical period for language acquisition. In the second interview, the anthropologist, mental health counselor, author, and Jaynesian scholar Brian McVeigh discusses the different features of Jaynesian consciousness, obstacles to understanding Jaynes's theory, the transition to consciousness in different cultures, and his own ongoing research into different aspects of the theory.

Next, rhetorician Ted Remington explains and clarifies Jaynes's discussion of how metaphorical language — specifically spatial metaphors of the physical world — is critical to the development of an inner "mind-space." Understanding the four components of metaphor that Jaynes identifies and why they are important is one of the more challenging sections in Jaynes's book, and Professor Remington does a wonderful job of explaining these difficult ideas in a manner that is easily understandable.

Bill Rowe discusses five behaviors shared between infant and caregiver that he suggests are related to the development of consciousness, including discussion of the concept of "theory of mind" and studies in child development that support Jaynes's idea that children learn consciousness as they learn language. In the last interview in this section, Dutch philosopher Jan Sleutels explains and refutes the critiques of Jaynes's theory by the philosopher Ned Block, discusses the concepts of "folk psychology" and "fringe

35. Daniel Dennett, in J. Brockman (ed.), *What We Believe but Cannot Prove: Today's Leading Thinkers on Science in the Age of Certainty* (Harper Perennial, 2006).
36. José Luis Bermúdez, "The Limits of Thinking Without Words," in J.L. Bermúdez, *Thinking Without Words* (Oxford University Press, 2003).
37. John Limber, "Language and Consciousness," in *Reflections on the Dawn of Consciousness*; Mulaik, "The Metaphoric Origins of Objectivity, Subjectivity, and Consciousness in the Direct Perception of Reality."

minds" in relation to Jaynes's theory, and explains Jaynes's definition of consciousness and how it relates to other theorists.

Hypothesis II: Bicameral Mentality

Jaynes's second hypothesis is that prior to the development of consciousness, humans operated under a previous mentality he called the bicameral mind. According to Jaynes, as humans developed language, the brain began to use language as an efficient method to transmit knowledge and experience from the non-dominant (usually right) hemisphere to the dominant (usually left) hemisphere.[38] This often took the form of a language-based command, or what we would today call an auditory hallucination. Bicameral people lacked an inner mind-space to introspect, so in stressful or non-habitual situations they would hear a commanding voice instructing their behavior.

We now know that hallucinations are found on a spectrum throughout societies worldwide, in both normal people as well as those with diagnoses of mental illness. Commanding voices that direct behavior, similar to those described by Jaynes in bicameral cultures, are still heard today by individuals diagnosed with schizophrenia, and voices that comment on or direct behavior are also heard by many "normal" people who present no clinical disorders. Archaeological and anthropological evidence for bicameral mentality in ancient China and Tibet has been found by scholars such as Michael Carr and Todd Gibson.[39] Much more is said about these topics, along with many others, in the interviews in this section.

In the first interview, I discuss how Jaynes believes the bicameral mentality evolved, how it likely worked, and some of the different lines of supporting evidence. Brian McVeigh then discusses the evidence for bicameral mentality in East Asia; cross-cultural evidence for vestiges of bicameral mentality such as spirit possession; modern changes to the human psyche; and evidence for bicameral mentality in ancient religions, the Bible, and in ancient Egypt.

In the following interview, Stanford University anthropologist Tanya Luhrmann discusses her ongoing research into a number of fascinating topics, many of which could be characterized by Jaynesians as "vestiges

---

38. My discussion here assumes a right-handed person, for sake of simplicity. The term "dominant" refers to the dominant hemisphere for language, or the hemisphere where language is primarily processed in a given individual. In left handed people, hemisphere dominance for language is often mixed or reversed.
39. Michael Carr, "The *Shi* 'Corpse/Personator' Ceremony in Early China," in *Reflections on the Dawn of Consciousness*; Todd Gibson, "Souls, Gods, Kings, and Mountains," and "Listening for Ancient Voices," in M. Kuijsten (ed.), *Gods, Voices, and the Bicameral Mind* (Julian Jaynes Society, 2016).

of the bicameral mind" — such as cross-cultural studies of hearing voices and "command hallucinations," hearing voices in homeless populations,
the experience of having an "imagined other," hearing the voice of God
and speaking in tongues in Evangelical groups, voices and visions as the
basis of modern religions, and cultural differences in theory of mind.

In the next interview, Dutch psychiatrists Marius Romme and Dirk Corstens and the late mental health advocate Sandra Escher describe the nature of the voice hearing experience, their many years of clinical experience
working with voice hearers, and strategies for learning to live with voices.
Michel Knols and the author Elisabeth Bell Carroll then discuss their own
experiences with hearing voices and, in Carroll's case, seeing visions.

Next, research professor, pediatrician, and hypnosis scholar Laurence
Sugarman discusses his insights into nonconscious learning, the nature of
autism, hypnosis as a vestige of bicameral mentality, placebo effects, and
the role of external authorization in both hypnosis specifically and society
in general. The University of Padova professor, cardiologist, anthropologist,
and hypnosis expert Edoardo Casiglia then discusses his research into the
historical evidence for bicameral mentality, voice hearing in ancient history,
the relationship between language and consciousness, hypnosis as a vestige
of bicameral mentality, and the nature of free will. The final interview in
this section is my wide-ranging discussion with the psychologist John Kihlstrom. We discuss his many years of research into nonconscious perception
and learning, the nature of the self and its relationship to consciousness,
the nature of hypnosis, parallels between bicameral mentality and hypnosis, theory of mind, and his course on consciousness, in which he taught
Jaynes's theory of consciousness and others to students.

Hypothesis III: Dating the Transition from Bicameral Mentality to Consciousness

Jaynes's third hypothesis dates the transition from bicameral mentality to
consciousness to roughly 1500 to 1200 BCE in Egypt, Greece, Mesopotamia,
and ancient Israel. The transition is documented by Jaynesian scholars to
have taken place during the same time period in China,[40] but likely trans-
pired later in the Americas and in isolated locations such as Easter Island.[41]

To arrive at his dating, Jaynes draws upon a number of different lines of
evidence. For example, Jaynes documents the linguistic evolution of words
such as *noos* in ancient Greek, that first referred to the physical body or to

---

40. See Michael Carr, "The *Shi* 'Corpse/Personator' Ceremony in Early China."
41. Ferren MacIntyre, "Talking Moai?" *Rapa Nui Journal*, 1999, 13, 4.

visual perception, but later came to mean "conscious mind." Jaynes argues that the evolving meaning of the words can be used to date the corresponding development of consciousness, as the ancient Greeks' introduction of mind-related words tracked their changing psychology.

Jaynes also analyzes ancient texts, finding that, in the *Iliad* for example, there is no evidence for subjective consciousness in the older layers (modifications to the *Iliad* are thought to have occurred over a span of hundreds of years, from the time period the epic reflects to the oldest surviving written versions).[42] The story is completely action-oriented, and in the place of introspection, a god appears and commands the characters' behaviors. In contrast, the *Odyssey*, which reflects a more recent mentality, is replete with introspection and deception. Jaynes also studied the evidence for the changing relationship of people to the gods. Initially the gods were ever-present, then later appeared to have departed as their bicameral voices grew distant. As the bicameral voices faded, Jaynes describes a number of entirely new behaviors that emerged as an attempt to regain contact with the gods, such as oracles, omens, divination, prophesy, and prayer.

Recent studies have offered further evidence for Jaynes's arguments that mental language both evolved and increased in frequency over time.[43] Furthermore, the evolution of mental language and the transition from bicameral mentality to consciousness has been further documented by a number of scholars in other ancient texts, including the Bible.[44] The psychologist Martin Seligman contrasts the lack of personal agency in the *Iliad* with an increasing sense of agency in the *Odyssey* and later works.[45]

In the first interview in this section, I explain evidence for dating the transition from bicameral mentality to consciousness from the perspective of cave art and dreams. Brendan Leahy then interviews the late Biblical scholar Rabbi James Cohn on his research on the Bible, particularly the Old Testament, as a written record of the transition from bicameral mentality to consciousness, and some of the challenges inherent in dating and translating ancient texts. Next, I interview Brian McVeigh on his research, which also looks at the Bible as a source of historical evidence

---

42. Steve Reece, "Homer's *Iliad* and *Odyssey*: From Oral Performance to Written Text," in M.C. Amodio (ed.), *New Directions in Oral Theory* (Center for Medieval and Renaissance Studies, 2005).
43. See, for example, Carlos Diuk, et al., "A Quantitative Philology of Introspection," *Frontiers in Integrative Neuroscience*, September 2012; Boban Dedović, "'Minds' in 'Homer': A Quantitative Psycholinguistic Comparison of the *Iliad* and *Odyssey*," *PsyArXiv Preprints*, 2021.
44. See James Cohn, *The Minds of the Bible* (Julian Jaynes Society, 2013); Brian J. McVeigh, *The Psychology of the Bible* (Imprint Academic, 2020); Jonathan Bernier, "The Consciousness of John's Gospel," *The Bible and Critical Theory*, 2010, 6, 2.
45. Martin Seligman, "Agency in Greco-Roman Philosophy," *The Journal of Positive Psychology*, 2021, 16, 1.

for bicameral mentality, discussing key traits of bicameral civilizations, the concept of "super-religiosity," evidence for the breakdown of the bicameral mind, the importance of poetry and music, the changing nature of Yahweh, and a number of other related topics.

The scholar of Tibetan studies Todd Gibson then discusses his research on the transition from bicameral mentality to consciousness in ancient Tibet; an evolution of mental language similar to what Jaynes describes in Greece; vestiges of bicameral mentality such as oracles, shaman, and spirit guides; and the connections between Jaynesian consciousness and Buddhism. In the final interview in this section, Boban Dedović discusses his research into the evolution of mental language in the *Iliad* and the *Odyssey,* including the concept of oral poetry, how the works are dated by scholars, Jaynes's "preconscious hypostases" and their different phases, and the methodology and conclusions of his research.

Hypothesis IV: Jaynes's Neurological Model for Bicameral Mentality

Jaynes's fourth hypothesis is his neurological model for bicameral mentality. It is what he posited might be taking place in the brain as it creates bicameral hallucinations. Jaynes wondered if auditory verbal hallucinations are generated in the language areas of the non-dominant hemisphere. Do they then travel across the interhemispheric bridge (corpus callosum) to be "heard" by the language areas of the dominant hemisphere?

In the early 1970s, the technology was not yet available to provide conclusive evidence to support his hypothesis, which Jaynes came to by deduction: if we have most of our language ability associated with the linguistic areas in the left hemisphere, and if auditory verbal hallucinations are of a linguistic nature, then perhaps they are generated in the corresponding areas of the right hemisphere. Traveling across the corpus callosum, they are then "heard" in the language areas of the left hemisphere. This made intuitive sense because these are the only areas of the brain believed to be capable of generating speech and understanding language.

This auditory-linguistic hypothesis is also informed by what we know about right hemispheric activity, which includes recognizing patterns, developing relationships, and meta-processing — functions that are similar in nature to the content of the voices. Further evidence for this part of the hypothesis comes from studies of brain stimulation during surgery: stimulation of the right temporal lobe elicits bicameral-like auditory hallucinations.[46]

---

46. Wilder Penfield and Phanor Perot, "The Brain's Record of Auditory and Visual Experience: A

Throughout the 1980s, studies occasionally appeared hinting that Jaynes's theory was worthy of further examination. But just two years after Jaynes's death in 1997, data generated with the emergence of neuroimaging technology strongly supported Jaynes's neurological model. A groundbreaking study by the British psychiatrist Belinda Lennox (then at the University of Nottingham, now a professor in the psychiatry department at the University of Oxford), showed that activation of hallucinations started in "the right middle temporal gyrus and then extended to a wider area of the right superior temporal and left superior temporal gyri (where the hallucination is 'heard'), right middle and inferior frontal gyri, right anterior cingulate, and right cuncus."[47] The data supporting this conclusion was obtained by brain imaging of a 26-year-old man who pressed a button to indicate the onset of a hallucination. These results were strikingly similar to Jaynes's predictions, and numerous other studies showing similar results soon followed.

The significance of Lennox's study for Jaynes's theory was noted by the psychiatrist Leo Sher in the *Journal of Psychiatry and Neuroscience* and Robert Olin, a professor of medicine, in *The Lancet*, who wrote that "neuroimaging techniques of today have illuminated and confirmed the importance of Jaynes' hypothesis."[48] More recently, the clinical neurologist Andrea Cavanna and the neuroscientist Andrea Nani stated that Jaynes's hypothesis "is consistent with the findings from recent neuroimaging studies, which identified the right temporal lobe as the source of auditory hallucinations in patients with schizophrenia."[49]

In my interview with Brendan Leahy, which starts off this section, I review some of the many studies that have emerged over the past three decades that provide a great deal of supporting evidence for Jaynes's neurological model. These studies use a variety of different technologies to explore the neurology of auditory hallucinations. I also discuss related lines of evidence, such as studies of language lateralization and auditory hallucinations, temporal lobe epilepsy and auditory hallucinations, and insights into Jaynes's neurological model that can be gleaned from split-brain experiments and hemispherectomy patients.

Final Summary and Discussion," *Brain*, 1963, 86, 595–702.

47. Belinda Lennox, et al., "Spatial and Temporal Mapping of Neural Activity Associated with Auditory Hallucinations," *Lancet*, 1999, 353, 644.

48. Leo Sher, "Neuroimaging, Auditory Hallucinations, and The Bicameral Mind," *Journal of Psychiatry and Neuroscience*, 2000, 25, 3; Robert Olin, "Auditory Hallucinations and the Bicameral Mind," *Lancet*, 1999, 354, 9173.

49. Andrea E. Cavanna and Andrea Nani, *Consciousness: Theories in Neuroscience and Philosophy of Mind* (Springer, 2014).

In the final interview, the Dutch psychiatrist and neuroscientist Iris Sommer — one of the world's foremost researchers into the neurology of auditory hallucinations — and her post-doctoral student Sanne Brederoo describe the results of their fascinating research. Professor Sommer's lab has done a number of different studies using fMRI (functional magnetic resonance imaging) technology to investigate the origin of auditory hallucinations in the brain, suggested factors that may give voice hearers the perception that their hallucinated voices are not their own, and explored potential non-invasive treatments for those suffering from auditory hallucinations that do not respond to medication.

Understanding Jaynes's Four Hypotheses

One of the key aspects of understanding Jaynes's theory through his four hypotheses is that each hypothesis is independent of the others and thus each hypothesis can stand or fall on its own. Consciousness, as Jaynes defines it, can be based on metaphorical language, whether or not it was preceded by bicameral mentality. Bicameral mentality could have preceded consciousness, even if Jaynes's neurological model for bicameral mentality turns out to be incorrect. Similarly, consciousness could be based on language, preceded by bicameral mentality, and the neurological model correct, even if Jaynes's dating for the transition from bicameral mentality to consciousness is discovered to be in need of modification.

The evidence for each of these four hypotheses is also fairly separate and distinct. It follows that one can accept one or more of Jaynes's hypotheses without accepting all of them. Presenting and discussing Jaynes's ideas in this way helps get away from the simplistic, binary, "either/or" type of thinking that tends to dominate so many discussions.

One final point of clarification is necessary. There is some confusion over the somewhat subtle distinctions between Jaynes's second and fourth hypotheses. Jaynes maintained that the bicameral mind is a psychological hypothesis having to do with a "god-side" commanding a "person-side," neither of which was conscious in the Jaynesian sense. This could have been based on the language areas of the brain's two hemispheres (his neurological model), or it could have been based on something else. The technology was simply not yet available to offer a definitive conclusion.

The term Jaynes chose to describe this phenomenon — "bicameral," meaning "two-chambered" — nevertheless furthered the idea that bicameral mentality was not just a psychological hypothesis but also a neurological hypothesis, based on the brain's two hemispheres operating more independently than they do today. His chapter "The Double Brain," which explains his neurological model for bicameral mentality, furthered this perception.

Yet Jaynes preferred to keep the bicameral mind hypothesis and the neurological model hypothesis distinct, so each could be evaluated separately on the merits of their respective evidence. In his Afterword, which appears in the 1990 and later editions, Jaynes makes this point clear:

> The two hemispheres of the brain are not the bicameral mind but its present neurological model. The bicameral mind is an ancient mentality demonstrated in the literature and artifacts of antiquity.[50]

Yet this somewhat subtle distinction is not recognized by many people — both proponents and skeptics of the theory.

At this point, because of advances in our understanding of the brain that support Jaynes's neurological model — as will be explained in the interviews in Part IV of the book — it is perhaps no longer important to keep these two hypotheses distinct. One could argue that it is now easier to think of bicameral mentality as one hypothesis, with both psychological and neurological components, rather than a psychological hypothesis with a separate, neurological explanation.

For those new to Jaynes's theory, the first interview provides an introduction to his ideas. I would, however, encourage anyone interested in a deep understanding of the theory to also read Jaynes's *The Origin of Consciousness in the Breakdown of the Bicameral Mind*. The Julian Jaynes Society has published four additional books that I recommend: *Gods, Voices, and the Bicameral Mind*; *The Julian Jaynes Collection*; *Reflections on the Dawn of Consciousness*; and *The Minds of the Bible*. Brian McVeigh has published additional related books, which will be described in some of the interviews that follow. Finally, I encourage you to visit julianjaynes.org, the Julian Jaynes Society website, where you can post questions and interact with others interested in Jaynes's theory, as well as access our Member Area, which contains many more resources, including articles, interviews, audio and video lectures by Julian Jaynes, and lectures on Jaynes's theory by other scholars.

---

50. Jaynes, *The Origin of Consciousness in the Breakdown of the Bicameral Mind*, p. 456.

1

Julian Jaynes, the Bicameral Mind, and the Origin of Consciousness

Marcel Kuijsten

Interviewed by Henrik Palmgren

Marcel Kuijsten is the Founder and Executive Director of the Julian Jaynes Society. He has bachelor's degrees in Psychology and English and a master's degree in Business Administration from the University of Nevada, Las Vegas. He has designed, edited, and published four books on Julian Jaynes's theory: the current volume, *Gods, Voices, and the Bicameral Mind: The Theories of Julian Jaynes*, *The Julian Jaynes Collection*, and *Reflections on the Dawn of Consciousness: Julian Jaynes's Bicameral Mind Theory Revisited*. He has spoken on Jaynes's theory at numerous conferences and he has been interviewed for many books, articles, podcasts, and radio programs, including the BBC's "The Why Factor." In 2013, he co-chaired (with Rabbi James Cohn) the Julian Jaynes Society Conference on Consciousness and Bicameral Studies — the largest conference ever held on Jaynes's theory.

HENRIK PALMGREN: All right, good day, and welcome. A warm welcome. If you are a regular listener, you will know that we have brought up the idea about the bicameral mind many times on this program. You have probably heard it in passing by other guests and researchers and you have probably heard the name Julian Jaynes as well. Well, we have invited Marcel Kuijsten on the program today, who is the Founder and Executive Director of the Julian Jaynes Society.

Their website is julianjaynes.org, where you can go to find out more information not only about Julian Jaynes but also about the Society itself, the books and the material that they offer in regards to Julian Jaynes's research and work. As you might know, he passed away back in 1997 — November 21st to be exact — when he suffered from a fatal stroke. We are going to talk more about Julian Jaynes later, we are obviously going to break down, as it were, the theory of the breakdown of the bicameral mind. But we are also going to talk about the book that Marcel has published titled *Reflections on the Dawn of Consciousness: Julian Jaynes's Bicameral Mind Theory Revisited.* That will be very interesting to talk about as well, so we have much to go through here. I also want to mention Marcel's own website, which is marcelkuijsten.com. So with that, welcome Marcel, it's fantastic to have you aboard today, thank you for coming on the program.

MARCEL KUIJSTEN: Thank you for having me.

PALMGREN: Before we go into Julian Jaynes and talk about him and his main theory, and present this idea to our listeners, why don't you just mention a little bit about yourself, your background, and also when you got involved in the work of Julian Jaynes, Marcel?

KUIJSTEN: My background is in psychology and I was working towards attending a doctoral program in neuroscience, but along the way I decided not to go into academia. I discovered Julian Jaynes's book in the early nineties and I was very interested in it, but like many other people, I didn't know where to go with it other than just being very interested — at the time there weren't many follow-up publications or organizations that one could get involved with.

So I had this interest in the back of my mind for a number of years, and at one point I wrote an essay about the theory for a psychology class, which I posted online — as the internet was just getting underway at that time in terms of mass adoption — and I was amazed to receive e-mails about the essay from people all over the world.

I discovered that many people around the world were very interested in Jaynes's ideas, but often they didn't have anyone else to discuss them with. Based on that interest, I decided to start a website dedicated to the theory. Shortly thereafter, I discovered that Jaynes had died, and I founded the Julian Jaynes Society in order to promote and expand upon his work. So that's how everything got started.

PALMGREN: So Jaynes's only book, *The Origin of Consciousness in the Breakdown of the Bicameral Mind*, is actually composed of three books in one. But he had planned books four and five, to be completed later on, but he never published that second volume, did he? To kind of finish off the theory, if you will?

KUIJSTEN: The follow-up book that he had planned was never published, and we spent quite a bit of time attempting to locate those writings. Eventually we learned that the second book was never completed — although there are several chapters. He wrote chapters on dreams, child development, and pre-literate societies. They are not available yet, but we are working on getting those published — along with additional commentaries — in the near future. But yes, unfortunately there is no completed second book, which he had tentatively titled *The Consequences of Consciousness*. Jaynes did add an Afterword to his book in 1990, however, and he includes some of his ideas on the consequences of consciousness there, and also provides further clarification of his theory.

PALMGREN: So was there anything in particular about Jaynes's theory that really drew you in? Had you ever come across anything like that before in terms of psychology studies or similar fields of research?

KUIJSTEN: I had always been interested in many of the non-mainstream aspects of psychology, so to speak — things like the nature of consciousness, hypnosis, fugue states, and dissociative disorders were fascinating to me. Since I already had an interest in a lot of the ground that Jaynes covers, when I read his book it had a profound impact on me. He was covering so much material that I was already interested in, and he was addressing it in ways that I thought were better than anything I had seen before.

Another topic that Jaynes delves into is the origin of religion, and ever since childhood, that is something that had always been in the back of my mind as one of the greatest mysteries of human civilization. His explanation for the origin of gods and religion — and maybe we will touch on that later — also struck me as better than anything else I had read on the subject.

So for a variety of reasons his book had a big impact on me. I had already done a lot of reading by that time, but I felt that Jaynes provided far better explanations for many of the somewhat mysterious phenomena in psychology, anthropology, and sociology than anything I had come across.

PALMGREN: Let's talk a little bit about Julian Jaynes, and then we can dive into the main theory. Perhaps you can give our listeners an overview of the theory and maybe talk about the term "bicameral" itself — what that means. It's dual chambers — that's the way I interpret it. But can you tell us your thoughts on that, and give us a summary of Jaynes's theory?

KUIJSTEN: Julian Jaynes taught at Princeton University in the Psychology Department for more than 25 years, and from a very early age he was interested in the nature and origin of consciousness. He came to define it very specifically as "introspectable mind-space" — so that which is introspectable. I think the definition of consciousness — which we will discuss — is something that is one of the problems today in consciousness studies — the term is used very differently by many different theorists. Often when people debate the nature of consciousness, they each define it in such different ways that they are essentially talking past each other.

PALMGREN: Yes.

KUIJSTEN: For Jaynes — and of course his precise definition of consciousness goes into much more depth, but to sum it up briefly — it's "that which is introspectable." Jaynes had thought about this problem of consciousness for many years, actually since childhood. In the beginning he started by doing experiments in the lab on learning in different types of animals. He pursued many different paths that he later came to see as incorrect, for example associating consciousness with learning and things of that nature.

Later, as his thinking on the subject progressed, he realized that consciousness had to be based on language, and specifically metaphorical language. Developing an introspectable mind-space is a process that is learned through metaphors of the physical world, and then taught to each successive generation. So it would then follow that only humans have consciousness, as Jaynes defines it, where one can introspect, see one's life on a timeline — reflecting on the past, planning for the future — visualize oneself in other situations, and have an interior dialogue going on in one's mind where decisions can be deliberated.

PALMGREN: Yes, and the question arises, and that Jaynes poses himself, is this idea of where consciousness comes from. How can it spring up in a world of matter, so to speak, and how can this externally perceived world be reflected upon internally — inside ourselves? Perhaps you can elaborate a little bit on that idea?

KUIJSTEN: Yes. Let's start by talking about what consciousness is for Jaynes, because I think it's critical to understanding the rest of his theory. Very often, if someone is learning about Jaynes's theory, but for whatever reason has not fully understood Jaynes's definition of consciousness, they often will reject it because they are thinking of consciousness as something other than how Jaynes defines it. In other words, they are trying to make sense of Jaynes's theory using their own, usually much broader definition of consciousness, rather than Jaynes's more narrow — and I think far more precise — definition.

So first of all, consciousness, as Jaynes defines it, is built up through metaphorical language — it's not a biological trait or evolutionarily-based characteristic. It's a learned process. Consciousness is learned by each successive generation through language, and taught to children by their parents and their culture in a process that now occurs very naturally, such that it's not something that we are aware of or that we think about.

But Jaynes stressed that this process was not a given. One could, for example, take a child from modern society and place them in an ancient bicameral civilization, and they would not develop subjective consciousness in that society. Whereas on the other hand, a child taken from an ancient bicameral civilization and raised among modern, conscious people today would learn consciousness.

This has been a point of misunderstanding: people think that the change in mentality that Jaynes describes — from a pre-conscious mentality to a conscious mentality — they think that it was a biological change, that it had to involve changes to the biological structure of the brain, but that's simply not the case. Culturally-based psychological changes and new skills can alter the way our existing brain functions, and decades of research into what is called brain plasticity have now demonstrated that conclusively.

In his book, Jaynes helps bring clarity to our understanding of consciousness by first explaining all of the things that conscious is not. And the first thing he explains is that it is not all mentality — it's not the sum total of all mental functioning. We now know that a great deal of our cognitive processing goes on outside of conscious awareness — most of it, in fact, is nonconscious. Consciousness is not basic sense perception, which we share with all animals. So you are not, for example, conscious of the bodily sensations of the chair that you are sitting on right now. Things like balance, motor control, the perceptual adjustments that the brain makes to account for distance, etc. — all of these things happen without consciousness.

Those that equate the experience of sense perception with consciousness, and don't take the time to understand Jaynes's definition, are simply not going to understand the rest of Jaynes's theory. That's why it is so important to understand Jaynes's definition first. If we are defining consciousness as the experience of sense perception, then really all living things are conscious — all animals and even insects that can also certainly perceive and react to their environment. Jaynes points out that, by this definition, even white blood cells would have to be considered conscious, as they are able to navigate their environment and identify and respond to foreign bacteria and viruses.

Jaynes's second point is that consciousness is not a copy of all experience. That was something that was a popular idea in the past — that the mind is like a recording device. But in fact, if you think about a memory you might have, often you will see yourself from a third-person perspective or from a bird's eye view. Jaynes uses the example of swimming. You generally don't have a precise memory of the sensations of yourself in the water from a first-person perspective. For some reason this third person perspective is particularly true of embarrassing memories. You generally see yourself as if you're an observer, which is something that you never actually experienced.

Thirdly — and this is important — consciousness is not necessary for learning. In fact, most learning takes place without consciousness. Jaynes provides examples such as Pavlovian conditioning and operant conditioning. But if we think about our own life, as we improve on skills like typing, playing tennis, or learning a musical instrument — most of the improvements happen completely outside of conscious awareness. So consciousness is not necessary for learning.

The fourth thing, which is a little harder to understand, is that while sometimes consciousness is involved in thinking and reasoning, often it's unnecessary. You can come to conclusions without introspection, just through nonconscious processes. A simple example Jaynes provides is an experiment where people were asked to pick up two weights, one in each hand, and then try to determine which one is heavier. The solution, or the judgment of which weight is heavier, comes instantly — the process of how you arrive at your conclusion is not something that you can have any insight into, it's not something that is amenable to introspection. And while this is a simple example, even more complex ideas come to us quite automatically.

Another example Jaynes provides is to look at a series of figures — a circle, a triangle, another circle, etc. — and then you are asked, "What's the next figure in the series?" You simply know the answer instantly, it's not something that you are able to deliberate on. Yet you have nonconsciously engaged in some type of process of thinking and reasoning.

Jaynes also relates anecdotes of scientists and mathematicians who describe sudden epiphanies while working on a difficult problem. After a period of incubation, often overnight, the next day while taking a walk, shaving, or engaged in some unrelated activity — when they are not actively thinking about the problem at all — suddenly the solution will come to them in a flash of insight. The solution to the problem was worked out nonconsciously.

So in this way, problem solving and thinking and reasoning can happen without consciousness — although in the case of the scientists, perhaps consciousness was used to set up the problem, the solution came without consciousness. Jaynes also points out that things like speaking and understanding speech all happen nonconsciously — you form an idea, and then the words just come to you. You can't introspect upon how you arrive at certain words.

So we are now reaching an understanding that we can have a human culture that is intelligent, social, has basic language, and can learn and solve problems, but yet does not have subjective consciousness — that lacks an analog 'I' narratizing in a mind-space. It's important to first understand these concepts before we then talk about ancient civilizations not having consciousness. There is a misconception that Jaynes was describing some type of "zombie-like" people, but of course that is not at all the case. Prior to the development of what we might call "Jaynesian consciousness," people were social, they had basic language, they were intelligent — all that was lacking was the ability to introspect, and of course, everything that comes with that.

In fact, you might think of your own life, perhaps in the morning driving to work, and arriving at your destination and not having any real awareness of the act of driving or the route that you took, especially if your consciousness was focused on some issue in your life that is troubling you, or maybe a phone conversation that took place. The key point is that through a combination of habit, routine, instinct, and nonconscious problem-solving, people can accomplish a great deal without consciousness ever being involved. And of course all non-human animal behavior is nonconscious, by Jaynes's definition.

PALMGREN: So consciousness was learned through our ability to form language? Jaynes suggests that ancient civilizations had various writing systems and such, but they did not have the same level of consciousness that we have today, is that right? How exactly then does Jaynes define consciousness and when did it emerge?

KUIJSTEN: Yes, so if consciousness is not necessary for these things that I've just described, then what is consciousness? And how did it come about? And here Jaynes offers a more technical explanation, that I would encourage people to read in his book, but in a nutshell what he describes is that through metaphors of the physical world, we create a metaphorical "inner space," or mind-space, that does not actually have a location. We think about consciousness as being located in our head, and of course at the most fundamental level it is based on brain activity, but it does not have an actual physical location. Jaynes describes it as being "an operator, not a thing," similar to mathematics.

Consciousness is built up through describing mental events that are based on metaphors of things we do behaviorally. When you "see" the solution to a problem — "seeing" something in your mind — it builds up associations of the inner space of consciousness, all based first on the metaphor of the physical act of "seeing" — of visual perception. Jaynes goes through a much more detailed explanation of this process in his book.

A culture can have simple language without having the ability to introspect. It's through complex metaphorical language that we develop introspection and, for example, the ability to think about time. Jaynes describes work by other scholars, such as the historian Chester Starr, who describes how the ancient Greeks did not develop the concept of history until around this time when Jaynes suggests consciousness first developed.[1] This is one of the features of consciousness: seeing time as spatialized out in front of us and going back behind us. This process is all facilitated by metaphorical language.

Jaynes calls this feature of consciousness *spatialization* — our ability to think about time and space. Other features of consciousness that Jaynes describes are the *analog 'I'* — essentially our self concept, or a first person view of ourselves; the *metaphor 'me'*, or a third-person view of ourselves;

---

1. Chester Starr, *The Awakening of the Greek Historical Spirit* (Knopf, 1968).

narratization, and *excerption*. Later he added things like *concentration* (the analog of sensory attention) and *suppression*.[2]

PALMGREN: This seems to suggest a linear progression, from the nonconscious or bicameral mentality to consciousness. If that's the case, do you think that there is an ongoing refining process that is taking place? In other words, are we gradually becoming more conscious as time goes on, or is the opposite the case — is it that consciousness is breaking down, so to speak?

KUIJSTEN: Yes, I think that even through the Middle Ages, one could argue that consciousness has been increasing to this point. If we contrast the psychology of even, for example, the twelfth century, we can observe differences when compared to our modern society. I think that much of it has to do with the proliferation of reading, writing, and more widespread education.

What is going to happen next is an interesting question. I have heard some people argue that as technology increases, and is doing more and more of our thinking for us, we could actually see consciousness start to diminish — at the very least for some people. On the other hand, we could develop more effective ways to teach the various features of consciousness, and over a period of generations, perhaps consciousness could develop further, or at the very least, be more uniformly acquired.

This also raises another, related topic: that if consciousness is learned, then like other learned skills, it can be highly variable. So I think you can have different levels of consciousness in different individuals and in different cultures, and it all depends on what is happening in that individual's environment and in the broader culture.

So as to the future of consciousness, I would just say that it is anything but certain, and it certainly could go either way. But for there to be a fundamental "breakdown of consciousness," so to speak, I think would require a widespread societal collapse, and a near complete abandonment of education, literacy, and these types of things.

PALMGREN: Indeed. Let's go back for a moment and talk about nonhuman animals and their form of consciousness — if they can even be considered conscious in the Jaynesian sense? What did Jaynes have to say in terms of what separates us from the animal mind?

---

2. See Julian Jaynes, *The Origin of Consciousness in the Breakdown of the Bicameral Mind* (Houghton-Mifflin, 1976/2000), pgs. 59-66 and p. 451.

On this program we have talked many times about the idea of catastrophe — that major events have occurred in the past that perhaps changed the trajectory of human civilization. Jaynes suggests that certain catastrophic events perhaps exacerbated the breakdown of the bicameral mind, and thus put us on the path of developing consciousness, whereas nonhuman animals did not. Can you talk about that?

KUIJSTEN: Sure, and I think this would also be a good point to introduce Jaynes's ideas on the bicameral mind. The question of course being, "If consciousness was a relatively recent development based on metaphorical language, then what was our mentality prior to that?"

But as far as nonhuman animals, Jaynes was a strict behaviorist. He thought that animals can be intelligent, can learn complex tasks, and can accomplish all kinds of sophisticated things, but that they do not have this ability to introspect — in other words, they do not have an analog 'I' narratizing in a mind-space, because that would require metaphorical language. Many animals have sophisticated communication systems, but they do not have the metaphorical language that would be necessary to develop the mind-space Jaynes describes. One can stop and think, "What would my thoughts consist of if I had no language as a vehicle to attach them to?"

PALMGREN: Yes, that's interesting.

KUIJSTEN: One can have impulses, drives, urges for hunger or for rest, fight or flight responses, and perhaps some type of proto-conscious thoughts, but language is a necessary vehicle for higher, or more sophisticated, forms of thought.[3] So for Jaynes, animals are all nonconscious — again keeping in mind his narrow definition of what consciousness is.

Again, animals can be highly intelligent, learn complex tasks, and accomplish all kinds of wonderful things, all without an introspectable mind-space. So this underscores the fact that the ability to introspect is not as involved in as many things as we tend to think it is — we tend to have the illusion that consciousness is necessary for everything, but we now know, experimentally, that that's not the case.

Jaynes dates the development of consciousness to about 3,500 years ago, in places like Egypt, Greece, and Mesopotamia — the transition took place at different times in other parts of the world. This dating is a controversial aspect of the theory, because other people have generally speculated that

---

3. See also, José Luis Bermúdez "The Limits of Thinking Without Words," in J.L. Bermúdez, *Thinking Without Words* (Oxford University Press, 2007).

the date for the development of consciousness is much further back — depending again on how they define consciousness, anywhere from a million years ago to 50,000 years ago, with the emergence of cave art.

But again, Jaynes argues that art can be produced non-consciously. And in fact, the British psychologist Nicholas Humphrey has addressed this issue quite persuasively, in my view.[4] He describes the case of an autistic child named Nadia, who had no language when she was three or four years old, and she produced art that was strikingly similar to the kind of thing we see in cave art. This case presents a major problem for scholars who have traditionally argued that cave art was a hallmark of the emergence of the modern mind — when you have a three-year-old non-linguistic child producing very similar things. And this is part of a much larger problem in the study of history, where people have a strong tendency to impose their modern consciousness upon ancient peoples — assuming, in this case, that these were "artists" in the modern, conscious sense.

So getting back to the question of "what came before consciousness?" — prior to the development of consciousness, Jaynes felt that we had a previous mentality that he called the bicameral mind. Bicameral mentality was a type of mental operating system, if you will, which involved a "god-side" and a "follower side," both of which were nonconscious. So "bicameral mind" refers to it being a "two-chambered mind," based on the metaphor of a bicameral legislature.

PALMGREN: Yes.

KUIJSTEN: And Jaynes argues that as language evolved — say over the last 50 to 75,000 years — the brain began to use language as the most efficient way to transmit information between the two brain hemispheres, which are connected by a band of nerve fibers called the corpus callosum. He speculated that the auditory verbal hallucinations that people still hear today, and that often direct their behavior, originate in the language areas of the non-dominant (usually right) hemisphere, travel across the corpus callosum, and are subsequently "heard" by the language areas of the dominant (usually left) hemisphere. The term "dominant" that is often used with regards to the brain hemispheres simply means "dominant for language."

Jaynes argues that these auditory verbal hallucinations served several functions. First, as I just mentioned, they allowed for the efficient transfer

---

4. Nicholas Humphrey, "Cave Art, Autism, and the Evolution of the Human Mind," *Cambridge Archaeological Journal*, 1998, 8, 2.

of information. Jaynes felt that the brain's hemispheres were less integrated at this time than they are today — for reasons that were psychological, not biological. So one would have a great deal of experience stored up in the right hemisphere, and the brain used language as the code to transmit that experience to the left hemisphere when a person was in a situation where a decision was required. So in a stressful situation, rather than deliberate as we might do today, a bicameral person heard a voice that commanded their behavior. The voice was an auditory hallucination, but they attributed it to the voice of their chief, king, dead ancestors, or a god. And as I mentioned, this still takes place in millions of people today — they routinely hear commanding voices that direct their behavior.

Secondly, Jaynes suggests that the bicameral voices may have helped to keep an individual focused on a task. The direction of the chief or the leader of the group could be repeated through these auditory hallucinations — keeping in mind that there was no ability to introspect at this point. This repeating voice would help keep them focused on tasks for longer periods of time.

Finally, the bicameral voices also served as a form of social cohesion, the way pheromones might operate in a beehive. They likely helped to facilitate the hierarchical structure of these early human groups.

The evidence Jaynes provides for all of this is quite compelling. For example, he did an analysis of some of the oldest written texts that are of a sufficient length and of a reliable translation. And in both the older parts of the *Iliad* and the older books of the Bible, we see evidence of bicameral mentality. When a decision needs to be made, the characters in the *Iliad* — such as Achilles, for example — do not reflect but rather they hear the voice of a god telling them what to do. In some cases a god also appears before them — they have an accompanying visual hallucination.

This is how the people of ancient cultures interpreted what we now call a hallucination. For them it was experienced as an external voice or presence, and it was interpreted as the voice of the chief, king, and eventually the gods.

Other evidence includes the fact that, in ancient civilizations, we often see practices of burying the dead as if they are still alive. This suggests they were still hearing their voice and so in some sense they were still interacting with them. There was also the proliferation of idols in many of these cultures, which likely served as hallucinatory aids.

Now in regards to the catastrophe that you mentioned, that comes into Jaynes's theory as one of the possible triggers for why this whole process broke down. Around the Mediterranean, there were many bicameral civilizations that were perhaps beginning this transition to consciousness through the development of metaphorical language and writing, as we discussed, and another catalyst may have been a massive volcanic eruption on the island of Thera. The explosion created a massive tsunami on a scale that we have not seen in modern times. The 2004 tsunami in Indonesia was much smaller, but gives us something of a feel for what it must have been like for these people.

So there was a devastating tsunami for the civilizations around the Mediterranean, and it is now very well documented that this occurred, although the precise date is still debated.[5] And the thinking is that this could have resulted in massive migrations, with different cultures then being interspersed and forced into contact, and each with different systems of gods. So although the dating now suggests that this event took place slightly longer ago than Jaynes's dating for the emergence of consciousness, it's possible that this nonetheless served to hasten the speed at which the entire bicameral hierarchical system started to break down in the civilizations around the Mediterranean. It's important to keep in mind the transition also took place at different times in other parts of the world, as other cultures followed their own trajectories.

PALMGREN: That's very interesting, that this served as possibly another trigger for this breakdown. With regard to these other cultures, there is a theory that language and even the ability to begin making tools and pots and things like that popped up in different regions around the world approximately around the same time — they were not just restricted to one area. What do you attribute that to? Is this related in any way to the phenomena known as the hundredth monkey effect? Did consciousness begin to take place in a smaller population of the human species, and an effect of that was that other human beings around the world began to learn the same thing? Or do you or Jaynes attribute that to other factors?

KUIJSTEN: Jaynes makes the case that the skill of consciousness, if we can call it that, was primarily transmitted through trade, migration, and then, for example in the Americas, it appears that the transition happened

---

5. Walter Kutschera, "On the Enigma of Dating the Minoan Eruption of Santorini," *Proceedings of the National Academy of Sciences of the United States of America*, 2020, 117, 16.

largely independently, but hundreds of years later. So different cultures are very likely to independently progress along this path toward subjective consciousness as their language becomes more complex.

Having said that, we still have some cultures today that are completely isolated from the modern world, and are still living essentially as preliterate societies did 10 or 20,000 years ago. At one point it was thought that perhaps there were none left, but there have been some recent discoveries, as well as rediscoveries, of some very small, isolated groups. For example, several of these groups live on Andaman and Nicobar Islands in the Bay of Bengal, in the Indian Ocean. There are others in the Amazon. These tribes may be the last living remnants of perhaps bicameral or semi-bicameral groups, although because they have not been carefully studied, we really don't know for sure.

Another place where we see evidence for the transition from bicameral mentality to consciousness is China. Jaynes did not know Chinese, so he could not investigate this himself in great depth. However, Michael Carr — who is an expert on Chinese linguistics and ancient history and who is also very interested in Jaynes's theory — published a series of articles documenting the same transition from bicameral mentality to consciousness in China, around the same time that Jaynes describes this taking place in the civilizations around the Mediterranean.

PALMGREN: Let's talk more about your book, *Reflections on the Dawn of Consciousness*. Are there any major points of disagreement with regard to Jaynes's theory in the book, or does it primarily try to clarify the theory or extend the theory into new areas?

KUIJSTEN: The book contains contributions from a number of different scholars, so it looks at Jaynes's theory from a variety of different perspectives: psychology, psychiatry, anthropology, ancient history, linguistics, etc. There is also a biography of Julian Jaynes. Additional support is provided for Jaynes's theory in all of these different areas, as well as new evidence for the theory that has emerged since Jaynes first published his book. The catalyst for the book was the new evidence for Jaynes's neurological model that began to appear starting in 1999. These were fMRI brain scans showing "bicameral" activation and interaction of the right and left temporal lobes of individuals experiencing auditory hallucinations, just as Jaynes had predicted. These findings, which have since been confirmed by a number of different studies, both vindicated Jaynes's neurological model and reignited interest in the theory. So that was what initially prompted me to start the project, and to begin looking at other areas of new evidence for Jaynes's theory. There is not a lot in the book that takes issues with Jaynes's ideas — it's more refinements, new evidence, and discussion of theory.

PALMGREN: Let's talk about the new evidence. There has been quite a bit of new research on the brain over the past several decades. Does any of this research support Jaynes's ideas?

KUIJSTEN: Yes, in fact one of the things that I focus on in my chapter in *Reflections on the Dawn of Consciousness* is "What is the new evidence for Jaynes's theory?" There's so much to cover here, so I will just briefly touch on a few of the different areas.

In regard to Jaynes's first hypothesis, that consciousness is based on language, there has been a great deal of new interest in this idea since Jaynes's book was first published. We see much more discussion of the importance of language for consciousness and higher forms of thought by a number of different philosophers. We also see this idea now being explored by developmental psychologists, and we now have studies looking at the development of consciousness in children as they learn language. There are also cases of children who don't learn language that support Jaynes's theory.

Jaynes's second hypothesis is the bicameral mind, and here we see a great deal of new evidence as well. It's easy to forget that when Jaynes's book was first published, hallucinations were not being studied in the general population. The generally accepted view was that they were relatively rare and only seen in mental illness.

The history of auditory hallucinations is quite fascinating. For hundreds of years, they were perceived as spiritual contact or divine revelation — anyone who experienced this was thought to be in contact with God, or gods, angels, demons, or dead ancestors. And then, at a certain point, and really only beginning in the late 1700s, hallucinations began to be seen as a symptom of mental illness. That is when the stigma around hallucinations began to develop, and this idea that if you experienced hallucinations you were mentally ill. So for the next two hundred years, there was very little interest in hallucinations in the general population — largely because people began to keep the experience to themselves.[6]

Jaynes's book to a large degree inspired the modern interest in hallucinations in the general, non-clinical population. There was an early study

---

6. A rare exception was an 1881 study by Francis Galton titled "The Visions of Sane Persons."

by Posey and Losch looking at the prevalence of hallucinations in the normal population that was inspired by Jaynes's theory.[7] Not long after that, and also inspired by Jaynes, John Hamilton discovered auditory hallucinations were common among nonverbal quadriplegics.[8] Soon after there was something of an explosion in this type of research, and hallucinations were found to be much more common throughout society than was previously known. They have been documented in high altitude climbers and solo explorers, people in social isolation, people in sensory deprivation, people under intense stress, in children, in the elderly, etc. While many of these cases involve a voice that is heard only occasionally, we also now know that there are many people who hear voices on a daily basis and live perfectly normal lives. This very much supports the idea that hallucinations once played a major role in our psychology.

We also now know much more about the content of the voices that people hear. I think that there is a tendency to think that they are of a completely random nature, but this is not the case. Auditory verbal hallucinations tend to be focused on people's behavior: commenting on it, criticizing it, and commanding it — there is now an entire literature on "command hallucinations." Of course this makes perfect sense if we see it as evidence for vestiges of bicameral mentality. To put it another way, without Jaynes's theory, it makes absolutely no sense. There's simply no other viable explanation for why people today would hear voices guiding or commanding their behavior.

There is also new evidence regarding dating of the transition from bicameral mentality to consciousness, or Jaynes's third hypothesis. Scholars such as Michael Carr and Todd Gibson have documented evidence for this transition in cultures that Jaynes did not investigate, such as China and Tibet. James Cohn and Brian McVeigh have looked at the evidence for the transition in the Old and New Testaments, and Boban Dedović has studied the development of mind-related words in several ancient languages.[9]

Finally, when Jaynes first proposed his theory in the late 1970's, he had what he called a neurological model for the bicameral mind. And this was that the language areas of the non-dominant (usually right) hemisphere

---

7. Thomas B. Posey and Mary E. Losch, "Auditory Hallucinations of Hearing Voices in 375 Normal Subjects," *Imagination, Cognition and Personality*, 1983, 3, 2, 99–113.

8. John Hamilton, "Auditory Hallucinations in Nonverbal Quadriplegics," *Psychiatry*, 1985, 48, 4; reprinted in M. Kuijsten (ed.), *Reflections on the Dawn of Consciousness* (Julian Jaynes Society, 2006).

9. See the interviews with James Cohn, Boban Dedović, Todd Gibson, and Brian McVeigh in this volume.

were responsible for auditory verbal hallucinations, and that these hallucinations then traveled across the corpus callosum or anterior commissures to be "heard" or "perceived" by the language areas of the dominant (usually left) hemisphere.

His neurological model was speculative, simply because the technology was not yet available at the time to test his ideas. But he based it on several lines of evidence, such as the brain stimulation research by Wilder Penfield; split-brain research of Roger Sperry, Michael Gazzaniga, and Joseph Bogen; and the known functions of the right hemisphere.

The split-brain research was based on a group of patients who had the corpus callosum, or the primary connection between the two hemispheres, severed in order to treat cases of severe epilepsy. This prevented the seizures from spreading from one hemisphere to the other, as they did not have the kinds of medications for epilepsy at that time that we have today. After this procedure, many experiments were conducted to try to determine what, if anything, was the result of the disconnection of the two hemispheres. And for anyone not familiar with the split-brain experiments, this is a truly amazing thing to read about.

What emerged from these experiments is the idea that the two brain hemispheres, after disconnection, often act very independently, and this was especially noticeable under controlled laboratory conditions. And while this idea is still controversial, the researchers concluded that the procedure resulted in two distinct, independent "spheres of consciousness," or "selves" — however you want to put it — one per hemisphere.

Their research also suggests that the two brain hemispheres can operate independently, each solving a task simultaneously, for example. And this of course lends support for Jaynes's idea that the two hemispheres could have operated more independently during the bicameral period than they do today.

Beginning in 1999, studies began to emerge using fMRI to look at what was happening in the brain while people were experiencing auditory hallucinations. There was a study by Belinda Lennox in the UK that took brain images of someone who, while in the MRI machine, would press a button at the onset of their hallucinations. This study showed a right/left temporal lobe (or "bicameral") interaction during auditory hallucinations, exactly as Jaynes has predicted.[10]

---

10. Belinda R. Lennox, et al., "Spatial and Temporal Mapping of Neural Activity Associated with Auditory Hallucinations," *Lancet*, 1999, 353, 644.

This created a lot of renewed interest in Jaynes's theory, and different psychiatrists mentioned this study in terms of Jaynes's theory.[11] Since then there have been many replications of these findings. Researchers that have investigated this and noted similar findings are Iris Sommer in the Netherlands[12] and Renaud Jardri in France,[13] but there are many others as well. There is such a growing consensus around this now that two neurosurgeons suggested severing the corpus callosum as a potential treatment for persistent, debilitating hallucinations that don't respond to medication. So here we have a surgical procedure being recommended based on Jaynes's theory and the follow-up research.[14]

Taken together, this new evidence from neuroscience very much vindicates Jaynes's fourth hypothesis — his neurological model for the bicameral mind — which prior to 1999 had mostly been either ignored or dismissed. So this is a very exciting new area of evidence for Jaynes's theory, because it's not historical or speculative in nature — we can see the areas of the brain that are active during auditory hallucinations on a brain scan right in front of us.

So to sum up, there is a great deal of new evidence for Jaynes's theory from a wide variety of disciplines and sources that has emerged since the publication of Jaynes's book, and there has been very little that contradicts anything that he had to say.

PALMGREN: Excellent. It's great to learn about all of these different lines of new evidence for the theory. I think that's a good place to wrap things up. Thank you so much for your time Marcel. I appreciate you coming on and discussing these ideas. Keep us posted on what's going on.

KUIJSTEN: Thank you for having me, it's been a pleasure.[15]

---

11. Robert Olin, "Auditory Hallucinations and the Bicameral Mind," *Lancet*, 1999, 354, 166; Leo Sher, "Neuroimaging, Auditory Hallucinations, and The Bicameral Mind," *Journal of Psychiatry and Neuroscience*, 2000, 25, 3, 239-40.

12. See Iris Sommer and Sanne Brederoo's interview, "Auditory Hallucinations and the Right Hemisphere," in this volume.

13. Renaud Jardri, et al., "Activation of Bilateral Auditory Cortex during Verbal Hallucinations in a Child with Schizophrenia," *Molecular Psychiatry*, 2007, 12, 4, 319.

14. Mousa Taghipour and Fariborz Ghaffarpasand, "Corpus Callosotomy for Drug-Resistant Schizophrenia: Novel Treatment Based on Pathophysiology," *World Neurosurgery*, 2018, 116, 483-484.

15. Additional portions of this interview discussing more nuanced aspects of Jaynes's theory can be found in the Appendix.

HYPOTHESIS I

Consciousness Based on Language

2

Consciousness and Language

Marcel Kuijsten

Interviewed by Brendan Leahy

BRENDAN LEAHY: Can you start by telling us about Julian Jaynes's background and how he became interested in the problem of consciousness?

MARCEL KUIJSTEN: Sure. Julian Jaynes tells us that he first developed an interest in consciousness as a child. He relates a story about looking at a forsythia bush outside his family home in West Newton, which is outside of Boston, and wondering if the color of the bush that he perceived was the same color that was perceived by someone else. And so he held on to this single-minded purpose to understand consciousness throughout his life.

Jaynes's father, Julian Clifford Jaynes, was a Unitarian minister who died when Jaynes was very young, just a few years old. After his death, Jaynes's mother, Clara Bullard Jaynes, collected his best sermons into a book called *Magic Wells*. Julian Jaynes surely read this book, and there is a lot in the sermons that has to do with introspection and self-reflection and similar themes. So we can see the seeds of some of Jaynes's later ideas in his father's sermons.

Jaynes went on to study at Harvard, and then at Yale, where he did his Ph.D. Initially he didn't accept his Ph.D., and there are at least two different stories about this. One explanation is that the dissertation committee required changes to his dissertation that he felt were wrong and that he refused to make. It's also been said that he felt that the Ph.D. was something that was constraining and that encouraged conformity, rather than the freedom to pursue one's own ideas. He was fairly critical of the whole system, as he felt it discouraged originality. Some years later, however, after the publication of his book, he was awarded his doctorate from Yale, which he accepted.

Initially Jaynes had started out his quest for understanding consciousness by looking at animal behavior, and things like studying learning in rats, and even observing learning in paramecium in mazes, and these kinds of things. However after some time he realized that this was the wrong approach to understanding consciousness, and that he was not making progress with this type of experimentation. Eventually he hit upon the insight that consciousness is something that is learned through language, and thus had its origin in human history. At that point Jaynes began to look back through human history, studying the oldest writings that were of a reasonable length and a reliable translation. And lo and behold, he found that introspective consciousness is absent in ancient texts such as the *Iliad*, and I think that's when the whole theory started to come together.

LEAHY: How was Jaynes's theory first received back in the late 1970s?

KUIJSTEN: That's a great question. We have to remember what the climate was like when Jaynes first published his book. Psychology was coming out of a long period where behaviorism was the dominant school of thought, and consciousness was regarded as an unproductive field of study. It had been studied in the late nineteenth and early twentieth centuries, but then it went by the wayside as the focus shifted to behaviorism — the study of learning and observable behavior. Even in the late 1990s, when I was considering graduate programs in psychology or neuroscience, there still was this sentiment that consciousness was not something that could be seriously pursed.

So Jaynes published a book on consciousness at a time when very few people were talking about consciousness. In addition to that, he takes a very broad, multidisciplinary approach that people in academia normally are not able to do — the various fields have all become so highly specialized that typically one has to become an expert in a very narrow field in order to make meaningful contributions. And typically these contributions add additional knowledge that is just beyond the most recent discoveries in a given field.

So it was very unusual for someone to draw upon so many different fields, such as psychology, anthropology, linguistics, ancient history, religion, and neuroscience, and to see the connections and put all of the various pieces of evidence together the way Jaynes did. In a traditional academic career, that kind of multidisciplinary approach is just not possible. And one of the reasons why Jaynes was able to take this approach was because he was not concerned with pursuing a tenure track position — he wanted the freedom to pursue his ideas wherever they led him. It's also important to note that he was unmarried, he did not have children, and he lived very frugally, so he had the time to study all of these different fields in the pursuit of his ideas. So Jaynes was publishing a book on consciousness, which was not a popular topic at the time, and he was taking this maverick, multidisciplinary approach.

In terms of the book's reception, his book was very well received by the general public. It received many positive book reviews, it quickly sold out its first print run, and it has remained in print and very popular ever since. It was of course viewed as controversial, and among academics there was something of a mixed response. Jaynes had both critics and supporters. Jaynes was a very popular lecturer, and he was frequently invited to speak about his theory at universities all across the country, as well as abroad.

I think that there are two main reasons for why, initially, there was not a great deal of follow-up on Jaynes's theory by others. The first reason is that members of academia are generally not incentivized to champion other people's theories — they are much more interested in trying to come up with their own ideas. The second reason is that Jaynes' theory is so multidisciplinary that people perhaps did not want to endorse something that may turn out to be wrong in areas that were outside of their expertise.

For example, a psychiatrist may have patients that experience command hallucinations, and so the theory very much resonates with them, and from their area of expertise, it makes sense. However, they may not have studied ancient history to the extent that they feel comfortable supporting the overall theory. People in academia are human beings just like everyone else, and they often have the same reluctance to stand out from the crowd, or to risk being ridiculed for endorsing a theory that later turns out to have a flaw in an area they are unfamiliar with.

That being said, with the books that the Julian Jaynes Society has published and the conferences that we have held, as well as the many new publications by others, the theory has become much more acceptable to discuss, and every year more and more scholars are writing about Jaynes's theory and expressing an interest in it. So over the years it has become less controversial than it used to be, even within mainstream academia.

LEAHY: Jaynes breaks his theory down into four main hypotheses. What is his first hypothesis?

KUIJSTEN: The first hypothesis is that consciousness is based on language. It's not biologically innate, it's not something that evolved the way physical characteristics evolved and simply resulted from a certain level of brain complexity. It was something that had to be learned, and it was only able to be learned when language developed to a certain level of sophistication. So that is the first hypothesis.

LEAHY: Can you explain how Jaynes defines consciousness?

KUIJSTEN: Jaynes defines consciousness as "that which is introspect-able" — the contents of our introspection. One of the ways he tries to get at the definition of consciousness is by first very meticulously stripping away all the things that consciousness is not. Jaynes explains that consciousness is not necessary for learning, sense perception, visual perception, attention, and many of the other things that tend to get wrapped up into these vague, broad definitions of consciousness. By first explaining what consciousness is not, we can then begin to get to the heart of what consciousness is.

Jaynes demonstrates that much of our mental activity takes places non-consciously, despite the fact that we often have the mistaken common sense intuition that consciousness is involved in all mentality. Consciousness for Jaynes is our learned ability to have what he calls an "analog 'I' narratizing in a mind-space;" a "metaphor me," which is our third-person view of ourselves; as well as a number of other features. This mind-space, he believes, is built up through metaphorical language. So the internal "space" that we have — where we narratize our life story, reflect on our decisions, reflect on the past, and plan for the future — is built up through metaphors of physical space, of the physical world.

For example, say we are sitting on the beach and looking at the ocean. Like all non-human animals, we nonconsciously perceive our surround-ings — the sand underneath us, the warmth of the sun, the sights and sounds of the ocean. For Jaynes, that's sense perception, not consciousness. At the same time, perhaps we are reflecting on a problem or an idea or thinking about a plan for our evening. That's one of the functions of con-sciousness. Because of the tremendous amount of confusion over the defi-nition of consciousness, I highly recommend Jaynes's detailed discussion of consciousness in order to fully understand his arguments.[1]

---

1. See Julian Jaynes, *The Origin of Consciousness in the Breakdown of the Bicameral Mind* (Houghton

LEAHY: So consciousness in the Jaynesian sense is something that is learned?

KUIJSTEN: Yes. One of the important things to understand about Jaynes's definition of consciousness is that it is something that is learned based on language, and specifically metaphorical language. The mainstream, broad view of consciousness is that it's genetic, it's biologically innate, it evolved as we did over millions of years, and it's present not just in humans but to varying degrees in many of the higher mammals — and so that is a major distinction that we see with Jaynes.

However, the problem with these broad views of consciousness is that very often they fail to properly define the term, or they define it very vaguely. They often include things like visual perception, that we share with all animals, including insects. Jaynes argues that that is not what was traditionally meant by consciousness, and furthermore, by defining consciousness so broadly, we then miss many of the important distinctions that seem to be learned, based on language, and uniquely human.

It then follows that children learn consciousness through language. It's important to understand this idea that consciousness is actually taught to each successive generation. This opens up the possibility that perhaps there are ways that we can teach it more effectively. There are developmental psychologists that are now doing research that supports this idea, and this is a direct extension of Jaynes's theory.

For example, the psychologist Philip Zelazo has done research documenting how stages of consciousness develop as children acquire language.[2] If consciousness was biologically innate rather than learned, then we would not expect to see these types of developmental stages. We also would not see the great variety and plasticity of consciousness throughout history, among different cultures, and in children who don't acquire language — nonlinguistic children who don't develop the features of consciousness that we see in children who are taught language.

LEAHY: So then, are there examples of feral children that have been studied in this regard?

KUIJSTEN: Yes, there are examples of feral children — or children who are, for example, raised in isolation without learning language. Probably

---

Mifflin, 1976/1990), Chapters 1 and 2, as well as the Afterword to the 1990 and later editions.
2. Philip Zelazo, et al., "The Development of Consciousness," in P. Zelazo, et al. (eds.), *The Cambridge Handbook on Consciousness* (Cambridge University Press, 2007).

the most famous case is Genie. Genie was a girl living in the Los Angeles area who was a victim of extreme abuse, neglect, and isolation. She came to the attention of child abuse authorities in 1970, at the age of 13. This is an interesting case because, unlike many of the other cases, Genie was studied extensively by psychologists. I think the key finding from this case, from our perspective, is that because Genie did not learn language during the critical window for language acquisition, she did not develop many of the features of consciousness that Jaynes describes.[3]

There are actually many other cases of so-called feral children, but generally they are less well documented. Another interesting case is that of Kaspar Hauser, in nineteenth century Nuremberg. Kaspar Hauser was a boy who unfortunately was raised in isolation and who was not taught language. While he was not carefully studied in the modern sense, he did have teachers and people around him that documented many interesting observations. It is interesting to note that, in a book that was written about him at the time, not only do we see predictable deficits in the features of consciousness, but the author describes him experiencing what we might call aspects of bicameral mentality, such as visual hallucinations and visitation dreams.[4]

Then there is the famous case of Helen Keller, who was not a feral child but was deaf, blind, and without language until a relatively late age — I believe six or seven years old. Her case very much speaks to the idea that language is critical for the development of Jaynesian consciousness, and highlights the relationship between thought and language.

Helen Keller wrote an autobiography, and in it she describes the transition she underwent — first not having any language, to then, working with a teacher, acquiring sign language. She describes in great detail the remarkable transition that took place in her thought processes as a result of the acquisition of language.

This is another case that supports Jaynes's idea that without language, we do not have the necessary tool to create an inner mind-space, or the vehicle to tie complex thoughts to. Without language, we can have impulses, fear, hunger, drives, and things of that nature, but we cannot have complex thought, or the kind of thought necessary to develop Jaynesian consciousness.

---

3. Susan Curtiss and Harry A Whitaker, *Genie: A Psycholinguistic Study of a Modern-Day Wild Child* (Academic Press, 2014).
4. Elizabeth Edson Gibson Evans, *The Story of Kaspar Hauser from Authentic Records* (Swan Sonnenschein & Co., 1892).

The late, well-known neurologist Oliver Sacks describes the more recent case of a deaf boy named Joseph that is very similar to Helen Keller.[5]
Joesph was raised on a farm in Mexico, and did not acquire language until
the age of 10, when the family came to the United States. Sacks relates how
Joseph appeared to be confined to the present moment, without the ability
to reflect on the past, plan for the future, or engage in abstract thought.

We have to be cautious with evidence from case studies, particularly
historical ones, but nonetheless cases of children raised without language
do support Jaynes's arguments about the necessity of language for consciousness. This is an area that could greatly benefit from further research,
and there are many cases of children with autism who are non-linguistic
or minimally linguistic.

LEAHY: Can you describe specifically how Helen Keller described the
transition?

KUIJSTEN: Yes, there are a number of interesting quotes on her life before acquiring language and her transition to consciousness. I'll read one of them:

> Before my teacher came to me, I did not know that I am. I lived in
> a world that was a no-world... I had neither will nor intellect. I was
> carried along to objects and acts by a certain blind natural impetus.' ...
> I never viewed anything beforehand or chose it. ... My inner life, then,
> was a blank without past, present, or future, without hope or anticipa-
> tion, without wonder or joy or faith... Since I had no power of thought,
> I did not compare one mental state with another... When I learned the
> meaning of "I" and "me" and found that I was something, I began to
> think. Then consciousness first existed for me.[6]

She goes on to say that when she began to learn sign language, she felt
as though she "thought" and "desired" with her fingers and states: "If I
had made a man, I should certainly have put the brain and soul in his
fingertips."[7] This is quite interesting, because she is placing the location of
thought in her fingers, where she communicates.

---

5. Oliver Sacks, *Seeing Voices: A Journey into the World of the Deaf* (University of California Press, 1989).
6. Helen Keller, *The World I Live In* (The Century Company, 1908), Chapter 11, pgs. 113–117.
7. Ibid., p. 116.

3

Julian Jaynes and the
Features of Consciousness

Brian J. McVeigh

Interviewed by Marcel Kuijsten & Brendan Leahy

Brian J. McVeigh received his BA in Asian studies and political science, MA in anthropology, and MS in counseling from the University at Albany, State University of New York, as well as a Ph.D. in anthropology from Princeton University. He works as a licensed mental health counselor and is also a scholar of China and Japan, where he lived and worked for 16 years. He taught in the Department of East Asian Studies at the University of Arizona for ten years. The author of 16 books, he has published widely on pop culture, politics, gender, education, religion, nationalism, the history of psychology, and archaeopsychology. His latest publication, *The Self-healing Mind: Harnessing the Active Ingredients of Psychotherapy* (in press), combines his interests in how humans adapt, both through history and therapeutically. His current projects include *The Psychology of Ancient Egypt: Reconstructing a Lost Mentality* and *Julian Jaynes for Beginners*.

MARCEL KUIJSTEN: You knew Julian Jaynes when you were a doctoral student at Princeton University, and have been studying, writing, and speaking about various aspects of his theory for more than 30 years. What in your view is the primary obstacle to people understanding Jaynes's theory?

BRIAN J. McVEIGH: Well, the first issue is the word "consciousness" itself. It seems to me there is an almost irrational obsession surrounding this term, a sort of fetishism, if you will. In both the academic literature and scientific journalistic writings it appears quite frequently. I say this because it appeals to many who are attracted to the mysterious nature of the mind but perhaps don't want to do the heavy-lifting of disciplined research. It is often used with an aura of mysticism. Witness the recent upsurge in talk about panpsychism. Such discussions are fine for philosophical speculation, but they do little to advance scientific understanding of psychology. And then those who practice science do not define what they mean by consciousness. Are they talking about perception, thinking, deep reflection, self-awareness, or something else? But note Jaynes was very careful with how he defined consciousness, or as I like to say to be clear, conscious interiority.

A second and related problem concerns how, since we are conscious, we assume we must understand it. It seems so personal and intuitive. In the same way we experience space and time on a daily basis, we conclude we understand these phenomena as well. We each possess, as it were, our private stage of consciousness. However, in fact, astrophysicists have very different definitions of space and time. It makes no difference how intellectually trained someone is. If they have not explored and questioned their own consciousness in a methodical manner themselves, it ends up becoming a very elusive and indefinable thing. This leads to fetishism.

A third problem is that Jaynes's work does not fit neatly into a conventional genre. His claims are admittedly ambitious and grand. He deals with neurology, the origins of religion, historical change, linguistics, etc. A person needs to have an open-mind and inquisitive spirit to appreciate his arguments.

Finally, people want easy answers and look for "single key" explanations. Media treatments and the works of popular science writers sometimes encourage simplistic and reductionistic accounts. But the human mind and how it emerged from historical forces is multi-faceted and complex. There are no easy answers.

KUIJSTEN: Yes, I will never forget listening to two back-to-back conference lectures on the development of consciousness in children. Both professors used the word "consciousness," but one was clearly talking about sense perception (in infants, for example), while the other was implying a definition of consciousness that struck me as being very similar to Jaynes's. In a discussion that followed, the two professors were completely talking past each other, because there had been a failure to first properly define the term.

Among the general public, I've noticed that the response to Jaynes's book tends to fall into three groups. The first is the group of people that never read Jaynes's book because they essentially jump to conclusions about what they think Jaynes means by consciousness. In other words, they dismiss his book based on their own broad definition of consciousness, without ever realizing that Jaynes defines the term in a more careful, more narrow, and I would argue, much more useful way. It's based on a snap judgment or one might say a knee-jerk reaction.

There is a second group of people that actually read Jaynes's book, but for whatever reason they still do not fully grasp how he is defining consciousness. I think this is a much smaller number — primarily people who are, for a lack of a better term, perhaps a little out of their depth in terms of the content. Yet unfortunately, they often still see themselves as being in a position to provide their opinion, in the form of a blog post, book review, or what have you.

Finally, there is a third group of people that read Jaynes's book and come away with a clear understanding of how he defines consciousness. They understand the very important distinction that Jaynes is making between our ability to narratize in an inner mind-space, versus things like sense perception, learning, and problem-solving. It's not something that is easy to fully understand right away, and this can sometimes take multiple readings, or reading Jaynes's book and then following that up by reading some or all of the follow-up books we have published. But without a clear understanding of this very important distinction that Jaynes is making, unfortunately I don't see how much progress will be made in the field of consciousness studies. There will be a lot of discussion of reactivity, sense perception, learning, and that type of thing, all labeled as consciousness — mistakenly, in my view.

McVEIGH: I think what you said about the need to tackle Jaynes with multiple readings is absolutely true. That's very good advice. Jaynes is inviting us to view matters from a very different perspective, one that takes getting used to. I would also say that as a field, psychology simply lacks the scientific rigor and preciseness you find in the natural sciences. This is not necessarily a bad thing, since psychology is very much concerned with subjectivity, and to my mind, historical changes in mentality require subtle analyses. But not a few psychologists suffer from natural-science envy — so they are severely challenged, even put off, by cultural and historical studies. I just wish that the same attention they give to rigorous statistical analyses they would give to the terms they employ when writing about consciousness. Psychology, because it utilizes both objective and subjective approaches, will probably never settle on a well-defined list of concepts, as you find in, say, chemistry. But at the same time injecting some definitional parameters into psychological studies would certainly advance the field.

KUIJSTEN: I can relate to how difficult having a deep understanding of Jaynes's definition can be. After having read Jaynes's book the first time, I can recall how over time the ideas start to slip away, and it's easy to fall back into the more vague, messy types of thinking about the subject that is so common in the literature.

Julian Jaynes — as well as others, such as the philosopher Daniel Dennett and now some developmental psychologists[1] — argues that we learn consciousness in childhood through language. I recently have had the opportunity to observe a non-linguistic child — a friend's developmentally disabled son. This boy — let's call him Eric — is currently limited to understanding a few hundred words or so. The number of words that he can articulate is far fewer. He also uses an iPad with photos of items that he can point to, which he uses to express what he would like to eat, for example. He certainly does not have the level of language sophistication that Jaynes describes as being necessary to develop Jaynesian consciousness — or conscious interiority, as you say.

He has provided something of a living reminder for me of all of the things that Jaynes describes that can be accomplished without consciousness: how one can perceive, learn, problem solve, exhibit intelligence, eat, laugh, play, explore, and move about the world — but still lack consciousness as Jaynes carefully defines it. Essentially Eric, as far as anyone can tell, is always living in the present moment. He does not seem able to reflect on the past, plan for the future (beyond the immediate present — getting dressed, getting in the car, for example) — understand the concept of time, or any of these types of things. He understands concrete terms and actions like "banana" or "get dressed," but not abstract concepts like "how was therapy today?" or "what would you like to do tomorrow?" It would seem as though his language ability is not sufficient for the development of what Jaynes calls an "analog 'I' narratizing in a mind-space." He doesn't seem to be able to imagine what he would like to dress up as for the next Halloween, for example. Yet if you show him several costumes, he can of

---

1. See for example, P.D. Zelazo, H.H. Gao, and R. Todd, "The Development of Consciousness," in P.D. Zelazo (ed.), *The Cambridge Handbook of Consciousness* (Cambridge University Press, 2007).

course express a preference. In his case, because he very much wants to express himself and his preferences, it seems fairly clear when he has a concept that he wants to express, but can't, and when he simply doesn't comprehend the question.

From brief observations, it seems as though the parents and caretakers of non-linguistic individuals often experience frustration as a result of interacting with the person as though they are in fact conscious (in the Jaynesian sense), and as though they understand complex language. They speak to them in ways that the individual likely cannot understand, rather than communicating via known, established words. This speaks to the fact that there are different ways of communicating with non-linguistic people — or non-human animals, for that matter — versus those with highly developed language skills, and yet this distinction is lost on many people. Thus working with minimally linguistic individuals could perhaps be both a practical application and a opportunity to further elucidate the "consciousness based on language" hypothesis of Jaynes's theory.

McVEIGH: This is an extremely salient issue and I'm glad you brought it up — are individuals with intellectual developmental disorders and those on the autism spectrum disorder conscious? Or, better yet, to what degree are they conscious?

First, I would say that it depends on the nature of the disability. Obviously the more severe the intellectual disability, the more the development of consciousness would be hindered. It has to be stressed that consciousness is not an either-all-or-none proposition, as if all it takes is flipping a switch to be conscious. Building upon Jaynes, I have identified about a dozen or so features or functions of conscious interiority. So the question, "is this person conscious?" is not very useful. A better question would be "what features of consciousness does this person with special needs possess?" as well as "how robust are the particular features of consciousness for this individual?"

A second point. We have lots of psychological assessments and instruments to test and measure all types of things. What we need is the development of tests that assess the various facets of consciousness, to see how developed they are in individuals. Such assessments could have neurodevelopmental as well as neurocognitive applications, helping us with patients who suffer from various forms of dementia, etc. Perhaps some assessments are already in existence that could help us measure the features of conscious interiority.

A final point I'd like to make is that having a discussion about special needs individuals is vital to understanding not just the relationship between consciousness and neurodiversity, but what it means to be neurotypical, as well. In a discussion like this, we can only skim the surface, but as should be evident to the inquisitive reader of our exchange, there are many exciting possibilities to pursue.

KUIJSTEN: It's interesting that what's called Applied Behavior Analysis (or ABA) Therapy — which is often the preferred approach to working with such individuals — is largely based on John Watson's and B.F. Skinner's operant conditioning. Practitioners of ABA work at improving social, communication, and other skills through positive reinforcement. The basic principles are not that different than what trainers use when working with non-human animals. It was through my exposure to animal training that I came to appreciate the tremendous role of positive and negative reinforcers in all of us. I think that even in "normal," linguistic people, operant conditioning plays a much larger role than we generally like to acknowledge. But this gets back to the idea that consciousness plays a far more limited role in our day-to-day lives and behavior than most of us like to recognize or like to admit.

McVEIGH: Yes, you're absolutely right. Consciousness plays a very small part in our everyday lives. But because we cannot be conscious of being nonconscious, as obvious as that is, we often assume we are conscious more times than we actually are.

* * *

BRENDAN LEAHY: Could you discuss the features of consciousness?

McVEIGH: Yes. Perhaps the most important — and the one I think most of us can relate to — is the idea of *spatialization*, or what Jaynes calls "mindspace." The idea here is something that we do all the time. We can picture in our minds — using our mind's eye to see things in an imaginary space in our head — where we can move things around, where we can imagine for example the past or something in the present or the future. I can stop and think about, for example, what I had for breakfast. And again, this is something that we take for granted. But for Jaynes, if you go back and look at the historical record, there's no evidence that people were spatializing their experiences until about 1000 BCE.

Another feature of consciousness, which builds upon the idea of spatialization, is *excerption* — the ability to "perceive," and again, perceive should be in quotations — this mind-space and to move things around in it. Jaynes notes that reminiscence is a "succession of excerptions."[2] Or as Nørretranders notes, interiority is the "instance of selection that picks and chooses among the many options" that psyche provides us.[3]

Then there is *conciliation*, which is our ability to bring different ideas together in this mind-space. According to Jaynes, "it brings together conscious objects just as narratization brings episodes together as a story."

Another important feature — and this Jaynes did not discuss, but I have added it — is the ability to *introceive*. I use that term in order to distinguish from "perceive" or "perception." The reason I'm mentioning this is because many people assume that consciousness is just perception, but in fact that's not true, and this is what has led to a great deal of confusion. To *introceive* — or *introception*, which is the term I use — is the ability to stop outward perception and only look at things in our mind. So this ability to introceive of course is something that is built upon the different features that I already mentioned, for example *spatialization*, the ability to hold a mind-space in our heads, and *conciliation* and *excerption*. This is only a partial list, there are other features as well.

LEAHY: What was it like for bicameral people to lack these abilities? Could you give an example of what it might have been like?

McVEIGH: Yes, when people first hear about Jaynes's ideas they often ask, "What was it like for people if they weren't conscious?" I think it sounds bizarre for most people, to hear that argument — that people were not conscious. But you have to remember that even for people today, thinking — for the most part — is not conscious. We are not aware of our thoughts, unless some novel situation arises and we have to stop and become more conscious of what we are doing. Well, according to Jaynes, in ancient times, before people learned consciousness, if they did encounter a strange or novel situation and they weren't sure of what to do, that's when the voices of chieftains, ancestors, or gods would kick in. So the voices or supernatural entities took the place of consciousness, and if you stop and think about it, we are only conscious when we decide to be conscious about something, or when we confront some challenging situation. But most of

---

2. Julian Jaynes, *The Origin of Consciousness in the Breakdown of the Bicameral Mind* (Houghton-Mifflin, 1976), pgs. 64-65.
3. Tor Nørretranders, *The User Illusion: Cutting Consciousness Down to Size* (Viking, 1998).

the time we are not conscious of what we are doing. That's one of the great myths about consciousness — that it's like a light in our head that's always turned on. But in fact that's not true. Another interesting thing is that consciousness also occurs in dreaming — in fact that's what dreaming is. Dreaming is essentially consciousness operating during sleep.

LEAHY: How did Jaynes develop this theory?

MCVEIGH: Jaynes said in interviews and in his writing that as far back as he could remember, he was always interested in consciousness — even as a small child. So that's why he pursued studies in psychology and philosophy. He wanted to find out exactly what consciousness is. Of course he encountered many obstacles, and in fact he decided to become a comparative psychologist. Basically, a comparative psychologist is someone who studies animals, and so he spent much of his time in the laboratory studying single celled organisms, for example. He was trying to find out how they learn things, assuming that that must have something to do with being conscious.

But when he was taking this type of conventional psychological approach, Jaynes kept running into all of these brick walls in trying to find out what consciousness is. So he decided, "Well maybe what I should do is see what the great historical thinkers and the great philosophers have said about the nature of consciousness." He started to do a lot of reading and going back through history, because the first people to talk about what we might call psychology of course were the ancient Greek philosophers. But he found something very bizarre: people stopped talking about consciousness, or people stopped talking about what we call psychological events, between the seventh and ninth century BCE, depending on where you looked. There's no record of people talking about their psychological experiences, and that's when it occurred to Jaynes that maybe what we need is not a conventional research psychological approach to consciousness, but an historical approach to consciousness.

We have to look for consciousness outside of the laboratory, we have to look for consciousness outside of psychology. In fact, to follow a purely psychological approach for many problems — not just consciousness — really does not necessarily take you very far. So this is why he started to read about religion, and he started to encounter strange phenomena that still exist, for example spirit possession and hypnosis, and he realized that these things had to be explained. There was really no current theory in psychology that dealt with these phenomena in any serious way.

This is a big problem for many people who study consciousness and try to relate these phenomena to what I would call establishment or conventional research psychology. They don't look at history. And many things don't make sense unless you take a historical perspective. The problem as I see it in research psychology is how they think of time. Most psychologists have only two ways to view time. They view it in developmental terms, or as the lifespan of the individual — they're born, they become adolescents, they go through middle age, they grow old, and then they die. That's one type of time, we might call it an individual developmental range of time.

The other, second range of time, is what evolutionary psychology uses. They look in segments of perhaps tens of thousands or hundreds of thousands of years. But I think that these two ways of looking at time limit us in research. We need a third measure of time, that lasts several thousand years, or even several centuries. Because there are certain periods in the history of human civilization where we can see huge changes when we look at just the space of a few centuries, or a few thousand years. That third measure of time — as I said, several centuries, several millennia — that's also tremendously informative. It's shorter than the time span the evolutionary psychologists use, and it's not limited to the individual, developmental range of time. I think that range of history is where psychologists are missing out on many very interesting things.

LEAHY: Could you clarify how the breakdown of the bicameral mind and birth of consciousness happened in different cultures at different times?

MCVEIGH: Yes. When we are talking about the birth of consciousness in Jaynesian terms, we have to remember that it is not as if people woke up one day and everyone around the globe was conscious. It followed different trajectories, but basically, we can say that most civilizations had people who were conscious by around 1000 BCE. There is some variation, because the growth or the evolution of consciousness, if you will, involved different features of consciousness, and some societies might emphasize some features more than others. But in any case, I think it is pretty clear that if you look at Chinese civilization, if you look at India, Mesopotamia, Palestine, the ancient Greek world, clearly by the eighth or seventh century BCE, everyone was conscious.

Except for people in Mesoamerica and North and South America. If you look at their civilizations, it seems to me that the Maya, for example, probably did not become fully conscious until maybe the seventh or eighth century CE. So they were much later in terms of the development of consciousness. I think that the ancient Inca and the Aztec people probably were conscious when the conquistadors came to the New World, however if you study their religions — if you study their civilizations carefully — it is clear that they had many vestiges of bicameral mentality. So even though Mesoamerica and South America don't fit into the timeline of the evolutionary history of consciousness that we find in the old world, it basically followed the same trajectory — it's just that it occurred later.

LEAHY: What was it like to study under Jaynes?

McVEIGH: Well, I found him to be a quiet and humble individual, but I think you wouldn't know that if you pick up a copy of his book on the origin of consciousness, because it's such a challenge to conventional wisdom. I guess what struck me about Julian Jaynes is how he allowed me at the time — when I first met him, as a lowly grad student — to do all of the talking. For example, I would go to visit him in his office with a question or two. I would ask him my question and he would sit back in his chair and say, "Well, what do you think? I want to hear what you have to say, what are your ideas on the topic?" As a grad student at Princeton University, I found that shocking. And I don't mean to insult the fine faculty of Princeton University — but I found many of them to be quite arrogant. It was refreshing, but shocking, as I said, to meet an individual who was so open to hearing what other people had to say. And related to this, I think it demonstrates how open-minded he was.

4

Metaphor and the Rhetorical Structuring of Consciousness

Ted Remington

Interviewed by Brendan Leahy

Ted Remington received his Ph.D. in rhetorical studies from the University of Iowa. He has taught a wide range of academic writing courses at a number of colleges and universities, including the University of Iowa, Kirkwood Community College, and the University of Saint Francis in Fort Wayne, Indiana, where he served as the Director of Writing and, later, Director of General Education. He currently teaches communication at Western Governors University. His article "Echoes of the Gods: Towards a Jaynesian Understanding of Rhetoric," appears in *Gods, Voices, and the Bicameral Mind: The Theories of Julian Jaynes.*

BRENDAN LEAHY: Can you talk about the topic of metaphor and its relation to subjective consciousness?

TED REMINGTON: As a rhetorician what's most interesting about Jaynes is the way he deals with metaphor, because I think in talking about the way metaphor generates consciousness — to do that he has to really dig into how metaphor works. What's fascinating is the way Jaynes breaks down the concept of metaphor into four categories: *metaphier, metaphrand, paraphier,* and *paraphrand.* So the idea that consciousness is actually created through metaphor is provocative — for someone who comes from a field where we've been preoccupied for 2,400 years with how metaphor works, why it works, what it does, and frankly never coming to any real clear consensus about it. When I read Jaynes, suddenly it became much clearer to me.

Jaynes gives us a vocabulary to talk about metaphor, and he's using that language to talk about how it generates consciousness by using the idea of mind-space as an analog to the physical world. From my point of view, that's interesting, but it's the byproduct of the deeper understanding of metaphor and the mechanics by which it works, which I think is fascinating. In particular, the idea that metaphors don't simply point out existing similarities: they actually create. That's really where metaphor intersects with consciousness: Jaynes says that consciousness — in his fairly strict sense of it as subjective awareness — is something that metaphor creates, rather than something that metaphor simply points to. I think that's the key for Jaynes in terms of his linking of metaphor to consciousness.

As a rhetorician, it's also intriguing because it has implications beyond just consciousness. It talks about how metaphor in general works — that it's not simply the "cherry on top of the sundae" that we use to make a rather ordinary observation about reality fancier, more palatable, or more interesting. Metaphor is inherent in the thought process itself. It creates rather than just describes. That's the mechanism that Jaynes is using as a way of describing the emergence of consciousness. I think — as I've said before in things that I've written — that even if one doesn't go along fully with Jaynes's conclusion that metaphor creates consciousness, simply the way Jaynes understands metaphor and breaking it down the way he does is really valuable to thinking about how language works figuratively; how metaphor is a process, not simply a static thing; and that thought is metaphoric — that all thought is metaphoric by nature. To me that is what is really interesting about Jaynes.

LEAHY: Can you elaborate on this idea of metaphor and its relation to consciousness?

REMINGTON: For Jaynes, consciousness is created through metaphor, and what I see him doing is working actually in sort of a line that goes back a ways in talking about how metaphor is not simply this extra element added to language or an unusual, "artistic" use of language — metaphor is intrinsic to how we think about ourselves and think about the world around us. Language is inherently metaphoric, and what Jaynes is saying — as I understand him — is that the way that consciousness developed or came about is by using metaphor to create an analog of the outside world within our own heads. And again even in phrasing it that way, I'm using his kinds of metaphors.

But the idea is that by talking about things like "I see the solution to a problem," I'm describing an intellectual activity, but I'm doing it in terms of a physical interaction. If I say, "I see something," I suggest that I'm actually visually observing something. That's of course not what's actually going on, but by choosing to use that metaphor, I am creating in a small way, contributing to the idea of an inner mind-space in which I can see myself walking around. I describe mental activities in terms of interacting with the physical world. Metaphors for Jaynes operate by taking these seemingly innocuous verbal descriptions of mental processes, but by using those metaphors, we're actually creating this inner mind-space that we take for granted after that. That is, the metaphors become our internal reality by creating this mind-space that we now take for granted.

By the way, a helpful addition to understanding Jaynes's approach here is the work of cognitive linguist George Lakoff and philosopher Mark Johnson, particularly their book *Metaphors We Live By*, in which they point out the extent to which some of our most fundamental ways of discussing abstract concepts are rooted in metaphors based on our physical existence. Our embodied nature determines how we conceptualize abstractions essential to our way of thinking, such as time, knowledge, and causation. If we connect this to Jaynes, it raises some interesting questions about topics such as artificial intelligence, and if consciousness in the sense of self-awareness is possible in a non-organic entity, or at least if it would be something utterly distinct from how self-awareness is experienced by human beings.

Jaynes is saying that there's no hardwired necessity for us to say things like, "I see a solution." That is a linguistic phenomenon, a metaphor that, while rooted in our biology, is in no sense "automatic." Its use is a cultural phenomenon developed at a particular place and time. That is I think the fascinating insight that Jaynes has: that consciousness — again in the way that he's talking about it; subjectivity — is something that's culturally constructed through the way that we use our language. One of the interesting things about Jaynes for me is the way he ties these very specific uses for language. Something as innocuous as "I see a solution," or "I find what you said interesting" — even these kinds of phrases, that don't seem to be terribly metaphoric to us — in fact if we go back far enough, there was a time in which that idea of attributing or describing mental processes in terms of physical interactions with the world was new. And through that process these phrases created an inner mind-space and the idea of an 'I' that can wander around in a mind-space and interact with it.

I can then project that mind-space into you, and imagine what it's like to experience this interaction from your point of view, by assuming that you have that mind-space. So for me that's one of the most interesting things about Jaynes: the fact that he sees consciousness in terms of a linguistic construct rather than a biological construct, which has all kinds of ramifications. For someone coming from my disciplinary background of rhetoric, that's the gospel to us. That the way we use language is important and not only reflects the world but changes the world, and that's ultimately what Jaynes is saying in his book — that when it comes to metaphor and consciousness, we've created this sense of self by these seemingly innocuous uses of metaphor.

LEAHY: Can you discuss Jaynes's analog 'I' and metaphor 'me,' as well as what the *metaphier, metaphrand, paraphier,* and *paraphrand* relationships are?

REMINGTON: This is a famously complex part of Jaynes, so let's start with a basic understanding of the relationship between those four terms and then move on to the 'I' and the 'me'. The way I explain it is basically to take Jaynes's metaphor that he uses when he describes those terms, and then unpack it. I've been through that chapter numerous times, and every time I go through it I have to reorient myself, because it is really dense stuff.

The metaphor that Jaynes uses when he's describing these things is, "the snow blankets the ground." A fairly random, simple metaphor — nothing terribly artsy about it, but it serves its purpose. Anyone who's taken a middle school English class can say that "the snow blankets the ground" is a metaphor. But then, as Jaynes notes, that doesn't really help us a whole lot if we want to dig into how that metaphor actually works to construct a meaning or understanding. So he breaks down the idea of a metaphor into its constituent parts. He begins the process by looking at, "Well, what are the two moving parts in that metaphor: the snow blankets the ground?" On one hand, you have something being taken out of its literal meaning and being used figuratively — in this case, "blankets." And then we're using that term to describe something about the world around us, in this case something about the way the snow is lying on the ground. He calls those two things the *metaphier* and the *metaphrand*. First, the use of the word "blankets" figuratively is the *metaphier*. Then the thing that it's describing — the snow on the ground — is the *metaphrand*. So that already is helpful because it breaks the idea of a metaphor into two distinct parts.

Now this is something that's not new to Jaynes, other people have done this as well. Probably most famously — from my point of view — I.A. Richards, a well-known rhetorical and literary scholar, used the terms *vehicle* and *tenor* to make that same distinction between the term being used figuratively and the idea that's being expressed with it. Jaynes is aware of Richards and doesn't really like his terminology, for a variety of reasons, and from my point of view actually develops the terms more robustly. Without getting into whether the terms *metaphier* and *metaphrand* or *vehicle* and *tenor* are better or worse, Jaynes takes that idea of breaking the metaphor down and goes even further with it.

So we have "the snow blankets the ground" — "blankets" is the *metaphier* being used to describe something to better understand something about the way the snow is lying on the ground. That's the *metaphrand*. So far so good, but that doesn't really get us to where we want to go, which is to figure out how it is that that actually constructs a new meaning — how we are seeing the snow on the ground *differently* through that metaphor.

So he goes down a level and talks about how you have these associations with the word/concept "blanket," and those can't be listed in some sort of concrete way because they are going to vary from person to person — there's no finite list of things. But what do you think about when you think about blankets? You think about a bed, you think about sleep, you think about warmth, you think about coziness. You might think about snuggling up with somebody. Blankets have these connotations that go with them — those are what he calls the *paraphiers*. So these are associations that go along with the *metaphier* "blankets."

What happens then when we say, "the snow blankets the ground?" Jaynes is saying that when we use that metaphor, we are then mapping the *paraphiers* onto the way the snow blankets the ground. And when we do that, we're not simply pointing out — and this is the key thing to me — some preexisting similarities between blankets and the way the snow is lying on the ground. We're creating similarities; we're generating new understandings about the way the snow is lying on the ground. In this case, the way that works is that we're taking associations with the idea of blankets, the *paraphiers*: warmth, coziness, sleep, etc., and then we're superimposing them or projecting them onto the way the snow blankets the ground.

What does that give us? Well, if the snow is "blanketing the ground," and we understand all those *paraphiers* we just listed as being part of that, you start generating understandings of "Well, does that mean that the ground is a person? The earth is a person?" It's sort of anthropomorphizing the earth. Simple enough. The earth is sleeping, the ground is sleeping... does that mean that winter is like night? Spring is like day? It's a very different understanding than if you used a different metaphor, let's say, "The snow was smothering the ground." It's a metaphor but it has all kinds of different connotations, and I think the neat thing about Jaynes is that he identifies the moving parts of metaphor.

So again, to recapitulate, "The snow blankets the ground":

- blankets = *metaphier*;
- the way the snow is lying on the ground = *metaphrand*,
- *paraphiers* are those things we associate with blankets,
- *paraphrands* are the new understandings about the way the snow is lying on the ground — the associations generated once we understand it in terms of a blanket.

This brings us to the $64,000 question, which is "how does this generate something called the 'I' and the 'me'?" Jaynes is savvy enough to point out that that is a much more difficult thing to figure out. Because in thinking about that, we are engaging in the very process we're trying to describe. It's not as simple as describing the snow on the ground, which is outside of us; we can look at it, I can point at it, it's something that exists outside of us.

In trying to talk about one's own mental processes, it's much more complicated. But as I understand Jaynes, what he's essentially saying is that metaphors began being used to describe mental processes that had as their *paraphiers* aspects of the real world we move around in. So again, things like "I see a solution," "I see where you're coming from," "I grasped that idea" — these are metaphors that parallel the real world, they make mental processes and they describe them in terms of dealing with physical reality around us. So when I say something like "I see the solution," (if we're using that metaphor) I am taking a *paraphier* in the metaphor of "seeing" — which means something that actually has eyes and can see something — and I'm superimposing that onto this idea of seeing a solution.

If I do that, then what I'm creating is this sense of something in my mind-space that is "seeing" a solution. What is that? Well that's what Jaynes is going to call the analog 'I'. When you use a phrase or a metaphor like

"I see a solution," that's presupposing something that is seeing something else. So if the solution is something being seen, what's doing the "seeing?" That becomes the analog 'I'. The metaphor 'me' is this ability to not only think of myself in terms of my subjective experience of seeing the solution to the problem, but also my ability to stand outside of that process and look at me seeing the solution of the process from a third-person perspective.

It's easier to understand if you think of something that's less abstract — and again I'll use an example that Jaynes uses — and think about swimming. If I say, "do you remember when you went swimming last summer?" If you call up that memory, you might think about a first-person experience of being in the water and swimming through it from a first-person point of view. Jaynes suggests that more likely — and I think this rings true with my experience — if I remember myself swimming, what I actually do is I see myself swimming from a third-person perspective. I'm standing from some outside point of view, looking at myself swimming, and that's what Jaynes calls the metaphor 'me' — this being able to see oneself from an outside point of view.

The analog 'I' and the metaphor 'me' can only exist in some sort of setting. The setting is what Jaynes calls "mind-space," which is generated from our use of metaphors where we describe mental processes in terms of physical interactions with the world around us. When we use those metaphors collectively, we create this mind-space inside of ourselves, which we can inhabit both in terms of a first person point of view, but also we can stand outside of ourselves (almost like a movie camera) and watch ourselves doing these things. So you can easily call up memories not simply from your own first person point of view, but you can imagine what the interaction was like for the person you were speaking to — or what I looked like when I was swimming in the pool last summer. That's the difference between the 'I' and the 'me', but they are both products of seeing or of understanding mental processes in terms of a metaphor of physical, interactive experience.

LEAHY: What are some of the similarities and difference between Jaynes's ideas on metaphor and I.A. Richards's earlier work?

REMINGTON: One of the things that really popped out at me is that Jaynes isn't arguing against Richards. He's taking Richards's ideas and developing them in a really profound way. I found the way that Jaynes alludes to Richards, which is literally a footnote in the book, a bit odd. I almost wonder if Jaynes was only aware of Richards's terminology for metaphor, rather than the full content of work in which Richards introduced these terms. What I imagine happening — and I grant I have no hard evidence for this — is that Jaynes was doing some work on metaphor and said, "Well, who else has talked about metaphor? Has anyone else really dug down and tried to figure out how to talk about metaphor in terms of the various moving parts, and how they work together to create meaning?" And he, being a former literature student as an undergrad, remembered I.A. Richards's neat terms *tenor* and *vehicle*, but sort of ended it there.

He somewhat dismisses I.A. Richards's terminology, saying, "Well, yes, Richards did this and he has these terms *vehicle* and *tenor*, and they're ok and somewhat getting at what I'm getting at, but they seem too literary." It almost sounds as though he didn't actually read I.A. Richards's book where those terms come from, which is *The Philosophy of Rhetoric* — not the philosophy of literature or the philosophy of poetry.

The whole book that Richards writes — or it's actually a series of lectures that are assembled into a book — these are all about the fact that metaphor isn't simply a poetic figure; that metaphor is the way that we think about the world, including ourselves. And there are a number of spots in Richards's lectures that seem profoundly Jaynesian. There's one point where he says — and he's paraphrasing Bentham when he's saying this — that if you really begin to think about how integral metaphor is to the very process of thinking itself, one of the things you end up concluding is that perhaps the mind and everything it does are in some way fictitious. And you read that and think, "well, that's Jaynes right there in a nutshell, almost."

I do think it's very important though to notice that there are some important differences that show that Jaynes is taking some insights that Richards has and going beyond them. So, for example, we can go back to our old trusty metaphor of "the snow blankets the earth," — and let's use "earth" here rather than "ground" to make it a little easier to follow, because Richards uses *ground* as one of his terms. Richards would say, "Okay, let's break that down. We have the word 'blankets,' that's the term we're using figuratively, we're going to say that's the *vehicle*. And we're going to say that the *vehicle* is going to be used to describe something about the way the snow is lying on the earth. The way the snow is lying on the earth is going to be the *tenor*." So we have *vehicle* and *tenor* — okay good. Those correspond quite closely to Jaynes's *metaphier* and *metaphrand*.

Here's where things get interesting. Both Richards and Jaynes say that's not enough. You've identified the two kinds of moving parts of the metaphor, but how do those two moving parts create new meaning? Richards says that the *vehicle/tenor* relationship points out similarities between the two things being compared, in this case "blanket" and "the way the snow is lying on the earth." But the way Richards phrases it, he suggests that these are preexisting similarities. In this case, it's a preexisting similarity between a physical blanket on a bed, and the way the snow is lying on the earth. And those preexisting similarities are what he calls *ground*.

Now, it may be something else if you use a metaphor that's less physical. If you say, "so and so is a pig," it might not be that so and so resembles physically a pig, it may be that they resemble a pig in terms of our attitudes towards the person and pigs. The same thing applies: the idea is that the metaphor is pointing to some preexisting set of similarities between the two objects being compared, whether those similarities are physical or attitudinal.

But the important thing is that Richards is suggesting that the similarities are already there and the metaphor simply points them out; that they are there in the real world and we're pointing them out. Jaynes says — and again he doesn't specifically frame his discussion in terms of a development of Richards — "No, we need to break out the term that Richards is calling the *ground* — this idea that preexisting similarities that are out there. That's not really what's going on. We need to break that up into its constituent parts, and those two parts are the *paraphier* and the *paraphrand*. *Paraphiers* are the attitudes we have about the *metaphier* — in this case 'blanket' — and the *paraphrand* is not a preexisting set of similarities; it's *the result* of what happens when we use that metaphor."

When we use the metaphor, "the snow blankets the earth," we are not simply pointing out some objectively existing similarities, we are creating similarities. Because even the concept "similarities" presupposes someone making the connection. The idea of "similarities" existing objectively apart from any subjective experience of them does not make a whole lot of sense. Jaynes cannily realizes this and says, "No, metaphors don't just simply — as Richards suggests — artfully point out similarities that might otherwise go unnoticed, they create new things, they create new understandings." It's not simply pointing out similarities, it's creating something new — a new concept.

What's paradoxical is that this is a way of thinking about metaphor coming from a psychologist. I.A. Richards is a rhetorician, but it's actually Jaynes's way of talking and thinking about metaphor that's more thoroughly rhetorical, because now a metaphor becomes not simply a passive way of pointing to something in reality, it becomes a way of making an assertion that becomes reality. It's changing reality by framing something in a certain way linguistically, which is rhetorical. As a rhetorician, I think, "Wow, that's right on the money," because it talks about how language changes our relationship to the world.

Whether it's physical objects in the world and the way we understand them, whether it's our own social interactions, language changes the way we interact with the world around us, social and physical. And that's coming from Jaynes. That's something that comes out more clearly and emphatically in Jaynes's idea of how metaphor works than it does in even Richards's, who's ostensibly a rhetorician.

So again, one of the many reasons I think Jaynes is really valuable to us thinking about rhetoric — and interested in the way language works socially — is that he gives us a vocabulary with which to talk about that, and an understanding of metaphor that truly does emphasize its rhetorical component: that it's making an assertion that creates something new. Jaynes is focused of course on how those metaphors assert the reality, and in fact create the reality of this subjective 'I' and the mind-space that 'I' inhabits, but that same process can be used to help us understand how we metaphorically create all of our understanding of the world. And does so in a way that gets at the "rhetoricity" of our understanding of the world in a way that even Richards didn't fully grasp.

So I see Jaynes as taking Richards's insights and developing them to a logical next step in that line of thought. I think of Jaynes as a successor and expander of Richards — to what extent Jaynes himself was aware of that is up to debate — he obviously understood Richards's notions of breaking up metaphor into its parts, but whether he fully appreciated how he was coming up with an understanding of metaphor that was as thoroughly rhetorical as it is, I don't know, I can only guess. I suspect that he wasn't fully aware of it. But as a rhetorician, when I read Jaynes I think, "Wow, that guy understands the way metaphor works rhetorically, and gives us an even better vocabulary in which to talk about it, which is great!"

LEAHY: Do you think language is necessary for consciousness?

REMINGTON: The word "consciousness" is a loaded term, and Jaynes spends a lot of time in the book explaining what he means by "consciousness." I think from my point of view, his use of that word is kind of a double-edged sword. On one hand I think it leads a lot of people astray because they assume that when he says "consciousness," he just means being awake. And that if he says, "people in the *Iliad* were not conscious," that somehow he thinks that everyone was like "the walking dead" — walking around like zombies. And of course that's not what he means at all.

On the other hand, if he said something less dramatic like, "subjectivity depends on language," I think it would dramatically undercut the importance of what he's saying. That's the caveat you always have to deal with when discussing Jaynes — what he means by the word "consciousness." If you agree with his definition of "consciousness," if you say, "Okay, we're talking about subjectivity," then I think the answer is yes, not only is metaphor or language necessary for consciousness in his sense, language as a metaphoric process is necessary for thought — that thought itself is metaphoric.

So the short answer is yes. To have the sense of a subjective 'I' is a metaphorical understanding, and metaphors are inherent in language. Perhaps the best analogy I can come up with is if you try to think about time. Time is something we experience — we're aware of it, we live through time moment by moment, but you can't really think of time beyond the here and now unless you make it into a metaphor. So we have lots of metaphors for time. Most of them are spatial, linear — I talk about "this summer has gone by really quickly," or "I'm looking forward to next year." We have other metaphors as well, "I spend my time," so time is money, or "I'm killing time," like time is an organism that I'm killing.

And consciousness is like that, it's something that is inherent in our lived experience, but we can't understand it outside of metaphor and language. Consciousness in the sense of a subjective sense of self is predicated on language because language allows us to abstract from our lived experience and talk about it. If you don't have that, then you can't create this inner mind-space. So if the question is, "is subjective experience of the sort that Jaynes defines as consciousness based on language?" then I think the answer is, "yes, you have to have language to be able to do that." Which is why we don't see that in animals. We have no evidence that animals have this same sort of subjective experience, and it's because animals don't have language in the way we do. They have communication, but they certainly don't have the ability to use language metaphorically. In many cases they may have some signaling or communication system, but that's not the same as "language" in the Jaynesian understanding of language, which is as an inherently metaphorical process. So, if one stipulates that we're talking about a narrow idea of consciousness in the terms that Jaynes is using it, then yes, I think language is a prerequisite for that kind of consciousness.

LEAHY: Do you feel rhetoric was developed out of a need for an expanding consciousness, or was consciousness created out of the development of rhetoric?

REMINGTON: This is a sort of chicken and the egg kind of question, and it depends on how one defines "rhetoric." Simply using language to influence other people might be one way of thinking of it, but for purposes of this discussion I'd go with a more Aristotelian definition, which is the ability to think clearly about how to persuade people. In other words, rhetoric is not merely using language to get people to do something, but the art of *thinking* about how that process works.

What I found interesting after reading Jaynes's book, and thinking about what it might have to say about the history of rhetoric, was to look at the timeline of the development of rhetoric and put that on top of the timeline that Jaynes outlined for consciousness. And when I did that, what emerged — for me at least, and I'm probably out there on my own on this — is that it seemed to dovetail nicely. Jaynes is talking about the social structure of bicameral society being shaken by this fact that suddenly now people don't have these voices telling them what to do. Suddenly they're able to stop and think about, "Well, if I did this, then this would happen" and "If I did that, then that would happen." They're able to project themselves further into time and say, "Well if this happens, then this would happen to me." And social control becomes a problem at that point.

As you have more and more complex societies, with people actually thinking of themselves as individuals, then suddenly you need another sort of mechanism with which to keep society coherent — to keep people working together. How do you do that? Well, you need to use something, some sort of linguistic process to do that. Rhetoric as a discipline develops roughly when Jaynes's understanding of ancient Greece would suggest it should — which is the early fifth century BCE. You're beginning to have society needing to deal with the consequences of the loss of bicameral identity and the loss of these voices telling people what to do. At about that time you have people beginning to think seriously about "Well, how can we use language to get someone else to do something that we want them to do?"

This goes hand in hand with the growth of democracy as well. The origin story for rhetoric, if you look at the ancient Greek sources — and the ancient Greeks are famous for wanting to ascribe complex events to specific individual people, which is a simplistic way of understanding it, but that's how they told their story — the idea is that in the fifth century BCE tyrants were overthrown in the Greek city states in Sicily. They then needed to figure out, "Well, what do we do now? We've gotten rid of the tyrants, that's great, but what do we do now that we have all this land that used to belong to these tyrants, and now we want to split it amongst our-selves, but how do we go about doing that?" That is, how do we self-govern, how do we have this proto-democracy?

That's a problem if you don't have some means of doing it, if you don't have someone telling you what to do. And the story that the Greeks tell is that there were two guys named Corax and Tisias who said, "We've got a solution for you guys — it's called rhetoric. We will use these arts of verbal persuasion and making arguments to hash out what land should belong to whom and move on from there." From Sicily then you have people moving into Athens — which was becoming a democracy — and teaching them how to use rhetoric. That's the story that the Greeks tell about it.

Even if we discount the idea that there were two specific guys who came up with rhetoric out of the blue, the idea that rhetoric developed as a way of dealing with the breakdown of aristocratic rule fits very well with the idea that society was changing at this period — where the Greeks were moving out of a bicameral era into an era where people were expe-riencing themselves subjectively. At that point there was a need to find a way of maintaining social cohesion, and the story about how rhetoric develops at this time and place coincides very nicely with this idea Jaynes has of the breakdown of bicameral society. Suddenly there is a need to find a way to maintain social cohesion, when you no longer have this very autocratic understanding of the way the world works, which is inherent in bicameral society.

I also think it's important to note that in saying that — picking up on what Jaynes is saying — Jaynes is not alone in talking about this change in mindset. Perhaps the best example is Eric Havelock, and also some people who have worked after Havelock, such as Walter Ong, who has written a lot about orality and literacy.[1] At the same point that Jaynes is talking about the breakdown of the bicameral mind and the societal impact of that — at the same time rhetoric is developing in ancient Greece — is also the time when literacy is developing — moving ancient Greece from a primarily oral culture into a written culture. All of these things for me are all of a piece. I think that trying to say that this one caused the other ones to happen sort of misses the point — which is the reinforcing dynamic? Walter Ong said of Jaynes, "Well, it seems to me that, as interesting as that is, Jaynes is just coming up with another way of saying that Greece moved from an oral to a literate society." I think that's too simplistic. I think it's a both/and. You have these combinations of moving from an oral to a literate society and, as Jaynes notes, literacy itself contributed to the breakdown of bicameral society. One of the results of that is if you no longer have bicameral voices telling people what to do and you now have autonomous people wondering, "How do you get people to do things?" Well, you need to persuade them, and there you have rhetoric.

LEAHY: One of the definitions of rhetoric is "language designed to have a persuasive or impressive effect on its audience" but often regarded as lacking in sincerity. How do you feel the development of language and metaphor helped bring individuals from only listening to being able to create it on their own?

REMINGTON: Right, I think you're putting your finger on some important things there. You're right that that is one of the early knocks against rhetoric, almost from the beginning. The most famous naysayer here is Plato, who had a very negative view of rhetoric because he saw it as basically being an art that could be used to manipulate people. Here again, what immediately comes to my mind when you think about the long association of rhetoric as being potentially insincere or manipulative, is going back to what Jaynes said, which is that before the breakdown of bicameral mentality, you couldn't have lying in the sense that we talk about it today. That is, the ability to say something that is not true with the idea of misleading someone can only happen after the breakdown of a bicameral society.

So again, that's one of the offshoots that makes me fascinated with the linkage between Jaynes and the art of rhetoric. People like Plato and people after him considered rhetoric dangerous because it can be used to

---

1. Eric Havelock, *Preface to Plato* (Belknap Press, 1962); Walter Ong, *Orality and Literacy: The Technologizing of the Word* (Routledge, 1982).

misrepresent reality, it can get people to think in ways that they ought not to think. But that only happens if you have transitioned from bicameral mentality.

I think one of the most fascinating things about Jaynes's hypothesis is the idea that lying — in the sense that we use that term today — that kind of deception isn't possible unless you have a subjective 'I' where you can say, "I'm going to tell him something that's not true, because I want to get this effect later on." That's a kind of thought process that can't exist in a bicameral world.

I think there's that linkage between rhetoric and the breakdown of the bicameral mind — in terms of this awareness that people can now be misled through language use. For me, the link that is more interesting — given that rhetoric is where I'm coming from, that's what I focus on — and to see rhetoric a little more positively, I would take a definition more like what I.A. Richards uses, which is that the study of rhetoric is the study of misunderstanding and its remedies. Which is to figure out "how do we negotiate our very fragmented individual experiences with the rest of the world around us and come to some common understanding?" That to me is the art of rhetoric, and it's an art that only works if we understand the way our experience is subjective. And we can only engage in that if we have some language to talk about the way we generate that subjectivity.

So one of the many ways that Jaynes's ideas are valuable is the fact that they gives us a vocabulary to talk about how we take our lived experiences — which is by definition individualistic and not sharable, directly — and how we use language to share those experiences and negotiate them. And only by being aware of that do we have any hope of actually correcting misunderstanding.

One of the things that I love about Jaynes's way of thinking about the way our mind works is that he's not simply highlighting metaphor — interesting as that is — but he's suggesting that consciousness itself is metaphoric. And the consequence of that is that we have to study the way that we represent our experiences to each other through language — if we're going to have any hope of forging commonality with one another. What I'm describing there is, from my point of view, rhetoric. That is, the use of language to get things done, to share our experiences in order to forge something: a meaningful coexistence. I think that's much more difficult unless one starts from a place where we understand that even our conceptions of ourselves are inherently based in language, to the extent that language structures the way we think about ourselves.

LEAHY: You mentioned that rhetoric provided the tool needed to create political and philosophical realities. Are there other areas that rely heavily on metaphors that rhetoric was able to give rise to, other areas that may have played a large role in expanding and maintaining these large societies without the need for a bicameral mind?

REMINGTON: For me, the biggest example of this is what would fall under the heading of *ideology* — that is, taking things that are inherently abstract and giving them some sort of reality in this mind-space that we inhabit. These include things like law, justice, virtue — these big abstractions that we need to have some common agreement on to function in society. In my view, what those are — if you think about it from a Jaynesian perspective — are landmarks in the mind-space that we inhabit.

If you take Jaynes, from the beginning he's talking about a subjective 'I', where one says, "I see a solution to a problem." He talks about this lone figure, this analog 'I' wandering around mind-space. But what happened — what I suspect happened with the breakdown of bicameral society and the need to find some way to forge cohesion among a large disparate group of people who suddenly were now thinking about themselves as individuals — is to create landmarks that everyone could agree on, more or less, in this mind-space. That takes the forms of things like law, justice, truth, virtue, and their opposites: cowardice, venality — all those kinds of things that we use as terms to say, "Here's what our society is about. It's about freedom. It's about justice. It's about law and order."

These are things that we unproblematically throw around in our language even today. But like consciousness itself, these things can't be understood in total because they're abstractions and we don't understand the world abstractly — we understand it through concrete actions. So we have to come up with a metaphorical way of understanding things like law. Even the word "law," if you go back etymologically, the original meaning is a plot of land. As Jaynes points out, many things like "law," "virtue," "truth" — if you go back far enough you can see that these abstract concepts are often based, etymologically, in physical metaphors.

So what I think rhetoric does more than anything, as far as performing a role to keep society cohesive in a post-bicameral world, is creating through give and take the ideas of these abstractions as having a reality so we think that, "Law and freedom are these actual things, right?" Well no, they're abstractions that we've created from actual individual experiences of things, that we then decided to label "law" or "justice" — that's a just act, that's a virtuous act. We try to say that there's some sort of actual preexisting commonality that these things have, but they don't. We've created that as a metaphor — "virtue," "truth," "justice" — and decided to treat those things as if they were real things, the same way we would treat our analog 'I' as if it's a real thing.

The way I tend to describe it is that rhetoric does two things: first, it creates these things so that if you imagine walking through your mind-space, if you live in a society that has some fairly firm ideas about what "freedom" and "justice" and "the law" are, you can imagine them as the landmarks — the buildings, the forest, the trees that you walk around in your internal mind-space. "Virtue is on the corner of truth and duty" — almost. You're walking around this mind-space that is populated or structured by these things that exist metaphorically, but which we don't treat as metaphorical — we treat as real because we have to. If we don't treat them as real, society breaks down. So rhetoric is the way in which we create ideas about law, virtue, justice, etc.

Second, it's also the way that we can step outside of ideology and look at the way it's constructed — in the way that I just did — and say, "you know what, yes, freedom is good, truth is good, let's accept that. But let's also think about where we came up with these concepts. What abstractions have we made from real events that have created these things?" So rhetoric is both the means by which ideology — which I think of as being the scenery in the mind-space we move through — in our given society is created, and it's also the means by which we can talk about, "Well, is this really the scenery that we want? Do we want to change the scenery? Is this scenery serving us?" So rhetoric is both the creation of ideology and also the way we can critique ideology. That's a very broad answer, but that to me is how I think about the way rhetoric serves as a tool with which to maintain social cohesion in a post-bicameral world — it's through the creation and critique of ideology.

LEAHY: Elizabeth Bell Carroll, during temporal lobe epilepsy seizures, would hallucinate a garden of Eden where she was searching for answers.[2] Could you speak to the idea of hallucination as metaphor?

---

2. See Elizabeth Bell Carroll's interview, "A Vestige of the Bicameral Mind in the Modern World," in this volume.

REMINGTON: I can give it a shot, but it's going to be on much thinner ice because you're talking about something that's a medical condition, and I'm only a doctor in the old-fashioned academic sense [laughs]. To me, when I read about hallucination in the context that Jaynes describes it, what I imagine is something that's a visceral unsubjective experience that parallels what we do on a day-to-day basis when we walk through these virtual mind-spaces that we've created for ourselves.

So again, as I was saying earlier, as we wander through this mind-space and imagine ourselves doing things and interacting with these entities called "law" and "justice" and "love" — and we don't actually believe that. I'm aware that I'm sitting in this room talking to you, even as in my mind I'm walking through this virtual reality that I have created for myself. My sense is that hallucinations occur when the metaphor becomes real; that is, when the metaphorical space intrudes on our actual visceral experience of the world and substitutes itself for it.

Most of us, as I say in our normal thinking, are very much aware of the fact that there's this physical world around us and there's our mental mind-space. And if we go along with Jaynes and say that our mental mind-space is an analog of the outside space, and follows some of the same rules and we conceptualize it in the same way, we're very much aware of the separateness. And when I'm reading about hallucinations — whether auditory or visual — what comes to my mind is that it's basically a case where this internal mind-space is then being projected outwards and is taking the place of our actual physical perceptions in a way that makes it hard to distinguish between the two.

That's a layperson's point of view on this. But if I'm trying to understand how Jaynes is understanding hallucination and connecting it to how I'm thinking about language and rhetoric and ideology, that's where I make the connection: that hallucinations are where this analogous relationship between mind-space and the physical world collapses, and is undistinguished. I've never had a hallucination myself, so I can only go from reports, but that's what it sounds like is happening, from my point of view. Hallucination in the Jaynesian sense is when that separateness between mind-space and the physical world collapses, and that goes along with his whole idea that the breakdown of bicameral mentality — that everyone was like that before we suddenly created this internal mind-space.

Again, Jaynes is not alone in saying that. Other scholars have pointed out that if you look at the *Iliad* and the Old Testament and early Greek philosophers, there's clearly a vastly different sense of subjectivity. Even if you don't accept his arguments regarding auditory hallucinations, I don't think there's any disagreement that there was a vastly different way of understanding oneself and the relationship between oneself and the world. That is, if you look at Homeric era Greeks, the idea of saying something like, "well I did that, but that wasn't at all like me. It's not like me to do something like that." What do you mean, "it's not like you to do something like that?" You did that. Your actions are you, so this idea that somehow there's a "you" that's independent of what you do when interacting with the world around you is a novel concept — that's not something that's always been around.

Jaynes is saying, I think, that in the bicameral age, actions and one's sense of self were the same thing, and only with the advent of consciousness — in Jaynes's strong sense of the term — were you able to separate those two. What he points to in the case of schizophrenics, or other people with hallucinations of an auditory or visual nature, is how those things collapse back onto each other. So again, take that with a grain of salt because it's coming from a non-medical person. But to me that's how I understand the relationship, again this momentary re-collapse of mind-space and the physical world into something that's indistinguishable from each other.

LEAHY: Where do you think things are going in terms of your field?

REMINGTON: Looking at rhetoric from a Jaynesian point of view, on one hand, the pessimistic part of me feels that academics in general have become more and more siloed, and there's less and less people who are willing and able to look at issues like consciousness and metaphor from a multi-disciplinary point of view — and Jaynes is nothing if not multidisciplinary.

I mean that's the whole magic of Jaynes to me: his ability to draw from all of these different ways of thinking about the world, all these different disciplines — psychiatry, anthropology, archeology, classics — and to be able to put them together. That was a rare gift when Jaynes was writing his book, and I think it's even rarer now. I think we've made academia into this very siloed thing. But if there's one discipline that I think has been showing the promise of breaking that down — and has a lot to gain by doing that — it's rhetoric.

There is actually some work being done in that regard. I have a colleague who is very interested in cognitive linguistics and the connection between cognitive linguistics and rhetoric. I think that is an area that's going to be mined in the future. For example, we might think about the way the mind actually processes language, and then take that seemingly technical information and use it to better understand how those processes play out socially and politically. And I think there's a tendency for those things to be separated and thought about in a very tactical way: the way the brain works and the way language is processed, and thinking about the way language has actually worked socially in the world as being separate things. But I think we're beginning to see a move towards understanding that fields like cognitive linguistics, rhetoric, the sciences in general, and the humanities do have these areas of overlap, and I think rhetoric is a place where enough thought has been done already that it serves as a natural place where insights like Jaynes's can flourish.

My experience with Jaynes has been that there are still a lot of people who will dismiss him precisely because of his ability to draw on all of these different areas. So classicists will say, "Well, I don't really agree with his reading of the *Iliad*." Literary critics might say, "I don't care for his description of metaphor" — you know people will do that. But I think that's missing the forest for the trees.

In my experience, rhetoric is a place where there's a growing awareness of the importance of people who think about language and consciousness from a scientific point of view, and thinking about it from a social point of view. Those two camps need to come together, and it's not a matter of one has to subdue the other, it's saying these are both lenses that we can use to understand the world around us. So I'm cautiously optimistic that ideas like Jaynes's lend themselves to language and that rhetorical critics are in a position — given that we've traditionally been this vagabond discipline that's drawn on a lot of other disciplines — to make use of that. I'm cautiously optimistic, and I'm very encouraged by the increasing dialogue among cognitive linguistics and humanists that this is something that is going to bear fruit down the road. And I think, to the extent that it does, Jaynes is a great representative anecdote of the fruitfulness of that mixing of perspectives.

Further Reading

Ted Remington,"Echoes of the Gods: Towards a Jaynesian Understanding of Rhetoric," in M. Kuijsten (ed.), *Gods, Voices, and the Bicameral Mind* (Julian Jaynes Society, 2016).

5

The Development of
Consciousness in Children

Bill Rowe

Interviewed by Brendan Leahy

Bill Rowe retired from the University of California Santa Cruz where he worked for 27 years as a staff research associate for the Santa Cruz Institute for Particle Physics. Since retiring he has worked as an independent consultant for medical device companies developing models and neural implants for various neurological disorders. His four part article, "Retrospective: Julian Jaynes and *The Origin of Consciousness in the Breakdown of the Bicameral Mind*" was published in the *American Journal of Psychology*. Updated and revised portions appear as three chapters in *Gods, Voices, and the Bicameral Mind*, and he was an invited speaker at the Julian Jaynes Society Conference on Consciousness and Bicameral Studies.

BRENDAN LEAHY: What are some of the prerequisites for consciousness, as consciousness is defined by Jaynes?

BILL ROWE: Well in children, there's a capacity and a context. There has to be a capacity for language — language is an absolute requirement. Then the group that the child is born into has to have the need to build cognitively flexible individuals who are comfortable with making a lot of choices. Julian Jaynes's theory is a constructivist one. So, to put together a child development component, we have to look for features in childhood that link the child to the group or to other people, because you have to learn consciousness through other people.

When we look at the trajectory from birth to seven years of age, we have to find features that are species-specific — unique to humans — and that reasonably can contribute to the final product: consciousness as Julian Jaynes defines it. Over the course of human development, there's an intimacy between the human infant and the caregiver that we don't see in any other species. This is referred to in the literature as intersubjectivity, and this intersubjectivity is probably the core from which later humans' subjective consciousness emerged.

I see in intersubjectivity the formation of something like a virtual third-person. At least to the degree that the two parties are interacting rhythmically, that behavior can't be predicted on the basis of either one of them alone. That means it's more than the sum of the parts. We have to look for some species-specific behaviors that are shared between the infant and the caregiver, and I suggest there are five. So it's a small set, but there are five things from birth to about seven years of age which are reasonable suggestions that are necessary for the origin of consciousness.

The first one is very early in the first year of life, and that's rhythmic entrainment. What is shared with rhythmic entrainment is affect. Affect is the outward expression of feelings or emotion. So the rhythmic entrainment is just what you might think — the adult, more formal version of it is singing and dancing together. What is really remarkable in the human species, and only humans, is we see this in childhood — the infant and the caregiver interacting rhythmically.

The next thing we see is equally remarkable, and it's the ability to share subjective experience. And the vehicle for this is what the psychotherapist Daniel Stern called "affect attunement." Affect attunement looks like imitation, but it's not. In fact, we all do it all the time. Instead of duplicating what a person did, you abstract the way they did it, the intensity, shape, and then you play it back in another modality. So, if the infant did something with his hand, pounding a block of wood, for example, that increased in loudness and beat, the mother — in order to regulate the infant — would not do the same thing (the infant would hardly notice if she did). Instead, she will, with her voice or her body, duplicate it. So if he goes *knock, knock, knock* on the wood the mother might say "oh, oh, oh." So for the infant, this is completely different behavior going on, but in that is a ghost of what he or she just felt. It should have a déjà vu feeling to it, it could also have the feeling like "I've just been penetrated; this person can get inside of me." We do this all the time, but it is a transcendental moment for the infant when this happens.

Coming up on nine months, some people call this the nine-month miracle. At nine months for a typically developing infant, the pattern switches from dyadic (person to person) to triadic (two people engaged in sustained attention on a third object), and the vehicle for this is shared focal attention. It's important because the child is not attending to this third object for his or her own sake; he or she is doing it because of the previous nine months of living inside the affective states of another living person. It's a rather monumental phase — that's nine months.

As we move into the teen months, we see pretense emerge — pretend play. This is very important for Jaynes's theory. Most other animals at a similar stage are trying to get the world right, but the human infant at this stage is launched off into imaginative excursions. It should be high risk, but it's not — it turns out to be very useful. So that's pretend play, and what is shared is a social script. The first examples of pretend play that we see in the infant are not capricious, they're not random, they are social interactions that they've had before, with caregivers as a witness. But now they're generating it on their own, and this is evidence that they have internalized a generalized other. They're doing it for this imaginative person, and maybe for a live person.

In the last feature, between ages three and seven, we then see the ability to share knowledge. And this now goes under the rubric of "theory of mind." Theory of mind is where children are taught to interpret other people in terms of invisible things: belief, desire, thought, memory. So, at about four years of age, a child might say "Sally is crying because she wanted to go to the zoo, but the trip was canceled." So you interpret other peoples' behavior, and predict their behavior, based on these hypothetical mental states.

So those are five features that are unique to the human species. That makes them candidates to be necessary — but maybe not sufficient — for Jaynes's theory of consciousness. The first one I consider to be the most important: rhythmic entrainment. Without that, you don't get that first intimate coupling, which has the same intimacy that we all know when we dance or sing with someone — that's not available to other animals. Other animals can feed together, they can groom, they can fight, but it's nothing like this. This is special to the human species. And that's the core of what I think is the developmental component to Julian Jaynes's theory.

LEAHY: At what age do you see children fully developing consciousness in the Jaynesian sense?

ROWE: I would say seven is the point in which many of the things we just talked about plateau, and the child is now ready to go beyond that. So by plateau I mean that a typically developing child will pass all of the theory of mind tests. At seven, they're not only interpreting other people in terms of these invisible things — thoughts and memories and desires — but by age seven, they're also turning it back on themselves, and they're explaining their own behavior in terms of these social constructs: thoughts, memories, and beliefs.

An intriguing corollary to age seven are rites of passages. For example, the Catholic Church has never had the rite of confirmation below age seven. Confirmation is a type of rite of passage: "Welcome into the community now." Why age seven? The Church has always said that that's the "age of reason" — even though most parents would raise an eyebrow that their seven year old is reasonable. However, it does make sense from a scientific point of view, because as I was just saying, the child now passes all these false belief tests, and other tests, such as theory of mind.

Also, by age six, typically developing children are able to decenter in time and tell a story about themselves in this imaginary space called time. So because they can talk about themselves — "what I thought, what I wanted, what I did" — in a past and in an imagined future, they can now be held guilty. That's the main reason why the Church has confirmation: they can know that they've sinned, and there needs to be a rite of passage for this. So I would put the realization of consciousness at around age seven.

LEAHY: Can you delve a little more into what theory of mind is, and touch on the theory of mind tests?

ROWE: So theory of mind is a version of "attribution theory" in psychology, which has been around for some time. In this case, you attribute mental states to other people. Examples would be desire, belief, thought and memory, intention, regret. You use those to interpret other peoples' behavior. It's only been around as an experimental paradigm since the early 1980s. But very quickly, a handful of measurements came to be operationalized.

So typically measurements are "source of knowledge" tests. That is, if you know something, do you understand how you came to know it? Did someone tell you, did you reach into a bag and feel something, or did you see it? That's source of knowledge. There is also what's called "appearance reality." When does a child know that the way something appears is not what it is? Also deception; this is an interesting one because there is such a thing that all primates can do — it's called tactical deception in the wild. They can learn when to hide food and other things; these are non-conscious skills that can be understood from a basic behaviorist point of view. Children can do that by age three. By age four, they begin doing something different. Since they are conceiving other people in terms of thought and memory and beliefs, they begin to try to manipulate those thoughts, memories, and beliefs. Then, and only then, do we have true deception. But the test that everyone talks about when you discuss theory of mind is the "false belief test." That's the one that is probably used the most often, to my knowledge.

I'll give you an example of the false belief test and its rough trajectory through time. So this is the content false belief test, the "Sally-Anne false belief test." So in this test, you have 3-year old Sally, and you show her a box of candy marked "candy." And you say "what's in here?" and she'll say "candy." Then you open it, and it's pencils. So you close the box. Now Anne comes in. Now the question for Sally is, "What will Anne think is in there?" Three-year-old Sally will say "pencils." She doesn't know that other people don't know what she does. But more importantly, she doesn't yet conceive Anne, in terms of mental states and beliefs, so she can't imagine that Anne can be wrong in a belief.

Four-year old Sally is a little different. At four years old, most children begin passing this false belief test. By six and seven, pretty much everybody passes the false belief test. So theory of mind is the arrival at a state in which you can interpret other peoples' behavior in terms of invisible things. These are social constructs, you can never find belief in the brain. And there's probably one other important facet to this, at least for Jaynes's theory. Going beyond interpreting other people in terms of these, the child, probably by age seven, begins turning it on herself and thinking of herself in the same terms that she initially learned to talk about other people. And that's a remarkable phase, because you're beginning to be able to view yourself as an object. So it's one of the first steps to viewing yourself objectively, which is important for human consciousness.

LEAHY: You point out in your article the differences between the theory of mind test given to children in China versus the test in the U.S., and how some difference within societies and social expectations pushed the Chinese children to develop some skills a little bit sooner?

ROWE: Right, they develop executive skills sooner. We talk about the terrible twos, when the child is developing a lot of rapid motor sequential skills, they are able to do things quickly. The bad side of that is they do it with everything around the house — they turn every button on. So executive skills are what adults impart to children to get them to take context into account. "You don't push the button on the stereo," and things like this. So Chinese children hit this a little sooner than American children. But it doesn't influence the rate at which they go through theory of mind. So I was using this as an example because there are some debates which say that theory of mind is present right away, it's just not expressed, it's just waiting to be expressed. And I made the claim in the article, that the particular relationship of Chinese children arriving at executive skills earlier than American children, but going no faster in theory of mind skills, makes a case that we don't have these theory of mind skills in the early months shortly after birth, they are acquired in a social context. That was the point I was trying to make there.

LEAHY: Can you talk about developmental disability as it relates to bicameral mentality and the development of consciousness?

ROWE: Autism is most likely the one to focus on. Jaynes's theory is a social constructivist one, and autism is a deficit in social interactions. Autistic children have trouble holding gaze, they have trouble with touch, they're very anxious in any social interaction. So, since Jaynes's theory is a social constructivist one, it depends on a very intimate relationship between people, and autistic children have a problem with this. I would say that learning more about autism could shed light on how children come to be conscious in Jaynes's sense. From my point of view, since I put a lot of stock in this first year of life, the rhythmic entrainment, even though there may be multiple routes to autism, one of them I would propose is that the child has missed this rhythmic entrainment phase; they've missed this opportunity to establish this intimacy and intersubjectivity with another person, and so they don't know what it means when another person is talking. They have trouble with theory of mind mental states, because they've never experienced the world through another person the way a normal child has when they go through that first year of life.

LEAHY: Could you speak about children and their use of metaphor?

ROWE: Actually, children's first use of metaphor is surprisingly early — eighteen, nineteen, twenty months? However, they're not called "true" metaphors; sometimes they're called "child metaphors," and they happen at a stage that is referred to as symbolic play. In the teen months, the symbolic play that you see children going through is the ability to use an object or event to represent another object or event. An example of what is often called "first metaphor" would be a child will see a ladder and say "scissors," or they will point to a green rug and say "grass."

So why aren't these real metaphors? There's a symmetry to those sentences, and true metaphors are considered to be asymmetric. An example of asymmetric, true metaphor would be from *Hamlet*, Act 1, Scene 2. Hamlet says, "the world is an unweeded garden." The reason that's asymmetric is the purpose of that sentence is to recontextualize the topic, the world, in terms of an unweeded garden. So, it works one way; the unweeded garden works on the world. Whereas what the child just said, at eighteen months or twenty months, pointing to the green carpet saying "grass," could have equally pointed to a well-tended lawn and said "carpet." Now this changes as you move from second year to fourth year. Coming on four or five years of age, you see a child who is able to either generate, or definitely to understand, a sentence like "the car is dead" — so that's getting there metaphorically. However, the same child can stumble on a sentence like "the idea blossomed" — which is still a little too abstract.

But as we hit ages six, seven, and eight, we do see significant development in the use of metaphor. There was one experiment they did on I think three- to nine-year-olds: A story is read to the children about a girl going home, and the story has two endings — a literal one, and a metaphoric one. In the literal one, the story ends with "Sally, the girl ran to her home." The metaphoric one ends with "Sally, the bird flew to her nest." Then the test is — let's take the six-year-old — they would give the six-year-old a doll and say, "Act out the metaphorical ending." The six year old, probably still a little too tightly tethered to symbolical play, will take the doll and fly it through the air like a bird. Not true for the eight-year-old, the eight-year-old will understand that "Sally, the bird flew to her nest" was metaphoric, and they will take the doll and run it along the ground quickly to home. So, somewhat like theory of mind and other milestones, again, it's age seven in which we see an inflection point. Children will still fail various tests of metaphors, but adults fail tests of metaphors too. They are complicated, and depend on context, previous knowledge, how it's asked. But again, I would place it at age seven when they're beginning to be pretty confident at the use and understanding of metaphorical language.

LEAHY: What causes the cessation of imaginary companions?

ROWE: The adults either discourage the imaginary companions or ignore them. The reason they do it, at least in our society, is that to the degree that imaginary companions are echoes of bicameral volition, they don't fit. Today, we need to raise children to be very cognitively flexible, to be decision-makers, and that means "you're on your own, you're making your own decisions" — so you can't go around depending upon the voices, which is really an echo of the executive skills that you learned going through the terrible twos. So, adults either explicitly discourage them or ignore them, and as the child grows up herself, she will realize "this isn't working." Some people do keep their voices though — their companions — their entire life. But it generally doesn't fit within the context of our modern society.

LEAHY: If you could, you were talking about how the first time you read Julian Jaynes's work and how you understood it then versus how you understood it twenty years later, if you could talk about that... and how your understanding shifted?

ROWE: Well I first read it 1977, the year it came out. And at the time, I don't think I understood a thing, I was bewildered by it. But I was so taken with the meter and the beat and the prose that I read it again. I think the way he wrote just instilled in me a sense of confidence in this man. So I kept reading it, and every re-read I would get something new. And that sort of snowballed over the years; I began to gain more confidence in this writing.

But I would say the breakpoint for me was in the early nineties, when I went to a summer-long seminar on the University of California, Santa Cruz campus in the philosophy department. And there I learned about the psychotherapist Daniel Stern, who's written a book called *The Interpersonal World of the Infant*, and that changed everything for me. To see the social construction of a child, immediately I saw how that would fit in, or was needed, in Julian Jaynes's theory. So that was the biggest, most important change for me — to come in contact with people who studied children.

Daniel Stern was part of a cadre of developmental psychologists in the seventies who could afford video equipment — it became less expensive then, so they began filming infants and their caregivers, just for the purpose of doing what they did: studying children. They would do frame-by-frame analysis, and then it was amazing! The titles of their papers, through the seventies, were filled with musical terms. "Orchestral" relationship between mother and child, "rhythmic" entrainment between infant and caregiver — so that resonated with me. And it was importing that into Jaynes's theory which gave a second life to it, because there were lots of things left undone.

That led to studying theory of mind, and then that helped me with another component of Jaynes's theory, and that is his description of mentalities in bicameral times: Mycenae and the Greeks, and the oldest parts of the Old Testament. Because he said, as well as other classicists say, that people in those ancient cultures were not like us. Indeed, they don't have mental state terms like we do. So that was always a puzzle to me — how am I going to come to grips with Jaynes's theory? At first I didn't know how to interpret it. So access to this way of studying children, and seeing how theory of mind is actually optional, and then turning it on yourself is actually optional — that was a turning point in helping me come to grips with Julian Jaynes's theory.

LEAHY: Where do you think consciousness is headed? Currently we still have remnants of bicameral mentality present today — do you feel like those are going to disappear completely?

ROWE: Consciousness in this view is infinite. Given that consciousness is a metaphorical construct, well metaphors are infinite, there's no limit to how you can conceive of yourself. And I think Jaynes believed this. It's simply ongoing, it's difficult to predict what another subsequent consciousness will be.

There is an interesting thing along these lines though that I think is worth noting, that is theory of mind around the world. People are now taking tests on theory of mind and looking at other cultures, particularly traditional cultures which don't have writing. That's a window into the variation which consciousness is capable of, because theory of mind began in the eighties, and it was done by WEIRD people studying WEIRD children. "WEIRD" is a technical term, it's W-E-I-R-D… Western Educated Individual Rich and Democratic. When this whole thing started, it was American and British scientists, all Western Educated Individual Rich and Democratic countries, and they were studying the children of people just like them — that's who they had access to. So there was an initial bias to theory of mind studies. But it was known. So, now it's operationalized, it's stable. If you look at the psychologist Angeline Lillard's paper, "Ethnopsychologies: Cultural Variations in Theory of Mind," it's stunning to see how traditional cultures construct the mind.[1] We try to find the terms that are just like ours, and they're not there.

In fact, most traditional cultures' words for "mind" are inseparable from words for "feeling." And often words for "mind" are not located in the head at all, they're located in the heart. They don't have it wrong, and we don't have it right. It is dependent upon what the culture needs, what they will index it on. I have a feeling that traditional cultures have it more right than we do. We inherited a Greek Platonic version of the mind, which sort of puts thinking and reasoning somewhere "out there," that it's decoupled from the body.

There is another thing from neuroscience that I've learned, and that is that there is no such thing as a thought that's non-emotional. That's what we are, we are our body. I think this is an important thing — that even what people call thought (if you read about "aha" moments that people have), those are emotional shifts. When you know you figured out a formula, you have a feeling. So I can't find anything in human cognition that is not part of feeling. In fact if you ask someone to describe what it's like when you're thinking, they can tell you, but it's all feeling states.

So in any case, looking at ethnographies around the world can really give us a sense of how highly variable this sense of self is. What's it going to be like when we become increasingly dependent upon and intimate with machines? It could get very strange. But it is going to happen. One interesting thing you can do to see how variable personal experience is, is to close your eyes and take a pencil and drag the tip of it along a rough surface. Your experience will not be at your fingertips, you will experience that point. So that gives you a sense of what it's going to be like if we increasingly add prosthetics to our bodies, as we see people doing. So I think consciousness is infinitely variable. It will change. It has to, because it depends on the context. The culture has to raise its young to fit that context, and I just don't have any idea of how it might go, but it's probably going to be pretty exciting.

---

1. Angeline Lillard, "Ethnopsychologies: Cultural Variations in Theory of Mind," *Psychological Bulletin*, 1998, 123, 1.

6

Julian Jaynes and
Contemporary Philosophy of Mind

Jan Sleutels

Interviewed by Brendan Leahy

Jan Sleutels is Professor of Philosophy at Leiden University. His teaching and research interests include metaphysics, philosophy of mind, and media philosophy. His article on Jaynes's theory, "Greek Zombies," was published in the journal *Philosophical Psychology*, and a revised version appears in the book *Reflections on the Dawn of Consciousness*. He has spoken on Jaynes's theory at several conferences, including the Julian Jaynes Society Conference on Consciousness and Bicameral Studies.

BRENDAN LEAHY: How did you first become interested in Julian Jaynes's theory?

JAN SLEUTELS: I read Julian Jaynes's book when I was a first-year student, a few years after it was published. It was not part of any of my courses, but so were most of the books I read. I absolutely loved it. Amazing claims, an inspiring mix of archaeology, psychology, and philosophy, and a very engaging writing style! Then I put Jaynes on the shelf and went on reading lots of other books that took my fancy.

Apart from a passing reference in my Ph.D. thesis, I never did anything with Jaynes's theory, until a little over 10 years ago. I became interested in the question of whether it is possible, or under which conditions it is possible, that human mentality — the way human beings experience the world — went through substantial changes in the near or distant past.

That question arose when I decided to include evolutionary psychology and cognitive archaeology into a philosophy course I was teaching. These disciplines raise questions about the architecture of the minds of our distant ancestors, for example a million years ago, 500,000 years ago, or 20,000 years ago — Stone Age people, so to speak. How did Stone Age people experience the world and organize their behavior? Did they have motives? Desires? Beliefs?

It struck me that most work in evolutionary psychology and cognitive archaeology is based on a typical way of thinking about the psychology of our distant ancestors, by projecting our own self-image as mindful beings onto all predecessors. It is presumed from the outset that their psychology must have been roughly like our own, but then with a prehistoric twist. It reminded me of the Flintstones cartoon series that I watched as a kid. In cartoons the effect is very enjoyable, of course, but I don't think it is wise to use that strategy in science.[1]

When thinking about the possibility that the human mind may have undergone substantial changes in the course of history, I remembered Julian Jaynes. How did philosophers, psychologists, and archaeologists respond to his theory? What were their arguments to choose a Flintstones approach, as you might call it, rather than a Jaynesian approach?

LEAHY: What did you find?

SLEUTELS: To my amazement: almost nothing. The general public loved Jaynes's book, but in the academic world it was for the most part ignored. Jaynes was simply dismissed as a maverick, without discussion. I found that very intriguing. Why was that? What is so outrageous about the idea that the minds of our not-so-distant ancestors, a mere couple of millennia ago, may have been very different from our own?

Jaynes's hypothesis is that consciousness as we know it today is of a fairly recent date, roughly 1200 BCE. Consciousness as we know it today: an inner world of thoughts, memories, beliefs and desires, mental items that you can internally manipulate and process, for instance when you are deliberating or planning future action. Before 1200 BCE. (or maybe later in places where the change occurred more recently) people had a different sort of mind, according to Jaynes, a mind not marked by this inner world where we engage in deliberations. What makes this suggestion so outrageous that it can be dismissed?

---

1. See Jan Sleutels, "The Flintstones Fallacy," *Dialogue and Universalism*, 2013, 1, 65-75.

I wrote a paper about the question of "Greek Zombies," as I called it, which was published by the journal *Philosophical Psychology* in 2006.[2] I focused on one of the very few philosophers who actually had something to say about Jaynes, the American philosopher Ned Block. He wrote a short review of Jaynes's book in 1981.[3] There as well as in his later work on consciousness, he argued that Jaynes's theory is "ludicrous" and "obviously false."

LEAHY: What specifically were Ned Block's arguments and how did you respond to them?

SLEUTELS: Ned Block is known for making a distinction between a number of functionally different types of consciousness. The two most important of these are "A-consciousness" — A for *access* — and "P-consciousness" — P for *phenomenal*.

Phenomenal consciousness is the consciousness in which you have something "appear to you." You open your eyes in the morning and you see bright colors, or maybe you awake to the smell of freshly ground coffee. If you were blind, by contrast, nothing would be visually appearing to you in phenomenal consciousness — you would not have a visual world being phenomenally presented to you.

Access consciousness refers to the fact that our type of consciousness is something like a "storage place," so to speak, or an inner realm, in which you have different items present, as in memory. Think of memory as the storage place where you can put away memories to store them, and then later retrieve them — have "access" to them. We have the same sort of "access" to mental items such as beliefs and desires in all sorts of rational processes. For instance, you have access to a number of ideas, or propositions, when you are trying to figure out how they are logically related, which of them you should discard, and which you should keep.

Now, Block raised the question whether it would be possible for P-consciousness or A-consciousness to be something that emerged relatively recently in history. Could it be that before, let's say, 1500 BCE people did not have P-consciousness? Could it be that they did not have A-consciousness? On both counts, Block says that this is literally "unthinkable" to him. It's unthinkable that our ancestors did not have anything phenomenally "appear" to them when they woke up in the morning. And it is "perfectly

---

2. Jan Sleutels, "Greek Zombies," *Philosophical Psychology*, April 2006, 19, 2, 177-197. Revised version in M. Kuijsten (ed.), *Reflections on the Dawn of Consciousness* (Julian Jaynes Society, 2006).
3. Ned Block, "Review of Julian Jaynes' *The Origin of Consciousness in the Breakdown of the Bicameral Mind*," *Cognition and Brain Theory*, 1981, 4, 81-83.

obvious" that even animals have P-consciousness. As for A-consciousness, Block says that "even higher primates have it," and therefore it would be "silly" to claim that it is something that emerged only in the course of cultural history.

It should be clear that Block is simply stating a prejudice here, not giving an argument. He is spelling out an intuition about what it means to be a being that is even remotely like us — an ancestor in the recent or distant past, or a biological relative like the higher primates. The basis for this intuition is our own self-image as mindful beings, which is then used as a psychological gold standard: any being that is sufficiently like us, must have a mental structure just like us, A-consciousness and P-consciousness included. This intuition may be widely shared, but it does not amount to an argument. It just begs the question against Jaynes.

LEAHY: So Block had no real arguments against Jaynes?

SLEUTELS: First a word about Jaynes and P-consciousness here. I don't think Block is right in suggesting that Jaynes denied that the Mycenaean Greeks, or other ancient cultures, had P-consciousness. As I read Jaynes, his theory is strictly about A-consciousness, not about P-consciousness. P-consciousness is not something that Jaynes would call consciousness at all, but rather "awareness," which is something he was glad to grant to higher primates, lower primates, all other sorts of animals, as well as to all sorts of human beings, including distant ancestors. So I think that Jaynes's theory is about A-consciousness, which he himself described in terms of a "mind-space" in which your "analog I" can perform operations on mental items.

Now, in addition to the intuitions I just mentioned, Block offers the following line of argument against Jaynes. He points out that the basis for Jaynes's theory seems to be that the "concept" of consciousness in the modern sense of the word was absent in ancient Greece. But from this it does not follow, Block says, that they did not have consciousness. To think otherwise would be committing a so-called use/mention fallacy: to mistake *using* a concept with *mentioning* a concept.

To illustrate this fallacy, let's compare consciousness to gravity. For the sake of convenience let's assume that it was Sir Isaac Newton who single-handedly introduced the concept of gravity. So before Newton there was no concept of gravity. But from this it obviously does not follow that there was no gravity before Newton. Before Newton there was gravity (the thing), even though there was no "gravity" (the word referring to the thing). Similarly, it would be a mistake to claim that before the concept of consciousness was introduced, there was no consciousness.

According to Block, the case of consciousness is just like that of gravity. And because of this giant logical blunder, Jaynes's theory can be safely dismissed. I don't think this alleged refutation is as straightforward as Block makes it appear, however. I think Block seriously underestimates what it takes for a concept to be completely absent, especially in the case of a concept like consciousness. To explain this, we need to take a closer look at Jaynes's theory of what happened when the ancient "bicameral mind" (as Jaynes called it) was replaced by consciousness in its modern form.

According to Jaynes, between 1200 and 800 BCE a new cultural technology emerged and developed in ancient Greece, with at its core a new way of using language. It has been noted by scholars before Julian Jaynes, most notably the German classical philologist Bruno Snell, that until roughly 800 BCE the Greek language did not have verbs for describing mental acts, nor nouns for describing anything like the mental items we are now familiar with.[4]

The ancient Greeks had a rich vocabulary for describing all sorts of public transactions such as communication between persons, and also for the specific things that get transacted, or are conveyed from one person to another. But it had no nouns for pointing out items in one's mind, nor verbs for denoting the mental actions we are familiar with. Think of "speaking to yourself," or "thinking to yourself," or for "finding an explanation," "finding a reason for things," or even for "reasoning," for that matter.

Somewhere around the year 1000 BCE, Jaynes argues, the Greek language was enriched with this new vocabulary that made it possible for people to describe what goes on in their minds, in language. Until then, they had only been able to describe things that happened "outside" of them, but from that moment onward, once that change in their language spread throughout their community, they were also able to describe things that went on "inside" them.

According to Jaynes, this new vocabulary made it possible for them to get a handle on what was going on in their minds. In the ancient framework of the "bicameral" mind, people typically described what went on in their minds as "alien" events that they were not in control of — as "hearing voices" (that are not your own), "seeing things" (that are not really there), or

4. Bruno Snell, *The Discovery of the Mind: In Greek Philosophy and Literature* (Dover, 1951).

as a "blindness" (that makes you do things in a way you don't understand). Not knowing what else to make of these "alien" events, they typically attributed them to the gods, who spoke to them, made things appear to them, and made them do the things they did.

You and I also "hear voices" and "see things," but we know how to identify with the internal mental agent that is speaking, making things appear before the mind's eye, and making you jump into action for specific reasons. We have acquired a set of skills for this, presumably at a very early age. It may be like second nature to us, but it is a skill nonetheless, one which the ancient Greeks had not yet acquired.

According to Jaynes, the switch from bicameral mentality to modern consciousness was made possible by a new language technology that enabled people to "take control" of their A-consciousness, so to speak. The new verbs and the new nouns derived from interpersonal communication were now used for identifying intrapersonal activity, and the events that used to be experienced as "alien" could now be conceptualized as being part and parcel of a person's own mental agency.

There is also a neural story to be told about the switch from bicameral mentality to modern consciousness. Along with the acquisition of new language skills and the changes in social life that go with it, something must have changed in people's brains as well. Jaynes explored possible explanations for bicameral mentality in terms of neuroscience, focusing on the communication between the brain's left and right hemispheres. While he didn't propose a neurology of consciousness, my personal feeling, with the benefit several decades of new research, is that the shift to consciousness may have involved the natural plasticity of the neocortex, to explain the acquisition of cultural skills and habits. I will leave the brain issues aside for now, and focus on the role of language technology.

Now that we have seen some of the details of Jaynes's theory, how does this affect Block's alleged refutation in terms of the use/mention fallacy? If the modern concept of consciousness was lacking in 1000 BCE, is it still a logical blunder to conclude that consciousness was lacking as well? I think Block's argument loses much of its force.

Block thinks of the concept of consciousness as merely a word in a language that can be absent or present. Whether it's absent or present wouldn't then make much difference to the reality of the phenomenon, as in the case of gravity. You can lack the word for X, and still have X. On the other hand, if "having the concept of consciousness" really translates as "possessing a number of relevant skills," then the concept of consciousness does not so much describe something that was there in the first place (like gravity), but rather serves to establish a new way of arranging, organizing, and taking control of one's mental life.

It is only when you become aware of the fact that there are many different items that you have access to — things that you can say to yourself, things that you can use for planning future action, or that you can use for narrating something about your past — that you can start actually trying to accomplish them. This awareness emerges as you acquire the skill of taking charge of your mental life. The voices you are hearing are not those of the gods telling you what to do, but your own!

LEAHY: In your article you mention the concept of "folk psychology." Can you say more about that?

SLEUTELS: When we think about the mind, both in daily life and in scientific psychology, we use a specific set of concepts like belief, desire, perception, memory, and imagination. We have all learned how to use these concepts that are part of our "folk psychology," as it is sometimes called. Folk psychology expresses the self-image that we have of ourselves as thinking beings. It's something that we have acquired, and that is culturally variable: we have our "Western" folk psychology, while other cultures use slightly different sets of concepts.

This folk psychology, or "theory of mind," is something we use in everyday life for describing our mental states, but it is also the starting-point for scientific psychology, or any other discipline that sets out to explain the mind. Scientific psychology needs folk psychology to identify its *explananda* — the set of phenomena that need to be explained in the first place.

Now an interesting question poses itself: when confronted with a culture that is using a different set of concepts to describe the mind, would it be fair to use our folk psychology to describe their mental lives?[5] Think of this as a thought experiment: imagine that you come across a culture — in the past, present, or future — with a folk psychology that is substantially different from your own. How should that culture be studied from a psychological point of view? Is it fair to use our contemporary, Western set of concepts to describe and explain what is going on in their minds? I don't think so. We should rather try to use that other culture's folk psychology

---

5. See Jan Sleutels, "Fringe Mind Strategies," *AVANT: Journal of the Philosophical-Interdisciplinary Vanguard*, 2013, 2, 59-80.

to describe their mentality, for the same reasons that *our* folk psychology is the best starting-point for studying *our* type of mind. This is a *parity argument*, because of the parity of reasoning involved in selecting the appropriate set of concepts for describing and explaining the minds to go with that folk psychology. With a different folk psychology you get a different sort of mind.

Now, is it conceivable that we should run into a culture with a folk psychology that is substantially different from our own? Maybe one that lacks all concepts relating to memory, or all concepts relating to imagination, beliefs, or desires? I think we should say, "Yes, that is absolutely conceivable, at least in theory." In practice it remains to be seen what would convince us of the fact that a culture is actually based on a substantially different folk psychology. What sort of evidence does it take to establish this? Sources need to be translated and interpreted. Doesn't this inevitably mean that we use our own concepts to describe the other culture's psychology, and hence "contaminate" it with our own folk psychology?

What I find particularly fascinating about Julian Jaynes's approach, is that he took his sources at face value, so to speak. The ancient Greeks, Mesopotamians, and Egyptians left records of their mental goings-on — not only obliquely in the form of the artifacts they created, the buildings they erected, and the battles they fought, but also in the form of actual written records based on a preceding, pristinely oral tradition. What the records suggest, taken literally and at face value, is that these ancient cultures described their minds in terms of a folk psychology that was substantially different from our own.

And why not take them at face value, as literally true reports of a radically different type of mental organization? We do the same with our own folk psychology, so shouldn't we make allowance for other cultures as well? There is the parity argument again!

That brings me back to Block's line of argument against Jaynes. If you look at the balance of evidence, I think that Jaynes is holding his ground, and is actually doing better than Block. Block's arguments turn out to be intuitions drawn from present-day folk psychology, while Jaynes presents arguments based on empirical evidence. Block's appeal to intuitions puts up an *a priori* block against alternative folk psychologies, while Jaynes, when backed up with the parity argument, paves the way for taking them seriously.

LEAHY: Indeed. You also introduced the concept of "fringe minds." What do you mean by that?

SLEUTELS: Think of a collection of people, or even beings in general, in terms of a spatial metaphor, as forming a field that has a core and that has fringes, or outskirts. You find yourself at the center, right in the core, together with all others who organize their behavior and mental activity in roughly the same way. The people at the core use a shared folk psychology, in the sense that I just explained.

The closer you are to another person, in terms of distance in this field, the easier it is for you to guess what the other person is up to — what he or she believes, desires, is feeling or thinking, etc. For instance, you, Brendan, are really close to me in terms of this field. I know why you are here, what you're planning to do in the foreseeable future, and even roughly what you're thinking right now. I can read your mind. It's even easier with my wife, my brother, or my closest friends, whom I know so much better. Taking myself as a reference point, we form a sort of core.

You can apply this idea of a field with a core and fringes to wider communities as well, for instance to all people living here in the Netherlands, or in Western Europe. Surprisingly, many people are very close to me, in the sense that I can read their minds. Even strangers that I've never met before, that I might meet on a train. I can more or less easily read their minds, just like they can read mine. Why is that? Because we share a common folk psychology, or "theory of mind," we organize our behavior and mental activity in roughly the same way, and we know what to expect from one another.

But there are also persons who are slightly different from you and me, who behave in slightly different ways, who do things that we cannot really understand, and whose minds are much more difficult to read. They find themselves, not at the core, but at a greater distance from the core — so to speak, at the fringes.

For instance, this is true of my own children, who are now young teenagers. They clearly have a different mindset from mine. At times I honestly don't know what they are up to or how they manage to do the things they do. The younger the children are, the more difficult it is to read their minds. A newborn infant, lying in a cradle, and crying: what's going on in there? I can imagine that she wants a new diaper, or is hungry, or is otherwise feeling uncomfortable. But otherwise? Infants don't organize their crying behavior in the same way as adults do. I wouldn't even know where to start when trying to answer the question of what goes on in their minds.

What is true of young children here is even more true of non-human animals. Dogs and cats — what are they feeling or thinking? What do they desire or believe, if anything at all? Sure, to some extent I can make sense of their behavior by interpreting it in "human" terms, but I know that I am projecting something onto them that may not really be there. With goldfish or spiders this is even worse. At the distant fringes of the field I'm a lousy mind-reader.

Now apply this idea of core and fringes to our ancestors. My parents, my grandparents, my great-grandparents — presumably they are relatively near to me, still at the core of the field. But what happens as you go deeper down into history, one generation after another? What happens when you reach prehistory? As you go deeper down, it becomes increasingly difficult to be sure about the experience and mental architecture of distant ancestors. Based on material traces of their activity, which are studied by archaeologists, we try to figure out what their behavior must have been like, which already involves some tricky guessing. But when it comes to reading their minds, we're at a loss. How did they mentally organize that behavior? Did they have beliefs and desires; did they plan their behavior on the basis of motives and deliberate choices in the way that we do? I know how to read minds at the core, but I don't know how to do that at the fringes, where I cannot be sure that the core set of concepts still applies.

What I find particularly interesting about Jaynes's theory is his suggestion and that the fringes of mind may be closer to home than is usually expected. You don't have to go down into deep history, say 500,000 years or 50,000 years, to find beings whose mind worked in a way that is radically different from ours. Jaynes boldly suggested that we might run into fringe minds a mere 3,500 years ago. We are talking about human beings in the relatively recent past, who are considered "modern" by all the usual standards of biologists, archaeologists, and historians, who to all appearances must have been quite like us — but then with a "bicameral mentality" — without consciousness in the Jaynesian sense of the word.

LEAHY: How does Jaynes define consciousness?

SLEUTELS: Julian Jaynes tries to be as precise as possible about what he means by modern consciousness. "Basic awareness" is not part of that, Jaynes said — being there when you engage in public activities, like playing ball, sitting in a chair, preparing food, simply doing things. We would say that you know what you are doing when you are doing these things, even if you're not consciously thinking about them. That's basic awareness. It's like being "switched on," so to speak.

Consciousness, in the sense that's really distinct from bicameral mentality, takes much more than basic awareness. Jaynes uses a spatial metaphor to describe it as being a private "inner world" where you are king and ruler. An inner world where you contemplate, store, and manipulate mental items "before the mind's eye," as we sometimes say. In this inner world you engage in private mental activities that are not publicly observable, and that do not necessarily result in observable behavior at all.

It's the sort of mental activity that you typically engage in when you sit in a chair thinking, musing, reviewing the day, or planning the next day. Maybe you make up the balance at the end of the day — what went well and what went wrong, how you could have done better, what needs to be done tomorrow. Or maybe you mentally rehearse what you are going to say next to your colleagues across the table — before actually saying it out loud.

This inner world is certainly a crucial aspect of consciousness as we know it today. A second crucial aspect of consciousness is the idea that there is a "ruler," someone in charge of what goes on in this inner kingdom, and that it is you, or rather 'I'. It is 'me' who is in charge of the musing, thinking, planning, and other mental activities.

This internal ruler is not quite the same as the actual 'I', the real 'me' who is walking, talking, shaking hands, tending to the fields, etc. The 'real me' obviously includes the body that is engaged in doing all these things. The "internal ruler" is something analogous to the 'real me'. It is what Jaynes called the 'analog I'.

LEAHY: How does Jaynes's idea of consciousness compare to that of other philosophers?

SLEUTELS: Most modern philosophy and psychology tend to identify the 'I' that performs the publicly observable feats with the 'I' that does the mental feats. Or rather, they tend not to make a distinction between the two.

One example is Ned Block's account of consciousness in terms of A-consciousness and P-consciousness, which we discussed earlier. Block makes no distinction between what you might call the "operators" of these forms of consciousness, nor does he distinguish them from the embodied person, or the embodied cognitive system that features consciousness. That is also one of the reasons why Block thinks that straightforward biological considerations should be enough to refute Jaynes's theory. If the biologically embodied 'I' hasn't changed, then the conscious 'I' can't have changed either.

In terms of Block's terminology, Jaynes introduced a strict distinction between the "operator" of A-consciousness on the one hand (which he called the 'analog I'), and the embodied person on the other hand (what I have just called the 'real me'). Moreover, Jaynes reserves the word "consciousness" for A-consciousness, and attributed P-consciousness (which he calles "basic awareness") to the embodied person (the 'real me'). On that basis, Jaynes is able to argue that the development of consciousness and of embodied persons are quite different processes, both in an evolutionary and in a historical sense.

It is particularly interesting to compare Jaynes's view to that of Immanuel Kant, the famous eighteenth century Enlightenment philosopher. In his famous first critique, *The Critique of Pure Reason*, Kant came close to suggesting that the 'I' of consciousness, like Jaynes's 'analog I', is not the same as the 'real me'. All conscious thought and experience, Kant said, revolves around a single 'I' that does the experiencing, for otherwise it would be impossible that one's experience is a logically connected whole. Kant distinguished this single 'I' (which he called the "transcendental self") from the real 'me' (which he called the "empirical self"), which is reminiscent of the distinction made by Jaynes.

The resemblance between Kant and Jaynes may be merely apparent, however, depending on how you explain Kant's distinction between the transcendental self and the empirical self. But even apart from that question, there is still a capital difference between the two. Kant thought that the 'I' of consciousness is a universal characteristic shared by all human beings. If Jaynes is right, that certainly needs to be corrected!

Further Reading

Jan Sleutels, "Greek Zombies," in M. Kuijsten (ed.), *Reflections on the Dawn of Consciousness* (Julian Jaynes Society, 2006).

HYPOTHESIS II

Bicameral Mentality

7

The Bicameral Mind Explained

Marcel Kuijsten

Interviewed by Brendan Leahy

BRENDAN LEAHY: What were the origins of the bicameral mind? How did the bicameral mentality come about?

MARCEL KUIJSTEN: So roughly 50,000 to 100,000 years ago we have the beginnings of language. There is a lot of speculation around the actual date, and no one really knows for sure when language began. But as our use of language developed, Jaynes argues that the brain began using language as a tool or vehicle to convey knowledge and experience from one hemisphere of the brain to the other. This occurred in the form of what today we call auditory hallucinations. What Jaynes proposed is that, during an auditory verbal hallucination, the language areas of the non-dominant hemisphere become active, facilitating the transmission of information to the dominant hemisphere across the corpus callosum, via language.

Jaynes speculates that it was often the stress of decision-making that triggered this process. This voice, which generally has an external quality to it, was interpreted by bicameral people as the voice of their chief, dead ancestors, and eventually the gods. Jaynes thinks that bicameral mentality helped with decision-making, helped keep nonconscious humans focused on tasks, and also reinforced the hierarchical social structure that allowed these early civilizations to function.

LEAHY: So if a family member died, did Jaynes propose that the remaining relatives would hear the voice of that family member, or would the commanding voice be of the chief or ruler of the society?

KUIJSTEN: Depending on the culture, I think we see both. We see the dead being fed via feeding tubes, as if they were still alive. In some cases, we see dead family members' skulls placed in dwellings, perhaps as a source of bicameral hallucination. So various props were used to help facilitate the hallucinations. First the skulls of dead ancestors, and later, in Mesopotamia, we see the use of the small, large-eyed idols that were found in nearly every dwelling.

There is a large degree of cultural variability. In ancient China, for example, there was a greater focus on the voices of dead ancestors than on gods. Whereas in Egypt and Mesopotamia, we see elaborate hierarchies of gods. The great gods issued commands to the king or priests that were concerned with the major decisions of the community. In addition, each individual likely had a personal god, heard only by them, whose commands would be related to their day-to-day issues.

LEAHY: Were these voices constant, or did they only occur at specific times?

KUIJSTEN: Most likely, the hallucinations were not constant. Rather, when a person was in a situation where a decision was required, a build-up of stress hormones would trigger a bicameral hallucination. Most of daily life was probably fairly habitual. To a large extent even today, where introspection has, for most of us, taken the place of bicameral hallucination, much of our everyday lives is habitual behavior, and we could often get through most of our day without introspection.

In terms of the frequency of the voices, we also have evidence from present-day voice hearers. There are some people that only hear a voice occasionally, whereas with others the voices seem to be fairly predominant throughout the day. I have personally spoken to voice hearers who tell me that they hear their voices throughout the day. People often hear multiple voices, which is something that was not well known at the time Jaynes was writing his book. We are still learning a great deal about both the content and the frequency of the voices in present-day voice hearers. A point to emphasize is that the voices generally seem to center on the person's behavior — commanding it, criticizing it, and commenting on it — and this of course is very much in line with what we would predict based on Jaynes's theory.

LEAHY: How did people function in these large cities with everyone hearing different voices?

KUIJSTEN: This is a great question, and one that I've heard before. I think people often forget that in these early bicameral civilizations, like us, people were intelligent, they had language, and they were communicating with one another. The major decisions — for example, where to build a temple, issues regarding the harvest, and these kinds of things — were commands that were issued by the great gods and were hallucinated by the leaders, either in waking life or in dreams. Then these commands were communicated down the hierarchy through spoken language, through the clergy and the different social structures that they had in place — just as an order would be passed down today, in a modern military hierarchy, for example. Individuals in these cultures relied on their personal god for making their own day-to-day decisions. It is the strict hierarchical nature of these civilizations that allows the bicameral mentality to function. We can also imagine in our society today what happens when someone low in the social hierarchy has an idea that would impact the entire group, or a different way they want to do things — generally they are just ignored.

LEAHY: How did civilizations progress and eventually have this issue of bicameral mentality transitioning to consciousness?

KUIJSTEN: Jaynes suggests that bicameral mentality functions well up to a certain point in a civilization's population growth and complexity — so it functioned well in these strict hierarchical societies of a certain size. But as a society became too large and too complex, and perhaps began intermingling with other nearby societies, or suffered from natural disasters or invasions, it could no longer function and could no longer maintain the type of social control that it did in smaller, more stable populations.

So when civilizations encountered other groups — through migrations, war, and marauding — there was a lot of intermingling of different societies with different gods, and the voices perhaps became confused: different groups had different hierarchies of gods and so the whole system broke down. Jaynes points to examples in different cultures, such as the Maya, where societies were built up, reached a certain level of complexity, and then mysteriously broke down again — they abandoned their cities and returned to the forest. We see similar breakdowns in Egypt as well as the Late Bronze Age collapse around the Mediterranean.

Jaynes thinks that what we are seeing in these examples of societal collapse are periodic breakdowns of bicameral mentality. Then after a period of time, various groups coalesce, and these societies build back up again.

So bicameral civilizations were stable up to a certain point, but could not handle social complexity beyond that point. And eventually, as language grew in complexity, this led to the development of the new, more flexible mentality of consciousness.

Jaynes argues that this process was facilitated by the evolution of language. As metaphorical language developed and became complex and widespread, through metaphors of the physical world we developed an interior mind-space that allows us to introspect, reflect on the past, deliberate on our decisions, and think about things like history in completely new ways. Jaynes argues that the development of writing was also a factor. So as this new way of thinking developed, based on the new technologies of metaphorical language and writing, bicameral hallucinations began to be suppressed.

LEAHY: Can you talk about examples from ancient texts that tell us how bicameral societies worked?

KUIJSTEN: Yes, Jaynes describes an example from the *Iliad*, where, at the time of a decision, Athena appears before Achilles and issues a command. We also see examples from other civilizations, such as ancient Mesopotamia. Ancient Mesopotamia is quite interesting because there we have a situation where the gods owned all of the land and the gods were essentially the leaders of the civilization. Imagine if your local city council consisted only of gods — this is a very difficult idea for modern people to relate to, and it reflects a very different psychology than our own.

In Mesopotamia, ancient texts tell us that the high priests would enter the temples to interact with the great gods. Often they would sleep in the temple and receive the will of the gods in bicameral dreams, also called "visitation dreams." The idols in the temples were not seen as statues "representing the gods," but rather they believed that these *were* the gods themselves — and every other instance of a statue of that god in the city was also that god. They fed and bathed these idols, and took them on parades.

Coming from our modern, conscious perspective, these concepts are very difficult to comprehend. There are many descriptions of how all of this worked, and none of it makes much sense without the perspective of Jaynes's theory. In other words, why would any of this have taken place — why would people in ancient cultures engage in these bizarre rituals and behaviors — if they were psychologically identical to us, as some scholars would have us believe?

Their psychology does indeed seem to have been very different from ours, and it was these differences that Jaynes took note of, and began putting the various pieces of the puzzle together. I think that Jaynes was able to look at these various lines of evidence very objectively, whereas historians and classicists have a well known tendency to project our modern psychology into the past — something called the *presentist fallacy*.

It's fascinating to read the descriptions of these rituals by the classicists. They describe things that are truly bizarre from our modern perspective — but they simply describe them without offering any interpretation. In other words, it was just something interesting that went on.

Part of the reason for this is that generally scholars are heavily specialized in their fields, often creating a disconnect between the academic disciplines. On the one hand, we have classicists describing these very strange and interesting behaviors, but ignoring the psychological implications. And on the other hand, psychologists and psychiatrists are primarily focused on the mental health issues of today — with a few exceptions, they generally don't concern themselves with the psychology of people in the past, let alone in ancient civilizations.

I think this is one of the reasons why much of the evidence for bicameral mentality went unnoticed for such a long time. Jaynes was the first to look at this evidence in ancient history from a psychologist's perspective. Equally important, he took a literal interpretation of these events — rather than impose a modern psychological interpretation. In other words, if we are told by the ancient Greeks that Achilles saw Athena and heard her command, then perhaps they are describing their actual experience. There is no *a priori* reason to impose our modern psychology and assume that this was some type of literary device, as has so often been suggested. So these are some of the factors that I think helped Jaynes to develop his theory.

LEAHY: What are some of the things we see in history as bicameral mentality starts to break down?

KUIJSTEN: As bicameral mentality starts to break down and consciousness begins to develop, we see many different behaviors taking place that are otherwise fairly inexplicable. What drives this process is the fact that people were accustomed to hearing the voices of the gods — experiencing auditory hallucinations to direct their actions — and when the voices begin to disappear, we see a lot of anguish, fear, and confusion. And in various ancient texts we see people lamenting the loss of the gods.

Then an entire repertoire of new behaviors come into place, designed to attempt to try to still determine what the gods want them to do. We see the emergence of things like oracles, omens, prophets, prayer, astrology, and divination — and there were many different types of divination. Interestingly, the oracles in Greece were typically illiterate peasant girls, who were still able to more easily enter into trance states and thus have hallucinatory experiences.

So initially, everyone heard the voices of the gods. Then, as bicameral mentality broke down, eventually only certain people continued hearing the voices of the gods — for example, the early prophets of the Old Testament. And then it became only certain people in specific places, such as the Oracle at Delphi. Eventually the gods fell silent altogether, and people turned to the last writings of the gods in order to try to understand their will, and these writings were gathered together into things like the Old Testament. Even today, we continue to look to these texts for guidance as to what we should do — as basically the last known commandments of the gods. So this quest for external authorization continues in the form of modern religions, cults, celebrities, and charismatic leaders.

LEAHY: What are some of the other vestiges of the bicameral mind?

KUIJSTEN: So even in the modern world today we see many vestiges of this earlier bicameral mentality. The first vestige that I will mention is what is commonly termed schizophrenia. There is a lot of controversy about schizophrenia, and whether or not it is actually one definable mental illness, or a variety of different symptoms that are being placed under the umbrella term of "schizophrenia." I prefer to focus on the most common symptom, which is auditory hallucinations, and to just avoid the term "schizophrenia" altogether.

The modern psychiatric approach to auditory hallucinations has generally been to view them rather simply as a sign that for some reason the brain is not functioning properly — that there is some type of brain pathology. But if we look more carefully at the content of hallucinations, we come to find that they almost always center on the person's behavior: either describing it, criticizing it, or, perhaps most frequently, commanding it. We now even see the term "command hallucinations" frequently in the medical literature, because it is such a common form of hallucination.

Looking at this through the lens of Jaynes's theory, the fact that hallucinations often direct behavior makes perfect sense. It fits perfectly, and there are no compelling alternate interpretations as to why this would be the case. So from the perspective of Jaynes's theory, what we have are modern, conscious people that are having what we might call a relapse to bicameral mentality, and thus they are hearing hallucinations that command their behavior. There are even cases of people who refer to their hallucinations as "voices of the gods."[1] Often in modern culture, the voices are also attributed to political or religious figures, but they are nearly always attributed to someone that would be above the person in the social hierarchy.

There are many other vestiges as well, such as "spirit possession," hypnosis, and even inspired poetry. Often people do not realize that many of the great poets in history heard voices from which they transcribed their poetry.[2]

LEAHY: Can you say more about the hierarchical aspect of the voices?

KUIJSTEN: Yes, so people today normally interpret their voices in terms of our modern social structure — so typically political figures such as the President, or religious figures such as God or Jesus — but it is generally someone who is above them in their perceived hierarchy, just as it would have been during the bicameral period. And as I mentioned, there are still many cases today of people who perceive their voices as coming from gods, particularly in non-Western cultures. Like anything else, there are always exceptions, but attributing one's voice to someone above oneself in the social hierarchy seems to be the general rule.

It is the hierarchical aspect of the voices that gives them their authority. It is why the command hallucinations are often obeyed. As a species, humans naturally form hierarchies, as do many other mammals. As we developed language and bicameral mentality emerged, the voices helped enforce these hierarchical structures. I think this had a survival value, and it is otherwise somewhat of a mystery as to why the right hemisphere seems to "look down" upon the left hemisphere. But this hierarchical aspect to the voices again fits perfectly with Jaynes's theory, and without his theory, it becomes much more difficult to explain.

---

1. Russell T. Hurlburt, "A Schizophrenic Woman Who Heard Voices of the Gods," in M. Kuijsten (ed.), *Gods, Voices, and the Bicameral Mind: The Theories of Julian Jaynes* (Julian Jaynes Society, 2016); see also T.M. Luhrmann and J. Marrow (eds.), *Our Most Troubling Madness: Case Studies in Schizophrenia across Cultures* (University of California Press, 2016), pgs. 99-126.

2. See Julian Jaynes, "The Ghost of a Flea: Visions of William Blake," in M. Kuijsten (ed.), *Reflections on the Dawn of Consciousness* (Julian Jaynes Society, 2006); Carole Brooks Platt, *In Their Right Minds: The Lives and Shared Practices of Poetic Geniuses* (Imprint Academic, 2015).

LEAHY: Do children also experience hallucinations?

KUIJSTEN: Yes, we see hallucinations in children as well. In the seventies and eighties we started to see more discussion of children's "imaginary playmates," but there is a book on this subject that dates back to 1918.[3] Today the phenomenon is typically referred to as "imaginary companions." And with imaginary companions, children are often seen interacting with a companion that does not exist.

Initially people thought that this was just children's imagination and role-playing and this kind of thing, and some researchers still maintain this view. But other developmental psychologists that study this now suggest that, at least in some cases, the phenomenon involves actual hallucinations. And the numbers are much larger than what was initially believed; something close to 50% of children have this kind of experience.[4] Then there are also other studies looking at hallucinations in normal, non-clinical child populations that do not necessarily involve an imaginary companion.[5]

So the situation is likely complex: some children likely have imaginary companions that are purely imagination-based, and don't involve hallucinations; others have imaginary companions that do involve hallucinations; and still others experience hallucinations in the absence of an imaginary companion.

Jaynes suggests that in bicameral societies, that voice or companion would have grown up with the person and become their personal god. Today, parents often try to socialize that experience out of the child, but some people continue to hear their voice into adulthood. If you gain people's confidence on this topic, you would be surprised by the number of people who have had this experience. I like to encourage people to do their own personal survey of their friends and family as to whether or not they have had an imaginary companion or experienced hallucinations. I should add that it is only recently that we have begun to learn more about adults who experience an imaginary companion, or whose childhood imaginary companion persists into adulthood.[6]

So there is still much more that we can learn about both the phenomenon of imaginary companions and hearing voices in children. How often do they occur? What is the exact nature of the experience? What is the

---

3. N.A. Harvey, *Imaginary Playmates and Other Mental Phenomena of Children* (State Normal College, 1918).
4. D. Pearson, et al., "Prevalence of Imaginary Companions in a Normal Child Population," *Child*, 2001, 27, 1.
5. D. Pearson, et al., "Auditory Hallucinations in Normal Child Populations," *Personality and Individual Differences*, 2001, 31, 3.
6. See the interview with Tanya Luhrmann, "Hearing Voices, Sensed Presences, and Imagined 'Others'" in this volume.

content? How often does the experience of imaginary companions involve actual hallucinations, and how often do children experience hallucinations but not develop an imaginary companion? How often does it simply fade away, and how often does it progress into adulthood? There is a lot that we still don't know, but the main takeaway is that these experiences are much more common in children than was previously known, and they strongly support Jaynes's theory. Alternate explanations as to why this occurs to me seem unconvincing.

LEAHY: Can you talk a little more about the experience of hearing voices in the general, non-clinical population?

KUIJSTEN: Yes, the phenomenon of hearing voices among everyday, "normal," non-clinical people is also much more common than was previously known. Jaynes's book inspired the modern interest in this subject, and it has since been studied in a wide variety of populations. Hallucinations are often induced by stress, and they have now been documented in soldiers in combat situations; in the elderly, especially after the loss of a spouse; in wilderness explorers and high altitude climbers; in people in social isolation, such as solitary confinement; in people under sensory deprivation; in various ethnic populations — there are a wide variety of studies that show auditory hallucinations are not at all uncommon among the general population. There is also now an organization called the Hearing Voices Network, that seeks to both remove the stigma of the experience of hearing voices as well as teach people how to better live with their voices.

In terms of the actual experience, there is a wide variety in the type of experiences that people have. In some cases it is perceived as an externally produced voice. The voice is often associated by the person with the left ear or the left shoulder, which is interesting because that is the side that is associated with the right hemisphere. The occultist Aleister Crowley described hearing voices and associated it with his left side. One woman I spoke with who had this experience called it "the crow on her left shoulder." This gets to the next point, which is that it is often a critical voice — the voice often comments, criticizes, or commands their behavior. There is often a negative quality to it, as though the right hemisphere is "looking down" on the left hemisphere in a critical way. However this is also not always the case — less frequently, people enjoy their voice, and think of it more like an imaginary friend or a helpful, guiding companion.

In other cases, people describe hearing voices that are coming from their own mind, so to speak, but that are not "theirs" — so it is a voice that is perceived internally, but that they feel is not their own and that they do not associate with their sense of self. It is not perceived as their own internal dialogue — the way you or I might continually have an inner narrative of thoughts, things that we have to do, etc. They feel as though this is a voice coming from within them, but it's a separate voice that they don't associate with themselves.

There's another variety of voice hearing called "inserted thoughts" that is somewhat similar to this. And with inserted thoughts, people feel as though someone else is inserting thoughts into their own mind.[7] So they feel as though the thoughts are their own, but they are being put there by someone else.

The frequency of the voices varies widely as well — from something that happens quite rarely to almost non-stop. So the experience of hearing voices is quite varied as well as difficult for the average person to relate to.

LEAHY: Occasionally I suffer from sleep paralysis — it tends to happen more if I'm very tired. Typically I hear something like a woman crying or calling my name. Sometimes the experience can be terrifying. That has typically been the only time when I've experienced hearing a voice.

KUIJSTEN: It has been found that, for the person that rarely hears voices, the most common time for them to experience an auditory or visual hallucination is when they are just falling asleep or just waking up. In some cases, people will be caught in a state where they have woken up, but they are still experiencing a dream. So, yes, for someone that rarely has this experience, that is the most frequent time that they will occur.

But I should also point out that just about anyone can have the experience of hearing voices. And if you are skeptical about hallucinations, there are a number of different ways that you can induce this experience. First, you can stay up for more than say 24 to 30 hours, and you will likely start to hallucinate. An easier method is to visit a sensory deprivation tank, often called a flotation tank. These have become increasingly popular in recent years, and these types of sensory deprivation experiences often induce hallucinations. Similarly, if you were placed in solitary confinement for a number of days, you will very likely start to hallucinate.

---

7. G. Lynn Stephens and George Graham, *When Self-Consciousness Breaks: Alien Voices and Inserted Thoughts* (MIT Press, 2000).

Very stressful situations often induce hallucinations — for example, in life or death situations, people often experience a voice or vision that helps guide them to safety. Finally, there are a number of psychedelic substances that one can take that will induce hallucinations. So there are a number of different paths to hearing voices, even for the average person that has never had this experience.

LEAHY: Can you say a little more about the role of psychedelics in the hearing voices experience?

KUIJSTEN: Yes, this is something that many people are interested in. People often ask about hallucinatory substances and whether or not they can be used as a method to get back to what we might call a bicameral state, or state where one could hallucinate external guidance, or what they might characterize as spiritual or divine guidance. We do see that in many different cultures, hallucinogens are one of the methods that are used to have this type of experience. It has become more popular even in Western culture to seek this out, for example there are organized retreats that people go on for the express purpose of consuming hallucinogens such as ayahuasca.

Here again, the types of experiences that people have vary widely. Some people do experience things like actual voices and visions. Others are not always having direct hallucinations per se, but it is a way for them to feel like they are opening up to receiving insights or inspiration from "the universe," or from some type of spiritual entity. In my view, these thoughts or insights are coming from their own nonconscious mind or what is more popularly referred to as the "subconscious mind." And there is an element here of our longing for the lost guidance of the bicameral mind and seeking ways to re-experience it. The breakdown of the bicameral mind has left us forever searching for answers from external authorities — from the "lost voices" or a "higher power." I should also add that various forms of psychedelics are also now being looked at again as possible treatments for things like depression and post traumatic stress disorder, with some success.[8]

Hallucinations have also been associated with other types of drug use. There are cases of people using drugs like methamphetamine and they can experience what's called "drug induced psychosis." So for a brief period of time, the drug causes them to hallucinate. So again, this is just one of the myriad ways to trigger a hallucinatory state. In some cases, with enough

---

8. Michael Pollan, *How to Change Your Mind: What the New Science of Psychedelics Teaches Us About Consciousness, Dying, Addiction, Depression, and Transcendence* (Penguin Press, 2018).

drug use, people can develop what would be diagnosed as schizophrenia permanently. So this is another interesting and of course unfortunate thing that has been documented. And exactly how it all works biochemically, I don't think anyone really knows.

LEAHY: A friend recommended a documentary called *The Devil in Daniel Johnston.* At one point this guy, Daniel Johnston, takes LSD, and that tips him over the edge. He starts focusing on how people need to beware of the devil and look out for the number six, as well as the number nine, and that different people are "possessed." Can you comment about possession as a vestige of the bicameral mind?

KUIJSTEN: Yes, Jaynes suggests that "spirit possession," which is a type of dissociative state, is likely another vestige of bicameral mentality. Many people don't realize that the phenomenon is still widespread. It also varies widely in different cultures. Like glossolalia ("speaking in tongues"), there are also a variety of forms. The key connection is that these phenomena suggest a bicameral-like propensity for seeking external authorization, but instead of a hallucinated voice, it's in the form of a possessing spirit.

In terms of the neurology, these phenomena are quite difficult to study. An intriguing possibility is that the more extreme cases involve a temporary shift from left to right brain hemisphere dominance for language. Do some cases involve the non-dominant language areas temporarily controlling speech, or the right hemisphere controlling behavior? While speculative, there is suggestive evidence. For example, we know that in some individuals the right (or non-dominant) hemisphere language areas can at times produce speech.[9] Further, the kind of speech that we see when a person is in a possessed state is indicative of the non-dominant hemisphere. In some cultures, rhythmic drumming and chanting is involved, which are thought to increase right hemisphere activity.[10] There have also been studies of trance states similar to spirit possession that show a shift toward right hemisphere dominance.[11]

So possession and glossolalia are both suggestive of bicameral mentality. It's quite possible that a shift in brain hemisphere dominance is involved,

---

9. E. Schechter, *Self-Consciousness and "Split" Brains: The Minds' I* (Oxford University Press, 2018).
10. J.H. Hageman, et al., "The Neurobiology of Trance and Mediumship in Brazil," in S. Krippner and H.L. Friedman (eds.), *Mysterious Minds* (Praeger, 2009).
11. S.C. Krippner and A. Combs, "The Neurophenomenology of Shamanism: An Essay Review," *Journal of Consciousness Studies*, 2002 9, 77–82; D. Lehmann, et al., "Brain Sources of EEG Gamma Frequency During Volitionally Meditation-Induced, Altered States of Consciousness, and Experience of the Self," *Psychiatry Research: Neuroimaging*, 2001, 108, 111–121.

but more research is needed. Somewhat related to this are cases of temporal lobe epilepsy. In these cases we often see a normal, ordinary person, who is not particularly religious, but maybe mildly so. For whatever reason they experience temporal lobe epilepsy — which is an excitation of the temporal lobes — and in some cases they begin to exhibit what is called "hyper religiosity" as a result.

If we set aside Jaynes's theory, what could explain the fact that activity in the right temporal lobe would be implicated in auditory hallucinations, the feeling of a sensed presence, and hyper religiosity? What explains the existence of spirit possession? Alternative explanations are lacking. But if we look at these things through the lens of Jaynes's theory, they begin to make sense. We would expect to see religiosity associated with the right temporal lobe, along with the voices, because in order to function, the voices had to be perceived as all powerful and something that could not be questioned.

LEAHY: Jaynes also suggests that hypnosis is a vestige of the bicameral mind. Can you say something about hypnosis?

KUIJSTEN: Hypnosis is still very mysterious in many ways. We still do not have a good explanation as to exactly what is happening in hypnosis. People unfamiliar with hypnosis often mistakenly think that it is just a stage trick, that it doesn't exist — but it's a real phenomenon. I have practiced hypnosis myself on and off for many years. What we see in hypnosis is the hypnotist taking on the role of the guiding bicameral voice. And we can accomplish all kinds of things with the aid of hypnosis that we generally seem unable to do on our own. For example, with hypnosis people can often quickly break bad habits that they are unable to change through willpower alone.

The point is that we seem to be oddly predisposed to responding to an external, authorizing, guiding voice, and it is hard to explain why this predisposition exists without the bicameral mind theory. So while the exact mechanisms of hypnosis are still not understood, the main point with regard to Jaynes's theory is that hypnosis is probably effective because we have an underlying predisposition to respond to an external guiding voice. This predisposition likely exists because for thousands of years we were responding to bicameral hallucinated voices. We have a tendency to take things like hypnosis for granted, but the fact that it exists at all is very bizarre, unless we look at it from the perspective of Jaynes's theory.[12]

---

12. For more on hypnosis, see the interviews with Edoardo Casiglia, John Kihlstrom, and Laurence

LEAHY: I also wanted to touch on Jaynes's discussion of poetry. How is poetry related to the bicameral mind?

KUIJSTEN: Poetry is interesting because it has gone through a change in relatively recent history. Today we have what we might call modern, conscious poetry, and, at the risk of offending some people, generally it is considered to not be very good when compared to what is often referred to as the "inspired poetry" of past centuries. People often are unaware that many of the great poets that we are familiar with — such as William Blake and Rainer Maria Rilke — felt that their poetry was in a sense being dictated to them by, in some cases, an angel, a spirit, or God — by something outside of themselves. This occurs with novelists as well, such as Virginia Woolf. In the case of Blake, he often felt as though he were merely transcribing what he was hearing. So he was often in something like a trance state — a highly creative trance state — where he experienced auditory and visual hallucinations of his poetry, which he then wrote down. We see this with many of the great poets — they are not sitting down, going through a conscious, deliberative writing process as we might do today, but they are in a state where they feel that they are perhaps divinely inspired. So inspired poetry is another vestige of bicameral mentality.[13]

LEAHY: In *Reflections on the Dawn of Consciousness*, you also talk about religion as a vestige of the bicameral mind. Can you talk about that?

KUIJSTEN: Yes, another vestige of bicameral mentality that Jaynes does not delve into extensively in his book, but it's there if you read his book carefully, is religion itself. Jaynes perhaps downplayed this aspect of his theory somewhat, not wanting to offend anyone or turn anyone off to his ideas — he was primarily interested in people understanding his theory on the origin of consciousness. But it's quite clear that his theory is also perhaps the best explanation for the origin of religion.

So as we discussed, humans developed language and along with language, developed bicameral mentality. People would then hallucinate the voice of the chief or king. And when that leader died, they would continue to hear his voice. We see several lines of evidence for this, such as treating

Sugarman in this volume.

13. See Julian Jaynes, "The Ghost of a Flea: Visions of William Blake," in M. Kuijsten (ed.), *Reflections on the Dawn of Consciousness* (Julian Jaynes Society, 2006); Judith Weissman, *Of Two Minds: Poets Who Hear Voices* (Wesleyan University Press, 1993); Carole Brooks Platt, *In Their Right Minds: The Lives and Shared Practices of Poetic Geniuses* (Imprint Academic, 2015); Julie Kane, "Poetry as Right-Hemispheric Language," *Journal of Consciousness Studies*, 2004, 11, 5, 21-59.

the dead as though they were still living — using feeding tubes and similar kinds of things. They also sometimes propped up the dead as though they were still alive. We also see evidence of multiple burials — presumably the initial burial when the person first died, and then a second burial sometime later, perhaps when the person's hallucinated voice had faded away. We see evidence for secondary burials in a number of different cultures, not just around the Mediterranean but in places like Mexico and China as well.[14]

Jaynes suggests that the continued hearing of the leader's voice after his death gave rise to the concept of gods and an afterlife: "the king dead is a living god."[15] Then over time, societies built up these very large hierarchies of gods. During the bicameral period, cultures such as those in Egypt and Mesopotamia had thousands of gods — all very well documented. Then, as bicameral mentality breaks down, the voices fall silent, and consciousness develops, we see a transitional period — termed the "Axial Age" by the German-Swiss psychiatrist and philosopher Karl Jaspers — where the thousands of gods began to merge and blend. Eventually they are combined into the notion of a one, "true" God. So in many different cultures, during roughly the same time period, we see a transition from polytheism to monotheism. This is quite fascinating, and again, it is more supporting evidence for the bicameral mind theory.

Today, we are left with modern religion, which is very different from ancient religion. In ancient religion, the gods were not far away in an abstract place like "heaven," they were very much with us right here on Earth — giving advice and directing people's behavior. One person I know compared the gods of ancient civilizations to a high school football coach: they are right there with you, telling you what to do. They are not uncommunicative and in some remote, far away place.

All of our modern notions of religion arose from the idea that the gods had departed — that they had left us and went to some type of remote, unattainable location, such as Heaven. Since we no longer hear their voices, we are left to try to discern their will through divination and the last utterances that were perceived of them by the prophets. The world's major religions were all initially founded on divine revelation — the voices of the gods — and in that sense, all religion is a vestige of bicameral mentality.

---

14. Michael Carr, "The *Shi* 'Corpse/Personator' Ceremony in Early China," in M. Kuijsten (ed.), *Reflections on the Dawn of Consciousness* (Julian Jaynes Society, 2006).

15. Julian Jaynes, *The Origin of Consciousness in the Breakdown of the Bicameral Mind* (Houghton-Mifflin, 1976), p. 143.

8

Vestiges of Bicameral Mentality

Brian J. McVeigh

Interviewed by Marcel Kuijsten & Brendan Leahy

MARCEL KUIJSTEN: Some people may think of Jaynes's theory as only being concerned with a psychological change that took place in ancient history. I think that understanding the transition from bicameral mentality to consciousness is absolutely essential to an accurate view of human history, but Jaynes's theory is also very relevant to modern life. In fact, one of the early appeals of Jaynes's theory to me personally was that it allowed me to make sense of so many different aspects of modern life that, without Jaynes's theory, seem more or less inexplicable. What are some of the modern day implications of Jaynes's theory?

BRIAN McVEIGH: This is an extremely crucial issue, and I'm glad you asked the question. Jaynes's work actually has numerous practical and therapeutic implications. For instance, he noted that those who suffer from auditory hallucinations, sometimes referred to as "voice hearers" if they do not suffer from a serious mental health disorder, could benefit from psychoeducation. They could be told that the voices are a vestige of an earlier mentality. This might help ease their concerns and feelings of stigma. Another example: understanding the nature of consciousness helps us see the complex interplay between what Jaynes calls sensory pain and conscious pain and why, for example, some amputees still feel sensation in missing limbs. Though phantom pain has something to do with the mapping of the sensorimotor cortex, consciousness no doubt plays a role as well. Pain is a major complaint among patients seeking care, and many times it lacks a clear physiological basis. Perhaps there is a conscious component to the experience of discomfort that we need to investigate.[1] But progress on this front can only be made once we fully understand the nature of conscious interiority. Also on the practical front — understanding the culturally-constructed nature of consciousness aids us in seeing what I call the "active ingredients" of psychotherapy work.

KUIJSTEN: As an anthropologist, you specialize in East Asian cultures: you've studied East Asian cultures for more than 30 years, you've published numerous books and articles on various aspects of Japanese culture, you spent a year studying at Beijing University, you lived in Japan and taught at Japanese universities for about 16 years, and you speak Japanese. One of the persistent misconceptions about Jaynes's bicameral mind theory — and I attribute this primarily to those that have never actually read Jaynes's book — is that it doesn't apply to cultures outside of Egypt, Mesopotamia, and the Eastern Mediterranean. How do you respond to this misconception, and can you describe some of the evidence that has been published for bicameral mentality in East Asian cultures, both by yourself and the sinologist Michael Carr?

MCVEIGH: Even a cursory view of Asian cultures, whether South, Southeast, or East, shows patterns of civilizational development that fits into a Jaynesian interpretation. The research of Michael Carr has made it abundantly clear that Jaynes's theories have relevance outside the Eastern Mediterranean sphere and nearby areas. His work is crucial because it puts Jaynes's theories to the test. By a meticulous linguistic analysis of ancient Chinese language and texts, he convincingly demonstrates how the bicameral thesis goes a long way in solving what he calls the "hermeneutic puzzles" that have perplexed scholars for centuries. For example, he solved the question of how "to dead father" and "think" are linked. The idea is that "to dead father" means to communicate with the spirit of one's deceased father.[2] His investigations have also examined the role of visions, divination, and "personation," or *shi* in Chinese, which describes how spirits of the dead spoke through "personators" — a type of spirit possession.[3]

---

1. See Julian Jaynes, "Sensory Pain and Conscious Pain," *Behavioral and Brain Sciences*, 1985, 8, 1; reprinted in M. Kuijsten (ed.), *The Julian Jaynes Collection* (Julian Jaynes Society, 2012).
2. Michael Carr, "The *Kʼóg* 'To Dead Father' Hypothesis," *Review of the Liberal Arts*, 1989, 77.
3. Michael Carr, "The *Shi* 'Corpse/Personator' Ceremony in Early China" in M. Kuijsten (ed.), *Reflections on the Dawn of Consciousness* (Julian Jaynes Society, 2006).

It's important to point out that "spirit possession," though it goes by different names, has been a staple of anthropological research. But we also find it in ancient civilizations, including Mesopotamian and Egyptian. Biblical prophecy was a type of spirit possession. So Michael Carr has identified something important and linked it to a Jaynesian interpretation.

As for my own research, my dissertation examined a modern religious organization that practiced spirit possession, a clear vestige of bicameral mentality. Indeed, "spirit possession" is common in modern Japan, as well as in other cultures, for that matter. And speaking of modern Japan, my book, *The History of Japanese Psychology*, not only shows the relevance of Jaynes to an East Asian culture but demonstrates how his findings have significance not just for ancient civilizations but for more recent historical changes. Using Japan as a case study, I explore how the birth of psychology as a discipline signaled a transformation of conscious interiority itself. More specifically, I explain how the forces of modernity, such as industrialization, shaped understandings of the "inner experience." The result was a psychological revolution that produced a new definition of our interior life, among other things. This coincides well with a Jaynesian understanding that consciousness is following a historical trajectory and is increasing.

KUIJSTEN: That's very interesting. You touched on one of the fascinating pieces of the puzzle of the origin of consciousness — the linguistic analysis, or the changes in the meanings of words over time. Jaynes describes how the meanings of words in ancient Greek transition over time — words that initially described actions of the physical body later refer to mental processes. For example, the ancient Greek word *noeein*, which means "to see," transitioned over time to *noos*, which means "conscious mind." This linguistic analysis provides evidence for when the transition to consciousness occurred — the idea being that the meanings of the words coincided with changes in their psychological experience. It's quite interesting that Michael Carr was able to document a similar transition with the meaning of the word *xin*, which provides evidence for a similar transition from bicameral mentality to consciousness in ancient China.[4] Could you elaborate on this?

McVEIGH: Yes, of course. Michael Carr examined the evolution of mind-words in the *Shijing*, a collection of songs and odes composed approximately

---

4. Michael Carr, "Sidelights on *Xin* 'Heart; Mind' in the *Shijing*," *Proceedings of the 31st International Congress of Human Sciences in Asia and North Africa, Tokyo and Kyoto*, August 31-September 7, 1983.

from the eleventh to seventh centuries BCE in China. He focused on *xin*. This word is often translated as "heart," but it actually means something more like "heart–mind." This is a critical analysis because Carr found the same general pattern of linguistic evolution that Jaynes found in his own study of ancient Greek psychological terminology. The trajectory, in both China and Greece, reflects a transition from bicameral mentality to a conscious mentality. We need more studies like Carr's.

KUIJSTEN: You've written two books looking at religious history through the lens of Julian Jaynes's theory: *How Religion Evolved* and *The Psychology of the Bible*. Gods and religion are central themes of Jaynes's theory, yet the tremendous implications of his theory for the origin of religion was something Jaynes did not emphasize — it's been explained that he wanted to keep the focus on his ideas about the origin of consciousness, and he did not want to turn people off who might have been more religiously-inclined. So Jaynes walked a fine line between discussing ancient religious texts and practices — which provide some of the most compelling evidence for the existence of bicameral mentality and the transition from bicameral mentality to consciousness — and perhaps downplaying some of the implications for present-day religions. Can you talk about some of the evidence that you've discovered, or areas where you've expanded on what Jaynes discussed?

McVEIGH: The first book, *How Religion Evolved*, is an updating and expansion of Jaynes's ideas. If Jaynes was correct, we should find the same patterns worldwide, and this is in fact what we see. For example, some key similarities include treating the dead as if they were still alive, feeding statues as if they were living beings, texts recounting divine visitations, monumental mortuary architecture, and how the landscape of the ancient world was dotted with "houses of gods," or what we call temples. I also investigate how as bicameral mentality collapsed, people had to replace the gods with new cognitive capabilities. This psychological interiorization of spiritual experience is another major world pattern that deserves attention, since it established the foundations for the world's great religious and philosophical traditions that eventually arose in India, China, Greece, and the Middle East.

The second book you mentioned applies Jaynesian thinking to the Bible. It attempts to account for what I call the "super-religious" nature of the Old Testament. It is important to note that the books making up the

Old Testament were written in the first millennium BCE. They are nostalgic recountings of what had become an obsolete mentality from the Bronze Age. This collection of sacred texts gives us an unparalleled look into the transition from a preconscious mentality to an interiorized psychology and a new introspective religiosity. To make my case I analyze the role of visions, angels, and prophets, as well as the divinatory function of idols and oracular aids, such as the Ark of the Covenant. I also look at the linkages among music, poetry, and inspiration.[5]

KUIJSTEN: You're also working on a new book looking at ancient Egypt through the lens of Julian Jaynes's theory. Would you like to give us a preview of some of the things you've discovered or some of the topics you'll be discussing?

McVEIGH: Yes, of course. So far I haven't found anything that contradicts Jaynes's thinking and ancient Egypt fits nicely into the Bicameral Civilization Inventory.[6] With that said, I would note an examination of Egypt does complicate a Jaynesian interpretation. First, Egyptian history presents us with a more nuanced view of the transition from preconsciousness to consciousness. The change was gradual. Jaynes himself discusses what can be referred to as transitional mentalities. This describes periods of history when proto-subjective mentation existed, or when individuals were in some ways semi-bicameral and semi-conscious.

Second, from what I've seen so far in the early periods, say from around 3000 BCE, high-ranking deities rarely if ever communicated with the average person, though in later periods of pharaonic history such communication did seem to occur. Instead, the priesthood would broadcast divine messages to the populace that the pharaoh heard directly. Just as importantly, the common person was most likely in divine communication of some sort with ancestors and personal and domestic spiritual beings. These more local-level hierarchies were nested within larger theopolitical structures topped by the monarch.[7]

* * *

BRENDAN LEAHY: Could you address "spirit possession" in Asian cultures, perhaps focusing on Japan and the similarities or differences from Western cultures?

---

5. See Brian McVeigh's interview, "Evidence for Bicameral Mentality in the Bible," in this volume.
6. For more on the Bicameral Civilizational Inventory see pages 277-278 and p. 358.
7. Additional portions of this interview on other aspects of Brian McVeigh's research can be found in the Appendix.

McVEIGH: Spirit possession, for many people, especially if you are from the Christian tradition — or perhaps the Western tradition — is something that many of us associate with, for example, the movie *The Exorcist*. The idea that evil spirits come in and take you over, and you need a priest to perform an exorcism to get rid of this terrible demon. So in Western culture, we think of spirit possession more in terms of "demon possession."

But in many parts of the world, and Japan is a good example, spirit possession — while it can be a negative, threatening experience — actually is generally not seen as negative. This is because spirit possession has been a part of the Japanese spiritual scene for centuries. In Japan there are many people who join one of the new religions, and most of these new groups practice a type of spirit possession. Of course there is some variation, but if you look at this from a grand historical perspective, basically what they're practicing is a type of shamanism — and shamanism is often a form of spirit possession. So the roots are deep.

This is important for Jaynes's theory because it illustrates how the vestiges of bicameral mentality are found all over the world, as they are found throughout history. And I think Jaynes is able to offer a very convincing theory, from a scientific point of view, of what is going on neurologically in spirit possession.

LEAHY: Could you explain what you found while you were doing your field work in Japan, and how that ties into Jaynes, in terms of building on your understanding of his theories?

McVEIGH: In Jaynes's book about the origin of consciousness, there's a entire chapter devoted to spirit possession. And for Jaynes, this is important because spirit possession is a phenomenon that really has not been explained in a serious scientific manner. In fact, I should add that this is true for hypnosis. We actually know much about hypnosis, but it's a bit of a mystery as to why hypnosis occurs, or why people are able to be hypnotized. And for Jaynes, spirit possession and hypnosis are vestiges of an earlier mentality and of course this earlier mentality is what he calls the bicameral mind. It gets somewhat complicated on what the neurology of spirit possession is, but the idea, as I said for Jaynes, is that this is a holdover of this earlier mentality. So is, by the way, glossolalia, or "speaking in tongues." But we don't have an overarching theory to tie together hypnosis, glossolalia, and spirit possession. The only person who has attempted to tie these strange phenomena together of course is Julian Jaynes.

LEAHY: The religious group you were studying — that was a new religion?

McVEIGH: It's a term in Japanese that they call a "new religion." They have the traditional religions — Shintoism, Buddhism, and some Confucianism. The new religions are groups that, unless you live in Japan, you generally would not know about. These are groups of people that want to practice some form of religion in Japan, but they don't turn to Shintoism or Buddhism, so they join one of these new religions — and there are probably hundreds of them.

LEAHY: How do they think about spirit possession in these new religions versus the more traditional religions?

McVEIGH: In Japan, to put it simply, you basically have two types of religions, you have what we may call the established faiths that we discussed — Shintoism, Buddhism, and Confucianism. And then you have another type of religion, the "new religions." And the new religions trace their roots back to the nineteenth century in Japan. The new religions emerged because of all the socio-political economic turmoil in Japan after World War II, for example — to provide another way apart from the established religions.

So the first question I think we want to entertain is, "What is the relationship between the new religions and the established religions?" On the surface they don't necessarily look very different, but with closer observation, what we notice is that most of these new religions borrow ideas from Shintoism, from Buddhism, even from Christianity and Islam, and they sort of put it all together and — if I can use this term — create a stew of different ideas. But something that is interesting about these new religions, versus the established faiths, is that they actually incorporate very ancient ideas — ideas that can be traced back to ancient history. Some people use the terms "folk tradition" or "folk religion."

What's important for our purposes — how this relates to Jaynes — is that an important part of this folk religion is shamanism, and shamanism is a type of spirit possession. So I think it's very interesting — it's very important — that Japan today is supposedly a very modernized, in fact in some ways a super-modernized society, yet they still resort to a type of vestigial, psychological process that we call spirit possession.

LEAHY: What surprised you the most when you finally started doing research in Japan? Was there an "aha" moment that made you think that your research there very much clicks with Julian Jaynes's theory?

MCVEIGH: When I was a grad student I was interested in Asian culture, specifically Japan. I was interested in religion and I wanted to study spirit possession in Japan, so I started to do a lot of reading in the library at my university, before I went into the field as an anthropologist. One of the things I learned is that spirit possession is actually quite common. It's been common historically in the ancient world, during medieval times, and it's still a common phenomenon around the world today. What I also learned is that actually there's no real theory of what spirit possession is. People who have studied possession in modern times will say "This is a type of trancing; it has something to do with hypnosis." And they have these circular arguments — they would never really define what spirit possession is or what causes people to have this overwhelming experience where they feel that they're possessed by a supernatural entity.

It occurred to me that I had actually read an interesting book that touched upon spirit possession, and this book of course was written by Julian Jaynes. I was at Princeton University at the time, and I said to myself, "This book that was given to me when I was in high school was written by a professor who's in the building right next to my department!" So I made an appointment to go see Julian Jaynes and I told him what I was interested in. Of course before I went to see him, I read what he had to say about spirit possession, and that's where it all started to come together for me. And when I met Jaynes, he was very gracious and interested in my research. Eventually I ended up doing my fieldwork in Japan with a new religion called Sukyo Mahikari. Like many other religious groups in Japan, they practice spirit possession — in fact spirit possession is a salient aspect of Japanese religiosity.

LEAHY: Aside from Japan, are there other cultures with religions that have this type of non-negative relationship to spirit possession?

MCVEIGH: Well I can say that all over the world — in almost all subcultures in fact — you are going to find something like spirit possession. So yes, wherever you go in the world, you would find phenomena that we would classify as spirit possession. Of course, the particular manifestation, the particular expression of spirit possession, depends on the cultural context, but what's important here is that this is very much a universal type of phenomenon. In fact, I don't think you'll be able to find a culture that does not practice or has not practiced some type of spirit possession. We call it by different names and it changes somewhat, I suppose, by definition.

To give you an example, take what's called "channeling." This sort of New Age practice I think can loosely be understood as a type of spirit possession. Another example is what's know as "hypergraphia." In hypergraphia, a person writes something out rapidly and has a feeling that they are not in control, as if something is taking over their body — is taking over their hand — and is doing all of the writing for them. That's not exactly "spirit possession" defined classically, but it's certainly a type of vestige, it's certainly related to this class of behaviors.

So glossolalia, channeling, spirit possession, hypnosis — all of these things prior to Jaynes have not been adequately explained. And it's easy to say, "Well, all of these phenomena are just loose neurological wiring." For example, hallucinations — that's another important type of vestige of bicameral mentality. It's easy to say, "Well, there's just something wrong with the person, that's why they're hallucinating." But that does not offer much in the way of an explanation of hallucinations themselves, when you stop and think about it. Similarly, these other phenomena have lacked adequate explanations.

Actually, most people are able to experience a type of hallucination, what I would define as a type of quasi-hallucination. What I mean by that is the ability to use our mind's eye, to stop and, for example, think about what you were doing last week. Who did you meet, this morning, or this afternoon for lunch? Most of us can imagine that in our head — we can see that. And while that's not exactly a hallucination, it comes close, and I think it demonstrates how modern consciousness is actually related to ancient examples of hallucinations.

I think one way to appreciate what Jaynes had to say is to look at things from a grand historical perspective. What I mean by that is we can ask a question, for example, "Why did modern research psychology develop?" And we have to be a little bit careful here, because when you're in college and you take a course in psychology, they might have a short section on the history of psychology. And they trace it back to Locke and Hume, or back to the Middle Ages. They'd go back to the great Greek philosophers, and the assumption is that these people were talking about psychology. Of course, there's something psychologically-related to what they were talking about, but certainly they were not practicing modern research psychology as we think about it today.

So the first question is, "When and why did modern research psychology emerge?" And it's clear in the historical record that modern research psychology developed in the mid- to late nineteenth century. The next question is, "Why? Why didn't it develop much earlier?" Well, I think it developed for the same reasons that people started to become conscious — according to Jaynes about 1000 BCE. And that's because society's political and economic systems have become more complex.

Now, when you reach the late eighteenth and the early part of the nineteenth century, there are huge changes, primarily the Industrial Revolution, which really was an earthquake that eventually spread around the globe and changed our economic relations, our political systems, and it changed society in fundamental ways — some obvious, some not so obvious. One thing the Industrial Revolution did was it forced us to focus on new types of knowledge: chemistry, biology, new inventions — and not just in the natural sciences, but also the social sciences.

For example, the birth of political economics, of political science and very importantly, psychology. And so, psychology — it may sound strange to say this — but the birth of modern research psychology is really evidence that the human mind is still changing, is still evolving. It did not stop about 3,000 years ago, when according to Jaynes, we learned consciousness. It's going through a series of ruptures, a series of changes — a process that continues today.

9

Hearing Voices, Sensed Presences, and Imagined "Others"

Tanya M. Luhrmann

Interviewed by Marcel Kuijsten

Tanya Luhrmann is the Watkins University Professor in the Stanford University Anthropology department, with a courtesy appointment in Psychology. She is a medical and psychological anthropologist who more recently describes her work as an anthropology of mind. She received her bachelor's degree in Folklore and Mythology from Harvard University and her Ph.D. in Social Anthropology from Cambridge University. She has done ethnography on the streets of Chicago with homeless and psychotic women, and worked with people who hear voices in Chennai, India; Accra, Ghana; and the San Francisco Bay Area. She has also done fieldwork with evangelical Christians who seek to hear God speak back, with Zoroastrians who set out to create a more mystical faith, and with people who practice magic. She was elected to the American Academy of Arts and Sciences in 2003 and received a John Guggenheim Fellowship award in 2007. She has written and edited numerous books, including *When God Talks Back, Our Most Troubling Madness,* and *How God Becomes Real.* She has published over thirty Op-Eds in *The New York Times,* and her work has been featured in *The New Yorker, The New York Review of Books, The Times Literary Supplement, Science News,* and many other publications.

MARCEL KUIJSTEN: To start with, in a *Chronicle of Higher Education* article that asked you and eleven other scholars the question, "What book changed your mind?" you answered Julian Jaynes's *The Origin of Consciousness in the*

Breakdown of the Bicameral Mind. You said that after finishing Jaynes's book, "readers find that they think about the world quite differently. At least I did. I think the book crept up on me year by year until suddenly I decided that this odd book I'd read in college had a fundamental insight and had presented to me the puzzle that became my life's work."[1] What led you to read Jaynes, what was the fundamental insight that his book provided, and what was the puzzle that Jaynes's book proposes that became your life's work?

TANYA LUHRMANN: So I did some classics in college, and I think it was in the context of talking to a classics professor — I expect it was Bennett Simon, who is actually a psychiatrist and a scholar of psychiatric illness among the Greeks — who said that Jaynes's book was a really interesting book that I should read.

The reason that it captured my attention was that people have these auditory experiences, and not everybody has them. They are distributed differently in the social world. And I think that for me, as I now remember that book — which of course is a different experience of the book than when I first read it — for me the deep puzzle is whether different ways of representing the mind and experiencing the mind enable or make possible these different kinds of experiences, in particular the experience of voices.

So what's been fascinating to me is whether different ideas about the mind enable or create these experiences of somebody else talking back. And the specific thesis that Jaynes lays out is the idea that if you don't have a lot of words to describe mental events — he has a thesis about the brain that I don't feel like I can speak to or deeply understand — but there is that amazing section on the *Iliad*, where he leans on the ideas of Bruno Snell's argument in *The Discovery of the Mind*.[2]

The claim is that in the world of the *Iliad* and the archaic Greeks, they didn't yet have a word for "mind" per se, and didn't have a word for body per se. They had words for body segments — they could talk about pieces of the body — but they don't talk about the body as a whole. They are speaking to mental processes, but there's not the mental.

So I think part of what it is to be human is to be aware, but that the way that people map that awareness varies enormously. And Jaynes invites us to think that if you don't map the awareness specifically, then when people

---

1. Tanya Luhrmann, interview in "What Book Changed Your Mind?" *The Chronicle Review*, November 7, 2014.
2. Bruno Snell, *The Discovery of the Mind: In Greek Philosophy and Literature* (Dover, 1951).

have powerful feelings, they are more likely to experience themselves as coming from the outside, and they're more likely to experience that as a voice that speaks back.

And so trying to make sense of these things is something that I've really been thinking a lot about. What I see in my own work is that even in a Western context, where people have very sophisticated ideas for describing awareness, there's still something deeply true that when people have very powerful feelings, very powerful ideas, they're a little more likely to feel as if they're spontaneous — to feel as if they're not theirs. And when they do that, they're a little bit more likely to feel as if not only do their thoughts not have their own agency, but they actually originate from outside of themselves. They come as if they're not their own voice. And so that's the puzzle that Jaynes laid down for me — this model of representation, this texture of thought, and these phenomenological experiences in which people hear voices — are those connected?

KUIJSTEN: Yes, that's very interesting. And not to get sidetracked with the neuroscience, but you're touching on this interesting puzzle of why the feeling of a sensed presence and the experience of auditory hallucinations don't seem like they're coming from ourselves. Something that I've been interested in that first came out of the split-brain studies is that for some reason our sense of self seems to be in some way associated with our primary language areas — the language areas that for most people are in the left or dominant hemisphere. Then — as Jaynes had speculated but now some brain research supports — when the language areas of the non-dominant hemisphere become active, for some reason it's experienced as coming from outside of ourselves, or as the presence of an "other." This fascinating relationship between consciousness, language, and our sense of self I think is still very poorly understood.

So, before we delve into all of your research, I wanted to quickly touch on an early connection that you had to Jaynes's theory and a topic that also comes up in another interview. It was very interesting for me to learn that your undergraduate degree at Harvard was in the Folklore and Mythology department, created in part by Albert Lord.

LUHRMANN: Yes.

KUIJSTEN: As you know, he is known for the Parry-Lord hypothesis, and Jaynes refers to this hypothesis to support his argument that the *Iliad* and the *Odyssey* reflect different psychologies from different time periods, and they were not written by one man named Homer. I wanted to hear your take on this — do you agree with the Parry-Lord hypothesis that epics such as the *Iliad* and the *Odyssey* were sung by Greek bards over generations before they were written down, and not composed by one person named Homer, the first in his youth and the second in his old age?

LUHRMANN: I think that the scholarly support is pretty strong for that. You get to the idea that there is this story, the story is retold and retold, and it's remembered because it has a structure. There are two pieces to this structure: words that hang together — so "the wine-dark sea," "the rosy fingered dawn," little phrases that hang together — and then there are subplots that hang together — for example a wedding scene hangs together. It's through these linguistic tags and these plot tags that they can remember and elaborate the story. And Lord went to Yugoslavia and spent time with the closest analogue to these great singers who can memorize and sing a tale.

He did point out that they were great singers, and at one point he took the person that he thought was the best singer and had him listen to a new story, and then tell it to him the next day. And he was able to sing it for hours with a great deal of detail. So one can say that there's room for a little bit of a "Homer" — an individual who is skilled and is able to hear a story and then retell it with richness and structure. But I think there's no question that the Parry-Lord hypothesis shows that we remember and construct narratives differently than we do in a literate world, with room for an individual storyteller, and in an oral world, where people need to remember differently.

KUIJSTEN: Thank you for commenting on that — I know that that question was probably going back in time a bit and not a subject that's part of your own research. As a psychological anthropologist or an "anthropologist of mind," I think you bring a different perspective to psychological subject matter than one might get from psychologists and psychiatrists, and one of the topics you've researched extensively is hearing voices. I have a number of questions on this topic, but let's start with your research on differences in hearing voices in clinical versus non-clinical populations. You discuss this subject in your article "Living with Voices" in *The American Scholar* — where you also talk about the Hearing Voices Network, which seeks to depathologize hearing voices and promote the idea that hearing voices is part of the human experience, and that not everyone who hears voices requires psychiatric treatment.[3] You also discuss this subject in your book *When God Talks Back,* among other places.[4] Do you agree that the phenomenon of hearing voices is more widespread throughout society than is still commonly known, and can you describe some of the differences between hearing voices in clinical versus non-clinical populations?

LUHRMANN: So I think it is more widespread, depending on how you count. In other words, what scale you're using, how you're collecting your data. For example, are you sitting and talking with people or are you showing up at their door with an NIH [National Institutes of Health] clipboard. You will get a rate of somewhere between 5% and 80% of people who have had some kind of experience in which they feel that they've heard a voice but there was not a human speaker of that voice — so there's some sense of "you've heard a voice when alone."

So it really is not at all uncommon, but that said, there are some pretty broad brush differences. I've spent a lot of time talking to Evangelical Christians, who seek to have an intimate relationship with God and they want God to talk back. I've also spent a lot of time talking to people who meet the criteria for schizophrenia — so, hundreds of interviews in total.

In some broad sense, there are two kinds of phenomena. People who meet criteria for schizophrenia — so I'm not making the diagnosis, they meet the DSM-III/IV/5 criteria — when they talk about their experiences, typically the experiences are frequent. So they can hear words, language, voices many times a day, many times an hour, or even continuously. Often what they hear contains a lot of content. So for example, sometimes people just hear single words, but many people who are psychotic will hear sentences, paragraphs, and conversations. And often a lot of what they experience is negative — not everything they experience, but a lot of what they experience. And they also experienced this kind of array of "other stuff" — such as sounds, or whispering, or scratching.

There's often a very physical component as well — there's a lot of sensory stuff. People talk about — and [Daniel Paul] Schreber talked about this — the words pushing down on their head.[5] They talk about the voices hurting. So it's not only that what the voices say is mean, but they "feel" the meanness — it's like it stabs them.

3. T.M. Luhrmann, "Living with Voices," *The American Scholar,* Summer 2012.
4. T.M. Luhrmann, *When God Talks Back: Understanding the American Evangelical Relationship with God* (Knopf, 2012).
5. Daniel Paul Schreber, *Memoirs of My Nervous Illness* (NYRB Classics, 1903/2000).

People who don't meet criteria for schizophrenia, for example people that I meet in the context of interviewing people at a church, are likely to remember a handful of experiences — maybe one voice, and if you push people, sometimes they will say, "Well I have this experience about once per month." But they often can't remember the details.

If you're talking about an auditory event, what they experience is typically brief. So typically four to six words: "I will always be with you" or "I love you." And they will usually ascribe this to God, at least the folks that I'm talking to, but there are other groups as well.

And typically what they remember and report is not negative. It might be disconcerting — for example, God might want them to tithe or to start a school, or to go do something that they don't want to do. But it's not things like "you stink," "you're scum," "you're worthless," "you should die." So the type of content is very different. It's also typically less physical. It feels less commanding, even though often there's a quality of — all of these voices often involve imperatives. So people feel spoken to. When reporting these events, the voice doesn't show up and talk about what a lovely day it is. There is a sense of being spoken to, of being told something, being told what to do.

So those are the big distinctions, but there are also complicated puzzles — many complicated puzzles. There are people who are not considered ill, but their experiences are somewhat more frequent than in the religious group. So there are people in the middle. There are also debates about what's different. A voice carries two qualities: it feels as though it's not you, as though you did not generate it. But also, we think of a voice as coming from outside — an external, auditory voice. But those experiences are probably pretty rare for everyone — even in psychosis. The more time that I've spent talking to people about this, the more I see the interaction between the language — the term "voice" — and the experience, and the more I think that the phenomenological quality is a little more interior, but it feels like it comes from outside.

KUIJSTEN: That is a fascinating level of detail that you've discovered about these experiences. I've heard what you're referring to, or something similar, described as "inserted thoughts" — they don't have the full external quality of talking to another physical person, but rather they are experienced as thoughts in their mind that they don't attribute to themselves.

LUHRMANN: Right.

KUIJSTEN: What you mentioned about the content of the voices being imperatives — the fact that the voices often comment on behavior or command behavior — I think is another very interesting connection with what Jaynes suggests was happening in the ancient world. In other words, if not for Jaynes's theory, why are these voices so focused on behavior?

In your book *Our Most Troubling Madness: Case Studies in Schizophrenia across Cultures*, you and the other contributors studied voice hearers among the homeless in Chicago, Caribbean immigrants in London, and in places like Ghana and India.[6] How widespread is the phenomenon of hearing voices in non-Western cultures, and what are some of the cross cultural differences? One of the things that you mention that stood out to me, for example, was that people in India were more likely to experience their voices as gods. Can you say something about the cross cultural differences?

LUHRMANN: Yes. So to answer the question of "how common are the experiences?" it depends to some degree on how you do the work. If you think like a psychiatrist and you do that kind of epidemiological work, you come up with rates that are sort of in the same ballpark, say roughly one to two percent. Somewhere between half a percent to four percent of people in the community would meet criteria for schizophrenia, and of those people, sixty to eighty percent hear voices.

There are also social worlds, outside of the West, where hearing a voice is more — the language is more appropriate to the experience. So in Ghana, there are people who talk to the gods — that's their job. And so they will use this language of talking to gods, and some of them use that language and don't have a phenomenological experience — but some of them do.

The direct comparison that I did, with colleagues, was to talk to folks in San Mateo, and in a Chennai hospital in South India, and folks in a hospital in Accra, Ghana. And we did a direct comparison of 20 people from each place.

The striking thing was that in U.S., there was much more violence in the voice, and the voice was less personal. People were less likely to say, "Oh I know this person who's talking... this is my mother. I know my mother, I've heard my mother, she's just not here right now." Both of those are more common in Chennai and in Accra. In Chennai, it was interesting that indeed people were more likely to report that God was speaking. After all, all of the Americans in the sample were Christians, and for them, God is

---

6. T.M. Luhrmann and Jocelyn Marrow (eds.), *Our Most Troubling Madness: Case Studies in Schizophrenia across Cultures* (University of California Press, 2016).

sometimes speaking, but it's not a primary feature of the voice. In Chennai it's more often a feature of the voice.

What was really striking about the South Indian sample is that it was more often attributed to people that they knew — it was kin: mother, father, brother-in-law, sister. And in Accra, there it was God. And it's really important not to be romantic — by that I mean, it would be pretty lousy to have schizophrenia in any of these settings. But in Accra, people were much more likely to say "Oh I hear God. If I didn't hear God, my troubles would have been much worse." So that was a striking difference. And of course there were other differences as well.

KUIJSTEN: These cultural differences in hearing voices are quite interesting. Thanks to your research and the research of others, we now know so much more about these kinds of cross cultural differences than we did just 25 years ago, when I first began investigating Jaynes's theory and these related topics.

One of the things that you noted in your introduction to *Our Most Troubling Madness* is the association of schizophrenia with a number of cultural or environmental factors, such as living in an urban environment, living as an ethnic minority, and being detached from family and community support. Would you agree that these factors all fall under the broad umbrella of "stress"?

LUHRMANN: Yes.

KUIJSTEN: So besides genetic factors, is it your view that stress is one of the primary drivers of unwanted auditory hallucinations?

LUHRMANN: So I use — and other people use as well — the term "social defeat," which is the sense of being "one down," or a social relationship in which you are "not as good as." So yes, "stress" works. But it's also this feeling of being physically or socially beaten up by somebody else. And it's remarkably robust. Schizophrenia used to be thought of as like a "genetic lightning bolt," and now people really talk much more about the social context which makes it more likely that, whatever your predisposition is, it's going to push you into the condition.

KUIJSTEN: That makes sense. Another thing that comes to mind from your book are the case studies involving newly married women in India, and how stressful those circumstances can be.

LUHRMANN: Yes, absolutely.

KUIJSTEN: Yes, very interesting case studies on these cultural differences. In a 1990 article titled "Verbal Hallucinations and Preconscious Mentality," published in the book *Philosophy and Psychopathology*, Julian Jaynes presents data that many homeless people frequently hear voices — he had a student that went out and conducted interviews with the homeless in New York City.[7] You spent quite a bit of time studying the lives of homeless and mentally ill women in Chicago.[8]

LUHRMANN: Right.

KUIJSTEN: You've also discussed some of the major problems, at least here in the United States, that there are with regard to the treatment of people who are diagnosed with schizophrenia and other mental illnesses. So due to a variety of factors — such as lack of state funding, legal issues surrounding institutionalizing people against their will, lack of available places for treatment — many voice hearers end up homeless and drifting in and out of shelters, or in some cases they end up in and out of prisons. Based on your first-hand research, as well as some of the recent surveys that you describe, are auditory hallucinations widespread among homeless populations?

LUHRMANN: Yes, so if somebody is on the street for a short amount of time — a lot of people periodically lose their home or become homeless for a couple of months — but if somebody is on the street for six months or more, the chances that they struggle with what we call psychosis or hear voices is pretty high. And it's often a very stressful experience. I'm actually willing to say that becoming homeless increases your chances of developing schizophrenia or psychosis. Being homeless is pretty scary, and often people start self-medicating — using crack or using meth, and those all increase the chances that you will have some type of hallucination-like experience.

KUIJSTEN: So is psychosis one of the primary drivers of homelessness, or is it the stress of homelessness and the subsequent self-medicating and drug

---

7. Julian Jaynes, "Verbal Hallucinations and Preconscious Mentality," in Manfred Spitzer and Brendan A. Maher (eds.), *Philosophy and Psychopathology* (Springer-Verlag, 1990).
8. T.M. Luhrmann, "The Culture of the Institutional Circuit in the United States," in T.M. Luhrmann and Jocelyn Marrow (eds.), *Our Most Troubling Madness: Case Studies in Schizophrenia across Cultures* (University of California Press, 2016).

use that then triggers psychosis — or is it impossible at this point to tease that out?

LUHRMANN: It's very hard to tease that out. I thought about how you might try to do it, but it would be very difficult because you would have to follow people who looked as if they carry the same risk factors for psychosis — and it's very hard to find those people — and then see if some of them became homeless and some of them did not, and follow them and see what happens. But again, being beaten up — somebody that's living on the streets and then starts using drugs — it's just going to exacerbate something that looks like psychosis.

Psychosis is really hard. You can identify flagrant psychosis pretty much everywhere. And pretty much everywhere, dramatic psychosis looks kind of the same. People are having these experiences, often auditory, of things that other people can't hear. They're having some thoughts that seem like really whacked out — really disconnected from reality. They're behaving in very odd ways and they're not following social norms. And many social worlds have names for that kind of person, and the name includes the idea that they've lost their minds.

So who's at risk? But we can't find the disease — we haven't been able to find a gene for schizophrenia, despite decades of searching. And we haven't been able to find "a thing." It's really hard to draw a line in the sand — there are these lists in the DSM, but even so, it's hard to feel that you're confidently identifying early psychosis, rather than just some unconventional person. It's very difficult to ascertain.

But it is certainly true that the American love of independence, and the American assumption that a child over the age of 18 should be independent of their families, creates the kind of conditions in which people who are at the risk of becoming ill, leave their home, don't want mental health care, and end up self-medicating on the street. And the economic conditions that make housing incredibly expensive also play their role.

KUIJSTEN: Indeed. And from my observations and the conversations that I've had with people, it seems to me that many of these issues — such as the prevalence of psychosis in homeless populations, prisons having become to a large extent de facto asylums, etc. — are just beginning to be understood or still have not been fully acknowledged. It's just in the past ten years that we've begun to see more investigative journalism on these topics, for example. Also, the issue of drug-induced psychosis — a great deal has been written on temporary drug-induced psychosis, but only recently have I begun to see more articles on the onset of schizophrenia having been initiated by drug abuse.

I actually have a friend from way back in college where that was the case. Unfortunately, she got involved with the wrong people and started using methamphetamine, and she didn't just experience a temporary drug-induced psychosis, but in fact it seems to have triggered a lifetime of what would be diagnosed as schizophrenia — she's been hearing voices every day since that time. Now perhaps in her case there were also earlier indicators, I don't know, but according to her, the drug use was what triggered the onset. The relationship of substance abuse to the potential onset of mental illness still seems as though it's not something that's widely known. I think the point to emphasize here is that there seem to be many different pathways to psychosis — suggesting more of a human predisposition rather than a rare pathology.

LUHRMANN: Right.

KUIJSTEN: So in several of your articles and book chapters, including a recent article that you co-authored, "Sexual Shaming and Violent Commands in Schizophrenia: Cultural Differences in Distressing Voices in India and the United States," you discuss command hallucinations in different populations.[9] How prevalent are command hallucinations that direct people's behavior, and what are some of the cross cultural differences?

LUHRMANN: It's difficult to say exactly how common they are, but they are fairly common. So if someone is diagnosed with schizophrenia, they often have some of the list of what are called first-rank symptoms, and command hallucinations are among them. And this is the sense of an imperative directed at you. What is really striking about comparing — this actually comes from the same sample of comparing 20 Americans with 20 folks in Accra and 20 in Chennai, and we actually now have a much larger sample — the commands in the States were much more likely to be violent. They were much more likely to order to "hurt," or "kill," or "wound" — to "kill yourself" or other people. And that was less common in India in our sample. I've also done some work with a student who spoke with folks in Russia who meet criteria for schizophrenia, and it's also a little less

---

9. Julia G. Lebovitz, R. Padmavati, Hema Tharoor, and T.M. Luhrmann, "Sexual Shaming and Violent Commands in Schizophrenia: Cultural Differences in Distressing Voices in India and the United States," *Schizophrenia Bulletin Open*, 2021, 2, 1.

common there. And my sense is — although I haven't quantified it sys-tematically — is that violent command hallucinations are less common in Accra and in Cape Coast, where I also did some work.

In these other settings, what you see is more along the lines of common-place household commands: "wash the dishes," "clean up," "don't smoke," "get dressed." So why is that? I don't know. I'm tempted to say that we live in a more violent society in the United States. I'm tempted to say that our current era is a little bit more violent — there's a paper that's compared voice hearing in a Texas hospital in the eighties and in the thirties, and in the eighties the voices were quite violent and in the thirties they weren't.[10] And so I think that the sense of commandment is pretty basic to the voice hearing experience, but the content of the commandment varies a lot.

KUIJSTEN: That is very interesting. And in terms of the more negative ver-sus more neutral or positive content of the voices, I also wonder to what degree some of the things that you've described — such as the differences in family support, community support, and cultural acceptance of voic-es — also plays a role in differences in the content of the voices? Also to what extent depression and anxiety are present in people with psycho-sis and to what degree that co-occurrence influences the content of the voices? And finally, to what extent are the voices replaying childhood ad-monitions — perhaps abusive childhood admonitions? There are so many possible factors and so many unanswered questions. But just the fact that the voices center on behavior to such a large extent I think is something that's very interesting — and I haven't seen a great deal in the way of expla-nations, or even speculation, as to why that might be the case, other than what Jaynes has proposed.

I'd like to touch on the topic of preliterate societies. I don't know that that's something that you've researched yourself, but you were speaking in another interview about how, as a graduate student, you had of course read Evans-Pritchard and the work of many other anthropologists on pre-literate societies. You spoke about how things like magic and witchcraft play a large role in many, if not all, of these societies, and how that in-spired some of your early research on witchcraft. Lévy-Bruhl, for exam-ple, documents accounts of missionaries that suggest that hearing voices and seeing visions — in the form of communicating with spirits and dead

---

10. J. Mitchell and A.D. Vierkant, "Delusions and Hallucinations as a Reflection of the Subcultural Milieu Among Psychotic Patients of the 1930s and 1980s," *The Journal of Psychology*, 1989, 123, 3.

ancestors — was relatively common in preliterate societies. I was wondering if you share that view?

LUHRMANN: Well I certainly think that secularism dampens these experiences, and you don't get secularism in preliterate societies, so preliterate societies are almost by definition more oriented towards a magical world. Secularism, science, and an enlightenment model of the mind all sort of hang together. There are different models of secularism, there are many different ways of "being modern," but I think one of the big differences between those two kinds of worlds is a model of the mind that is bounded, and a model of the mind that is more open, or more connected to the world.

KUIJSTEN: Yes, that makes sense. So in your most recent book, *How God Becomes Real: Rekindling the Presence of Invisible Others,* as well as in your recent article, "Sensing the Presence of Gods and Spirits Across Cultures and Faiths," you describe what one might call imaginary companions in adults and how the feeling of an external sensed presence is cultivated.[11]

I've wondered if, because of the different ways that these things came to be studied, there's something of a false distinction between imaginary companions in children and auditory hallucinations and the feeling of a sensed presence in adults. Do you feel that these are related and did you find in your research, for example, that some individuals had the experience of an "invisible other" since childhood, and that their imaginary companion simply stayed with them throughout life? Is it more that child psychologists were noting one thing with children — and many children also grow out of it, I'm sure — and then clinical psychologists were noting something else in adults, but that in fact these are related phenomena?

LUHRMANN: So that's a very big question, it's a very good question. I think that gets to this very basic question of the relationship between imagination and psychosis, and the capacity of what I would call "absorption," or the capacity to be absorbed. Absorption — which was named by a psychologist named Auke Tellegen — is usually measured by a scale that has 34 items, for example, "Sometimes I feel and experience things the way I did as a child." Or, "I can change almost any sound into music by the way I listen to it." So people who score highly on this scale are more likely to

---

11. T.M. Luhrmann, *How God Becomes Real: Rekindling the Presence of Invisible Others* (Princeton University Press, 2020); T.M. Luhrmann, Kara Weisman, Felicity Aulino, et al., "Sensing the Presence of Gods and Spirits Across Cultures and Faiths," *Proceedings of the National Academy of Sciences of the United States of America*, 2021, 118, 5.

score highly on dissociation measures. Things like dissociation, hypnotizability, trance, and absorption kind of hang together, and people struggle to understand the relationship between them. Absorption seems to pick up the central thing that people sometimes call "imaginative involvement."

So we've been thinking about this more recently as two factors: one more about the ability to have vivid mental imagery — which is pretty tightly bound with absorption — and the ability to suspend disbelief. And then psychosis crops up in clinical contexts — it is a clinical illness — and there is a relationship between people who are identified with schizophrenia and who hear voices — they are more likely to score highly on absorption measures. Is that because the imagination, absorption, etc., creates the auditory hallucinations? I actually think that it's two different processes and I think we're really struggling to disentangle them.

Now kids, people want to say, are high in absorption and high in hypnotizability, and they just do this imaginative thing very easily. It's also true, you could argue, that kids are different from that. And a group of people such as the psychologist Paul Harris say that "kids are really realists" — that's why they fail the False Belief Test. When they fail, it's because they assume that what they know to be true about the world, other people know to be true about the world. And to have an imaginative experience — the adults have to help them to do that. Margaret Mead, for example, says that a child will not fear the bear under the bed unless an adult puts the bear there. So this is a kind of funny thing about kids.

But it's also true that some kids show up with imaginary friends at the breakfast table. So what's going on with these kids? And what is the experience of having an imaginary friend? Are these kids having quasi-audible experiences in which their imaginary friend talks back? I don't think we know. Many, many kids have vivid imaginative experiences.

Marjorie Taylor — who is one of the primary researchers of imaginary friends — is pretty clear that the kids know that this is imagined. And Bradley Wigger just wrote a book in which he says, "Yes, that's true around the world. The kids know that the imaginary friend is imagined." But it is still vividly present. So I've been talking to tulpamancers — do you know about tulpamancers?

KUIJSTEN: Yes, I've heard the term, but I don't know a lot about them.

LUHRMANN: Okay, so tulpamancers are people who create imaginary friends as adults. And they use these training techniques that you would find in prayer practices, and that maybe some kids do naturally. So these are people who want to create an imaginary friend but they have no metaphysical commitments — so they know that they are making this friend up. So for example, you decide that you're going to talk to a fox — it's going to be your imaginary friend. And so one training technique — and there are books written by tulpamancers about how to do this — involves vividly representing this experience of seeing the fox. You're going to spend an hour looking at the fox's snout — really vividly visualizing the features of the fox or trying to auditorily imagine the fox.

There's also a training technique in which people say, "Okay, just talk to the fox. Just talk to the fox as if the fox is real." So there's this kind of attachment practice using language, and then there's this kind of mental imagery cultivation practice. So I've spoken with about 18 tulpamancers for two to four hours apiece, trying to figure out what they're experiencing.

And what I've learned is that, first of all, people do actually do this, and if they're going to do it then they're really going to spend hours and hours doing this over a period of months. And then they have these complicated metaphysical ideas about how to think about the ontology of the friend. So if they do this, it is true that they have a series of moments in which the friend starts to feel more real, and people will give different names to this. So there will be a moment of vocality. Does the friend talk back? There's a moment sometimes of autonomy — does the friend act different?

But what the people — the tulpamancers, the humans — really articulate are these surprising events in which their imagined companion feels like it's really not them. In my experience, relatively few of their experiences of the tulpa are auditory. So it's clear that the tulpa gets more and more autonomous, more and more external, more and more "not me" and there is more and more of a sensory dimension, but it's generally not as vividly sensory as the first tulpamancers had suggested that it was.

They're not really hearing voices in the psychiatric sense — however it's very complicated, because in the psychiatric world, when people are hearing voices they're also usually not having fully sensory experiences — they're having more inner sensory experiences. At least that's what the literature says as well as my experiences talking to people. So again, there's this really deep puzzle.

So this is the way that I think about it. I think that there's something really basic to the psyche of "another being," or "other people" in the psyche. There's a sense in which we all hear voices — that's too strong — but we certainly all have an experience of, for example "talking to oneself." It's kind of a mystery that you can experience your mom, and then your mom goes away, and yet you still have your mom — and your mom is somehow always with you, and some of the *sotto voce* comments that your mom makes, that's always kind of with you.

So we tend to think of the mind as a vast, immaterial, inner universe, and I think that's probably not a good way of thinking about it. I think that there's something more deeply social about the mind. We understand awareness through the understanding that other people have different beliefs, desires, and intentions. We experience — some of us more than others — but we're practicing talking to other people, rehearsing what we might say, and imagining how other people will respond.

[The German psychiatrist Emil] Kraepelin used the metaphor of an organ stop. So if you're playing an organ, if you open a stop, you have access to all of this sound. And different stops give you different access to different kinds of sound. And I think that imagination and psychosis are "different organ stops." I don't have a good defense of that, except that I'm not the only one — people really struggle to try to figure out these differences.

So I think that psychosis amplifies the sense of the dissolution of the difference between the self and others, or of the self and the world. And people say these strange things about "how the world is made of paper" — they get attracted by weird ideas. Or they might say that the lamp is talking to them. And in the imagination — if that's another kind of organ stop — they are using that capacity to bleed into the world, to make the world more alive. They have a little more control, but, for example, they want God to be more independent, they want the imaginary friend to be more autonomous.

So what I like about Jaynes is the idea that there's this very basic human capacity to mentally experience "others." And then I think of that as being amplified and made possible in different ways and by different pathways. But that's the big question — what the heck is going on? [laughs]

KUIJSTEN: Yes indeed, and thank you for that explanation. I think you're highlighting a very important point here about just how difficult it is in all of these different cases to delineate between what is imagination and what are the more externally perceived experiences. The example of the organ stops is an interesting metaphor that I hadn't heard before, and an interesting way to talk about the idea of psychic diversity. And just as an interesting side note, Julian Jaynes was actually an organist, and my mother was a church organist as well.

LUHRMANN: Oh really? How interesting.

KUIJSTEN: Yes, so I can definitely relate to that metaphor. Not to get on too much of a tangent, but I remember as a young child being on the organ loft with the massive pipe organ, and while my mother played the service, I was looking down from the loft at the congregation — my father never attended the services. Being on the organ loft was much more of an observational role, rather than a participatory role — I've often joked that my earliest experiences with religion were more anthropological in nature. Observing all of the rituals is what planted the seeds of my interest in trying to understand the mystery of the origin of religion, which is what ultimately lead me to Jaynes. Also, I wasn't aware that you had done that research on the tulpamancers...

LUHRMANN: Yes, I haven't published that yet.

KUIJSTEN: So a couple of things that came to mind — I know that in her book Marjorie Taylor definitely comes down much more on the side of the "imagination" interpretation of imaginary companions, and no doubt I'm sure that is true in many cases. But on the other hand we have clinical psychologists, particularly in the UK, that take what we might call a more Jaynesian interpretation — reporting that in many cases, actual hallucinations are involved. Perhaps an additional complication may be that some children experience auditory hallucinations but don't identify them as an imaginary companion. So in any case, as you said, it seems quite complicated trying to determine which children simply have a vivid imagination and are playing "make believe," and which children are having an actual hallucinatory experience that could be predictive of voice hearing and/or an imaginary companion that continues into adulthood.

LUHRMANN: Yes.

KUIJSTEN: You also mentioned absorption and the relationship of things like absorption and hypnosis to imaginary companions. That's a very interesting connection, and it reminded me of something that I read a long time ago by the psychologist and psychiatrist Josephine Hilgard — who was also at Stanford University for many years. Along with her psychology professor husband Ernest Hilgard, she primarily studied hypnosis. And I don't recall what prompted her to study imaginary companions, but she had studied that as well, and she talked about having discovered what she called a "conscience-related" imaginary companion — one that to some extent guided and commented on the children's behavior. She compared their imaginary companions to [the Walt Disney character] Jiminy Cricket, that served as Pinocchio's conscience.[12] If I remember correctly, she also discussed this connection between experiencing imaginary companions and hypnotizability. In any case, the possible connections between imaginary companions and both behavior and hypnotizablity are interesting.

I wanted to ask you about possible connections between people who experience imaginary companions today and similar experiences that are described in the ancient world. You were interviewed recently on your book *How God Becomes Real* by the Harvard theologian Charles Stang, and you referred to his book that discusses the phenomena of a "divine double" in ancient history.[13] I have not yet read his book, but this has a very Jaynesian sound to it. What are your thoughts on people experiencing a sensed presence or imaginary companion, as well as hearing voices, throughout history? Is that something that you've looked at?

LUHRMANN: Yes, reports of hearing voices go way back. Voices are foundational to most religious stories in some form. The sense of an "other" speaking back is again quite basic to the human experience. So Stang documents this in his work. But again, it's the basic idea of God — that there's this "being" who responds. I think that the "imperative" aspect to this is quite interesting, and I haven't quite sorted it out in my mind.

Because I see the imaginary companion typically... for example, Marjorie Taylor talks about kids who have imaginary companions and one of the imaginary companions is called "Doogie" — who is this kind of weird dog. And the "Doogies" are not commanding. Whereas God is commanding, psychotic voices are commanding — why is that? And I don't know exactly whether or not that is true or maybe it's that we're not asking the right questions to the kids.

KUIJSTEN: Yes, that's a great point — that's a very puzzling distinction. So, in your book *When God Talks Back*, you talk about training and almost what we might call a set of protocols that the Evangelical church members go through to elicit what they perceive as the voice of God, and this process

12. Josephine R. Hilgard, *Personality and Hypnosis: A Study of Imaginative Involvement* (University of Chicago Press, 1970).
13. Charles M. Stang, *Our Divine Double* (Harvard University Press, 2016).

seems to be effective for many of them, at least in terms of the more transient type of voices. They also regularly engage in glossolalia, or "speaking in tongues." I've read that there are at least two different forms of glossolalia — what one might call a more moderate, private form and a more extreme, public, dissociative form.[14] Does the more extreme form, in your view, involve an actual altered state of consciousness? Jaynes hypothesized that this more extreme form of glossolalia might involve something of a takeover by the right, or non-dominant, hemisphere language areas. What are your thoughts?

LUHRMANN: So it's a great question. I feel a little naïve about talking about brain structure. But it's clear that people both talk in tongues "on demand" — so you can be in a church in which people regularly talk in tongues, and the pastor will say, "pray," and everybody talks in tongues. And they can do it — and sometimes people talk about this as "faking it" — but people can talk in tongues when they choose.

It is also true that people will enter a state in which the tongues seem to happen "to them," and they seem to feel more caught up in the experience. We did work here in a local church, and a researcher named Josh Brahinsky was leading this project. And he would talk about them as "dropping in." So it's the moment when you're speaking in tongues and you "drop in," and it feels like God is more involved and that you are less involved with your tongue. And we've actually been doing some work with an fMRI to see whether we can catch that difference in the way that the brain seems to behave.

And in Accra, people talked about speaking in tongues in a way that would cure their cold. They were clearly going into trance — and they talked about feeling lighter, they talked about feeling cleansed, and they talked about how great it felt to be talking in this way.

For example, they would walk for an hour and be speaking in tongues. They would sometimes talk about speaking in tongues in their mind, for example, during a lecture, which I thought was particularly interesting. So they are listening to a lecture and they are talking in tongues in their mind. What is happening there? They're using linguistic practice to occupy some of their attention in powerful ways.[15]

---

14. B. Grady and K.M. Loewenthal, "Features Associated with Speaking in Tongues (Glossolalia)," *British Journal of Medical Psychology*, 1997, 70; see also Franco Fabbro, et al., "Contributions of Neuropsychology to the Study of Ancient Literature," *Frontiers in Psychology*, 2018, 9.
15. T.M. Luhrmann, et al., "Sensing the Presence of Gods and Spirits Across Cultures and Faiths."

KUIJSTEN: That is very interesting — yet another interesting piece of this whole puzzle.

LUHRMANN: Yes.

KUIJSTEN: So, as we've discussed, your research indicates the experience of hearing voices is fairly widespread and found on a spectrum in both clinical and non-clinical populations, as well as in different cultures around the world. Evidence suggests hearing voices has been present throughout recorded history and as well as in many, if not all, preliterate societies. We've talked about how hallucinations often comment on or command people's behavior and we've also touched upon your research of people's experience of a sense presence or an imagined, guiding "other." In your books and articles, you've also discussed things like prophecy, spirit and demon possession, automatic writing, and what I would characterize as a longing for external authorization in Wiccan and occultist groups.

With the exception of psychosis in the mentally ill, mainstream psychology for many years has marginalized or completely ignored many of these phenomena, and to the extent that they are discussed even to this day, they are typically treated as separate and distinct. However, looking at these different phenomena through the lens of Jaynes's theory suggests that perhaps they're related. Does Jaynes's bicameral mind theory offer the best explanation for why these phenomena continue throughout societies today, or is there something else in psychology or anthropology that you feel offers a better explanation for all of these different phenomena?

LUHRMANN: That's a great question. So again, I feel uneasy passing judgment on the brain structure argument. So Jaynes's key explanatory argument is about brain structure and about the way in which language operates on both sides of the brain. And I know that some neuroscientists support this theory and others do not. So I don't feel comfortable commenting on that.

However I do think that the observation that our mental world is social rather than singular and private is pretty fundamental. One of the ways that I've been talking about this with one of my colleagues, Kara Weisman, is that I think that all humans have conflicting intuitions about awareness.

So to be human involves being conscious — at least in the case of most humans. But consciousness varies extraordinary widely and nobody understands it. But there is a phenomenological sense of awareness that I think is pretty basic. And I think humans have conflicting intuitions about the relationship between awareness in the world. So, for example, is awareness located in the body, or is it not? I think we have this very basic sense that it's in the body and that if you die, the mind dies. Yet even most secular folks report that they believe that something of the dead person lives on — something that's "mind-like."

Are your thoughts private, or are they not? In the West, we have this very powerful idea that the mind is private, but at the same time we also think that, for example, twins might know what each other are thinking at the certain times when it matters.

Do your thoughts cause things? For the most part, we think not. But many people might have the sense that, for example, if there's been a fight, maybe something of the anger lives on in the room — the anger kind of seeps out somehow. Or if you've been really angry at somebody else, and then something goes wrong for them, you might have a little intuition of, "Did I do that? Should I apologize for that?" We used to say, "My prayers will be with you." Even if you're secular, you might say, "My thoughts will be with you" — as if the thought has power.

And so I think there are a lot of these conflicting intuitions, and I think that's pretty basic. Because thought is confusing. It's your thought, it's your mind. And yet you can't decide not to be angry or not to be in love. You can't decide not to grieve. So sometimes your thoughts don't feel as though they are yours, even though they are yours, and they have this quality of being yours. I think that's very conflicting and powerful and confusing.

And I think that that's connected to these unusual experiences that we have, because these conflicting intuitions also include the idea of the mind as being outside of ourselves. And I think that the possibility is there that the voice is part of that conflict. So that's kind of where I would go — I think there's something pretty basic about these experiences.

KUIJSTEN: Thank you for that explanation. You have also studied cultural differences in "theory of mind," and in a collection of papers titled "Toward An Anthropological Theory of Mind," you, along with others, report striking differences in theory of mind across cultures.[16] I realize that this is a big topic, but if you could perhaps offer a comment on that, and do those differences support the idea that consciousness in the Jaynesian sense is learned and is a cultural construction?

---

16. T.M. Luhrmann, et al., "Toward An Anthropological Theory of Mind: Position Papers from the Lemelson Conference," *Suomen Antropologi: Journal of the Finnish Anthropological Society*, 2011, 36, 4.

LUHRMANN: It's a big question — these questions are terrific. So theory of mind is often used to describe this one paradigm, this one experiment where a child is asked to judge whether somebody thinks differently from them, and at what point the child will say, "Well, I saw that the toy was moved. Sally didn't see the toy was moved, so Sally will say that the toy is here, even though the toy is now there." So that's usually what theory of mind is referring to, but I and others are starting to use it more broadly to refer to one's model of the mind: what can the mind do, and is one's model of the mind bounded — is it cut off from the world? So does one have private, interior thoughts that stay in the head? There are different ways of thinking about how thoughts work.

So a group of us, in what we call "The Mind and Spirit Project," were looking at different representations of mind in different parts of the world, and we found many different ways that people represented the mind. For example, Felicity Aulino, who's working in Thailand, talked about how "the mind is a kaleidoscope." So what was in the mind, or what somebody thought, was kind of connected to the world and kept changing. The world and the mind, they changed together in interlocking ways.

In social worlds where talk of witchcraft and sorcery are more present, for example in Vanuatu and Ghana, there's a more easy default to the idea that the mind is open — that the boundary between the mind and the world is permeable. And the idea that, at least in the case of some people in particular, their negative thoughts can go out and effect the world. So in witchcraft, the key idea is that somebody's bad feeling somehow goes out and attaches itself to somebody else's body and hurts their body — without the action of the person who is doing the thinking. The thoughts just do this.

So I think there are different models of mind. And I think that what makes it hard for Americans to experience God sometimes is that they have a model of the mind that the mind is behind a barrier, and God has to "break into the mind," and if you have an odd sensory experience, you have to discount it because it's not real.

So I think there are these differences. One of the things that we did find systematically is that within any particular social world — and people have a variety of points of view as to the degree that they accept the local ideas about mind or not — the more that somebody was committed to the idea that the mind/world boundary was porous, the more spiritual experiences they were likely to report — the more voices and visions they reported.

KUIJSTEN: That is fascinating research. It's great to see this kind of interdisciplinary research being done — this bridging of anthropology and psychology is so important. Okay, this is my last question. In a 2017 interview you stated that, "No great religion has been founded by someone without voices and visions of some sort."[17] And I was excited to read that, because it was one of the few times that I read someone saying that other than myself. [laughs] Do you see all modern religions as stemming from auditory hallucinations and visions?

LUHRMANN: I think they're pretty basic. I mean, to be clear, since that interview I went back and I was reading through a collection of creation stories, and not all of them involve a voice. But I think the big religions all involve something like that. Buddha is a little more complicated — he has this moment of enlightenment, but was there a voice there? I don't know.

But if there is another being, then the being has to speak. And usually you know that the being is there because the being speaks. So, for example, Zarathustra "sees," but the seeing also comes with a voice. And the voice commands — it says something, it matters. Again, a spirit doesn't show up and tell you what a lovely day it is. The spirit is there for a reason, to give you something to do. So I do think that voices are central to religion.

KUIJSTEN: Indeed. And I remember many years ago when I first took a look at this question in the context of Jaynes's theory, being interested to see that this pattern held up even in the case of religions that Jaynes didn't discuss. So, for example, Muhammad experienced the voice and vision of what he called the angel Gabriel after a period of fasting in a cave outside of Mecca, and Joseph Smith was known to go into dissociative states and claimed to have been visited by God and Jesus while alone in the woods on his family's farm. Voices and visions seem to have played a role in many cults as well, such as with David Koresh and the Branch Davidians and Marshall Applewhite and Heaven's Gate.

Well, thank you so much for taking the time today to share all of your fascinating research and insights on all these interesting topics.

LUHRMANN: Great questions — it was a lot of fun.

---

17. T.M. Luhrmann and M. Fortier, "The Anthropology of Mind: Exploring Unusual Sensations and Spiritual Experiences Across Cultures. An Interview with Tanya Luhrmann," *ALIUS Bulletin*, 2017,1.

10

Making Sense of Voices

Marius Romme, Sandra Escher & Dirk Corstens

Interviewed by Brendan Leahy

Marius Romme is a Dutch psychiatrist best known for his work on hearing voices. He is regarded as the founder and principal theorist for the Hearing Voices Movement.

Sandra Escher (1945-2021) received her Ph.D. from the University of Maastricht. She began working with voice hearers with Marius Romme starting in 1987. Together they published two books and many articles on the voice hearing phenomenon.

Dirk Corstens is a social psychiatrist and psychotherapist and has been a key collaborator in Marius Romme and Sandra Escher's Hearing Voices project at the University of Maastricht, Netherlands, since 1992. He was Chair of the Intervoice Board between 2009 and 2016 during which period hearing voices work was established in 11 new countries. During his work and research, Dirk discovered that many people who hear challenging voices found that a turning point in coping with the experience is finding different ways of talking with and understanding them. Dr. Corstens was a keynote speaker at the Julian Jaynes Conference on Consciousness and Bicameral Studies.

BRENDAN LEAHY: Can you please start by introducing yourselves?

MARIUS ROMME: I'm a psychiatrist — now not as active anymore because I'm retired, but I've worked in psychiatry for 60 years. I've been critical of mainstream psychiatry, because in my view they make human problems into symptoms of illness, including psychotic symptoms.

SANDRA ESCHER: I actually was trained as a journalist and then Marius invited me to help him with the Hearing Voices Project, back in the very beginning, when his patient, Patsy Hage, who was 30 years old at the time, challenged him to expand his thinking regarding her experience of hearing voices. She had read Julian Jaynes's book, *The Origin of Consciousness in the Breakdown of the Bicameral Mind*, and Jaynes's theory provided her with a historical context for understanding her voices. Then over time I became more and more involved. I think one of my advantages is that I don't see "diagnoses," I hear the experiences of people. We developed an interview process, and I've interviewed over 300 voice hearers. We've been working together since 1987.

LEAHY: Is that how you both first came to hear of Julian Jaynes's theory?

ESCHER: Yes, in 1986, Patsy Hage, who had been hearing voices for some time, read Jaynes's book. She asked Marius to read the book and she challenged him to see her voices in the context of Jaynes's theory. So Patsy's experience and Jaynes's theory changed Marius' opinion of hearing voices as a symptom of illness — as he had learned in his medical training — to a meaningful human experience with a historical context.

In 1987, Marius and Patsy appeared on Dutch television, asking the public to respond to a survey about hearing voices. And 450 participants responded — which at the time was quite surprising. Because of the large number of people that responded to the survey, a conference on hearing voices was organized in Maastricht (in the Netherlands), and the Hearing Voices Movement was founded. So, Patsy, Jaynes's theory, and the large response to the initial public survey were what started the quest to make sense of voices and inspired the founding of the Hearing Voices Movement.

LEAHY: Can you explain the difference between your approach and the traditional or mainstream psychiatric approach to hearing voices?

ROMME: We look at the experience — what people experience when they hear voices: what the influences are on that experience, and what influence that experience has on the person. By contrast, in the traditional Western approach, they just say "they hear voices" — but they don't go into anything about the experience. Right away they make it an "entity." And where they say simply "a person hears voices," we recognize that a person often hears different voices, and we are interested in how these different voices relate to different parts of the person.

ESCHER: For me, I became fascinated by working with voice hearers and helping them to write down all of their experiences in a structured way, which gives them a better understanding of themselves. This also allows them to more effectively explain their experience, so that they can be better understood by others. So that became my focus. I also conducted research on 80 children who hear voices, and I very much enjoyed working with these young people.

LEAHY: What were some of your findings?

ESCHER: About sixty percent of the children lost their voices within three years, during the research period. We also learned that the voices were related to their emotions and their development, so it was something you could work with. It was not an illness. It was something you could develop and use. Often the voices have a message to convey about the children's problems.

LEAHY: What are some examples of messages that the children's voices convey?

ESCHER: Well, for instance, if a child was bullied at school, often they hear the voices of the children that bullied them, so the message is that they have to deal with the emotions that relate to that bullying.

LEAHY: Is it your view that the phenomenon of imaginary companions typically involves actual hallucinations?

ESCHER: It depends on the individual. Children talking to their imaginary companions often experience more agency. The voices are experienced as more separate and they have their own agency. The voice hearer is not the author of the play anymore.

ROMME: You carry the voices of bullies with you during your life. It's nice to work together in that sense, because Sandra was educated as a journalist and a journalist interviews a person to know the person better. A mental health professional often interviews a person to affirm his or her own ideas about what they expect. So in terms of exploring the hearing voices experience, the journalistic approach is a much better way to get information about the experience, the influences on the experience, and the person themselves.

ESCHER: Marius and Dirk [Corstens] are not afraid of people's experiences, from a psychiatric point of view. And I believe I can be very open to their experiences because I have no clinical training — I became a researcher — but I meet people as individuals, not as patients.

ROMME: Yes, for example, we often have people over to our house, which you normally don't do as a therapist — but you do if you want to get to know someone better. That's the only way if you want to see them as persons and not as carriers of symptoms and illnesses.

LEAHY: Can you go into more detail about some of the experiences you have had with your therapy?

ROMME: Yes, for us it's not so much a therapy but the development of a person. In therapy, you want to change the person. In our approach, we focus on developing the person. It took quite some time before we realized that it's not about getting rid of the voices, but changing a person's relationship to their voices.

Like a Swedish woman named Ami said, in the beginning, when she looked in the mirror, she heard a voice telling her, "What a mess!" She was criticized by her voice. But when she changed her appearance, the voice still said "what a mess." Then she looked around and saw that she hadn't cleaned her apartment. So rather than criticizing her, she understood her voice to be giving her practical advice — because before living in her apartment, she had been homeless for six years. So the voice was helping her to adapt to living in an apartment.

Some researchers think that the voices are a misinterpretation of a perception, or are misinterpreted inner voices. We think that's not true. For the most part, it is very possible to analyze what the voices are related to — what traumatic or other essential problems in the life of the person that had an overwhelming emotional impact. So you can often find out quite easily the basis or the root of why a person hears voices. To learn to cope with emotions that cause the voices can be a very helpful process. We all talk to ourselves to learn to cope with the world, and surely that's more difficult when you are traumatized.

Adolescence is a difficult time for everyone, so it's not strange that we see a lot of voice hearing in adolescents. What is strange is that mainstream psychiatry isn't interested in this process, and only sees it in terms of its diagnostic value.

ESCHER: What you often see is that when a voice hearer tells the interviewer that they hear the voice of a seven-year-old child, you can be sure that something happened when the child was seven years old. Often it's trauma, or sexual abuse. So that's also a message. Through the voices, you can learn what problems are involved in the trauma.

ROMME: There are strong links between the characteristics of the voices and the problems of the person. For example, the identity of the voices — a victim of sexual abuses's voice might be associated with the identity of the abuser. Another voice might have the identity of the mother, who didn't believe that the girl was sexually abused. Or the voices have the identity of family members that were involved in physical abuse of the victim.

In order to better cope with the voices, you have to know yourself better: "Who am I? Where do I come from? How do I cope with what I have experienced?"

* * *

BRENDAN LEAHY: Can you start by introducing yourself?

DIRK CORSTENS: I work as a psychiatrist and psychotherapist in The Netherlands. I work with many voice hearers — not only as patients, but also as colleagues and friends — and I'm a member of the board of Intervoice, which is an international organization for voice hearers.

LEAHY: How did you first become interested in auditory hallucinations?

CORSTENS: I read about auditory hallucinations in a textbook and I thought it was fascinating. I also became acquainted with some fellow students who had psychotic experiences, and I was really puzzled by that. Later, when I became a psychiatrist, I met Marius Romme and Sandra Escher, who were working with people hearing voices, as well as doing research. I began getting involved and I came to know many people who hear voices.

LEAHY: Can you explain what the nature of someone's experience is when they are hearing voices?

CORSTENS: What I understand — and I know you'll be speaking with some actual voice hearers — is that they just hear voices, like I hear your voice or you hear my voice. The voice can be situated inside the head (or the body) or outside. The experience of hearing voices is very diverse. For example, the voice can be loud or soft, male or female, old or young. Even after having met many voice hearers, I still discover new ways that people describe the experience. Some voice hearers for example read what voices say, like subtitles.

LEAHY: Could you describe the difference between an internally and externally experienced voice?

CORSTENS: I can give a good example of someone who hears both internal and external voices. She hears three internal voices, and these voices represent her as a child. One of the three voices is a child, who calls the person "mother," and it's the voice of a very scared little girl, about eight years old. Then there are the internal voices of two women, who guide and correct her in daily life in a supportive way. So those are her three internal voices. Her external voices are those of people who she has met — people who in one way or another she had a negative experience with. For example, there is a grandfather who assaulted her sexually, a schoolboy who touched her, and a teacher who made fun of her. So those voices she perceives externally.

But internal versus external is also a categorization. Some people think that when you hear an internal voice, that you have developed your voice more, and it is associated more with yourself, whereas an external voice is more alienated. Sometimes that's perhaps true, but sometimes it's not. In psychopathology as a science, writers try to connect specific voices with a certain psychopathology. For example, internal voices are called "pseudo-hallucinations" and external voices are called "real" hallucinations. This endeavor is fruitless if you look at the bigger picture of voice hearers' experiences. There are no "psychotic" voices!

LEAHY: How prevalent is the phenomenon of hearing voices?

CORSTENS: In the Western world, population studies tell us that between 5 and 15 percent of the population hears voices, either short term or long term. That number goes up if you include the experiences that people report before they go to sleep and after they have slept. So it's a very common phenomenon, as common as many other things, for example left-handedness or dyslexia.

In psychiatry, it was long believed that hearing voices was a symptom of mental illness, but population research shows us that that cannot be true. It can be a symptom of illness, but not necessarily.

When I first became involved with The Hearing Voices Network, I learned that hearing voices is not necessarily a sign of madness, but if you hear voices and you cannot cope with them, then you can go mad. So we turn around the reasoning.

LEAHY: Can you talk about hearing voices in non-Western cultures?

CORSTENS: There haven't been a large number of studies of hearing voices in non-Western cultures, however a Dutch psychiatrist named Robert Giel researched hearing voices in an Ethiopian population. He found that 70% of the people there hear voices.[1] They generally attribute the voices to their ancestors. In that part of the world, it's abnormal not to hear voices. Another Dutch professor for a time taught medical students at Addis Ababa University, also in Ethiopia. He told me that when he told the medical students that hearing voices is the most common symptom of schizophrenia, a student bravely asked, "But professor, don't you hear voices?" So there, even in the medical school, it's accepted that people hear voices.

In some non-Western cultures, hearing voices is viewed as a means of connecting with their ancestors. It's very important for them to have a connection with their ancestors, and they view hearing voices as evidence of that connection. So again, for those cultures, it's seen as strange not to hear voices. But in our Western culture, it's still more frequently associated with having an illness.

There is also a developmental aspect to hearing voices — many more children hear voices than adults. Many people who hear voices as children no longer hear them as adults. So they just hear voices for a certain period of their lives. They are able to cope with it, and then eventually the voices disappear. Julian Jaynes's theory explains the evolutionary and historical ontology of hearing voices.

LEAHY: Do you think the reason that so many people hear voices today is because they are a vestige of bicameral mentality, as described by Jaynes?

CORSTENS: Jaynes's hypothesis of the bicameral mind teaches me, among other things, that hearing voices is a basic human capacity. The compelling quality of voices is stronger than words or commands spoken by other

---

1. Lars Jacobsson and Robert Giel (eds.), *Mental Health in Ethiopia* (1999).

people, like the voices of the gods and kings that Jaynes describes as generating decisions in earlier societies. It is extremely difficult for voice hearers not to listen to their voices and it takes a lot of energy to deal with them. In earlier societies, individuality was less emphasized. In our model, we link the voices to real people who acted in a way that was emotionally overwhelming for the individual who hears these voices.

LEAHY: Are there other environmental or cultural factors associated with hearing voices?

CORSTENS: We think that many people start hearing voices after they are unable to cope with certain overwhelming emotions, due to things that happened in their lives. Many people hear voices of people that they know or that they knew in the past. So one of our core questions we want to discover in developing a diagnosis (we call it "construct," because we construct it together with the voice hearer) is "who represents the voices?" People also hear voices of gods or other religious figures, of course. If I were to hear religious voices, I would probably hear the voice of Jesus, but most likely not Buddha or Allah, because the content of the voices is determined by our culture and our environment.

LEAHY: What is the difference between your treatment approach to hearing voices and what we might call the Western, medical approach?

CORSTENS: The approach, to start with, is that we consider hearing voices a natural phenomenon. So, we don't create panic or concepts of disease. Our attitude is very much informed by the idea that hearing voices is a normal experience that acts as a kind of indicator. It's a signal, in the same way that a fever can be a signal. People who can cope with their voices will not visit a psychiatrist. So most psychiatrists see only a selection of voice hearers.

The first step in working as a psychiatrist with voice hearers is asking people to tell you about their voices: "Who are they? What are they telling you? How do you cope with them? When did they first appear? What were the circumstances at that time? How do you deal with them? How do other people deal with you when you tell them you hear voices? Can you tell people about it? Can you share your experience? Do people criticize you about it? What do you think brought about your voices? What is your interpretation of the voices?"

The answers to these questions reveal a great deal about what is happening in someone's life. So in a way, we go from the voices to learning about their personal life story, and then you can discover what happened in people's lives, and what they can deal with and what they can't deal with. Then you can design your treatment to, on one hand, help them to cope with their voices, and on the other, solve the problem that created the voices.

The mainstream medical approach — which I think is slowly beginning to change — is if you tell a psychiatrist that you hear voices, you receive medication with the promise that they disappear. And that's what you want — if you seek help — you want them to disappear.

When someone approaches me and asks me "can you help me to stop the voices?" I tell them, "no, if that's what you want, then you have to go to someone else. But I can talk with you about the voices. And sometimes when we start talking about the voices, the voices disappear. But maybe your opinion about your voices will change, and maybe your voices will change." And that's often what happens.

In an ideal world a voice hearer would enter a pub and tell the other visitors: "I hear voices, who wants to hear my story?" And three of them would go with him to a table and listen to what he wants to share. Because it is a creative experience that has so many layered meanings.

LEAHY: If someone were to tell their doctor that they are experiencing auditory or visual hallucinations, in most circumstances would they be diagnosed with schizophrenia?

CORSTENS: People don't typically use terms like "auditory hallucinations" when they come to see you. They tell you "I hear voices," or "I hear music," or "I see things that other people don't see." So "hallucinations" is more of a medical term, not common language. So that's to start with.

But to your question, yesterday I met someone who hears voices and she is in treatment with a therapist who has a very positive approach towards the voices. But generally what we see is that many psychiatrists want to please their patients. When a patient says, "Please help me to get rid of the voices," then they prescribe medication. Sometimes it works, but most of the time it doesn't — the voices don't disappear, and people often become flattened emotionally, and are even less able to cope with the voices than before.

LEAHY: Can you talk a little about the content of the voices?

CORSTENS: We have learned that the voices often speak metaphorically. For example, when the voices say "you must kill yourself," you can translate that to the meaning "you must start a new life." Many voice hearers eventually come to agree with that. Not in the beginning, because the voices become quieter temporarily when they harm themselves. But if you use the metaphor, "this voice wants to change you," then you create another framework in which there is more space for understanding. If instead you think "this voice is just coming from a dark place in your brain," then you don't provide any understanding.

Often, voices that tell people to kill themselves are voices of people who have issues in their life that they need to address. They are at a dead end. When I talk with voice hearers, often we discover that the voices' intention is different from what they say. So in our opinion, voices generally have a protective function — even voices that say "you must kill yourself."

For example, I met a man who heard the voice of his father, telling him that he should kill himself. He went to a place where he could jump from a height, and he suddenly realized that he didn't want to do that. So he went to a psychiatric hospital. He had to stop working, and through this experience he came to realize the changes that he needed to make in his life — he was in a bad relationship, he couldn't cope with his work, he couldn't cope with his life. So this voice told him, "You should stop hurting yourself — you must take care of yourself." But it wasn't easy — he had to get a divorce, he had to find a new job, and he had to reflect on his life. But the consequence of what was initially seen as a negative voice was that he "took his life" — but in a metaphorical sense.

LEAHY: So there are some people that come to you because they have difficulty coping with their voices, but you've said that there are others who have a positive relationship with their voices?

CORSTENS: Yes, in fact many people can cope with their voices and some even have a good relationship with their voices. That's important to understand. Western society has focused on the negative aspects of hearing voices, but most people can cope with their voices. Some can't, and they seek help, and sometimes we meet them. Organizing these networks of voice hearers is therefore very important. It's very important that we give a positive message about hearing voices, because, over time, people can often learn even to cope with negative voices, and Michel can give you examples of that.[2]

2. See Michel Knols's interview "Living with Voices" in this volume; see also Michel Knols and Dirk Corstens, "Tuning In: A Story by A Patient and A Therapist about Making Sense of Voices," *Mental Health Today*, November-December 2011, 28-32.

11

Living with Voices

Michel Knols

Interviewed by Brendan Leahy & Dirk Corstens

Michel Knols is a voice hearer and former patient of Dirk Corstens living in The Netherlands. He now works as a counselor and peer worker with voice hearers in the mental health field.

BRENDAN LEAHY: Can you start by introducing yourself?

MICHEL KNOLS: My name is Michel Knols and I hear voices. Right now I'm studying again, trying to pick up my life, getting a nice job — fixing my life. It's been a difficult path that I've walked, but now my life is looking good — I feel more like me. That's about what my story is right now.

LEAHY: Could you explain the history of the experiences that you've had as a voice hearer?

KNOLS: When I was young, I could reasonably cope with them. But when I got older I ran into difficult problems at school and with other people. I started to use marijuana, and that actually increased the aggressiveness of my voices — they became stronger and stronger. I started using more and more marijuana to try to ease them down, but that actually made my life even worse, to the point that I had to seek for help. That's what happened in a nutshell.

LEAHY: Can you explain how the voices first started and how they manifest?

KNOLS: The first voice I heard I'm not really sure about — if I heard a voice or if it was just something in my mind. I don't have a very clear memory of that because I was only about three or four years old.

Later on, there came another voice in the period when I moved to a different part of town. I went to a different school, met different children, and I wasn't accustomed to that much change. Also during that period, we had troubles at home — my dad lost his job and there was a lot of stress. There was pressure at home, pressure at school — and then the voice started to manifest itself as a trainer or a coach. It was telling me things like, "You have to be strong, and a strong body is a strong mind. If you don't take care of yourself you will degrade as a person."

That voice started to increase when I went to high school. My high school experience was also not pleasant. I was the youngest one in my class, I was thin, and other kids ridiculed me. I always felt like I had to fight against both my own classmates and the school. That made me feel like an outcast. All of the teasing and bullying caused me to start experimenting with drugs. And initially, drugs provided a bit of a release, but over time it also made the voice grow stronger and more aggressive — because drugs are not good for your body or your mind, and especially not good for your school work. That's when it really became a problem.

After high school, I went on to study civil engineering. At one point I was in a class where we had to draw straws to form groups. I was picked to be in a group with two other students. We had to design a project and we were graded as a group rather than by our individual performance. Because my project mates didn't show up or didn't make the deadlines, we received bad grades. Even after having discussed this with the teachers, they still graded me from the group perspective That caused a lot of stress, and it was difficult to work together and stay motivated. It took a lot of energy to work on a project knowing that I would not get a good grade.

Some other stressful situations with my teachers and parents eventually drove me to start to use drugs on a daily basis, and basically just run away. This actually made the voice even more angry and aggressive — not only to me but also giving orders to hurt other people and saying things like "you can't trust anyone." But the release I got from using drugs made me keep using them. This was the start of the downward spiral.

At times the voice started to confirm my reality — what I mean is that things the voice told me actually started happening. And my voice would say, "See, I told you so." This made the bond with my voice stronger, or harder to sever. In hindsight, the voice was more wrong than right, but I started to lose who I was and started to attribute more power to the voice and what he told me. In this period my relationship with my parents degraded and it was increasingly difficult to stay in reality. The voice kept on repeating the same aggressive narrative to hurt myself and others. The line between being awake or asleep started to blur. Also, because of my drug use, I started to associate with some shady people and I started to go down a path of drug use and petty crime. I was in a state of mind where life was dark and I started seeing my existence as futile.

At one point I had a dream, and a different voice came in. In this dream, I died of a drug overdose and an unhappy life. This dream felt so real and scared me so much that I realized how far I had strayed from who I actually was. I realized that I was not a criminal and that deep inside I did not believe my existence was futile. This new voice gave me options — it gave me possibilities and choices. It wasn't aggressive, it just gave me choices like a wise elder or grandfather speaking in a calm, rational and accepting manner. But the aggressive voice was still dominant and relentless in his presence.

At that point, school was going bad and everything in my life was screwed up, so I decided to quit school in order to get out of this toxic situation. So I quit school, and in order to get a job I stopped using drugs and I got rid of all the bad people in my life. I was lucky that a friend notified me of a job opening in a nursing home as a kitchen assistant. So I got a job after roughly four months and I started working. That was actually the first time in a long time that I enjoyed myself, that I felt like I belonged somewhere, and that I was making something of my life.

But unfortunately that didn't last. I began to have conflicts at work due to changes in management and I also started to have trouble with my back. I had to go to the hospital, and they said I probably had a spinal tumor. After several months the diagnosis turned out to be false. But the feeling that I was going to die or remain paralyzed felt devastating to me, and I basically just disconnected from the world.

At that point, I started to lose control of what was happening and of what was going on in my mind. I started to realize I had to do something — that I had to get help. I was heading in the wrong direction again. Eventually I had to accept that I could not do this on my own and that I needed help. I decided to take a leap of faith and confessed to my parents how lost I was and that I needed their help. This was very difficult because my relationship with my parents was tense and damaged. But fortunately they listened to me and supported me.

LEAHY: Can you describe a little more in depth about the actual experience of the voices?

KNOLS: Well, what actually happened is someone started talking to me, and I didn't know where it was coming from. At first, I thought it might be ghosts, or something like that. But that didn't really make sense, because in my opinion ghosts don't exist. It was somebody talking to me who wasn't really there. I had to listen.

LEAHY: How do the voices sound?

KNOLS: They have their own personalities — they are just like other people that you meet on the street. They have their own character, their own way of speaking, and their own way of relating to the world. It's different from the experience of one's own internal thoughts. In my experience the voices are as real as it gets — it's just like you talking to me. For example, when you are thinking something over, it's as though I have more people thinking with me. I have more reference points, more people to ask questions.

LEAHY: How did you connect with Dr. Corstens and Dr. Romme?

KNOLS: I first met Dirk. He helped me a great deal by giving me an explanation for what was happening to me. He helped me to make connections to events that happened in my life, and that helped to clarify what was going on with me. I began to understand that what was happening to me is in part a reaction to what was happening in my environment. I started to understand the triggers and events, and that helped me to put things in perspective.

The first method we used was making an appointment to speak to the voices. Something as simple as that, I could never have imagined on my own — but it worked. And that gave me room to work on my own issues, to relate to the events and how everything worked for me at that time. Bit by bit we started to work on my emotional expressions. I worked on learning to express what I think, what I feel, and what I want — being able to clarify that for other people.

DIRK CORSTENS: Did your voices change as a result of this process?

KNOLS: It's not so much that the voices changed as it was my perception of the voices changed. I grew through the experience. The more I learned to express myself and tell people what I wanted and needed, the more I learned to find out who I really was. The stronger I became and the more my own identity grew, the less dominant and less intrusive the voices were.

The voices actually became an instrument that I could use to interpret my environment. I learned to use them. For example, if I began to run away from a situation, the aggressive voice might come up and say, "Hey, you have to do something about this — you have to address this situation."

CORSTENS: So did the voices help you to express yourself?

KNOLS: Yes, but they also helped me to look at my own position in the situation — my own position in the world, and my reactions to things. So they also helped me to reflect on who I am.

LEAHY: What was life like for you growing up?

KNOLS: I grew up in a very small town. Before that I lived in an even smaller part of this town. The social structure was different — we could walk around outside as small kids and everyone looked out for each other. You could walk into other people's homes with no problem.

Then we moved to a larger town and there people were more closed off. There you had to look out for yourself, in every way possible. If people felt like they could betray you, then they would. If they felt like they could use you, then they would. This didn't fit in with my way of being — concepts like this didn't even exist for me before I came to live there. You really had to fit in and behave in a certain manner in order not to be bullied. The fact that relationships were based on selfish motivations made trusting others difficult and made me feel isolated.

CORSTENS: So you felt unsafe?

KNOLS: Not only unsafe, but rejected. I couldn't build up normal social bonds. I thought I had friends, but then they would backstab me when it was convenient.

CORSTENS: And it was in this environment that you developed the voices?

KNOLS: Yes. That's when the "trainer" voice came, so I could take care of myself. The basic idea was, "When somebody tries to backstab you — get them. Be stronger."

CORSTENS: When we met for the first time, you told me that you were afraid that you would hurt other people because the dominant voice told you to. You asked for medication to stop the voices — you were desperate to make them stop. I explained that we take a different approach, and that we had found that most voices are related to life experiences. To my surprise, that immediately made sense to you.

LEAHY: How did that approach differ from what you might have experienced had you pursued a more mainstream pharmaceutical-based, psychiatric treatment?

KNOLS: Well, I didn't take that approach, so I really don't know. [laughs]

CORSTENS: If Michel would have been referred to a psychiatric program, he would have been diagnosed with schizophrenia, put on medication for many years, and, emotionally speaking, he would have become a zombie. He would have gained no perspective on his experience. They are very kind doctors and they have the best intentions — to help to stop the voices — but that's how they've been trained to approach the problem.

LEAHY: Do you have a message or advice for other voice hearers?

KNOLS: The most important thing for me was learning not to fight against the voices — accepting them as part of me. Fighting against yourself is a waste of energy, it doesn't move anything forward. It's like playing a game of chess against yourself. Learn to understand who your voices are. They aren't all evil. They may say evil things, but I'm still "me." I still decide what actions I take. I feel responsible for everything I do. I can't blame a voice if I do something stupid — I did it. That awareness of who I am is very strong in me, and that helped me to accept that the voices are part of my life. So my advice to other people who hear voices is, "Try to accept them as part of who you are." They always resemble a part of who you are or how you feel, so try to learn from them.

October 2021 Update: At the present time I'm married and a proud father, something I couldn't have imagined back when I first sought help with the voices. The relationship with my parents has improved greatly and we've found a balance that we never had before. I'm also working professionally in mental health care as a peer worker and I try to help other voice hearers to cope with their voices. Knowing that my life could have been very different makes me grateful for the help I received and the life I have now.

12

A Vestige of the Bicameral Mind in the Modern World

Elisabeth Bell Carroll

Interviewed by Brendan Leahy

Elisabeth Bell Carroll is author of *Chopin in the Attic*, which describes her experiences with temporal lobe epilepsy (TLE). She has lived with TLE since childhood, studied mathematics and was an in-house researcher, technical writer, and editor. Her forthcoming book, *Agnès & Oscara*, is set in fifteenth century France and our modern day world, with a time-travel — or time-slip — feel, inspired by her pre-seizure auras. Nods to the work of Julian Jaynes are woven throughout. She spoke about her experiences at the Julian Jaynes Society Conference on Consciousness and Bicameral Studies.

BRENDAN LEAHY: Could you please say a little bit about yourself and your experiences, just to start off?

ELISABETH BELL CARROLL: I'm a researcher and writer. I have a seizure disorder called temporal lobe epilepsy; the temporal lobes are here in the brain, near the top of each ear. Temporal lobe seizures are not obviously physical, at least for me, as in a grand mal, where one falls to the floor and rocks violently. The particular type of seizure that I have is called a Complex Partial seizure, or a CP seizure. For me, a seizure usually manifests as a deep, dreamy state. When I'm in this dreamy state, it's hardly apparent to anyone but me, since I experience an alteration of consciousness, not a cessation of consciousness, as in a grand mal.

My seizures grew in intensity over the course of 14 years, ages 4 to 17. As a child in a dreamy state seizure, I saw the Son of God, Jesus. Important to note, Jesus appeared as a young man before his crown of thorns, the assaults to his body, all the blood in the last days of his life. When I was a child, Jesus appeared to me as one finds him in a children's picture book of Bible stories, for example. A handsome young carpenter busy at his carpenter's bench in his village workshop, so a non-threatening Jesus. He spoke to me as a caregiver might, offering useful guidance. He was like an imaginary friend, yet there was a definite intentionality about his presence. He coached me. In particular, he helped me regain the desire to interact with family members after my long hospital confinement. Very much like the bicameral period described by Julian Jaynes, he was a participating God, a helpful God.

I was raised in Boston among an enclave of Irish immigrants, who held onto their Catholic religion as if holding onto their homeland. When I was age four, my appendix ruptured after a few days of excruciating pain. As peritonitis set in, a local doctor standing in my bedroom yelled at my mother, "She's green as a cabbage! Were you waiting for a miracle?" He put me on the backseat of his car, leaving my mother to watch from an upstairs window, and rushed the two of us to Massachusetts General Hospital. Shortly thereafter I was in an operating theater. A black mask that dispensed anesthetic ether was pressed over my nose and mouth, and as I swooned out, I yelled, "Don't kill me!" I fought that mask because I believed that the anesthesiologist was killing me with the approval of everyone there. No one had previewed with me what was about to happen in the operating room, since this was the early 1950s. We were not a child-centered society then, so I found no advocates as the mask pressed on my face. Later that day, after a last-measure second surgery, a family priest anointed my body in the final rites of our church, outside the operating room.

In my hospital crib, probably a week or so after surgery, I had my first vision, which may have been concomitant with my first seizure. A coal miner, black soot on his face and overalls and wearing a miner's cap lamp, stood at the foot of my crib. As I looked at this miner, he morphed into the Son of God, Jesus — a gentle and helpful man familiar to me from children's picture books and Easter greeting cards. How did my own brain know to do that?

In a singsong manner Jesus said, "*Bonne nuit.*" He said goodnight to me in French. Edith Piaf's records were often played in my home, so by age four I knew a bit of French. Isn't that funny? I find it humorous that the first words Jesus ever spoke to me were in French [laughs]. So, back-to-back surgeries in a single day may have created the scar on my right temporal lobe. It's also called a "seizure focus," and that is likely the source of my complex partial seizures.

LEAHY: During your hospital stay did you see Jesus again?

CARROLL: For weeks after surgery I was restrained in a crib, fixed still via straps. I was virtually incapable of moving so that intravenous medicine could flow as intended. Hospital policy guidelines advised parents against visiting an in-patient child — too much crying as the parents left — thus, Jesus visited my cribside and spoke to me, in lieu of my parents. "Soon the straps around your arms and tummy will be removed, and you'll be able to sit up. A playroom is across the hall. When you're feeling better, Libby, I will take you there."

The visitation of Jesus in my hospital room may relate to the phenomenon of sensed presences during extreme and unusual environments, according to the research of John Geiger and Peter Suedfeld.[1] In his book, *The Third Man Factor*, Geiger describes a fairly common experience that happens to people who confront life at its extremes — mountaineers and Arctic explorers who find themselves near death.[2] A sensed or hallucinated presence that is utterly compelling and vivid appears to them, a presence so real, they may offer it food. Suedfeld, a psychologist and a field researcher in the Antarctic and Canadian Arctic, interviewed solitary sailors, mountain climbers, and explorers of frigid lands who had survived desperate and prolonged near-death situations. They described to Suedfeld an incorporeal savior who assisted them, encouraging and cajoling in a clear voice to give them strength — a savior who helped these dying adventurers to survive, guiding them out of the impossible.

Although I was not on a forced march to reach the *Nimrod* as the Antarctic froze over, I was strapped down in a crib, alone in a stark, unfamiliar environment, forced to endure prolonged high stress. To a four-year-old weakened by illness, that's hostile terrain. Like those who spoke to Geiger and Suedfeld, a savior arrived on the desolate scene to help me survive.

1. Peter Suedfeld and John Geiger, "The Sensed Presence As A Coping Resource in Extreme Environments," in J.H. Ellens (ed.), *Miracles: God, Science, and Psychology in the Paranormal, Volume 3, Parapsychological Perspectives* (Praeger Publishers, 2008).
2. John Geiger, *The Third Man Factor: Surviving the Impossible* (Penguin Canada, 2008).

LEAHY: What were things like upon your return home?

CARROLL: It never occurred to me that I would ever go home from the hospital, since I was not told that going home was a future step in my recovery. One day, a mother arrived to take home a hospital roommate of mine. I asked, "Louis, are you going home to the house where you lived before the hospital?" Louis answered, "Yes." From then on, I hoped that I might go home one day, too.

At home, after a month as an in-patient, I chose to live under our dining room table. I resided there for perhaps a year, hidden from the adults who had abandoned me, who now allowed me the freedom to choose my living quarters [laughs]. I often heard the conversation of the women gathered around our dining table, drinking hot tea, eating sandwiches and smoking Herbert Tareytons. A favorite topic was the anointing I had received when everybody thought I was about to die. My family calls me Libby, and I'll give you an example of their dialogue. My grandmother would begin the conversation:

[Speaking with a strong Irish accent] "Already dabbed with the holy oil, Libby was in the arms of Jesus Christ himself in that hospital room, and he then gave her back to us."

"You see a reason in that, Helen?" an aunt would ask.

"Oh! Jesus would not have handed back Libby without a good plan in mind. She may already be a saint, she talks to Jesus. Isn't that true, Libby?"

These women spoke like they were across the lake, booming voices. An aunt would remark, lifting the tablecloth to peer at me sitting underneath, "You saw him there with arms wide open, and he nearly carted you off to Heaven!"

"Auntie, at first he had soot all over his face."

"Och, the imagination on you!" she would say.

Note the subtle indoctrination I received. I enjoyed a certain ease in hearing the voice of Jesus and seeing him face to face. With a family of collaborators such as mine, is it any wonder? Collaborators are important in a belief system. Julian Jaynes coined the term "the collective cognitive imperative" as it applied to the bicameral mind, when men and women lacked central analytical thinking skills and were unable to introspect. The imperative required that each person trust an external authority, accepted by the group members. In the bicameral period, that authority was actually his or her right temporal lobe, yet all the collaborators living then saw that authority as a god. I found this external authority in a hallucinated Jesus, and lucky for me, I was raised in a household where a young girl who saw Jesus, spoke to Jesus, and danced with him was not pathologized or medicated. That child lived among collaborators.

LEAHY: Can you talk a little more about the nature of your seizures?

CARROLL: Okay, yet it's always a challenge to describe them with pinpoint accuracy. A typical seizure at age six, for example, brought a simple dreamy state that passed in a few minutes while I did puzzles sitting on the floor, let's say, or while reading a book in a soft, comfy chair. While out for a family walk, I recall sitting on the knee wall of the strand while the dreamy state came over me for a while. The adults who accompanied me found nothing alarming about that and joined me for a sit on the wall. A typical seizure at age 14 began as a "pre-seizure aura" — its medical name. For me, that aura was a slow gliding into a pervasive déjà vu moment, "Uh oh, here we go again. I've been here before."

An orange, the smell of an orange being split open nearby, its particulates in the air, often accompanies the first three seconds or so of a seizure, while a perfect silence separates me from this world. A mystical, Dutch-master kind of light animates the reality I glide into, until I'm in a verdant paradise that I understand is the Garden of Eden. I feel my whole being assume the aspect of an inquiry — a vital secret is hidden in the Garden, and it's incumbent upon me to uncover it. Further, I feel received, welcomed into this secret place by an Other, who has an allegiance to me, who knows I have just crossed over the threshold into Eden. In a heartbeat, I understand that the Other is God the Father, almost identical albeit slightly different from his Son, Jesus.

My seizures were mostly the same. Also, the Garden of Eden had a kind of logic to it. First of all, consequential answers were available in the Garden, and it was to my great advantage to access them. Second, the tender voice of God coached me to persevere, to find those answers; he wanted me to have that vital intelligence. "Keep searching here, and you will find Secrets of Life that few are able to grasp while on Earth," was his message to me. Now, that was the incontrovertible logic of the Garden of Eden, and it was a reality that was as true as this one, right this minute. In fact, the Garden of Eden reality in seizure was even more real, more vivid than what I see as I sit in this chair. I felt valued there. I had an advocate there, someone who had an allegiance to me and wanted me to know the answers to eternal questions.

My seizures took a slight turn by age 16. The voice that I heard became more personal, more intimate. For example, "I am here for you, Libby. I will always be here for you." It was like a benediction, a perk, a sweetener for being a devoted visitor to the Garden. Again, that was the logic there. By age 17, the atmosphere got a little scary in seizure. I understood that I had to go deeper into the Garden to get the high-value answers to eternal questions like, "From whence have I come?" "Why am I here?" "Where am I going?" I knew those answers were hidden in the Garden, and I wanted to uncover them. I found this mission very alluring, yet there was a risk involved. If I went so deep into the Garden — like the rhapsody of the deep that a diver feels as he throws caution to the wind and continues to venture far too deep, where the undiscovered sea world is so gorgeous, so fascinating — I felt there was a possibility I might never return from Eden if I dared move into it too deep. If I failed to resist the richness of its treasure, I could die in there.

Since my seizures now had a scary edge, I made an appointment with a neurologist in Boston, for the first time. I told him my whole story, and he soon told me I had temporal lobe epilepsy. He prescribed anti-seizure medication. Well, I was on that medication for about two months, but the side effects were so dreadful that I refused to take it any longer. The upside could not possibly outweigh the negatives of the medication. And oddly enough, after that two-month experiment on medication, I rarely had a seizure after that.

However, a few times while I was on the medication, an anthropomorphic God appeared to me, just his face close up and in shadows. His face had the tenderness and mobility of a human face. God was trying to tell me something. He mouthed words he wanted me to hear, yet no voice came out. He kept mouthing the words slowly, and I couldn't get them. He wanted me to know what words he was saying, yet his voice was not transmitting. He had something important to impart, and I knew it, and I was trying to get it, but I could not decode what he was saying. I never did hear those final words that he had for me in Eden.

Every now and again over the next few years I would have a seizure, slowly gliding into the déjà vu and into the Garden of Eden. But in the Garden now I heard no voice. I did not feel received. I did not feel I had an advocate there. I did not think there were answers in the Garden now. A couple of times I saw the face and identified it as God's, even though I was moving away from my childhood Catholic beliefs. I began to feel that the "all-knowing" voice I had heard in the Garden was simply from another consciousness. I had been sharing my head with this other consciousness. I had my consciousness, and then there was the voice that was not my voice. It was simply the voice of a consciousness who possessed greater intelligence than I.

In Jaynesian terms, it could have been that my bicameral mind was breaking down. I almost never have a CP seizure now; however, I can recall the Garden of Eden, the voice that I heard, having an advocate in the Garden who valued me and loved me. I can recall the pleasure of being in that Garden like it happened this morning. At this point in my life, that's all I need.

LEAHY: When did you first discover Julian Jaynes's book?

CARROLL: I discovered *The Origin of Consciousness in the Breakdown of the Bicameral Mind* in 1977, the year it came out.[3] I was at a tavern with friends, in my twenties. We often met for frosty draft beers and BLTs. A person in our group, a staunch Catholic young man named Joseph, had just fled the seminary. Joseph brought Julian to lunch — his book, that is — and was singing its praises. Joseph particularly enjoyed the fact that, according to Jaynes, in bicameral days a god was always with each person and never left his or her side.

We were a group of Irish, Italian, and Lithuanian Catholics, and found that quite amusing since we had each read a similar assertion in our *Baltimore Catechism*. Catholic school children memorized this catechism from second grade on. "God sees us and watches over us always. God knows all things, even our most secret thoughts, words, and actions." Jaynes's new book espoused a theory that would be filed in the canon of neuroscience papers on the evolution of consciousness. That day, a group of Catholics in a tavern in Boston thought that the *Baltimore Catechism* should be filed alongside *The Origin of Consciousness in the Breakdown of the Bicameral Mind*, because it agreed entirely with Julian Jaynes.

LEAHY: What impact did Jaynes's book have on you at that time?

CARROLL: Jaynes's book influenced me in a very positive way. It was an "Aha!" moment: "That's it! That is it, of course!" By the time I had read the book in 1977, I was past the peril of psychiatric collapse myself. In Jaynesian terms, my bicameral mind had broken down, and it was time to

---

3. Although the book's copyright is 1976, it did not appear on store shelves until January 1977.

enjoy the happy hypostasis — the underpinning of my healthy conscious-ness, my healthy sense of self. Via a form of recapitulation theory, I assess Jaynes's millennial stages as congruent to my own growth into modern consciousness over the course of my first twenty years. And I must say this, Julian Jaynes was alive for twenty years after his book appeared in print, and I wish I had sought him out. I wish I had contacted him. I could have had a refreshing conversation with Julian.

LEAHY: When you talk about entering and exiting the garden, when you were having your seizures, did you actually have to — as you approach the space of the Garden of Eden — did you actually have to walk in and walk out? Or, how specifically did you...

CARROLL: No, no. It was all in my head. I would most likely be sitting down, as I am now, and I'd go into a deep, dreamy state. I never understood this state as a seizure until I was diagnosed. My particular brain chose to imagine Eden while in seizure. Those were all my own thoughts. So, no. There was nothing physical going on other than moving into a CP seizure, a place I understood as the Garden of Eden.

LEAHY: Did a family member advise you to see a neurologist? You spoke previously about how your family supported your unusual visions, corrob-orated them in many ways. Did their attitude shift?

CARROLL: My father heard voices, too. He suffered a complete psychiatric collapse when I was 13. A few years after that, an uncle noticed that I went off into a CP seizure, when my family and I visited his summer cottage. I explained that it was nothing — it just happens. His concern and questions may have helped me to accept, at age 17, that a scary aspect had emerged in my seizures. Soon, and on my own, I made an appointment with a Bos-ton neurologist. Here, I must underscore a nontrivial point — in an Irish household of recent immigrants, if a child complained of a sore throat or an injured arm, a parent would respond with a kick in the pants. "Off with you now! You're fine...!" The Irish child would be happy to receive even a rare gesture of caring such as that [laughs]. I'm relating my personal expe-rience, of course.

LEAHY: When you went into the Garden of Eden, did these answers ac-tually take any physical shape or form? Because you said you had to search around for them, so I was wondering if they took any sort of shape, or ...?

CARROLL: I understood that answers were hidden there, and it behooved me to uncover them. Inherent in this notion was a feeling that if I had answers to the eternal questions, I would rise to a superior position, above nearly all others. Certainly, my compulsion to find answers could be due to receiving no answers while an in-patient child. Further, being riveted to that eternal moment of "Don't kill me!" — the endless cry that moves through all nature — could account for something.

When I was back in this reality, consensus reality, I read everything under the sun from Baruch Spinoza to Teilhard de Chardin to Thomas Merton. I constantly searched for answers on my own. From my teen years on, I read widely: Franz Winkler and Teresa of Ávila and Pir Vilayat Inayat Khan. I read Fritjof Capra, *The Tao of Physics*. I never got any grand answers from the Garden; although, the notion that they were there remained.

LEAHY: Was your father's psychiatric breakdown and hearing voices ever given any sort of explanation? Do you think that hearing voices may have been passed on to you, and that the hospital experience that you endured brought out this genetic predisposition?

CARROLL: My father's experience of hearing voices and his profound decline frightened me. In my home, answers or words that might soften the hurt of his loss were never offered. I never asked questions, I just missed him terribly. Also, I learned never to talk about the voices that I heard or the visions that I saw to family members, or anyone at all. My father's illness was impossibly sad, and we didn't go there. He was committed to a psychiatric institution, and he never became a whole person after that.

As a result of my seizures and history, I have lived an isolated life, keeping stress to a minimum because I have to. There are so many dangers. I will add, doing an interview like this is a huge leap. My god, I can't believe I'm doing it! [laughs]

13

Authorizing Clinical Hypnosis: From Bicameral Mentality to Autonomy

Laurence I. Sugarman

Interviewed by Marcel Kuijsten

Laurence I. Sugarman is Research Professor and Director of the Center for Applied Psychophysiology and Self-regulation in the College of Health Sciences and Technology at the Rochester Institute of Technology (RIT); a developmental and behavioral pediatrician at the Easter Seals Diagnostic and Treatment Center in Rochester, New York; and Clinical Professor in Pediatrics at the University of Rochester School of Medicine and Dentistry. Over two decades of primary care pediatric practice, Professor Sugarman refined clinical biofeedback and hypnosis strategies that effectively increase resilience and coping skills for young people and families. Based on this experience, he produced an internationally acclaimed video-documentary, *Hypnosis in Pediatric Practice: Imaginative Medicine in Action*. At RIT, he has focused on (1) how best to evoke the abilities of young people with autism spectrum disorder and other chronic health problems, (2) innovative interactive media for health, and (3) pedagogy for professional development in psychobiological care. With Dr. William Wester, Dr. Sugarman has co-authored and co-edited the text, *Therapeutic Hypnosis with Children and Adolescents*. His latest book, coauthored with Julie Linden and Lee Brooks, is *Changing Minds with Clinical Hypnosis*.

MARCEL KUIJSTEN: To start with, let's talk about your background. How did you first become interested in medicine, how did you first become interested in hypnosis, and please tell us about the type of work that you're involved with.

LAURENCE SUGARMAN: I've always been interested in life sciences. I started to figure out how to bake bread when I was about 10, because I thought it was so cool that we could grow yeast and make it bubble into bread that tasted good. My mother was appalled at the mold I grew in the basement, in what I called my laboratory. Like many kids, I was fascinated about how things worked, and how they — and even we — became more than the sum of their parts.

When I went to college, I found myself taking all these courses with pre-medical students, and decided I absolutely would never go to medical school because those pre-medical students were so cut-throat, competitive, and after-the-grades, but not after the knowledge and understanding. That's how it felt to me, back then. My identity was so fragile. I thought if I attempted to become a pre-medical student, I would transform into what I saw as their personality and lose my own. But I worked in hospital labs from early in high school, and became enamored with the building blocks of how we — our bodies and minds — work. And so by the time I eventually — four years after graduating college — went to medical school, I was so thrilled and felt so fortunate to do this that it took hold.

I oriented myself towards pediatrics because I was excited about the potential for investing in a person's health early and intrigued by the mystery of human development. I didn't think of myself at all as a scholar or as a researcher. I wanted to get in there and do it and see what it was like, so in the mid-1980s I took out a loan and started a solo primary care pediatric practice — sharing call with like-minded pediatricians — in the city of Rochester, New York.

And very quickly I became disillusioned with my training, because I hadn't been well-prepared for the huge burden and volume of behavioral and mental health issues that young people and their families brought to my care. And I remember going to one of the senior clinical pediatricians in the community early on and saying, "I don't know what to do. I'm seeing all these children with sleep problems, and habit problems, and irritable bowel syndrome, and headaches, and anxiety, and depression, and dissolving and reforming families, and I'm seeing all of this, and my training didn't prepare me for this."

He was a wonderful man — he passed away last year — and he said, "Right, I know. Most of us deal with that by not *seeing* it." But I couldn't unsee it, and I became compelled to figure out how to integrate primary mental health care into primary care. That led quickly to thinking about self-regulation for children. And Karen Olness, Daniel Kohen, and certainly Milton Erickson, early on, wrote a lot about integrating hypnosis, the utilization of imagination, and employment of psychobiological reflexes in children into their health and care.

So I started studying that. I couldn't *not* study that. Since we check oxygen saturation with pulse oximeters in children, we listen to their hearts, and we do all sorts of other measurements, it became clear to me that simply giving children back the physiological measurement we were taking from them — basically doing biofeedback — could also have an important role in demonstrating a sense of their agency and helping develop resilience. So I became enamored with figuring out how to do that both with technology and as myself — the doctor who asks, "How do you know how to do that?" — in part to feel good about the effectiveness of my practice.

I think that many pediatricians — and primary care doctors in general — become disillusioned and frustrated because the individuals who come to them for care aren't having problems that they were trained to resolve. Feeling ineffective leads to burnout. Figuring out how to be more effective by addressing the person's capacity for resilience and self-regulation leads to the opposite of burnout: an enriched and intriguing practice of care.

I actually became excited and fell in love with my practice because there are so many opportunities to help children help themselves, to help them have a sense of success every time they get an immunization — "Look what I can do, I know how to turn that [pain and fear] down." To help children feel comfortable and empowered when they find out they have a chronic disease because there are ways that they can help themselves. And then, over the last 10 years of my 20 years in primary care, and certainly the next 10 years, as I focused on developmental-behavioral pediatrics, suddenly the number of children who met criteria for autism spectrum disorder — broadening, spreading criteria — exploded.

I realized that self-regulation therapies — hypnosis, biofeedback, relaxation training — had an incredibly powerful role in the lives of people with developmental differences. That focus shifted me to thinking more about health and care in general: "Why does our reductionist, allopathic model ignore the mind?"

Around that time I met another banjo player and collector of vintage instruments, Bill Destler, who also happened to be the new president of the Rochester Institute of Technology. He heard some of my music and he asked, "I like your music, it's really great. No offense, but what's your day job?" I explained to him what I was doing, and he was envisioning a new college — the ninth college at RIT — in Health Sciences and Technology. When he shared that, I said, "We already have a medical school in town." And he said, "I didn't say 'medicine', I said 'health'." And he got it, I mean, a physicist who really got it. He understood that we need to work on health and well-being — we're moving beyond medical care. So I'll always be grateful that I was fortunate to be given this place at RIT to wonder about how we change health care.

I'm still a pediatrician. I'm still a primary care doctor at heart. Two days per week I work with children — young people, and now even people older than me — who want to learn how to marshal their own aptitudes — and I'll jump ahead — and create their own autonomous authorizations for health. And I get to write. I get to collaborate. I get to do wonderful interviews like this.

KUIJSTEN: Fantastic. It sounds like those are strategies that everyone could benefit from. And that's a good segue to my second question, which is on autism. Autism has come up in connection with Jaynes's theory over the years because of the ideas about the relationship of consciousness and language and the role that language plays in Jaynes's definition of consciousness. I don't know that we will delve too deeply into that topic, but since you work with children with autism, I thought I'd ask you to comment on it. "Autism" is one of those words that we hear all the time, but I think that many people don't have a clear understanding of exactly what autism is. Could you give us your perspective?

SUGARMAN: Okay, but allow me to take one step back before moving forward. Over the last decade I have become a pretty rabid anti-diagnostician. Diagnoses are useful labels for models that we have developed to understand human conditions. We can use those models to prognosticate and as a basis to test treatment. We can even give people a sense of belonging by using them for social support. Significantly, we use them as a basis for reimbursement. They make money flow. But they're models, they're evolving concepts, and they're not real.

Diagnoses are not entities. They are not people. They represent uniquely lived experiences. In his beautiful book, *When Breath Becomes Air*, Paul Kalanithi wrote something about how our relationship with statistics changes when we become one. And I think this tension between the objective and subjective is played out even more in the field of mental health. It's played out in the study of what we call "autism" — which of course used to be called "infantile schizophrenia" — and it, too, keeps on evolving.

So, first of all, I don't say that people "have autism," and I learned to stop using "-ic" words for people, except when referring to their behaviors. Not "diabetic," "leukemic," or fancier terms like "migraineur." How is referring to a person by the diagnostic model we give them any better than objectifying them by race or gender or religion? A young man who *met criteria for autism* — my preferred figure of speech — says on video, "I have autism in disguise." Another young man once told me that "normal people are autistic about autism." I thought that was quite accurate and insightful.

So, we won't go into the derivation of autism and the origins of that diagnosis. I'll simply say that these days, autism spectrum disorder — not plural — which is what the *Diagnostic and Statistical Manual 5* of the American Psychiatric Association calls it, is a combination of difficulty with cognitive flexibility associated with language and social impairments. The *DSM IV* made language and social impairments separate aspects, and then they realized that human interaction and language were inextricable.

I think my definition of autism spectrum disorder has become, "A condition that applies to people who are more diverse than the rest of us are diverse." And the explosion in numbers of people who meet the criteria worldwide seems to be associated not only with a broadening of the definition to include a larger diversity. About 50% of the increase can be attributed to broadening the definition to include those with normal and higher intelligence, and looser criteria for social and language impairments and cognitive rigidity. But the other 50% cannot be explained by that inclusion. There has been too rapid an increase for the reasons to be purely genetic or generational. So we must consider that it may be environmentally based.

Anna Hope, who is attending this interview, and I did some research about this, and the bottom line — in a paper published in *The American Journal of Clinical Hypnosis* — is that we might be able to explain autism spectrum disorder as a developmental manifestation of autonomic dysregulation.[1] Stephen Porges has done a lot of work on the evolution of

1. L.I. Sugarman, B.L. Garrison, and K.L. Williford, "Symptoms as Solutions: Hypnosis and Biofeedback for Autonomic Regulation in Autism Spectrum Disorders," *The American Journal of Clinical*

the vagal — or parasympathetic — nervous system and how it informs development of social and emotional abilities. Porges posits that all of the abilities that are subsumed in the function of the vagus nerve — and that influence projects forward into the higher cortical functions and frontal lobes — are primarily (and intriguingly) on the right side: sensory, language, mirror neurons, gastrointestinal.[2]

When there is vagal impairment, the functional effects overlap well with the criteria for how people struggle with autism spectrum disorder. So we proposed that there could be early vagal impairment in development, such that the agility and the ability to modulate vagal tone is impaired.

This was kind of a reverse hypothesis, because it started when I was flooded clinically with kids who met criteria of autism who were being referred to me from the Autism Center at the University of Rochester and in the community, because medications either weren't effective or were not wanted and "Well, maybe Sugarman can help." And I would say "How can I help you?" And they would look away or stare. And I would say to myself, *Okay we're not going to use metaphors, and we're not going to do meditation. Wait!* — "Do you like to play with computers?" "Yes." "Alright, well let me show you how you can interact with your autonomic nervous system." And not with fancy interpretations of graphical user interfaces — we're just going to provide the data. Nothing implicit. "Here's your skin conductance, here's your heart rate variability, here's how you're breathing."

And we could teach them to increase their vagal tone, and later their parents would say "He's not having as many tantrums and his language is a little more fluent." So we proposed a vagal theory of autism, which still makes a lot of sense.

The question then becomes, "Okay, if vagal system dysfunction helps explain this developmental difference and it is increasing — why?" This is speculation on my part (although it's not only on my part), but this accelerating explosion of autism over the last 50 years — only half of which can be explained by broadening the diagnostic umbrella — also coincidentally accompanies a change in processing foods (think agribusiness, hormones, pesticides, antibiotics). The increased consumption of processed foods subsequently changes the microbiome, and gene products produced in the gut that are directly transferred to vagal nerve nuclei in the brain.

Hypnosis, 2013, 56, 152–173.
2. See Stephen W. Porges, *The Polyvagal Theory: Neurophysiological Foundations of Emotions, Attachment, Communication, and Self-Regulation* (W. W. Norton & Company, 2011).

So this phenomenon aligns coincidentally with a microbiome theory. Not the leaky gut theory, which is another theory that I won't go into. But changes in the microbiome alter psychoactive gene products within the gut, that in turn can affect vagal nerve development, and may increase the likelihood of autism. None of this is something that, until we talked earlier, I had ever aligned with Jaynes's theory. I love the idea and I need to do some thinking about that.

Strangely, this led to the development of a patent, because people who meet criteria for autism spectrum disorder are not only neurodiverse, but autonomically diverse. We needed to tune our biofeedback training to that diversity. So we developed an algorithmic method for tuning multi-channels of biofeedback — skin conductance, heart rate variability, electromyography, breathing, anything you want to measure and feed into the system — that tunes itself to whatever they know how to change best towards increased vagal tone. So it's kind of like positive psychology in an algorithm. So that's my learning from wonderful, amazing people who meet criteria for autism spectrum disorder, also known as ASD — which perhaps we ought to change to *A*utonomic *S*olution *D*eciders.

KUIJSTEN: Thank you for that explanation — that makes a lot of sense. The little bit of exposure that I have to this is through a friend with a child who has very limited language ability. What I've seen is that the approach that is being taken, through what I take is a more traditional ABA [Applied Behavior Analysis] therapy, has thus far not yielded a lot of results. So it's interesting to hear your very different approach.

SUGARMAN: And let me interrupt you to say one more thing. Do you want to know one interesting way to increase vagal tone?

KUIJSTEN: Yes.

SUGARMAN: Rock back and forth.

KUIJSTEN: Okay, that's interesting, because you see that a lot.

SUGARMAN: Absolutely, because it works. I'll say this, the title of the paper is "Symptoms as Solutions: Hypnosis and Biofeedback for Autonomic Regulation in Autism Spectrum Disorders." And the point is to ask, "What if we look at the 'maladaptive repetitive behaviors' of young people as their best effort to self-regulate?" And we utilize that to teach them how to do that even better — a strength-based, ability-based approach.

KUIJSTEN: Yes, that makes sense. That's a very interesting and creative approach. And I think this connection to Jaynes's theory in terms of the relationship between language and thought and consciousness — and perhaps studying those differences in individuals with limited language — is something that I hope will be taken up in the future. There have been some things in the past, having to do more with children that have been raised without language, but overall I haven't seen much published on this.

SUGARMAN: Well, the seed has been planted.

KUIJSTEN: Yes [laughs]. So before we get to hypnosis, one of the things that you mentioned is the use of biofeedback. I've actually had a chance to use a neurofeedback device to aid with meditation. But what's interesting to me about biofeedback from a Jaynesian perspective is that it really highlights the fact that learning can take place nonconsciously. This is still a point of tremendous confusion in the world of psychology and consciousness studies — where there are still vastly different definitions for what consciousness is and no widespread consensus as to what types of mental activities require consciousness and what do not. Of course, Jaynes tries to clarify this in his book, but can you tell us something about learning outside of conscious awareness through biofeedback, and how essentially that's what takes place — biofeedback trains the person nonconsciously to have greater control over autonomic processes, is that right?

SUGARMAN: So while reading Jaynes's book the first time — my copy of which is now held together by three layers of cellophane tape — I initially said "Yes!" out loud in that chapter about how much we can do without calling on consciousness. I would start by saying that *most* learning takes place nonconsciously and sometimes our vast nonconscious abilities choose to let our self-awareness in on it.

This shouldn't be a surprise. I read somewhere that if we look at energy transfer in the central nervous system, the energy efficiency, the economy of receptors and binding and nerve energy that goes into supporting consciousness — there are various numbers proposed, but the number I remember was that one percent of all of the effort in our central nervous system is used to support consciousness. And my response was, "I'm going for two percent — I want to double that" [laughs]. Three percent would probably be too much.

So in my clinical office, I have a mirror. It's a very cool mirror from Mexico that has tiles of lizards all around it — it's compelling. And when

I want to introduce young people to biofeedback, I say "Hey, do something for me, would you stand up and look there?" And they say, "Stare at the mirror?" And I say "Yes, look at that thing." Because I don't want to label it. I want them to label it. I want to encourage, implicitly, the novelty of a beginner's mind. And they look at it, and because of where I'm sitting, they are sideways to me. And I say, "You know, that's not the way that you look." And then, if they meet criteria for autism or just superior analytic ability, they say, "Oh you mean because my image is reversed?" And I say, "Yes, but not only. It's because you know you're looking in a mirror, and the moment you look in the mirror and those photons reflect back to your retinas and then to your brain, before you even know it, you change. For example, if you were looking in the mirror before your job interview and you saw the spinach in your teeth, would you leave it there?" It's great because the mother is usually sitting right there and you can see her tongue rub over her teeth beneath her lips as soon as I say that — she's not aware of it, or if she is, she can't help it.

Another way I introduce this is when I'm teaching professionals. I say, "How many of you have proposed marriage?" And some hands go up, mostly men's. And I say, "How many of you gave that some thought first?" All the hands go up again. "How many of you practiced?" Most hands go up. "How many of you practiced in a mirror? Even a rear-view mirror in your car on the way to the restaurant — a reflective surface?" Some hands and smiles. Then comes the punch line, "How many of you brought the mirror to the proposal?" That's when the laughter comes. They didn't do that. They internalized the image and the learning from the mirror.

So those two ways of teaching serve to show that the reflection of non-conscious material back to the conscious mind, to be utilized, is often at first met with confusion. And then, if we shut up, and let them interact with that signal cycle — skin conductance, heart rate variability, muscle tension in the "mirror" of the computer display — as long as they can somewhat understand what that is, what that reflection is in whatever version of that mirror we are giving them, then they begin to change it.

I have done autonomic biofeedback with a line graph with people with IQ's in the sixties who are non-verbal. I show them a line graph derived from their abdominal excursions measured from an elastic belt embedded with magnets around their waist so they can see their breathing. And I shut up and I wait. And they hold their breath, and they breathe fast, and they experiment with it — holding their breath then breathing rapidly — until they're done experimenting. And everybody eventually settles in to six to ten breaths per minute, because it feels good. And then, if the relationship allows it — the biofeedback connection to the computer is wireless so they can move with less restriction — I ask them to turn away from the screen, and we can keep recording, and internalizing. They can see the report screen later.

So that's the use of biofeedback clinically to teach people how to experience their nonconscious support. The goal is not to take it with you — not to whip out your mirror and say, "Dear, I've known you for this long and my heart is…" — not to do that. But to say, "I remember how that felt." The mirror is in the nonconscious mind, waiting.

One of the most wonderful things I get to hear in clinical practice is their response to my asking if they practiced. They usually say "Yes. I did practice. I went to a favorite place and I practiced doing my breathing and imagining what it was like to be there." So I ask if it would be safe for them to tell me where that "favorite place" was. Every once in a while, the answer is: "Your office." Wow. The problem with Zoom and telehealth encounters is that you can't hug people.

Now, most neurofeedback has been formalized as pure nonconscious learning. We're going to hook you up and we're going to increase frequencies in this area, and the movie or "reward" will stop or go based on how well you do that, and we're just going to condition your brain. But that doesn't develop a conscious skill or a sense of intentional self-efficacy. So I'm not enamored with only training conditioned learning beneath awareness, because it doesn't facilitate autonomous abilities.

KUIJSTEN: That's interesting — it had never occurred to me that something as simple as a mirror could be used as a biofeedback device. And hopefully we've managed to convince a few more people that most learning takes place outside of consciousness.

You have an extensive background in clinical hypnosis. For those who are not familiar with hypnosis, what is hypnosis? How do you define it? Is hypnosis an altered state of consciousness? I know the term "hypnosis" has probably as much debate over its definition as the term "consciousness." So what is your definition of hypnosis, and can you tell us something about it?

SUGARMAN: Right. So the good news about that lack of definition is that as long as we can use some support and empirically ground what we are attempting to say, we get to decide what the definition is. I do think that when anybody talks about hypnosis, or certainly does a clinical training workshop, or is putting a thesis together, they better define the term, because nobody agrees on what it is.

Anna Hope and I published a paper, and it attempts to ask, "Can we agree to call hypnosis this?" I do my best to practice humility, but I'm proud that this paper was twice-awarded by the American Society of Clinical Hypnosis. First it received the Milton H. Erickson Award for excellence in scientific writing. Then it received a unique recognition as the most downloaded paper in the history of the *American Journal of Clinical Hypnosis*. It's called "Orienting Hypnosis," and I still agree with it, although I've expanded and deepened my understanding.[3]

So I'm going to talk about that, but first I'm going to say that in that paper and since, I refer to the traditional, formal model of hypnosis as "the legacy model." And "the legacy model" — which is very much related to Jaynesian theory and what Jaynes wrote about in his book — is that hypnosis is a ritual. And hypnosis is a ritual that attempts to own an altered state of consciousness. And hypnosis is a ritual that attempts to own an altered state of consciousness that facilitates an external authorization — from or through the hypnotist. Or sometimes, it's the hypnotist saying the equivalent of, "You have all the power. I'm teaching you that you have all the power and you can change your mind. So shut up and listen to what I'm telling you." The ultimate hypocrisy.

If I'm a little biased in that, I own it. And we'll talk later about how that relates to Jaynesian theory, but that is how hypnosis is primarily taught by most professional organizations, and certainly lay organizations, like the National Guild of Hypnotists and other organizations that say, "This is how you do hypnosis, you get somebody to focus their attention and influence them."

People will say, "Hypnosis is focused attention." You get someone to focus their attention. You make sure they close their eyes, you put them in a trance, and then you craft suggestions that are based upon their problems. Then you take them out and wipe them off. I think of this as the marinade model. Trance is an immersion fluid that flavors the subject. And the international hypnosis listservs — there are two main professional ones: one is pediatric and one is not — the majority of postings on those listservs are: "So what suggestions would you use for this problem?" (Having told you previously that I'm an anti-diagnostician, you can imagine my squirming

3. Anna E. Hope and Laurence I. Sugarman, "Orienting Hypnosis," *American Journal of Clinical Hypnosis*, 2015, 57, 3, 212-29.

when I read that stuff.) And then having marinated them in this hypnotic trance and giving them these suggestions that you seem to understand better than they do, you bring them out. Perhaps you give them some posthypnotic suggestions, so it will be miraculously enacted when they reawaken or dehypnotize. And then you send them on their way and you see them back and see how the marinade worked.

KUIJSTEN: That's definitely the approach that I learned.

SUGARMAN: Yes, that's how it's usually taught. This legacy approach also supports a notion that there are "hypnotizable abilities" — a really interesting conception of phenomena that is very useful in research, because you can say that "This group of people is hypnotizable, so that means that whatever we do when we do what we call hypnosis is probably due to hypnosis. And we'll compare them to a group of people that are not hypnotizable, so it shouldn't work."

But hypnotizability really is about, "How well can you do these things that I'm calling hypnosis?" So there's a circular logic: I define hypnosis as this ritual in which you do the following things, and if you don't do them, then you're not hypnotizable." So I'm going to give us a ridiculous example. Here it is. If we proposed hypnotizability is one's ability to involuntarily raise their right arm, then we know that right arm amputees cannot be hypnotized. There ought to be more to it than that.

KUIJSTEN: Right.

SUGARMAN: That's where we were, and unfortunately still are, I think, in most organizations. And there are a number of flaws with that, and I'm not going to list them all — I refer you to our paper — but first, hypnosis doesn't own trance. We can define trance as our ability to change our embodied minds. Minds are always embodied. The brain is a very important central processing unit, but there is also information in the body — information is in our immune system, in our endocrine system.

I have been playing the banjo for 60 years this year. And I find myself putting my hands in that position when I want to feel competent. I have a picture over there of me, taken by Kathryn [Rossi], of me and her husband Ernest Rossi, and in it, my left hand is palm up and my right hand is palm down. If I want to feel completely incompetent, I just flip them over. That information is coming into my brain from my hands and assigned meaning. My mind is embodied.

We define trance as the *process*, not the *state*, of becoming *psychobiologically* plastic. It occurs in trauma — the sudden interruption of normal relationships. It occurs when we fall in love — a sudden interruption of normal relationships. It occurs whenever there is something novel. It occurs when we human organisms experience the orienting response: "What is that?"

Suddenly we pause our autonomic activity, the hippocampus says, "I better go check the reference library, I don't think we have anything like that in there." And we develop a moment of plasticity, of potential accommodation, a potential shift. We all — the most densely impaired, intellectually disabled person who meets criteria for autism, and the most brilliant of human beings — all know how to change our minds. And we do it with novelty, we do it with excitement, we do it with an activity, we do it with exercise, and we do it in relationships. Trance happens. *Hypnosis is a set of skills* that can be refined to a discipline — and like all disciplines, can be raised to an art — of interpersonal communication that is intentionally used to drive that plasticity. Unfortunately, 99% of hypnosis on the planet, or more, is used to drive that plasticity in ways that are not for the benefit of another person. At the very least, they are to get you to buy something, if not undue influence, cults, human enslavement, control, and the denigration of self.

There are the four World Health Organization ethical canons for clinical practice and research: doing no harm (non-maleficence), doing good (beneficence), respect for autonomy, and respect for justice. Doing no harm is a pretty low standard. Beneficence is harder than it seems, because it requires separating the clinician's needs from that of the persons in their care. Respect for autonomy requires that there is no deception — "I'm showing you what I'm doing, you need to know everything that you can understand about what this is" — and an appreciation of individuality. That means not seeing people as their diagnosis, as we talked about before. Justice means that everybody has equal access to the same quality of interaction, regardless of who they are or why they are seeking help. If we practice using the discipline of hypnosis within that ethical framework, we call that *clinical* hypnosis. So clinical hypnosis, by definition, ought not be a ritual procedure based on a problem. To practice clinical hypnosis in that procedural and problem-based — as compared to person-centered — way is neither the most beneficial, respectful of autonomy, or equally accessible.

Clinical hypnosis ought to be applied creatively to a unique individual, and the clinician's first requisite is to understand how that individual is unique. To not do what they — the clinician — always does when they encounter a problem (not a person) "like that." The goal is to facilitate that person's own development of new understandings of how to live a fulfilling life within their embodied mind. That's my definition of hypnosis: a skill-set, disciplined art to facilitate and drive plasticity towards benefit.

KUIJSTEN: So just so I understand you, while "trance" happens all the time, hypnosis is a set of tools to engage that process in a more formalized fashion. Can you elaborate on exactly what trance is? What is the current thinking on how trance is defined?

SUGARMAN: Let's call trance a process. Not a state. If you must use "state," let's call it a state of change. And trance is a process that intensifies novel experience within the entire system — that crosses the thresholds. And by thresholds, I mean new awareness. I mean changes in autonomic function. I mean changing receptors on cells. Receptors on cells get overwhelmed, so inside of the cell the clamor is so loud, that the second messengers inside of the cell say, "There's so much going on we have to knock on the door of the inner sanctum — the nucleus — and tell them to transcribe some new products, because we have to strengthen this and that connection."

Kathryn and Ernest Rossi and their group at the University of Salerno proposed that when you do these kinds of things, you actually change gene expression. So trance is the process of developing plasticity from consciousness to gene expression — which are intimately linked. Here's the conceptual: imagine that our nerves, all of our receptors — all of the communication within the embodied mind — which is really energy transfer — it's a whole system of pathways: highways, light rail, heavy rail, paths in the woods — all of those things. Trance is when they start melting.

So we say, "Whoa, we have to reconnect stuff." Then you know you've done it because things look different, and feel different. And when, in the office the person has that amazing, numinous "aha" moment — maybe their eyes are closed and they open their eyes and say, "Is the light brighter in here?" or "Were you always sitting in that chair?" Because they have been reoriented within and by themselves, by their inner experience.

KUIJSTEN: Let's talk about your forthcoming article in the *American Journal of Clinical Hypnosis*. You discuss the changing nature of hypnosis and you compare that to the transition from bicameral mentality to consciousness — you use that transition as a metaphor for the changing nature of hypnosis. Can you explain the main argument of your article, and also the contrast between what you call the legacy model of hypnosis versus the approach of people such as Milton Erickson and Ernest Rossi?

SUGARMAN: Sure. So what struck me first in my third reading of Jaynes was the importance of changing authorization. We'll get to the topic of authorization later, but for the sake of simplicity, let's just say that it's about changing who owns the inner voice — whether you know it's an inner voice or not.

And of course Jaynes is rare by including in his understanding of the evolution of consciousness an entire chapter on, "So what does that have to do with what we call hypnosis?" And including hypnosis as a vestige of bicameral mentality, in which the hypnotist, within the legacy model, replaces shamans, gods, and external authorizations, and says, "You will do what I say, just listen to my voice."

And our allopathic — meaning "other, non-self, treatment" — biomedical, reductionist model continues that tradition: "You can't heal yourself, you need this medication or this procedure or this device." We see this in the explosion of ads for expensive prescription drugs in the United States as external authorizations — "This is how you are broken. Healing is not about you; it's about what we do to you."

So hypnosis was evolved to fit into that model in order to be accepted. It's a health care intervention, so why shouldn't it fit into the biomedical model? What struck me in thinking about that is how Milton Erickson, over his lifetime, evolved from a very directive stance well within that legacy model into saying, "Wait ... people are individual collections of authorizations, people are individual collections of life experiences. How interesting and creative would it be to evoke those, and help people utilize them to change their own minds?" In that way he was directly countering the allopathic paradigm. He was claiming that each individual already has the experiential resources they need.

Then in the 1970s, Ernest Rossi comes along, and with his expansive mind, says, "Let's analyze what Erickson is doing. It's not idiosyncratic" — even though many refer to Erickson's practice as idiosyncratic — "There's a system to this. We don't even have to know what those resources are within an individual. They don't even have to label them. They just have to bring them to the surface, experience them, and repurpose them. And we can be change agents or provocateurs of their own unique autonomous authorizations."

And what struck me on top of that, from your book *The Julian Jaynes Collection*, Jaynes talks about developing one's own mind and consciousness to the point where one can be self-suggestive, where someone can be supple and agile in redirecting their own mind.[4] That they would no longer need a hypnotist — "I'm my own hypnotist" ... he didn't say that, I said that. So, in a nutshell, that's what it is about.

The title of the paper is "Leaving Hypnosis Behind?" The title is about whether we can agree that removing the trappings and *ritual* of hypnosis — that Jaynes posits was its original containing vessel — still leaves something we call hypnosis. I titled the paper "Leaving Hypnosis Behind?" with an important question mark — it's not a statement. I don't want to leave hypnosis behind, but I am proposing leaving behind the ritual and the external authorization. The "close your eyes, go to sleep, listen to my words, be passive, I will run your mind for you and then you'll reboot it, but differently" — leaving all of that behind in favor of having you do the hard work of the developing of higher consciousness by increasing your own ability in changing your embodied mind.

KUIJSTEN: Yes. And the question that you mentioned that was posed to Jaynes after one of his lectures — actually on several occasions — was, "If consciousness is something that's learned based on language and it's a relatively recent development in human history, and it's an ongoing process, then what is the future of consciousness? Where is it going from here?" And his response was something to the effect of: "Why is it that if we want to quit smoking, or stop biting our nails, overcome some type of phobia, or overcome anxiety, it's very difficult to do consciously? Yet through hypnosis, we can often have a better result. So in the future, perhaps we might be able to exert greater autonomous control over these kinds of nonconscious habits or behaviors than we are currently able to now, and without the aid of someone else." Can you explain the skills and the approach that is the alternative to the legacy model? Do you refer to it as the "Ericksonian" approach, or is there another name for this alternative approach to hypnosis?

SUGARMAN: Right. Not that I have a name or label for what I am claiming is a new approach. Maybe that's because I have the audacity to think that it is what we ought to be calling simply "hypnosis." I wouldn't call it "Ericksonian" because, as Steve Lankton, who is the Editor-In-Chief of

---

4. Julian Jaynes, "The Consequences of Consciousness: Emory University Discussion," in M. Kuijsten (ed.), *The Julian Jaynes Collection* (Julian Jaynes Society, 2012).

the *American Journal of Clinical Hypnosis*, has emphasized repeatedly, many misinterpret, or at least create their own interpretation of that adjective. Even Erickson at times rejected that adjective. I will leave it to others to name. The essence is that it emphasizes principles, skills, and an overall strategy for provoking and evoking the experiential cultivation of experiential resources that respects the autonomy of each individual. That leaves a lot to unpack, I know. I would refer you to our *Changing Minds* book for descriptions and illustrations.[5] Instead of inductions, directions, suggestions, and re-alerting in that linear, stepwise ritual of hypnosis, it involves an intentional conversational volley — both verbal and nonverbal — that intentionally enhances the relationship, questions and disrupts patterns of learning and experiencing, then supports development of new patterns. It looks a lot more like a weirdly intense, creative conversation than the normal hypnotic ritual. The goal is to drive epiphanies, realization, inspiration. Those, in turn, contain the solution to whatever problem the person brought with them.

KUIJSTEN: Let's talk more about the concept of authorization. In your paper you discuss the role of what Jaynes calls "external authorization," and in the case of the legacy model of hypnosis, this role is taken by the hypnotist. Authorization is one of these concepts that I think is difficult for people to relate to because it's so pervasive in our everyday lives that we tend not to notice it. We're responding to external authorization all the time in ways that we're not even aware of — beliefs and customs that we've internalized from our culture, for example.

It manifests itself more clearly in things like hypnosis and placebo effects. The question that comes up with placebo effects is, if our immune system already has the resources to address an illness, why can't it do it on its own? Oftentimes it does, of course. But in certain instances, why does our immune system require an external authority to provide a "cure," in the form of a placebo, in order to engage those processes? So if you could give us your thoughts on external authorization, how this developed as we learned consciousness, how you see it manifest more broadly in society, and perhaps more specifically in the case of things like placebo effects?

SUGARMAN: So authorization is never really clearly defined by Julian Jaynes, at least not in my reading. I think that authorization as a term has three

---

5. Laurence I. Sugarman, Julie H. Linden and Lee W. Brooks, *Changing Minds with Clinical Hypnosis: Narratives and Discourse for a New Health Care Paradigm* (Routledge, 2020).

overlapping meanings. The first is as a canon of doctrines. So, the United States Constitution is an authorization. It also refers to permission, or even compulsion: "You must do this," or "I have to do this, it's not a choice." But it also has an implication of origination: "This is the first source of this." For example, the Bible is an authorization. So I think that it's a combined meaning of a system of knowledge that is demanding or confining, and of the original, as in the author, or authority. And we make it real. Diagnoses are authorization. As Charles Rosenberg writes in his paper, "The Tyranny of Diagnosis":

> ...disease entities become indisputable social actors, real inasmuch as we have believed in them, and acted individually and collectively on those beliefs...Once articulated, such bureaucratic categories cannot help but exert a variety of substantive effects on individuals and institutional relationships...Thus a poor or homeless person becomes visible to the health care system when diagnosed with an acute ailment but then returns to invisibility once that episode has been managed. It is almost as though the disease, not its victim, justifies treatment.[6]

KUIJSTEN: It's interesting that you say that. The book *Our Most Troubling Madness* presents case studies of schizophrenia across different cultures, and one of the points that is made is that individuals dealing with schizophrenia — or rather, the cluster of symptoms often associated with schizophrenia — often seem to have a better outcome in non-Western cultures, in India for example.[7] The thinking is that, generally speaking, they have more support from their extended family, but also that there is much less of an emphasis on diagnostic labels, in terms of what is communicated to the patient and the patient's family, as well as how the patient's family refers to their condition going forward. They are not labeled with what is often perceived in the West as an incurable illness, and there is a greater expectation of recovery. So as you said, the diagnostic label itself can become a form of authorization, and through its psychological impact, can become a determining factor in a patient's outcome.

SUGARMAN: Yes, a diagnosis is an authorization and can be a nefarious one. The whole notion of biomedicine is authorization. I'm going to avoid too much of this vortex, but conspiracy theories are authorization. They are

6. Charles E. Rosenberg, "The Tyranny of Diagnosis: Specific Entities and Individual Experience," *Milbank Quarterly*, 2002, 80, 2, 237-260.
7. T.M. Luhrmann and Jocelynn Marrow (eds.), *Our Most Troubling Madness: Case Studies in Schizophrenia across Cultures* (University of California Press, 2016).

things we make real. One of the conceptualizations that I took out of the paper but is foundational to our book [*Changing Minds*], was a reference to Thomas Kuhn and *The Structure of Scientific Revolutions*, and the idea that how minds and paradigms change has to do with anomalies.[8] I love the word anomaly, it means "I don't have a name."

We have a belief system, such as an idea of who we think we are and of what is wrong with us and how we are stuck. Or maybe the belief system is the authorization, such as how the universe fits together with the rules of physics, or the authority of the U.S. constitution. In any case, anomalies form — for example, somebody you value and respect loves you even though you think you are not loveable, the heavenly bodies on closer inspection do not move the way they are predicted to, interpretations of the second amendment to the U.S. constitution are becoming problematic. And they build and build until there are enough anomalies that don't fit. Our self-concept, our rules for the heavens, or the way that we apply the constitution must change. Suddenly we realize, "Okay, so maybe that person in the mirror is better than I thought. So Earth isn't the center of the solar system, the sun is. Maybe we rethink how people get and use firearms." None of the planets have changed, nothing that we're looking at has changed. Our orientation has changed. Then we have a new version of "reality."

So that's what an authorization is, in my view. And we human beings seem to need authorizations. And as matter of fact, even though human beings are the only species that believes in autonomy and liberty, we tend to say, "I am the author of my own mind! But tell me what I should do" [laughs]. It's so interesting. And that quest for autonomy, that belief in autonomy, gives us poetry, literature, great works of art, cults, war, and we are also the most aggressive and destructive animals on the planet. The last piece I added to my recent paper on Jaynes and hypnosis was a paragraph on our continued need to believe in these political entities — including conspiracy theories — to structure ourselves. It's an interesting side effect of developing consciousness and believing that we create our authorizations when we don't. That's authorization as a vestige of bicameral mentality.

I happen to teach a course on placebo research, and there are a number of wonderful placebo research labs across the world. And your point is the essence of one of the papers that I'm working on now, and the placeholder

---

8. Thomas Kuhn, *The Structure of Scientific Revolutions* (University of Chicago Press, 1996).

title, which may survive, is, "Placebo Effects and Hypnosis Effects: Dorothy and The Wizard." And the quote is — as Toto pulls back the curtain and reveals the wizard running the image of the Wizard of Oz — Dorothy says, "Who are you?" And he says, "I am the great and powerful Wizard of Oz," [in a weakening voice]. And Dorothy says, "You are a very bad man." To which he replies, "No my dear, I'm a very good man. Just a very bad wizard."

That gets to the essence: placebo effects are about authorization. So for example, a person comes to the doctor and says, "I have these amazing pills and they keep me from having headaches, and they keep me employed, but the doctor who prescribed them for me died. Will you please replace these?" And you analyze them and find out that they're made of a pinch of quinine, a lot of cornstarch, and a little cayenne, so they have a little bite if you taste them — none of which should be effective enough to cure this person's headache. What do you do? Well, if you say, "Listen, you've been conned. This stuff does nothing, you're doing this yourself." Then they likely go back to having headaches and they lose their job. Because they think, "I can't possibly be doing this to myself." They certainly don't come back to see you!

That's the essence of what happens with placebos effects. I believe it is true that placebos enact that authorization. The history of allopathic care, of substance care, of interactive care is the history of placebos. Because the majority of the effects, until we started doing prospective placebo-controlled randomized trials — a standard that is just over 50 years old — is the history of placebos. So we will not do things for ourselves that we feel the need to externally attribute.

Interestingly — and I'm not aware of any studies looking at this — the opposite is an interesting question. Somebody who self-regulates, practices self-hypnosis for example, says, "I do this meditative hypnotic practice to keep myself from having migraines, and it works." And I say, "But I've got a pill for you. It saves time and you wouldn't have to do that stuff." Would they replace it? I wouldn't. So it's an interesting question of whether placebo effects boil down to external authorization, and how we can look at that. Can people — and this is the essence of my clinical practice — replace pills with skills?

KUIJSTEN: That's fascinating. One of Julian Jaynes's arguments is that most of what is often placed under the umbrella of the term "consciousness" are in fact things like sense perception, learning, reactivity, and a number of other things that we share with all animals, and that consciousness, as he narrowly defines it, is something that is learned. It requires metaphorical language to create an inner mind-space — an inner space that is based on metaphors of the physical world. And it is only by understanding the recent transition from bicameral mentality to Jaynesian consciousness that we can make sense of many things in the modern world.

As Jaynes explains it, as we learned language, the brain began to use the new tool of language as a more efficient way to transmit information from one hemisphere to the other. That information transfer took the form of what we now refer to as an auditory verbal hallucination — so auditory hallucinations are a vestige of bicameral mentality. And Jaynes makes the case that our quest for external authorization is held over from this previous mentality where we were directly responding to voices — because for reasons that are not entirely clear, when the language areas of the non-dominant hemisphere become active, generating an auditory hallucination, it's interpreted as an "other," or alien to us — not coming from our "self."

So essentially we're predisposed to things like responding to the hypnotist's voice and the many other forms of external authorization, because of the thousands of years that we were responding to the voices of the right hemisphere. Do you feel that the bicameral mind theory is the best explanation for the legacy model of hypnosis and the predisposition that humanity seems to have for external authorization? Or is there another explanation that you think better fits these observations?

SUGARMAN: So I could save time and simply respond "yes" then leave it at that [laughs]. Yes, that's what inspired me for this paper, that's what gives me an orientation. I'll simply add though that I'm hoping that we are accelerating away from it. I love being gob smacked, while taking a walk, with a new idea. And I know that it feels that it came externally because we externally attribute our nonconscious abilities.

Where did that come from? From the "wellspring"? From God? It came from my internal machinations. And what I'm excited about is the increasing evidence that we can evolve faster than generations. We can change — and I give so much credit to the inspiration of psychosocial genomics, which Ernest Rossi seeded and cultivated — we can begin to intentionally and beneficially change our gene expression within our own lives. And because of epigenetic phenomena, extend that change in other people's lives within families and within communities.

So that we change the embodied mind's genomic expression to create self-autonomous authorization, and own our inspiration, and therefore own our plasticity. I purposely do not use the term "neuroplasticity," because it also involves my hands, my immune system, my hematopoietic system, and my heart, etc. And we can inspire that same capacity in others, we can contribute to that ability to develop autonomous authorization. It's not that it still doesn't feel like it came from someplace else. And I'm happy that it feels that way, because it's a nice feeling — but I know we own it. We are all in this together. And in that way, we become more powerful than we thought we were.

I think there's an important part that's left out of what Jaynes said about this evolution of consciousness. We need each other. All hypnosis is relational. There's a saying that "all hypnosis is self-hypnosis" — it's wrong. All hypnosis is self-hypnosis *that we learn from other people*. And most of the self-hypnosis that we develop, starting around nine or ten months of life is, "You're not really that good a person, you're a fraud, and you're not really that lovable." That's what gives the rest of us employment as health professionals. So our relationships drive change. I have a colleague who says, "Don't forget the biggest cult: the cult of believing that we have individual selves."

KUIJSTEN: Well, that's a great quote to end on. Thank you so much for sharing all of your knowledge and interesting insights on these topics, it's been very enlightening — and I enjoyed hearing your vision for the future potential of hypnosis and heath care.

SUGARMAN: My pleasure.

14

Consciousness, Hypnosis, and Free Will

Edoardo Casiglia

Interviewed by Marcel Kuijsten

Edoardo Casiglia is Senior Scientist at the Studium Patavinum (Department of Medicine) at University of Padova in Italy. He is a specialist in cardiology, pharmacology, anesthesia and intensive care, a European Clinical Hypertension Specialist, an anthropologist and forensic archaeologist, and a criminologist/criminalist. He is also a trained hypnotist, hypnotherapist, hypnosis instructor, and is former Editor-in-Chief of the journal *Contemporary Hypnosis*. He has published 14 books and authored or co-authored over 700 scientific works on a range of diverse subjects such as cardiology, hypertension, hypnosis, hypnotherapy, and consciousness. Professor Casiglia has a longstanding interest in Julian Jaynes's theory and related subjects such as consciousness, anthropology, archeology, hypnosis, volition, and free will. He has published numerous books related to these topics, including *L'io e le sue Voci: Antropologia e Archeo-psicologia della Coscienza Egoica* [The I and its Voices: Anthropology and Archeo-Psychology of Egoic Consciousness], *Decisione, Volizione, Libero Arbitrio* [Decision, Volition, Free Will], and *I Mondi della Coscienza* [The Worlds of Consciousness].

MARCEL KUIJSTEN: Can you tell us about your background and how you became interested in medicine and hypnosis?

EDOARDO CASIGLIA: I have always been attracted by hypnotism,[1] since I was a kid, but I would never have become a graduate and professional

---

1. The set of means useful, but not essential, to rapidly reach the hypnotic trance in particular settings.

researcher in the field of hypnosis if I hadn't encountered Julian Jaynes's work. I had a serious approach to hypnosis when I was in high school, reading many books on the subject. However, they were unable to explain *what* hypnosis was or *why* hypnosis works — it was a mystery. In the meantime, I became interested in depth psychology, which I explored further during my studies at the Medical Faculty of the University of Padua (Italy). After I became a medical doctor and specialized first in cardiology, then in pharmacology, and again in anesthesia and intensive care, my interest in hypnosis grew to the point that I felt the need to formalize it. This happened at the Italian Centre of Clinical and Experimental Hypnosis in Turin (Italy), where I learned many of the various induction techniques, the meaning of Franco Granone's *plastic monoideism*,[2] and the methods of hypnotic trance management. I understood immediately that the techniques were not important — what was of paramount importance was the relationship, what psychoanalysts call "the *rapport*."

KUIJSTEN: What was the connection between hypnosis and theories of Julian Jaynes in your life, from both a personal and professional point of view?

CASIGLIA: Well, at one point in my life, an event of great personal significance took place for me: I encountered the work of Julian Jaynes. His book, *The Origin of Consciousness in the Breakdown of the Bicameral Mind*, introduced me to a world that I had only touched on before, and without fully understanding it. I must say that I did not come to Jaynes as a novice, having previously assimilated all of Carl Jung and Erich Neumann's fundamental text *Ursprungsgeschichte des Bewusstseins* [The Origins and History of the Consciousness]. Both of these authors had introduced me to the subject of egoic consciousness[3] and the concept of the 'I'.[4]

Jaynes's book, along with the works of Jung and Neumann, sparked a deep interest in me in topics related to the origin and nature of consciousness. So while in daily life I continued to work as a cardiologist and a Professor of Internal Medicine and of Emergency Care at the University

---

2. For the Franco Granone School, the basis of hypnotic trance is "plastic monoideism," or the realization of a mental image leading — thanks to the hypnotic condition — to such a high level of concentration and intensity as to become "plastic," in other words, able to produce both psychic and physical effects.

3. The term *consciousness* was introduced by John Locke in the seventeenth century. Initially there was no distinction between moral *conscience* and egoic *consciousness*.

4. Two entities that — given the confusion existing in this field — I will treat here as synonyms, although Jung, a couple of times in his *Opera Omnia*, speaks of "the consciousness of the I" and Julian Jaynes considers the I "an aspect of consciousness." See Julian Jaynes, *La Natura Diacronica della Coscienza* [The Diachronic Nature of Consciousness] (Aldephi 2014). I strongly prefer the 'I' because it seems to me the "ego" sounds too Freudian. For Jaynes the 'I' is an analog.

of Padua, deep down I began to feel more and more like an anthropologist and an archaeologist. I formalized these titles through a post-university Masters degree — as if medicine was no longer enough for me, as if it were only a part of my being. Wolfgang Goethe stated: "Who for three thousand years has failed to account for himself to himself remains inexperienced in the dark and can only live day by day." I realized that living day to day means being trapped in an eternal present, as nonconscious animals are — if you don't know what is bubbling inside you, then you're not aware of yourself and you don't know where you're going.

And if you realize that you don't know where you're going, you only have one option: turn around and see where you came from. So, my interest in hypnosis and my interest in Jaynes's work went hand in hand. And if I weren't afraid of sounding immodest by claiming to be a hypnotist of some fame and skill today, I'd say I owe it to Julian Jaynes as much as to Carl Jung.

Naturally, as a university professor and a researcher, my interest in the themes of the mind, egoic consciousness, and hypnosis took the experimental path that marked my entire academic life. For this reason, almost all of my articles and books on hypnosis have an openly and decidedly experimental stamp.[5] For the same reason, I developed a university course called "Hypnosis in Medicine and in Research," which has now been attended by hundreds of students of both medicine and psychology.

Together with my staff, using hypnosis we have produced — in both experimental and didactic settings — positive hallucinations, delusions, neglect (in the psychological sense), i.e., negative hallucinations (in the hypnotic view), age regressions and revivifications, increases in physical and mental performance, control of blood vessel diameter, and so on. I try to give to all this an archaic interpretation, well expressed by the *ancient gaze*, which in my experience is typical of people in hypnotic trance. I did this through the theoretical and practical hypnotic models that I was building, because at that time these did not yet exist.

In short, hypnosis has always been, during my entire academic and personal life, a very interesting tool[6] to study the mind and an extraordinary way to communicate with the unconscious — both my own and that of the

---

5. See Professor Casiglia's Google Scholar profile for details: https://scholar.google.it/citations?user=-C34e8ocAAAAJ.

6. My first scientific publication on hypnosis, also presented to a congress of internal medicine, was titled "Hypnosis as a Tool for Evaluating the Cortical Component of Haemodynamic Variations." Many years later, with much more experience and many more experiments to my credit, I published an article titled, "Measured Outcomes with Hypnosis as an Experimental Tool in a Cardiovascular Physiology Laboratory," which was very successful.

subjects that I've worked with. My research convinced me that conscious-ness continuously emanates from the unconscious, and pushes into it many of its contents — such as repressions, forgotten memories, thoughts, psy-chic traumas, dreams,[7] and unresolved conflicts. Consciousness, therefore, is never the same, and only a single idea can occupy the mind in a given instant (whatever the mind is).

KUIJSTEN: That's interesting to hear how Jaynes's book had such a signif-icant impact on you — I can certainly relate to that. While working as a medical doctor and professor, you've also published a number of different books in Italian based on your extensive study of pre-history, recorded his-tory, anthropology, archaeology, hearing voices, and origin of our internal di-alogue. Can you first talk about the concept of the self, or Jaynes's analog 'I'?

CASIGLIA: Yes, although I am not formally a historian, I am, as you said, a lifelong scholar of cultural and physical anthropology and archaeology, in addition to being a doctor. Consequently, the study of history and pre-history are now my daily bread. So, the present comes from the past, both my personal present and the collective present. When I say "the present," I mean "the unconscious of today" — because it is both from the personal unconscious and from the wider, collective unconscious that the egoic con-sciousness incessantly draws its source.

Until my encounter with Jaynes's work, exactly how this happened remained a mystery to me. Why is egoic consciousness formed? Is it a necessity or a mere epiphenomenon? Is the 'I' something of a monolith or an aggregation? These questions kept me busy without finding an an-swer — until Jaynes's book appeared before me. The 'I' is certainly a myste-rious phenomenon, even today, despite the widespread use of sophisticated tools such as functional magnetic resonance imaging that provide us with greater insight into precise brain activity.

Following my studies and research, which I will mix here for conve-nience but which actually occurred largely in parallel, I believe that the 'I' is an accident that the species *Homo sapiens* was predisposed to develop, but which could very well not have manifested at all. This predisposition is of a genetic nature, and has become evident over the millennia. It began with the evolution of the great apes, then the lowering of the larynx, then the development of the cerebral Broca's area (necessary to speak) and a few more millennia later that of Wernicke's area (to understand language),

---

7. "Dream" is called "*traum*" in German, the original language of psychoanalysis.

then with the development of "the unconscious" — our ability for mental images, abstraction, narratization, constellation,[8] etc.

For the sake of brevity, I won't go into more depth here, with the genetic process roughly outlined. But genetics interact with our environment, and epigenetics — which I studied experimentally in an epidemiological setting at the population level — taught me that the environment itself affects genetics in what we have defined as "the echogenetic context."

The environment that led to the development of the epiphenomenon called the 'I' is represented by a myriad of factors, many of which are unknown. I will summarize here those that I can document scientifically: spontaneous mutations (each human birth involves about 6 mutations, which ensure genetic diversity for *Homo sapiens*, preventing us from being copies of our parents — as is the case with many animals); unexpected mutations such as those due to β- and γ-rays;[9] the bipedalism consequent to the African drought (a drought that may or may not have occurred); the consequent development of larger pelvises which allowed the birth of fetuses with larger skulls and brains; maternal care due to infantile underdevelopment, resulting precisely from these large brains that could not stay too long inside the uterus; and so on.

The development of the hands allowed *Homo sapiens* to nonconsciously build lithic tools, and then to manipulate them three-dimensionally from all points of view, thanks to the great mobility of the wrist. This allowed us, over time, to develop a three-dimensional conception of the world. The two-dimensional conception, typical of Neolithic wall artists, but also of our painters, and of cinema and television, paradoxically came much later — show Leonardo's Mona Lisa to contemporary Amazonian Neolithic aborigines[10] such as, for instance, the Brazilian Amondava, discovered in 1986 and studied by anthropologists a few years later, and they will see nothing in the picture.

The hands developed the way that they did because the forelimbs were now useless for walking and useful for work.[11] During these phases, we

---

8. "Constellation" is the aptitude to group the things of the world, giving them an apparent meaning, a phenomenon called *pareidolia*. Four U.S. Navy ships were given the name *Constellation* in honor of the "constellation of the stars" of the American flag. My opinion is that all cognitive images of the world are constellations (of photons, if visual). See E. Casiglia, *L'Io e le sue Voci* [The I and its Voices] (CLEUP, 2015), pgs. 66-67. Jung was the first to talk about "constellation of the unconscious."

9. Such as those due to Supernova W44, which around 20,000 years ago exploded only 6,000 light-years from the earth, for many millennia spreading protons that, on impact with matter, produce highly mutagenic γ-rays, contributing to rapid changes in the course of terrestrial biology.

10. Present day *ab origines*, "since their origins."

11. But the same did not happen with the analogous upper limbs of certain dinosaurs, also not necessary

know little or nothing about the mind of the primitive individuals of the genus *Homo*. But we know enough about the mind of the individuals of the more recent species *Homo sapiens* living after the Würm glaciation (called the Wisconsian glaciation in the United States), thanks to information coming from settlements, places and methods of burial, the beginnings of writing, and from the analysis of the furrows and depressions left by the archaic right hemisphere on the inner surface of the fossil skulls, by brain structures that no longer exist today.

After the development of language, it is now beyond doubt that the late *sapiens* experienced inner voices originating from right-hemisphere homologues of the left hemisphere language areas. That these voices existed can be deduced from several documents which can be dated in the period during the transition from the bicameral mind to consciousness, such as the Jewish Bible (רנת), the Assyrian Tukulti-Ninurta saga, the Greek *Iliad* (Ἰλιάς), the more recent "Song of Sad Days" of the North American Paiute tribe,[12] and from the description of the so-called "big dreams" of the pan-Asian shamans.[13]

Let's consider Abrāhām or Ibrāhīm (אָבְרָהָב or مِيهاربا, whose meaning is "father of many"), a nonconscious man of the Bronze Age or perhaps a mere biblical character. A voice that he perceives as external tells him to kill his son, as sometimes happens today to modern schizophrenics: he heard the command and proceeded to carry out the action. Thanks to God — it is the case to say it — the voice also stops him in time. It is difficult to understand this biblical episode, which seems to be contrary to everything that the more recent books of the Bible say about God. And yet now a Jaynesian psychodynamic interpretation is evident: it was an auditory hallucination — one of the very common auditory and visual hallucinations that occurred at that time in bicameral people. Today, similar episodes of command hallucinations are an indication of pathology — although they are not always obeyed.

Even today, a modern person diagnosed with schizophrenia, or even a non-clinical subject, can see whole hallucinated scenes or written words, as happened to Nebuchadnezzar (Nabû-kudorri-uṣur), or characters can hover before him as Athena (Ἀαηνᾶ) in front of Achilles (Ἀχιλλεύς). It is interesting to note that Abrāhām (אָבְרָהָב), more bicameral, incapable of

---

for walking, because the echogenetic context was different as they lacked adequate brain development.

12. In: *Natives: Canti degli indiani d'America* [Songs of American Natives] (Mondadori, 2005).

13. Present even today among some preliterate peoples, who do not know the wheel or agriculture, and consequently of *civitas*.

feelings, is prepared to kill his son without asking questions. It is the son Yitzchak, or Isaac (יִצְחָק), of a later generation, or perhaps metaphorically of a more advanced evolutionary period — less bicameral, more subjective — who asks where the victim is.[14]

These voices and forms, perceived as external, that guided the life of archaic man, were real hallucinations. They appeared variously as voices, simple lights, and sometimes speaking figures — again, similar to the hallucinations of modern schizophrenics or to the physiological hallucinations that in particular conditions today also affect normal people.

According to Jaynes, to hear in the Bible the first subjective sentence ("vanity of vanities [...], everything is vanity") — a reflection that certainly implies an 'I' — it is necessary to arrive at Qohelet (תלהק, in Greek called ἐκκλησιαστής, Ekklesiastès, in Latin, Ecclesiastes). And in the original Greek *Iliad,* some statements of the so-called Mycenaean heroes (actually, mere unconscious puppets guided by externalized hallucinations) — statements which seem to prove the existence of an egoic consciousness[15] — are probably late glosses added afterwards, in a period that was now proto-conscious or conscious.[16]

These documents that have come down to us (no one knows how many have been lost) give substance to the theory of the breakdown of the bicameral mind. But this breakdown can also be deduced from the fact that these voices are still in us, albeit in a different form.

KUIJSTEN: Indeed — there are many great examples of voice hearers throughout history, such as some of the biblical prophets, the prophet Muhammad, Joan of Arc, Emanuel Swedenborg, William Blake, and Joseph Smith, just to name a few. I don't think it's an exaggeration to say that bicameral voices have shaped the modern world. Yet, there has always been an odd disconnect between the voice hearers of the past, who were often seen as prophets, and those of the present, who are typically viewed as suffering from mental illness — although we also now know that many people who hear voices are able to function quite normally. Jaynes was one of the first to connect the dots in this regard, demonstrating that there is this long trajectory from voice hearing during the ancient world, up through the Middle Ages, and continuing on to this day. We now know so much

---

14. Genesis, 22, 7.
15. For instance, *Iliad,* XXI, 663 or XXII, 99.
16. Julian Jaynes, *The Origin of the Consciousness in the Breakdown of the Bicameral Mind* (Houghton Mifflin, 1976/1990). See also the interview with Boban Dedović, "The Evolution of Mental Language in the *Iliad* and the *Odyssey,*" in this volume.

more about the experience of auditory verbal and visual hallucinations in a wide variety of populations than we did even twenty years ago, yet no one seems to be able to offer a convincing explanation for why hallucinations that command or direct behavior still occur, outside of Jaynes's bicameral mind theory. Can you explain what you mean by the idea that the voices are still with us, but in a different form?

CASIGLIA: Yes. The bicameral voices, which we no longer hear in their pure form even if we are schizophrenic,[17] did not die, did not dissolve, but they organized themselves into a new function, a new organ, which we call the 'I' or the "egoic consciousness." Using hypnosis, for example, we can bring to light these voices.[18] Another more complicated way to evoke the voices is to electrically stimulate certain cortical areas, a process that requires opening the skull, which today is practiced less and less.

Without the "death of voices" between 1500-1200 BCE, the 'I' would not have formed, because the 'I' is an aggregation of the voices. My experience with hypnosis has convinced me to view the 'I' not as a monolithic, Ptolemaic, stable, monarchical, centralizing entity as Renée Descartes imagined it, but rather as a federal republic, a fictitious identity whose parts change incessantly, as hypothesized by David Hume, or even as a parasite that presides over exchanges with the outside world as suggested by Schopenhauer.

Indeed, in hypnotic trance it is not difficult to dissociate the 'I' or produce many versions of the 'I' simultaneously active and present to themselves. Hume says that when we delve into what we call our inner space we can only grasp a perception. His idea is that when we sleep and have no perceptions, we do not exist, and we mask these voids with a fiction of continuity that we call the 'I', which unifies and holds together the bundle of perceptions. All this is ephemeral, because one thought drives out another one, and is in turn rapidly expelled.

Schopenhauer notes that in what should constitute the core of the 'I', in what appears as the hearth of identity, there is the absolute 'non-I'. As soon as one wants to know the 'I', one loses it in a void, from which a voice speaks with the words of an unknown, a parasite. We therefore have no real possession of ourselves, and we are not the owners of our existence, being mostly

---

17. Contemporary schizophrenics are "living fossils of bicameral people."
18. Which are many and could express the concept "My name is Λεγιὼν (legion) because there are many of us" as reported in the Gospel of Mark 5: 8-9. Note that in Greek δαίμων (*dáimon*, then usually translated into *demon*) is the equivalent of the Latin *spiritus* (spirit, i.e., a numinous agent, not necessarily negative, even divine).

in a state of turbid unconsciousness.[19] It is the first, confused perception of an Unconscious.

Furthermore, according to Rudolph Virchow, in the progressive ascent from mono- to multicellular organisms, the prerogatives of each single cell are assumed by a central hegemonic power that receives a delegation to represent it. This center, which in humans gives rise to the 'I', does not exist as an independent entity; it does not possess autonomy outside the system of proxies granted by the individuals of which it is composed.[20]

The 'I' therefore ceases to be a monolithic unit to become an unstable compound, an archipelago of islands of consciousness, a *coalition consciousness* not unlike coral polyps. The 'I' experienced by an individual at any given time is therefore the strongest one, not the only one. Its hegemony is based on a system of built alliances and balances that require a continuous expenditure of energy (*libido* in psychoanalytical terms).

Today, using a modern metaphor, we could say that the 'I' is not a monarchy, but rather, like the United Kingdom, *a family aristocracy tolerating a hegemonic sovereign*: the aristocracy is represented by what remains of the integrated bicameral voices. Julian Jaynes called the mind of primitive *Homo sapiens* "bicameral" not only because the two brain hemispheres were more independent than they are today, but also as a magnificent metaphor of many modern parliaments that are formed by different voices gathered in a bicameral structure acting as a unique entity.[21] Therefore, the items to which one had to obey in the bicameral period were the absolute preliminary condition to the modern conscious phase, to the 'I'.

The so-called "death of the voices" was a necessary premise for the birth of the 'I'. In fact, we are conscious because we became our own voices. Today the voices no longer speak to me as they did to my ancestors, because 'I' am those voices. They no longer arise from the right hemisphere to speak to the left, but they speak to each other by creating the 'I'. They coalesced in an internal space calling themselves 'I'.[22] So, modern people no longer usually hear voices in a direct and nonconscious way, as the bicameral person did.

---

19. Arthur Schopenhauer, *Der Handschriftliche Nachlaß* [The Handwritten Legacy] (Arthur Hübscher, ed.) (1885/1985).

20. Rudolf Virchow, *Die Cellularpathologie in ihrer Begründung auf physiologische und pathologische Gewebelehre*, 1858, in *Nederlands Tijdschrift voor Geneeskunde*, 2003, 147, 2236-2244.

21. See Jaynes, *La Natura Diacronica della Coscienza* [The Diachronic Nature of Consciousness].

22. In the absence of adequate semantics, I don't know how to better explain this concept. I think it is impossible, mainly because "being" is also a verb and 'I' is also a pronoun.

But there is a very important way for us modern people to hear bicameral voices, even if we don't perceive them as such; indeed, sometimes we do not perceive them at all, because the listening takes place *sub limine*,[23] but nevertheless they make us act. We have an unwelcome taste of it in neuroses: what is an obsessive-compulsive neurosis if not a condition due to unconscious voices that tell us *"wash your hands, wash your hands, wash your hands"*; these voices speak — it would be better to say they whisper — below the threshold of consciousness. We hear them without being aware of them, and often we obey.

But the same voices also speak to us in daily life and make us act. These are the admonitions of parents, teachers, grandparents, the catechist — admonitions that now act as conditioning which we may have lost conscious memory of, but which operate in us, giving rise to choices and actions. *"Don't run in the street, don't smoke, don't take drugs, avoid bad company, crime doesn't pay, be careful with boys, don't get pregnant at 16"* or even *"choose Medicine after graduation"* — these are conditioning, subliminal voices, true clockwork mechanisms that we often presume to consider conscious and the fruit of a presumed free will. As Homeric heroes or biblical patriarchs, we submit to their will without realizing it; and the mysterious process of volition is nothing more than acquiescence to our unconscious residual archaic voices.

KUIJSTEN: You're drawing an interesting connection between the non-conscious bicameral voices and modern, guiding voices that are not quite hallucinations but are still experienced as dissociated from our "self." I've always viewed bicameral hallucinations and our internal dialogue more as running in parallel, yet indeed much of our internal dialogue consists of these same types of behavioral admonitions. This brings to mind something Jaynes once said, in response to a question from the audience — that our modern conscience is like "a faint and wayward echo" of the bicameral voices.[24] I think there is much more to explore here, in terms of this relationship and the trajectory from bicameral voices to the varieties of internally perceived thoughts we experience today, some of which are dissociated. Drawing on your study of anthropology and archaeology, what

---

23. To be precise, we hear them in inner speech, on the occasion of silent reading and during some physiological hallucinations such as the hypnagogic and hypnopompic ones, which can be reproduced with hypnosis.

24. Julian Jaynes, "Consciousness and the Voices of the Mind: Open Discussion," *Canadian Psychology*, 1986, 21, 2; reprinted in M. Kuijsten (ed.), *The Julian Jaynes Collection* (Julian Jaynes Society, 2012).

can you say about the origin of language and the relationship of language to the development of consciousness?

CASIGLIA: An anthropological and archaeological view allows us to answer this question with some certainty. It is clear that egoic consciousness derives from language. Just reflect on the fact that it is nearly completely verbal. Most of our thinking is done verbally.[25]

We don't know how the mind of the oldest human species of the genus *Homo* worked, because they have not left any documents or myths. Because modern man has an 'I' and animals do not, we must assume that there was a progressive process of self-training, and that this took place over a long period of time. For millions of years, the first human species certainly acted following symbolic instinct, but when humans somehow became *Homo faber* (builder, craftsman), when they began producing tools and other artifacts, handmade articles — usually lithic and useful in daily life — following the indications of a mental image, something similar to the unconscious had to exist. These archaic human species obviously did not yet have an 'I', so they acted in a coordinated way thanks to unconscious commands of the *perceive* → *execute* type, without any intervention of an egoic consciousness (which had not yet developed), a mechanism not different from the neurological commands that constitute modern conditioning.

This system worked very well for a very long period of time — as it still does today for non-human animals. But, according to Jaynes, as language developed, the unconscious began to express itself in a verbal form, with the right hemisphere giving orders *ipso facto* executed by the left, like conditioning does today. So as the Wernicke center for language comprehension developed, the coordinated activity of the unconscious must have begun to be perceived as voices, which obviously were nonconscious, as man had no interiority.

Hence the projection of the bicameral voices on tombs, totems, monuments, mountains, natural phenomena, which gradually assumed the unconscious role of divinities and also ensured — thanks to a uniform and habitual behavior — the social cohesion of groups of limited size, such as tribes or small settlements (a *civitas*). This mechanism also worked well for a long period of time. Only much later, due to natural upheavals, mutagenic factors, enlargement of social groups, negative and positive selections,

---

25. The price of this verbalization was *Homo sapiens'* renunciation of the non-mediated understanding of the symbols of the unconscious. These symbols are now free to act but often are not understood, frequently generating neuroses and other pathologies, but also generating the egoic consciousness.

and, most importantly, the development of writing and more complex language, did the voices integrate, forming what we now perceive as the 'I' and we call the "egoic consciousness." In deep hypnotic trance we can both evoke these voices and collapse them into an alternate self or 'I' (some psychologists refer to this phenomenon as "dissociation").

KUIJSTEN: As you said, there is an interesting interplay between biological evolutionary processes and cultural and environmental factors, such that cause and effect can often be difficult to determine. In other words, language could not develop until the necessary underlying biological prerequisites were in place, but these biological changes were likely driven by earlier behaviors that conveyed survival value. Once developed, culturally driven, complex abilities such as early language do not only have a transformative effect on the psychology of an individual and of a culture, but can also in turn influence further biological changes to the brain over many generations, as these skills spread through a culture and are taught to each successive generation. You've written a book that discusses decision-making, volition, and free will. Can you say something about your views on these topics?

CASIGLIA: Ah, free will! How many things can be said about free will! One fact is certain: many people will be dissatisfied with what I will say now. To get straight to the point, I will say that there is no conscious personal freedom. The question is, "Who writes the story?" If you ask different people, they might answer God (or any god) writes the story, or the 'I', or "it is we as a people who write history" (this last interpretation is very American), etc. In my opinion, logically, the answer is that history is already written.

I'm afraid that I am a determinist. Any superior animal can perform an action (eat, move, reproduce, etc.). For this to be intentional and voluntary, however, the animal must be aware of the consequences of this action, that is, it must be able to narratize. Jaynesian narratization is a prerogative of modern *Homo sapiens*, and today we know, also thanks to some experiments of my research group with functional magnetic resonance imaging (fMRI), that it depends on the anterior cingulum and on the limbic structures responsible for emotions (or at least, these structures must be intact).[26] Only *sapiens*, thanks to the narratization function, can be assumed to act freely.

26. E. Casiglia, et al., "Granone's Plastic Monoideism Demonstrated by Functional Magnetic Resonance Imaging (fMRI)," *Psychology*, 2019, 10, 434-448; E. Casiglia, et al., "Hypnosis Meets Anaesthesia: Mechanisms of Hypnotic Analgesia Explained by Functional Magnetic Resonance (fMRI)," *International Journal of Clinical and Experimental Hypnosis*, 2020, 68, 1-15.

But is it really so or is it just an illusion? Is volition possible within the context of Newtonian determinism? Although I wish that were the case — I don't like feeling like I'm a puppet — it would seem that it is not so! Of course, we have the subjective feeling of being free. Nevertheless, from a naturalistic, scientific point of view, 'I' is an inconvenient pronoun because it forces us to confront a problem, that of personal identity, which, as long as we remain in the realm of naturalism, has only two alternatives: either it is reduced to the mere brain (which is also part of the Newtonian deterministic universe) or it is an illusion.

If we affirm that man is a consciously free entity, that he can make free conscious decisions, then where does this free will come from? From the brain? But if free will is determined by the brain, then it is preordained deterministically, therefore it is nothing more than an illusory freedom. This *free will* believes itself to be free, but this belief also belongs to determinism, because the succession of *cause* → *effect* obviously has never stopped from the Big Bang to this precise moment, albeit with the interposition of chaos and its laws.

So while I am a determinist, I am certainly not the first. Pierre Laplace affirmed in 1812:

> We ought to regard the present state of the universe as the effect of its antecedent state and as the cause of the state that is to follow. An intelligence knowing all the forces acting in nature at a given instant, as well as the momentary positions of all things in the universe, would be able to comprehend in one single formula the motions of the largest bodies as well as the lightest atoms in the world, provided that its intellect were sufficiently powerful to subject all data to analysis; to it nothing would be uncertain, the future as well as the past would be present to its eyes.[27]

In short, it would not be free. But this question was raised even earlier by Lucretius (99-55 BCE), who in *De Rerum Natura* [On the Nature of Things], discussed for the first time the problem of the material world, in a rational and surprisingly modern way. He found himself forced to hypothesize random "swerves" of atoms to justify human freedom. But the naturalistic universe does not make swerves.

KUIJSTEN: How is the concept of determinism best explained to the average person, or non-philosopher?

---

27. Pierre-Simon Laplace, *A Philosophical Essay on Probabilities* (1814), translated from the sixth French edition (John Wiley & Sons, 1902).

CASIGLIA: The point is that of the *event antecedents*. The knowledge of all the antecedents would make easily explainable what appears obscure — the inexplicable turns of nature and events. It is precisely by knowing the trajectories that mankind arrived on the moon and sent the Mariner probes to Mars. Even more incredibly, by knowing the trajectories, it was predicted decades ago — at the beginning of the Rosetta mission — that on November 12, 2014, at 17:03 local time in Frankfurt, and after a journey of 6.4 billion kilometers, the Philae probe would touch down on the surface of comet 67P/Churyumov-Gerasimenko, at a precise point called Agilkia, 511 million kilometers distant from Earth.

In Newtonian terms, it can be said that your decision to continue reading now was already decided immediately after the Big Bang — to be fulfilled in this moment. You seem to freely decide to continue reading by virtue of a free decision of your brain, but your brain too depends on naturalistic determinism. Determinism dictates why your brain operates in the way that it does.

Now, interpreting the thought of the Italian philosopher and theologian Vito Mancuso, if we accelerate the course of the birth of the universe — for example, if we were watching a film in fast forward — at some point we would see a mineral start talking and saying "I am," because this is exactly what happened: inanimate inorganic elements have progressively organized themselves and become organic, and they became life and then conscious life, without any interruption,[28] only over the course of a very, very long period of time. Of course, the biological trajectories — particularly the mental ones — are not linear and mechanistic like the cosmic ones, and the laws of chaos play a big role. But chaos is not freedom.

KUIJSTEN: I understand your explanation, and yet I think most people would object that this seems to be contrary to our perceived experience of making decisions. Are there experimental data in this regard?

CASIGLIA: It is quite scary to accept that, in philosophical terms, freedom does not exist. In everyday life we are sure to make free decisions. To tell the truth, the whole system represented by social life, work, individual responsibility, subjective merit, many religions, not to mention the judicial system, is based on this certainty. The freedom of the French Enlightenment is considered an achievement. The United States is founded on the

---

28. An interruption of the *cause* → *effect* principle should have the rank of a Big Bang or of a miracle. These events do not belong to the naturalistic Universe; they are outside of the Universe.

values of freedom and individual responsibility. The state of New Hampshire has the motto "Live Free or Die," which certainly dates back to the days of independence, but which today could be reworded more precisely as "live with the subjective and illusory feeling of being free or die." Paradoxically, I would die for my freedom, but I'm afraid I don't have it.

Unfortunately, the inner, subjective certainty of being free is the only proof of the existence of freedom: everyone can, mistakenly, experience it in himself. Yet, as I explained earlier, this is in conflict with the deterministic nature of the naturalistic universe; anyone who studies this cannot fail to recognize it. This poses insurmountable problems, because either (1) we accept the *cause* → *effect* principle which is the basis of our life, or, (2) we are satisfied with the mere feeling of being free, which is in any case the basis of our life. We are sure of being free on an experiential level, just as we are certain of existing on an experiential level. It is not a question of applying logic, but of feeling something intimately, even if it is clearly false and illusory.

And if philosophy with its determinism were not enough or unconvincing, experimental data now indicate that our decisions are not made consciously. Scientists have shown with both an electroencephalogram and fMRI that if I decide, for example, to move a finger or a hand at a certain moment, apparently *freely chosen by me*, the decision was made seconds before.[29] Indeed, they can predict whether I will move my right or left hand when I haven't decided yet![30] Decisions, even if not predetermined, do not belong to the domain of consciousness.

KUIJSTEN: Yes, the famous and controversial experiments by Benjamin Libet, and others. Because these findings run so contrary to our everyday perceived experience and common sense intuitions, they have been difficult for many to accept.

CASIGLIA: They are difficult to accept and they collide with common sense and with subjective experience. A solution commonly accepted by the philosophical community and by almost the entire scientific community is that, although we live in a naturalistic universe which is necessarily deterministic, human beings are not really determined because the number of

---

29. Benjamin Libet, et al., "Time of Conscious Intention to Act in Relation to Onset of Cerebral Activity (Readiness-Potential): The Unconscious Initiation of a Freely Voluntary Act," *Brain*, 1983, 106, 623-642.
30. C.S. Soon, et al., "Unconscious Determinants of Free Decisions in the Human Brain," *Nature Neuroscience*, 2008, 11, 543-545.

covariables acting on us — on our brain or on our psyche[31] — is so high, so overwhelming, that it does not allow us to foresee an effect from its causes. According to this view, the *cause* → *effect* principle, well understood, exists, but the great majority of effects depend on causes that are not the result of direct causal principle, but rather enormous degrees of uncertainty.

This uncertainty would be such as to touch on indeterminacy (apparent absence of determinism) to avert the bugbear of predestation. When you have many, indeed many, choices available, these can *falsely* appear infinite, which would explain the widespread tendency we have to perceive ourselves as free agents, rather than as actors governed by a director. In support of this hypothesis, chaos theories are often cited. In the past, between 400 and 40 BCE, with the arrival of the Roman Empire in Greece and the fall of certainties, providence of the gods has failed and the fallacious concept of chance was born.[32] Even today, most people believe in chance. For those who are satisfied by this, the *freedom of chance* is fine. But it is always determinism, even if masked by uncertainty: it is the vain freedom of chaos.

KUIJSTEN: Fascinating. Another topic that often comes up in the context of free will is quantum mechanics. There's also been a lot of talk about quantum mechanics with regards to consciousness in the past few decades, and things like so-called "quantum consciousness." Most — if not all — of this I think represents very confused thinking, albeit in some cases by otherwise very smart people. It often seems to boil down to little more than wild speculation and the basic idea that "Well, consciousness is highly complex and poorly understood, and quantum mechanics is highly complex and poorly understood, so perhaps the two are related, or one explains the other" — that's a paraphrase of a quote I once read, but I no longer remember where.

To be clear, these theories also tend to suggest a definition of "consciousness" that is very different from how Jaynes carefully defines it. And I say "suggest" because rarely is an actual definition provided. But putting that aside and getting back to free will — in your opinion, can quantum mechanics help to save free will?

CASIGLIA: This is a very good question. Actually, at an even greater level of uncertainty, today it is customary to refer to quantum physics. The brain, in the final analysis, is composed of atoms and these atoms are composed of

---

31. Externalized by the ancient Greeks as the goddess Psyché (Ψυχή).
32. Chance was externalized by the ancient Greeks by attributing it to the goddess Tyche (Τύχη).

subatomic particles, and it is now known by physicists — and to a certain extent even by the general public — that these particles (which perhaps are waves or vibrations or fields, or perhaps not) do not behave in a deterministic way. In particular, it is and it will always be impossible to determine (i.e., to reduce to determinism) all of the characteristics of a particle while leaving it undisturbed: when we observe it, the function collapses from "quantum" to "determined" — having been modified.

The highest degrees of uncertainty lead to the uncertainty principle, which can be explained in this way: at a fairly small level, which however exists and makes us up, we are indeterminate. The subatomic particles have unreliable aspects and do not allow excessive familiarity. For example, a particle can appear in the kitchen and then in the bedroom without going through the corridor, because in the interval from one room to another, in the corridor, it simply does not exist.

In this sense, the future can be considered unpredictable, which however does not reassure me about my freedom. And the quantum case is a true case, not ignorance of antecedents. Heisenberg's uncertainty does not confer freedom, however. At the most it makes the uncertainty total, as in the well-known theoretical experiment of the "cat in the box." The indeterminacy inherent in this experiment is now supported by a mathematically monolithic formula; however, the cat is not at all free to decide whether to be alive or dead, it can only experience or not its own existence while it is in the box, and it also loses this faculty when the box is opened.

KUIJSTEN: You've certainly given us a lot to think about! Do you have any final thoughts on Jaynes's theory?

CASIGLIA: Jaynes's theories provide a solid basis for the nature of hypnosis, which is still largely unknown. My experimental studies, my experience as a hypnotist, medical doctor, and my studies of anthropology and archaeology lead me to consider Julian Jaynes as a scientist who studied not only consciousness, but the mind in its totality. In ancient Latin, "*scientia*" (science) and "*conscientia*" (consciousness) have the same verbal root, but it is clear that the mind (whatever it is) cannot be studied with empirical science alone, but must also be informed by human disciplines such as literature, archaeology, art, museum conservation, and so on. There is still so much to do and to discover. *Ad majora!*

15

Hypnosis, Bicameral Mentality and the Theory of Mind

John F. Kihlstrom

Interviewed by Marcel Kuijsten

John Kihlstrom identifies himself as a cognitive social psychologist with clinical training and interests. He received his AB degree, with a major in psychology, from Colgate University in 1970, where he was introduced to hypnosis research by William E. Edmonston. He received his Ph.D. in psychology, with a focus on personality and experimental psychopathology, from the University of Pennsylvania in 1975, where he studied with Martin T. Orne. In the course of his doctoral training, he completed a clinical internship at Temple University Health Sciences Center. He began his academic career at Harvard University (1975–1980, and moved to the University of Wisconsin (1980–1987), the University of Arizona (1987–1994), and Yale University (1994–1997), before settling at the University of California, Berkeley (1997–2017). At the time of his retirement from Berkeley he was Professor in the Department of Psychology and Richard and Rhoda Goldman Distinguished Professor in the Division of Undergraduate and Interdisciplinary Studies. In addition to his extensive program of research on hypnosis, his 1987 *Science* paper on "The Cognitive Unconscious" is generally regarded as a landmark in the revival of scientific interest in unconscious mental life.

MARCEL KUIJSTEN: So to start with, we recognized coming into this that we have diverging views on certain aspects of Jaynes's theory, and that this would be part interview and part discussion. I think that this type of discussion helps to further elucidate and advance ideas, and will hopefully give readers greater clarity on some of the finer points of Julian Jaynes's theory. So I want to state up front that I appreciate both your willingness and your encouragement of this process.

JOHN KIHLSTROM: Thank you. For my part, I really appreciate the efforts you've made to keep Jaynes's ideas alive. I don't think our differences are all that great because we both accept his fundamental insight: that a major change in consciousness occurred not just in evolutionary time, but in historical time.

KUIJSTEN: Julian Jaynes cites your work in *The Origins of Consciousness in the Breakdown of the Bicameral Mind*, in his chapter on hypnosis. How did you first encounter Jaynes?

KIHLSTROM: I was surprised and pleased to see that footnote. I was a newly minted academic at the time, and this was almost my first recognition outside the relatively narrow circle of hypnosis researchers. Frankly, at this point I don't remember my discussion with him, some 50 years ago, but I do remember when I first heard his theory of the bicameral mind. Jaynes gave a colloquium at Penn when I was a graduate student — it may actually have been my first colloquium as a graduate student, in the fall of 1970. Penn had a very active colloquium series, everyone attended every week, and there was a tradition that the opening talk be something really special. At any rate, Julian got caught up in a debate with Frank Irwin, the *eminence grise* in the department — a debate about Greek philology! (It may have been Morris Viteles, another member of Penn's Old Guard.) This in one of the highest-ranked psychology departments in the country — the place where the American Psychological Association held its first meeting, which housed the first psychological clinic, where industrial/organizational psychology was invented, where mathematical psychology was practically invented, where our understanding of subjects as basic as color vision and classical and instrumental conditioning had been completely revolutionized; where Ulric Neisser wrote *Cognitive Psychology*,[1] and they were also talking about classical literature. It was my ideal of what academic life should be.

---

1. U. Neisser, *Cognitive Psychology* (Appleton-Century-Crofts, 1967). Neisser wrote this pioneering textbook while on sabbatical from Cornell in Martin Orne's laboratory.

I wish that I remembered our discussion. Jaynes refers to my early research on posthypnotic amnesia, some of which had not yet been published.[2] His note suggests that we discussed hypnosis at Harvard, where I was an assistant professor in 1975, while *The Origin* was being finished, and Jaynes may have given a talk there as well — but again, unfortunately, I just don't remember. That colloquium at Penn, though, really sticks in my mind — almost like a flashbulb memory.

KUIJSTEN: That's a great story. It's a shame that more of his early lectures and discussions weren't recorded. Over the course of your long career, you've studied many different subjects that are very relevant to consciousness in general and to Jaynes's theory specifically. Let's start with conscious versus nonconscious (or unconscious) learning and perception. In the literature on consciousness, learning and perception are still often lumped in with consciousness, but Jaynes gives clear examples of how learning and perception can take place nonconsciously. In other words, we often attribute much more of our mental activity to consciousness than is warranted. In the literature on consciousness, there is still tremendous confusion on this point. You've explored these ideas in articles such as "The Cognitive Unconscious," and chapters titled "Perception Without Awareness of What is Perceived, Learning Without Awareness of What is Learned" and "Unconscious Processes."[3] Can you describe some of your key insights on learning and perception without consciousness?

KIHLSTROM: It's commonplace to identify consciousness with thinking, broadly construed. William James did that in the *Principles*, which led his position on unconscious mental life to be widely misunderstood. But even James acknowledged, from the studies on hypnosis and hysteria that were available to him, that all sorts of mental activity could go on outside of conscious awareness. He disliked the term "unconscious," but he freely embraced terms like "co-conscious" and "sub-conscious," which amount to the same thing.

---

2. F.J. Evans and J.F. Kihlstrom, "Posthypnotic Amnesia as Disrupted Retrieval," *Journal of Abnormal Psychology*, 1973, 82, 2; J.F. Kihlstrom and F.J. Evans, "Generic Recall During Posthypnotic Amnesia," *Bulletin of the Psychonomic Society*, 1978, 12, 1.

3. J.F. Kihlstrom, "The Cognitive Unconscious," *Science*, 1987, 237, 4821; "Perception without Awareness of What Is Perceived, Learning without Awareness of What Is Learned," in M. Velmans (ed.), *The Science of Consciousness: Psychological, Neuropsychological and Clinical Reviews* (Routledge, 1996); "Unconscious Processes," in D. Reisberg (ed.), *Oxford Handbook of Cognitive Psychology* (Oxford University Press, 2012).

Consciousness has two aspects. First, *monitoring* ourselves and our environment, so that we become aware of the outside world and our relation to it. The monitoring function enables percepts, memories, thoughts, feelings, and desires to be represented in phenomenal awareness. Second, *controlling* ourselves and our environment, so that we voluntarily initiate and terminate various mental and behavioral activities. It is through the controlling function that we exercise what the philosophers (and lots of other people, too) call free will or agency.

When we talk about unconscious perception or learning, we mean that they are unconscious in both senses: they occur outside of awareness and outside of control. Perception without awareness was once very controversial, but now has been established to the satisfaction of just about everyone. It often goes by the name of "subliminal" perception, but there are cases where the stimulus is not, technically, presented below the threshold of conscious perception. Still, there is an external stimulus, which for some reason the subject does not consciously perceive, but which has some objective effect on the subject's experience, thought, or action. That effect must be mediated by some internal mental representation of the stimulus, and there's nothing else to call it but an unconscious perception. Actually, I prefer to call it "implicit perception," paralleling the concept of implicit memory.[4]

Now, one thing we've learned is that subliminal perception, and most other forms of implicit perception, is analytically limited. There is only so much processing you can devote to a subliminal stimulus, and only so much information you can extract from it. And the effect typically does not last too long, on the order of seconds. Hypnosis seems to expand these limits, as in the case of implicit perception during hypnotically suggested blindness, but that is a long story. The most important insights are (1) that unconscious perception is real, and (2) that it's typically limited. It's not the case that you can flash "Drink Coke" on a movie screen and have everyone run for the concession stand.

The same thing goes for unconscious learning — which, again following the example of implicit memory, I prefer to call "implicit learning." Actually, learning was the first domain in which the explicit-implicit distinction was applied.[5] We define learning as any relatively permanent change in

---

4. D.L. Schacter, "Implicit Memory: History and Current Status," *Journal of Experimental Psychology: Learning, Memory, and Cognition,* 1987, 13, 3.

5. A.S. Reber, "Implicit Learning of Artificial Grammars," *Journal of Verbal Learning & Verbal Behavior,* 1967, 6, 6.

behavior — or, from a cognitive point of view, knowledge — which occurs as a result of experience. Again, there are still skeptics, but it's been pretty well established that people can use knowledge that they've acquired through experience, without being aware of the knowledge that's guiding their behavior. This is different from source amnesia, a variant on implicit memory, in which the subject has conscious access to newly acquired knowledge, but doesn't remember the episode in which that knowledge was acquired.

KUIJSTEN: Another interesting aspect of consciousness is the notion of "the self." Julian Jaynes only touches on the idea of the self briefly in a few places in his book, but he did give a lecture on this topic that I've published in *The Julian Jaynes Collection*.[6] You've published a number of articles on different aspects of the self. Can you give us a brief summary of your thoughts on the nature of the self and how it relates to consciousness?

KIHLSTROM: I define the self simply as one's mental representation of oneself — a high-level cognitive structure that includes the person's knowledge of him- or herself.[7] This knowledge structure can take a variety of forms. The self-concept can be thought of as a prototype whose characteristic features tend to distinguish a person from everyone else — at least from his or her point of view. The self-image is a perception-based, analog representation of what one looks, sounds, and feels like. The self can also be construed as a network of semantic and episodic memories referring to oneself. Or you can think of it as a theory, which explains not just what you are like, but also how you came to be that way. However you think of it, it's a knowledge representation stored in memory.

And this mental representation of the self is critical to consciousness — at least the kind of consciousness that Jaynes is talking about. In the *Principles*, William James wrote that "It seems as if the elementary psychic fact were not *thought* or *this thought* or *that thought*, but *my thought*, every thought being *owned*." Without a sense of self, you can't have that. Jaynes's bicameral man has thoughts go through his head; after the breakdown of

---

6. J. Jaynes, "Imagination and the Dance of the Self," in M. Kuijsten (ed.), *The Julian Jaynes Collection* (Julian Jaynes Society, 2012).

7. J.F. Kihlstrom and S.B. Klein, "The Self as a Knowledge Structure," in R.S. Wyer and T.K. Srull (eds.), *Handbook of Social Cognition, Vol. 1: Basic Processes* (Lawrence Erlbaum Associates, 1994); J.F. Kihlstrom, "Searching for Self in Mind and Brain," *Social Cognition*, 2012, 30, 4; "Consciousness and Me-Ness," in J.D. Cohen and J.W. Schooler (eds.), *Scientific Approaches to Consciousness* (Erlbaum, 1997); "Consciousness, the Unconscious, and the Self," *Psychology of Consciousness: Theory, Research, and Practice*, 2021, 8.

the bicameral mind, people recognize them as the products of their own mental activity. All conscious mental states have this link to the self as the agent or patient of some action, or the stimulus or experiencer of some state. In unconscious processing, this link to the self is absent.

KUIJSTEN: Indeed. The relationship between the self and consciousness is quite interesting, as well as how and why some thoughts are perceived as not being associated with ourselves. I think there is much more to explore here.

You have studied hypnosis for many years. In the past, I've argued — as have others — that one of the major obstacles to progress in the field of consciousness studies in general, and to understanding Julian Jaynes's theory specifically, is the fact that there is no widespread agreement over the definition of the term "consciousness." Consciousness theorists and authors define it in wildly different ways, or fail to define it altogether. Do you see similar disagreement with regards to how "hypnosis" is defined? How do you define the term — is hypnosis an altered state of consciousness?

KIHLSTROM: I define hypnosis, pretty conventionally, as a process in which one person, whom we call the hypnotist, offers suggestions to another person, whom we call the subject, for imaginative experiences entailing alterations in perception, memory, and action. In the classic case, these experiences are associated with a degree of subjective conviction bordering on delusion, and an experience of involuntariness bordering on compulsion. The persisting theoretical debates in the field, and they're related, are (1) whether hypnosis is anything more than suggestion, and (2) whether it is an altered state of consciousness. But there are several different forms of suggestibility, and not all of them are "hypnotic" in nature. They're different, for example, from the suggestion that we go to lunch at the Omelet House. For many clinicians, "hypnosis" is little more than progressive relaxation and instructed reverie. But hypnotized subjects see things that aren't there, and fail to see things that are there, they don't feel pain, and they can't remember these experiences later. So it seems obvious to me that hypnosis is an altered state of consciousness.[8]

KUIJSTEN: Yes, and from my own limited experience with practicing hypnosis, I share that view. It's now been more than 40 years since Jaynes first

---

8. I analyze the components of this definition in "The Domain of Hypnosis, Revisited," in M. Nash and A. Barnier (eds.), *The Oxford Handbook of Hypnosis* (Oxford University Press, 2008). See also "Hypnosis as an Altered State of Consciousness," *Journal of Consciousness Studies*, 2018, 25, 11-12.

published his book. How does Jaynes's discussion of hypnosis hold up in your view? Do you see hypnosis as a vestige of the bicameral mind?

KIHLSTROM: I can understand why hypnosis appealed to Jaynes. Many aspects of hypnosis can be viewed within the framework of what he called the *general bicameral paradigm* (p. 323ff). There is a more-or-less formalized *induction* procedure, of course, resulting in an altered state of consciousness that some writers still call "*trance*," at least informally. And a transference-like "archaic involvement," which Ronald Shor thought was characteristic of deep trance, is similar to Jaynes's *archaic authorization*.[9] All the cultural stereotypes and expectations surrounding hypnosis, including what Orne called its chameleon-like nature — the fact that the core features of hypnosis vary over time and setting — reflects something like the *collective cognitive imperative*. It's clear that Jaynes had read widely in the literature that was available to him — both the nineteenth century authorities, even going back to Mesmer and the Franklin Commission in the eighteenth century, as well as much of the more recent research and theory. And apparently, he did a little bit of experimenting with hypnosis himself.

At the same time, one shouldn't get carried away with the parallels. Close your eyes: that's what it feels like to be hypnotized, so "trance" is some kind of holdover from the language of a previous era. Besides, anything that can occur in hypnosis can also occur posthypnotically, after the subject is out of "trance." And there are lots of ways to induce hypnosis, some of which are downright "nonhypnotic." George Estabrooks, an authority on hypnosis from the early twentieth century, who was still a presence at Colgate when I was a student there, was the first to record a hypnotic induction — on 12-inch Victrola disks, as part of an early effort to standardize procedures for hypnosis research (he also invented the short-answer academic test, to the everlasting gratitude of all classroom teachers, but that's another story). Anyway, one day when he was working with a subject, he put on a record, left the room, came back at the appropriate time to continue the experiment in person, and found the subject deeply hypnotized. But when he was preparing for the next subject, he discovered that he had accidentally played a recording of a Swiss yodeler! Apparently, the voice of the hypnotist isn't all that important, provided that the subject has the appropriate

---

9. Ronald Shor was a graduate student of Abraham Maslow, and his phenomenological analysis of hypnosis was widely influential. See, for example, R.E. Shor, "A Phenomenological Method for the Measurement of Variables Important to an Understanding of the Nature of Hypnosis," in E. Fromm and R.E. Shor (eds.), *Hypnosis: Developments in Research and New Perspectives* (Aldine, 1979).

expectations (and is hypnotizable). This was probably an experienced subject, so he knew what to do.[10]

KUIJSTEN: That is very interesting. So for experienced subjects, a formal induction process is not always necessary. We see that with post hypnotic suggestions for trance as well.

KIHLSTROM: Yes. One parallel between hypnosis and bicameral mentality that Jaynes discusses is "trance logic," which Martin Orne, who coined the term, liked to characterize as "the peaceful coexistence of illusion and reality." For example, in the double hallucination, we suggest that there is someone, familiar to the subject, sitting next to him, when the chair is actually empty, and the person is actually standing *behind* him, out of view. After the hallucination is established, we draw the subject's attention to the *real* person. Interestingly: the hallucination doesn't disappear, and the subject may do a kind of double-take. And the hallucination itself may be transparent: that is, subjects may see through the hallucination to the back of the chair. In either case, the subject is maintaining the hallucination and the veridical perception simultaneously. Orne was probably wrong to think that trance logic is a unique signature of hypnosis, but everyone who has done hypnosis research has seen it. And that's the sort of thing, I guess, a bicameral mind would do.[11]

Jaynes also discussed the hidden observer, which Jack Hilgard employed in some studies of hypnotic analgesia leading up to his neodissociation theory of divided consciousness. One of the puzzles of hypnotic analgesia is that it greatly reduces the subjective experience of pain, but has little effect on physiological responses to the pain stimulus. One interpretation is that the pain is still being processed at some level outside phenomenal awareness, and that this unconscious perception is driving the physiological response. The hidden observer is a metaphor for the technique that Hilgard used to gain access to that parallel, subconscious, representation

---

10. G.H. Estabrooks, "A Standardized Hypnotic Technique Dictated to a Victrola Record," *American Journal of Psychology*, 1930, 42. For his contribution to educational testing, see "A New Type of Objective Examination," *Pedagogical Seminary*, 1927, 34.

11. M.T. Orne, "The Nature of Hypnosis: Artifact and Essence," *Journal of Abnormal and Social Psychology*, 1959, 58, 3; K.M. McConkey, et al., "Trance Logic in Hypnosis and Imagination," *Journal of Abnormal Psychology*, 1991, 100, 4. There are several demonstrations of trance logic on videos that Orne made for television in the late 1950s and early 1960s: "Psychology 1 with E.G. Boring" (National Educational Television) at https://youtu.be/blZyGk-1K1U and "The Nature of Things" (Canadian Broadcasting System) at https://youtu.be/OVhGtrjgP7M.

of pain. And again, it's definitely the kind of thing you might expect with bicameral mentality.[12]

A third relevant feature of hypnosis, which was first documented after *The Origin* appeared, are dissociations between explicit and implicit expressions of memory and perception. Posthypnotic amnesia affects explicit expressions of episodic memory, such as recall (and to some extent recognition), but spares implicit expressions of memory, such as priming effects — much the way priming is spared in neurological patients with the amnesic syndrome. Similar priming effects have been observed in hypnotic blindness, in which case they count as expressions of implicit perception. And you can think of the physiological response to the pain stimulus as evidence of the implicit perception of pain. Explicit-implicit dissociations are evidence of unconscious mental life — you have a memory or percept that affects your experience, thought, and action outside of conscious awareness.[13]

KUIJSTEN: That's fascinating.

KIHLSTROM: Yes. These sorts of priming effects can provide the cognitive basis for intuition effects — which are definitely relevant to bicameral mentality.[14] Priming, whether it's associated with hypnosis or not, brings things to mind automatically, unbidden. Suppose that you memorized the word *ashcan*, among other words, while you were hypnotized, and then got a suggestion for posthypnotic amnesia. Later, you're asked to recall the words you memorized, and you come up blank. But if you're given a recognition test, with *ashcan* as one of the items, you might endorse it simply

12. E.R. Hilgard, "A Neodissociation Interpretation of Pain Reduction in Hypnosis," *Psychological Review*, 1973, 80, 5; J.F. Kihlstrom and A.J. Barnier, "The Hidden Observer: A Straw Horse, Undeservedly Flogged," *Contemporary Hypnosis*, 2005, 22, 3.

13. Priming effects in posthypnotic amnesia were first noted in J.F. Kihlstrom, "Posthypnotic Amnesia for Recently Learned Material: Interactions with 'Episodic' and 'Semantic' Memory," *Cognitive Psychology*, 1980, 12, 2. For a comprehensive review of posthypnotic amnesia, see "Posthypnotic Amnesia: Using Hypnosis to Induce Forgetting," in D. Groome and M. Eysenck (ed.) *Forgetting: Explaining Memory Failure* (SAGE, 2020). For priming effects in hypnotic blindness, see R.A. Bryant and K.M. McConkey, "Hypnotic Blindness: A Behavioral and Experiential Analysis," *Journal of Abnormal Psychology*, 1989, 98.

14. J.F. Kihlstrom, V.A. Shames, and J. Dorfman, "Intimations of Memory and Thought," in L.M. Reder (ed.), *Implicit Memory and Metacognition* (Erlbaum, 1996); J. Dorfman, V.A. Shames, and J.F. Kihlstrom, "Intuition, Incubation, and Insight: Implicit Cognition in Problem Solving," in G. Underwood (ed.), *Implicit Cognition* (Oxford University Press, 1996). For an analysis of priming effects supporting an intuitive "recognition by familiarity" in posthypnotic amnesia, see J.F. Kihlstrom, "Recognition in Posthypnotic Amnesia, Revisited," *International Journal of Clinical & Experimental Hypnosis*, 2021, 69, 3. For an analogous effect in tactile sensation, see D.J. Tataryn and J.F. Kihlstrom, "Hypnotic Tactile Anesthesia: Psychophysical and Signal-Detection Analyses," *International Journal of Clinical & Experimental Hypnosis*, 2017, 65, 2.

because it "rings a bell." You don't remember it, but it seems familiar to you somehow, and you infer that it does so because it was on the study list. This is, essentially, the judgment heuristic that Amos Tversky and Daniel Kahneman called "availability."

Or suppose you're asked to complete the stem *ash___* with a legal English word: by virtue of priming you're likely to respond with *ashcan* instead of the much more frequent *ashtray*. The experimenter asks you what made you think of that word. If you weren't amnesic, you'd say "Well, that was in the list of words you just had me memorize." But you are amnesic, so you don't know what to say. You might confabulate something plausible, like "Oh, I don't know, maybe there was a discussion of American art on the *PBS NewsHour* recently; and maybe they mentioned the 'Ashcan School'." Or, if you were a bicameral person, living in a bicameral society, you might say something like "The gods spoke to me."

KUIJSTEN: Yes, that's a great example of the role of information processing outside of conscious awareness.

KIHLSTROM: Along those lines, one feature of hypnosis that Jaynes did not discuss in any detail, probably because the main research on the topic was published only after *The Origin*, is what is known as "experienced involuntariness." When you give subjects the suggestion that their outstretched hand is holding a heavy weight, pulling it down, they don't just drop their arm; they hallucinate the weight, and they feel it pulling on them. Or you can give subjects a posthypnotic suggestion to touch their ankles when they hear a certain sound; when they do it, they will typically have no memory of doing so (not least because amnesia is typically included in the suggestion). To adopt a distinction introduced to hypnosis research by Theodore Sarbin, they experience the suggested effects as *happenings*, rather than as a *doing*.[15] Whether they're hallucinations or actions, the suggested effects are experienced as involuntary. But they're not, of course. Nobody is taking hold of subjects' hands and scratching their ankles. They're doing it themselves, even if they don't experience it that way. Again, this has some of the flavor of bicameral mentality — you can experience the effect as being instigated from somewhere outside yourself.

---

15. T.R. Sarbin and W. C. Coe, *Hypnosis: A Social Psychological Analysis of Influence Communication* (Holt, Rinehart & Winston, 1972). The distinction between doings and happenings was originally formulated in R.S. Peters, *The Concept of Motivation*, 2nd ed. (London: Routledge & Kegan Paul, 1958/1960).

KUIJSTEN: Indeed — very interesting, thank you for that explanation. For me, post-hypnotic suggestions are one of the most interesting aspects of hypnosis, as well as one of the aspects most relevant to Jaynes's theory. Do we have a better understanding of how they work?

KIHLSTROM: Well, we don't have a good account of how posthypnotic suggestions work.[16] They're often perceived as automatic, by both the subject and an onlooker, but they're not automatic in the technical sense of the term. In cognitive psychology, we define a process as automatic if it is inevitably evoked by a particular cue; if, once activated, it runs incorrigibly to completion; if it consumes little or nothing by way of attentional resources; and if its execution doesn't interfere with other ongoing processes. That's a kind of prototype of automaticity.[17] And posthypnotic suggestion doesn't seem to have these features. If you present the cue outside of the experimental context, the subject may not respond. Most important though, execution of a posthypnotic suggestion consumes attentional resources, and interferes with other ongoing processes. That shows that it's definitely not automatic, even though it may be *experienced* as involuntary. And the literature is clear that, for all its apparent power, a posthypnotic suggestion elicits no higher rate of compliance than an ordinary "waking" request to do the same thing. The difference between a posthypnotic suggestion, an ordinary instruction, and polite compliance is the experience of involuntariness.

At the same time, Jaynes talks about the voice of the hypnotist being akin to the voice of a god, but subjects don't usually perceive hypnotists that way, nor do hypnotists present themselves that way — at least, not in the laboratory. In fact, the most experienced hypnotist of all time is a former public-radio announcer named Lee Dumas, who made the standard tape of the Harvard Group Scale of Hypnotic Susceptibility. Dumas had no training in psychology, and had never hypnotized anyone in his life, but through that tape literally tens of thousands of people have had an experience of hypnosis. I never met him, but apparently, he wasn't particularly charismatic or authoritative — he had a great speaking voice, to be sure,

---

16. P. W. Sheehan and M.T. Orne, "Some Comments on the Nature of Posthypnotic Behavior," *Journal of Nervous & Mental Disease*, 1968, 146, 3; I.P. Tobis and J.F. Kihlstrom, "Allocation of Attentional Resources in Posthypnotic Suggestion," *International Journal of Clinical & Experimental Hypnosis*, 2010, 58, 4; A.J. Barnier and K.M. McConkey, "Posthypnotic Responding: The Relevance of Suggestion and Test Congruence," *International Journal of Clinical and Experimental Hypnosis*, 2001, 49.

17. J.F. Kihlstrom, "The Automaticity Juggernaut," in J. Baer, J.C. Kaufman, and R.F. Baumeister (eds.), *Psychology and Free Will* (Oxford University Press, 2008); A. Moors, "Automaticity," in D. Reisberg (ed.), *The Oxford Handbook of Cognitive Psychology* (Oxford University Press, 2013).

and could read a script with expression, and I understand that he lived next door to the researchers who were developing the scale. Those were more important qualities.[18]

KUIJSTEN: Here I think you are perhaps taking the idea of the hypnotist's voice "being like a god" too literally. Jaynes doesn't suggest that the hypnotist speaks in a "god-like" way or a booming voice or anything like that. What I think is important to the theory is that we seem (bizarrely) predisposed to respond to an external, guiding voice, and that the hypnotist in this way is taking the role of the bicameral guiding voice. What seems so puzzling is that we can't simply "decide" to quit smoking, stop biting our nails, overcome a phobia, etc., but somehow through hypnosis, behavior can often be altered much more easily — when the suggestion comes from an external source — and why this predisposition exists in the first place.

KIHLSTROM: OK, I'll grant you that, but Jaynes does describe the hypnotist as an authority figure (pp. 393-394). And that's just not how subjects generally perceive the hypnotist. In some respects, sure, he's an authority figure — the hypnotist is in charge of the experiment, or the therapy session, or whatever. But that's no different from any other experimenter or therapist. Experimenters have some structural authority, because they're the ones who determine what goes on in the experiment; and they have some sapiential authority, because they are presumed to have some training and expertise. But they don't have the charismatic authority of a priest. Same thing with a psychotherapist. Even the most client-centered Rogerian psychotherapist says to the patient, at the end of a 50-minute hour, "Our time's up for today — see you next week."[19]

There may have been a time when the hypnotist was a charismatic, Svengali-like authority figure, but those days are long gone — if they ever were.[20] The hypnotist today functions more like a coach or a tutor, whose job it is to help subjects have experiences that they are perfectly capable of having all on their own, if only they knew how. The hypnotist teaches them how, and after a while they don't need the hypnotist anymore.

---

18. On one occasion, Dumas became hypnotized while listening to his own tape. He relates the experience in L. Dumas, "A Subjective Report of Inadvertent Hypnosis," *International Journal of Clinical & Experimental Hypnosis*, 1964, 12, with commentary in M. T. Orne, "A Note on the Occurrence of Hypnosis without Conscious Intent," *International Journal of Clinical and Experimental Hypnosis*, 1964, 12.
19. The distinctions among structural, sapiential, and charismatic authority come from M. Siegler and H. Osmond, *Models of Madness, Models of Medicine* (Harper & Row, 1974).
20. J.F. Kihlstrom, "The Two Svengalis: Making the Myth of Hypnosis," *Australian Journal of Clinical & Experimental Hypnosis*, 1987, 15, 2.

Which is probably why Estabrooks was able to hypnotize his subjects with a record that lasted only 4-5 minutes; and why that Swiss-yodeler episode happened.

Anyway, the reason that people can't just "decide" to quit smoking is that nicotine is an addictive drug, and once you're hooked, going cold-turkey isn't usually going to work. That's why we have nicotine patches for people who want to quit. While hypnosis is better than nothing, it's probably no more effective than other scientifically validated treatments. Perhaps the most popular hypnotic treatment program for smoking cessation is one developed by the late Herbert Spiegel, of Columbia University. Immediate results were pretty good, but on 24-month follow-up the success rate was back down to about 25%, which is a pretty ubiquitous result for a behavioral treatment. Hypnosis can be a useful adjunct to cognitive-behavioral therapy, and maybe even psychodynamic therapy, but it's not a magic wand.[21]

Another problem is self-hypnosis: people can hypnotize themselves by reading the very same script that would otherwise be read to them. Self-hypnosis is just as effective as hetero-hypnosis, especially if you're hypnotizable in the first place. There are some complications, to be sure: it must be hard to suggest to yourself that you won't remember the things you've just been doing. But however the suggestion works, it's coming in your own voice, not the voice of another person, much less a god.[22]

KUIJSTEN: Yet on the most basic level, at least to me, there still seems to be something to the idea of self-authorization versus external authorization, and I don't think we have a good explanation for that. There are habits and behaviors that don't involve a physiologically addictive chemical, yet it seems easier to overcome with the aid of hypnosis, at least for the highly

21. J.P. Green and S.J. Lynn, "Hypnosis and Suggestion-Based Approaches to Smoking Cessation: An Examination of the Evidence," *International Journal of Clinical and Experimental Hypnosis*, 2000, 48, 2; I. Kirsch, G. Montgomery, and G. Sapirstein, "Hypnosis as an Adjunct to Cognitive-Behavioral Psychotherapy: A Meta-Analysis," *Journal of Consulting & Clinical Psychology*, 1995, 63; N. Ramondo et al., "Clinical Hypnosis as an Adjunct to Cognitive Behavior Therapy: An Updated Meta-Analysis," *International Journal of Clinical and Experimental Hypnosis*, 2021, 69, 2.
22. R.E. Shor and R.D. Easton, "A Preliminary Report on Research Comparing Self- and Hetero-Hypnosis," *American Journal of Clinical Hypnosis*, 1973, 16; J.C. Ruch, "Self-Hypnosis: The Result of Heterohypnosis or Vice Versa?," *International Journal of Clinical and Experimental Hypnosis*, 1975, 23, 4; L.S. Johnson et al., "Self-Hypnosis Versus Hetero-Hypnosis: Order Effects and Sex Differences in Behavioral and Experiential Impact," *International Journal of Clinical and Experimental Hypnosis*, 1983, 31, 3; M.T. Orne and K.M. McConkey, "Toward Convergent Inquiry into Self-Hypnosis," *International Journal of Clinical & Experimental Hypnosis*, 1981, 29.

hypnotizable subjects, than what they're able to accomplish on their own. We seem to see a similar phenomenon at work with placebo effects.

I have heard that some people can hypnotize themselves by reading a script, but does that actually work? I think the far more common method of self-hypnosis is to listen to a recording. In that case, the recorded voice becomes the external authority — even if it's their own recorded voice.

KIHLSTROM: Yes, but that's not really self-hypnosis. It's "heterohypnosis," induced by a recording, no different in principle than the recording that Lee Dumas made for the Harvard Group Scale. In self-hypnosis, as it's been studied in the laboratory anyway, the subjects actually hypnotize themselves. They're given a script, similar to one of the standardized scales used to assess measure individual differences in hypnotizability, and they're simply instructed to follow it. In some studies, the subjects are just given an abstract description of what to do, and they make up the details themselves. It's amazing that it works, but it does. That's because, in a sense, all hypnosis is self-hypnosis. On several occasions I've worked with highly hypnotizable, experienced subjects, and as I've started to go through my script, they've stopped me and said, "Never mind — let me do it myself and I'll let you know when I'm ready to proceed."

Now, many clinicians train their patients to use self-hypnosis, but that technique often involves little more than instructed reverie, and does not involve the distortions of perception and memory that are characteristic of hypnosis. No motor suggestions, no analgesia, no amnesia, no posthypnotic suggestions. Just something that's closer to progressive relaxation and daydreaming, and that's not hypnosis. True self-hypnosis is where the same person takes the role of both hypnotist and subject.

Finally, Jaynes cited some preliminary neuropsychological evidence that seemed to suggest that hypnosis was some sort of right-hemisphere function, which again would be consistent with his view that "hypnosis is a vestige of the bicameral mind" (p. 396). To make a long story short, subjects who showed a tendency to make reflective eye movements to the left, presumably demonstrating the dominance of the right hemisphere, were more hypnotizable than those who did not. Another study, which was published after *The Origin* came out, found that subjects were more hypnotizable if they were seated on the right side of the room, so that the hypnotist was in their left visual field (projecting to the right hemisphere). But there's been a lot of contradictory evidence since then. For example, there are no differences in response to motor suggestions targeting the left vs. right side of the body. Most important, there's no difference in hypnotizability between patients with left- and right-hemisphere damage. Our best guess now is that hypnosis involves the frontal lobe, not the right hemisphere — although a recent study did show right-hemisphere involvement in hypnotic visual hallucinations. But really, like pretty much everything interesting, hypnosis involves the whole brain.[23]

Jaynes asserted that his theory provides a better account of hypnosis than any other extant theory (p. 380). I don't think that was true, even at the time he was writing, and it certainly isn't true now. There are several theories that provide a better account of hypnosis than *The Origin*, including some "sociocognitive" theories that I don't personally favor. *The Origin* explains features of hypnosis that aren't critical, such as cultural variability and the relationship between hypnotist and subject. Hilgard's neodissociation theory, which Jaynes cited favorably, explains features that are critical, such as the dissociation between subjective experience and objective behavior.[24]

Now, to be clear, none of my critique undermines Jaynes's essential argument about bicameral mentality. His theory doesn't have to explain hypnosis in order to be viable — any more than it has to explain classical conditioning, visual illusions, or the five-factor structure of personality. It's a theory about the cultural evolution of consciousness — a contribution to cognitive anthropology — or cognitive archeology, if you will. It seems to me that Jaynes's theory stands or falls on philological evidence, about how Achilles and Odysseus, or Amos and Ecclesiastes, appear to think — or, I suppose I should say it better this way: how they appear to experience themselves thinking. *The Origin* would be just as good, just as provocative, just as convincing, if the chapter on hypnosis hadn't been included.

KUIJSTEN: Those are very interesting examples — it seems that our understanding of hypnosis is much more extensive and complex now than it was four decades ago. Let's turn to the topic of consciousness. You taught a course on consciousness at UC Berkeley for twenty years, and I think at other universities prior to that. What was your approach?

23. J.F. Kihlstrom, "Neuro-Hypnotism: Hypnosis and Neuroscience," *Cortex*, 2013, 49, 2; J.F. Kihlstrom, et al., "Hypnosis in the Right Hemisphere," *Cortex*, 2013, 49, 2; R.C. Lanfranco, et al., "Beyond Imagination: Hypnotic Visual Hallucination Induces Greater Lateralised Brain Activity Than Visual Mental Imagery," *NeuroImage*, 2021, 239, 1.
24. S.J. Lynn and J.W. Rhue (eds.), *Theories of Hypnosis: Current Models and Perspectives* (Guilford, 1991); P.W. Sheehan and C. Perry, *Methodologies of Hypnosis: A Critical Appraisal of Contemporary Paradigms of Hypnosis* (Erlbaum, 1976).

KIHLSTROM: My course focused on empirical research, and downplayed the philosophical issues. Personally, I haven't lost a single night's sleep over the "hard problem" of consciousness — nor the "easy problem," for that matter. I introduced students to the philosophical debates — Dennett vs. Searle, Chalmers, McGinn, etc., of course, but I didn't allow students to get bogged down in the philosophy — though I did have them read David Lodge's novel, *Thinks...*, which captures much of the philosophical debate. I began with introspective analyses of consciousness, especially William James's, in the *Principles*, which I think has never been equaled. I took students through psychophysics, which constituted the first scientific approach to consciousness. Then various aspects of the mind-body problem (there are at least four), the literature on conscious (controlled) and unconscious (automatic) processing, and the explicit-implicit distinction applied in various domains. Then surveys of various altered states of consciousness, such as coma and general anesthesia, sleep and dreams, hypnosis and hysteria, meditation, and drug states. Finally, the development of consciousness, which I approached from three different angles: ontogenetic, the development of consciousness in individuals; phylogenetic, across species; and finally cultural. That's where Jaynes came in: the idea that, in historical time, people were not conscious the way we are today.[25]

KUIJSTEN: So having taught Jaynes's theory in your university courses for many years, what is your view of his theory now?

KIHLSTROM: I think it remains one of the most interesting, provocative ideas in all of psychology. It does have some problems, but they are the kinds of problems that occur whenever we try to learn anything from ancient artifacts. So much depends, as I learned from watching Jaynes and Irwin debate the meaning of *thumos* and *phrenes*, about how words are interpreted, and how language evolves. And then there's the problem of what the literary critics call the authorial or intentional fallacy — that is, the idea that we can attribute to authors the views of their characters. Actually, it's the reverse, isn't it? All we know is what Homer wrote (you know what I mean). He portrays Achilles as having one kind of consciousness, Odysseus as having another kind. We don't have any idea how Achilles or Odysseus actually thought (you know what I mean). We only know how

---

25. My course, "Scientific Approaches to Consciousness," is documented online at https://www.ocf.berkeley.edu/~jfkihlstrom/ConsciousnessWeb/index.htm. My discussion of Jaynes is in the lectures on "Development."

Homer *portrayed* them as thinking, and he might have had reasons for doing this other than how they *really* thought.

On the other hand, I've always had a fondness for Karl Jaspers's notion of "The Axial Age." Jaynes doesn't cite Jaspers, whose treatise appeared in 1949, and Karen Armstrong, who popularized the notion, wrote long after *The Origin* was published. The essential argument is that, sometime in the first millennium BCE, the way we thought about thinking changed. Socrates taught that knowledge could be obtained by reason; Confucius that we should think for ourselves; Gautama Buddha that we could abolish suffering by changing the way we think. The dates don't exactly line up with Jaynes, but it's pretty clear that, by the middle of the first millennium BCE, something had seriously changed in the way we thought about ourselves, and about thinking itself. And it happened at roughly the same time, in very different places.[26]

KUIJSTEN: Yes, this grand historical transition from polytheism to monotheism and the change we see in behavioral control transitioning from external direction to internal thought are compelling evidence for Jaynes's theory. We could add Jesus to your list of religious reformers, although he came slightly later, and I should mention here that scholars such as Michael Carr and Todd Gibson have looked at ancient China and Tibet through the lens of Jaynes's theory, and documented many of the same things that Jaynes observed in ancient Greece and Mesopotamia.[27]

KIHLSTROM: I'll have to look at their work. We think of consciousness as something that every normal adult human has. But the developmental question is: How did we get it? In the cultural view of development, *Homo sapiens* evolves, and children become adults, but even among adult humans there appear to be cognitive differences between different cultural groups. That's where Jaynes comes in, because he argues that there was a historical time when even normal adult humans were not conscious in the way that we are today.

But I don't think it's right to think of consciousness as merely a sociohistorical construction, something that we've been taught to think we

---

26. K. Jaspers, *The Origin and the Goal of History*, trans. M. Bullock (Yale University Press, 1949/1953); K. Armstrong, *The Great Transformation: The Beginning of Our Religious Traditions* (Knopf, 2006); R.N. Bellah and H. Joas (eds.), *The Axial Age and Its Consequences* (Harvard University Press, 2012).

27. See M. Carr, "The *Shi* 'Corpse/Personator' Ceremony in Early China," in M. Kuijsten (ed.), *Reflections on the Dawn of Consciousness* (Julian Jaynes Society, 2006); T. Gibson, "Souls, Gods, Kings, and Mountains" and "Listening for Ancient Voices" in M. Kuijsten (ed.), *Gods, Voices, and the Bicameral Mind* (Julian Jaynes Society, 2016).

have, but really don't — which is what some skeptics seem to think. Nor, I think, is consciousness merely a product of language. My students often posed the question: "Which came first — consciousness or language?" I told them that I didn't know but that I was sure that consciousness gave us something to talk about. More seriously, I think that the Darwinian principle of evolutionary continuity requires us to ascribe at least some level of consciousness to nonhuman animals, who don't have language. Language is relevant to *The Origin* because it's by virtue of language that we communicate our mental states to other people — and, perforce, the means by which we learn that other people are thinking thoughts that are different from the thoughts we're thinking. At some point it sinks in that *My thoughts are my own; I'm thinking them all by myself.*

KUIJSTEN: This gets to the heart of the issue of definitions and exactly how we are defining the word "consciousness." As you know, Jaynes defines it very narrowly as introspection — or more specifically, possessing an analog 'I' narratizing in a mind-space — relegating other, more biologically or evolutionarily based functions to nonconscious reactivity, learning, sense perception, etc. I think that the distinctions that Jaynes makes are extremely important, and that these distinctions are often lost by more broad definitions of consciousness, but this is a complex topic that is probably beyond the scope of our discussion today.

KIHLSTROM: I agree that the connection to the self is critical to the kind of consciousness we're talking about, and that such a connection is lacking in unconscious processing.

KUIJSTEN: I'd like to ask you about new developments in the field of consciousness studies over the past several decades. Since the publication of Jaynes's book, have there been new developments that you feel are relevant to his theory?

KIHLSTROM: Mostly, the literature on consciousness has been taken up with various aspects of the mind-body problem — mostly the "easy problem" of establishing the neural correlates of consciousness. Lots of theories, most of which don't define consciousness properly, the way Jaynes does; not too much by way of evidence. And nobody has any idea about the "hard problem" — *just how* this neural activity generates conscious experience. None of this has much bearing on Jaynes's ideas, I think. The developments that do bear on Jaynes have come from a different direction entirely.

The Origin was published at the height of interest in hemispheric specialization. The work on "split-brain" patients by Michael Gazzaniga, Joseph Bogen, and Roger Sperry became widely known in the late 1960s. By the time that Jaynes started giving the talks leading up to his book, like the one I heard in 1970, the idea that the two hemispheres had different operating principles — left brain analytic, right brain holistic, that sort of thing — and even that the right hemisphere was in some sense unconscious, with consciousness another function of the left hemisphere, had thoroughly wormed its way into both the professional literature and the popular press.[28]

Any idea of bicameral mentality, in that atmosphere, naturally turns the mind toward hemispheric specialization, and some sort of hemispheric disconnection syndrome,[29] with "the speech of the gods" (p. 105) and other hallucinations arising from the right hemisphere and people listening and responding with the left. There are other ways to divide the brain in two — front-back, top-bottom, inner-outer, old-new. With all his rage, Achilles seems to be using his ancient "reptilian brain"; with his twists and turns, Odysseus seems to be all prefrontal cortex.[30] But none of these alternatives provides a normally silent right-hemisphere speech center, the way the left-right distinction does.

Jaynes was not immune to this attraction. After laying out what is essentially a sociohistorical argument based on philology, the reading of ancient texts, he immediately asks about the biological basis of bilaterality — he says that his argument "demands" (p. 100) a physiological mechanism. This may have seemed natural to him: he was, after all, trained as a physiological psychologist (what today we would call a behavioral neuroscientist). But psychological theories stand or fall at their own level of explanation: they never "demand" an account in terms of physiology. As one of my former colleagues at Wisconsin (himself a physiological psychologist) once said, physiology is a tool for psychology, but it's not an obligation.

KUIJSTEN: I have some thoughts here, but can you elaborate on that further?

---

28. M.S. Gazzaniga, J.E. Bogen, and R.W. Sperry, "Some Functional Effects of Sectioning the Cerebral Commissures in Man," *Proceedings of the National Academy of Sciences*, 1962, 48. Testifying to the enduring popularity of the left-right distinction, an Amazon search in June 2021 revealed over 1,000 titles on the subject.
29. N. Geschwind, "Disconnexion Syndromes in Animals and Man: Part I," *Brain*, 1965, 88, 2; "Disconnexion Syndromes in Animals and Man: Part II," *Brain*, 1965, 88, 3.
30. P. MacLean, "The Triune Brain, Emotion, and Scientific Bias," in F.O. Schmitt (ed.), *The Neurosciences: Second Study Program* (Rockefeller University Press, 1970). But see J. Cesario, D.J. Johnson, and H.L. Eisthen, "Your Brain Is Not an Onion with a Tiny Reptile Inside," *Current Directions in Psychological Science*, 2020, 29, 3.

KIHLSTROM: As Marvin Minsky put it, that "the mind is what the brain does," and connecting the mental to the neural is an interesting and important project, but psychologists don't *have* to do it. Psychology is, essentially, a dualistic enterprise in which psychologists can study mental structures and processes with behavioral tools, like self-reports and reaction time, and just assume that the brain does it somehow. Some theorists argue that psychological theories must be constrained by the findings of neuroscience, but in fact the reverse is the case: understanding neural function depends utterly on the findings of psychological research. As I've written elsewhere, "Psychology without neuroscience is still the science of mental life, but neuroscience without psychology is just a science of neurons."[31]

Jaynes may have thought that some sort of functional disconnection of the two cerebral hemispheres was the biological basis of bicameral mentality, but then he has to account in biological terms for the loss of bicameral mentality, a functional connection made some three or four thousand years ago. And I just don't think that there's any basis for thinking that the structure of the brain, like the corpus callosum bridging the two hemispheres, has changed much, if any, over that period of time. In fact, there's evidence that the structure of the brain hasn't changed at all for at least 35,000 years.[32] There are examples of fast evolution, admittedly, but it can't be that the fast evolution of the brain was promoted by language. We had language long before Jaynes thinks we lost bicameral mentality.

KUIJSTEN: So this is an issue that has been raised by others, but in my view it's a misunderstanding of Jaynes's theory that biological brain changes — changes to the corpus callosum — are necessary in the transition to consciousness. Jaynes was adamant that the transition from bicameral mentality to consciousness could occur culturally — for example, as societies developed writing and the kind of complex metaphorical language Jaynes felt was necessary to construct an inner "mind-space." In other words, to use the computer metaphor, consciousness was a new "operating system," so to speak, using the same biological "hardware." He cites studies of brain plasticity (pp. 122-125) — how brain function can change due to environmental factors — and this field has exploded since that time.

---

31. M. Minsky, *The Society of Mind* (Simon & Schuster, 1987), p. 287; J.F. Kihlstrom, "Social Neuroscience: The Footprints of Phineas Gage," *Social Cognition*, 2010, 28, 6.
32. S. Neubauer, J.-J. Hublin, and P. Gunz, "The Evolution of Modern Human Brain Shape," *Science Advances*, 2019, 4, 1.

KIHLSTROM: Well, maybe I'm reading too much into Jaynes. But it's he who wrote that cultural-historical changes in consciousness "demand" a physiological explanation. They don't: the psychological level of analysis is valid on its own, and there is no requirement for any reduction to biology or physics. And, frankly, brain plasticity doesn't really work as a mechanism, either. Brain plasticity is the neural mechanism of learning, the idea being that when you learn something new, some aspect of the wiring of your brain changes. But the plasticity that enables learning — whatever structural changes take place — remains a feature of that individual learning brain. There's no inheritance of acquired characteristics, so it can't be passed down from parent to child. The learning can be transmitted from one individual to another, by social learning processes of example and precept — especially by the medium of language. But what is learned? It's not *how to be* conscious, as the social constructivists might put it. Rather, it's *that we are* conscious. We don't teach children to *think of themselves* as conscious, but that *they are* conscious.

KUIJSTEN: OK, there's a lot to unpack here, but let's come back to this in a moment. Let's talk about the new developments that you feel are relevant.

KIHLSTROM: It wasn't long after Jaynes published *The Origin* before a new approach to psychological development appeared on the scene: the theory of mind — a term introduced by David Premack and Guy Woodruff in an article on language and cognition in chimpanzees like Premack's famous subject Sarah. Sarah had great symbolic skills: She learned to associate tokens with concepts, and she could string tokens together to form rudimentary sentences; she had simple concepts of number and proportion, she could perform some analogical reasoning tasks. And she also seemed to be able to impute mental states to other people — to infer what they knew or believed or wanted. In other words, Sarah had something like our folk psychology, with its vocabulary of mentalistic constructs like *belief* and *desire*. That's what Premack and Woodruff meant by a theory of mind.

The theory of mind was imported into developmental psychology by Henry Wellman, among others, resulting in a raft of studies trying to pinpoint exactly when children acquire it. The general finding is that, by the time children are four or five years old, they understand that what they know, want, and feel is not necessarily what other people know, want, and feel. The theory of mind was subsequently elaborated into a "theory theory" which views the developing child as formulating, testing, and revising theories that will predict events in various domains, including physical, biological, and social, as well as psychological. Debate continues as to whether nonhuman animals have a theory of mind. Sarah was a very special animal; attempts to demonstrate the theory of mind in other chimpanzees with nonverbal variants on the false-belief test, for example, have generally yielded negative results; but that may be the wrong way to ask the question.[33]

What does all this have to do with consciousness? The theory of mind is usually characterized as the ability to impute mental states to other people, and the understanding that other people's mental states might differ from one's own — fundamental aspects of social cognition. But the awareness that others' mental states might differ from one's own assumes the prior awareness of one's own mental states as such — that is, consciousness in exactly Jaynes's sense. This does not mean that children younger than five are not conscious. Nonverbal tests indicate that infants as young as 15 months can make inferences about other peoples' beliefs. But whenever it happens, the recognition of mental states as such, as something we possess, that we create, that our thoughts are our own, and not necessarily someone else's thoughts too — that's a cognitive achievement. When children come to that realization, it's at that point that they truly become conscious.

So, the theory of mind can be taken as one marker of consciousness in Jaynes's sense — that is, as Jaynes puts it in his very first chapter, "consciousness of consciousness" (p. 21). Or I suppose you could say, *metaconsciousness*. In fact, the concept of metacognition provides a related perspective here. The term, coined by Lila Gleitman in an article on language development, is another approach to consciousness which is compatible with my interpretation of Jaynes's view. "Metacognition" means cognition about cognition, or knowledge about cognition, and it quickly became a center of the post-Piagetian turn in developmental psychology toward the theory of mind. For example, John Flavell argued that cognitive development was marked by quantitative and qualitative changes in children's understanding of how their minds worked — a kind of intuitive psychology. Later, Thomas Nelson pointed out that another important aspect of metacognition was monitoring and controlling what goes on in (or through) our minds — in

---

33. D. Premack and G. Woodruff, "Does the Chimpanzee Have a Theory of Mind?" *Behavioral & Brain Sciences*, 1978, 4, 4; H.M. Wellman, *The Child's Theory of Mind* (Bradford Books, 1990); A. Gopnik and H.M. Wellman, "The Theory Theory," in L.A. Hirschfeld and S.A. Gelman (eds.) *Mapping the Mind: Domain Specificity in Cognition and Culture* (Cambridge University Press, 1994); J. Call and M. Tomasello, "Does the Chimpanzee Have a Theory of Mind? 30 Years Later," *Trends in Cognitive Sciences*, 2008, 12, 5; F.B.M. deWaal, "Apes Know What Others Believe: Understanding False Beliefs Is Not Unique to Humans," *Science*, 2016, 354, 6308.

other words, metacognition could be identified with consciousness itself. Developmental psychologists think of metacognition as an individual achievement, but we can also think of it as a cultural achievement.[34]

The idea of a theory of mind came along after *The Origin* was published, but I like to think that, had Jaynes been writing 15 or 20 years later, he would have viewed it as another important framework for his theory. That is to say, the origin of consciousness comes with the acquisition and cultural proliferation of a theory of mind — of a folk psychology based on mental states of belief, feeling, and desire. The people in the *Iliad* don't seem to have a theory of mind: there's a lot of rage, and other emotions, but not a lot of thinking and deciding, not too much thinking about what other people are thinking. Achilles makes one decision — to live a heroic, if short, life. The people in the *Odyssey* definitely do have a folk psychology: Odysseus is the man of twists and turns, always thinking ahead, always trying to outwit someone else. The Trojan Horse was his idea.

And that's what seems to be happening in Jaynes's theory. In my view, consciousness isn't a social construction. At some point in historical time, people discovered that what was going through their heads were their own thoughts — that what they have been thinking has not been injected into their minds by gods and demons, but rather that they have been thinking for themselves — sort of like Moliere's Bourgeois Gentleman who discovers he's been speaking prose all his life. It's not unlike what children discover when they acquire a theory of mind. Language is important because that's how we find out what other people are thinking. But, I think, the cerebral hemispheres, nor any other aspect of brain structure, don't have anything to do with it. So, the theory of mind is not just an individual cognitive achievement — it's also a cultural achievement. And it's a genuine discovery. Consciousness was always there, just like the New World was there before Columbus and the Pacific Ocean before Balboa, just like black holes were there before John Wheeler and Stephen Hawking. We just had to realize it. But once we realized it, there was no going back.

In my take on Jaynes, this discovery happened beginning about 3,000 years ago, and was consolidated by the time of the Axial Age. But apparently some people didn't get the memo. In a very interesting line of

---

34. The term "metacognition" was coined by Lila Gleitman in L.R. Gleitman, H. Gleitman, and E. Shipley, "The Emergence of the Child as Grammarian," *Cognition*, 1972, 1. See also, J.H. Flavell, "Metacognition and Cognitive Monitoring: A New Area of Cognitive-Developmental Inquiry," *American Psychologist*, 1979, 34, 10; T.O. Nelson, "Consciousness and Metacognition," *American Psychologist*, 1996, 51, 2.

research, Angeline Lillard has found that there are some cultures which have a very different theory of mind than we do in the West. In some cases they don't seem to have made the discovery yet. In other cases they just may not find the theory of mind useful. To give another historical analogy, these societies are a little like the Tokugawa period in Japan up to the mid-nineteenth century: they knew about the West, but they didn't want anything to do with it. In any event, the very fact that in the twentieth and twenty-first centuries there is still cultural variation in the theory of mind lends support to Jaynes's idea that, while consciousness is universal among adult humans, "consciousness of consciousness" is not. And if it's not universal now, after three thousand years, there's no reason to think it was universal then.[35]

KUIJSTEN: Yes, that's a great point. I agree there are some strong connections between Jaynesian consciousness and theory of mind — this is something that is discussed in another interview as well.[36] With regard to theory of mind in humans, I think that Jaynes might have viewed it as one of the features of consciousness, and perhaps also a metric for measuring the development of consciousness in children. With regard to theory of mind in animals, Jaynes discusses it briefly in a commentary on "cognition and consciousness in non-human animals," published after his book, stating:

> If the term simply means the recognition of a particular mental state in another animal and by mental we do not imply conscious, I do not disagree. But then we can apply such a phrase much more widely: to a dog that cowers to his master's scolding tone or wags his tail to praise; or to a four-year-old child who can choose appropriate gifts for a two-year-old. Both dog and four-year-old are recognizing the mental states of others, and I suggest that this is more automatic than introspective.[37]

Jaynes makes an important point here, and I agree that some of the research has been over interpreted — for example, I think that the inferences about other's beliefs as seen in 15-month old infants can be done

35. Angelina Lillard, "Ethnopsychologies: Cultural Variations in Theories of Mind," *Psychological Bulletin*, 1998, 123, 1; "Ethnopsychologies: Reply to Wellman (1998) and Gauvain (1998)," *Psychological Bulletin*, 1998, 123, 1.

36. See Bill Rowe's interview, "The Development of Consciousness in Children" in this volume.

37. J. Jaynes, "In A Manner of Speaking," *Behavioral and Brain Sciences*, 1978, 1, 4; reprinted in *The Julian Jaynes Collection*. Here and in the Afterword (which appears in the 1990 and later editions of Jaynes's *Origin*), Jaynes also refutes the popular misconception that the mirror recognition of one's body is evidence of consciousness in non-human animals.

nonconsciously — at least by the Jaynesian definition. These are things that can also be observed in some nonhuman animals. I agree with the view that one has to take care to parse out the differences between implicit (or nonconscious) versus explicit (conscious) inferences. Others have suggested that language acquisition plays a critical role in false-belief understanding.[38]

While I am certainly not up-to-date on all of the literature on theory of mind, my sense is that there is still a large degree of both confusion and debate in the literature as to what aspects of theory of mind require Jaynesian-type consciousness and what aspects can be accomplished nonconsciously. But in any case, I do agree that the connections between theory of mind and Jaynesian consciousness certainly deserve a great deal of further exploration, perhaps both as one of the features of consciousness and as a method of measuring the development of consciousness.

KIHLSTROM: Maybe 15-month-olds don't have a full-fledged theory of mind, but you've got to start somewhere, and what infants do nonverbally is a precursor to what four- and five-year-olds do verbally. I'm sure that language facilitates the process immensely. Consciousness does give us something to talk about, after all, and talking is the most efficient way for us to share our thoughts with others — and, therefore, the most efficient way to learn that our thoughts belong to us, and other people's thoughts belong to them.

KUIJSTEN: As to whether consciousness was always there, as you say, I think this brings us back once again to exactly how we're defining the term. Certainly things like learning, attention, and our ability to perceive and respond to our environment were always there. But I think the analog 'I' narratizing in a mind-space as described by Jaynes — for example, our ability to mentally visualize ourselves in other places doing other things, or the kind of mental rehearsal that is becoming popular among athletes — is indeed something more like a learned skill that I think requires metaphorical language as a prerequisite, although the details of this process are complex and certainly require further exploration.[39]

38. J. Perner and W.A. Clements, "From an Implicit to an Explicit Theory of Mind," in Y. Rossetti and A. Revensuo (eds.), *Beyond Dissociation: Interaction between Dissociated Implicit and Explicit Processing* (John Benjamins, 2000); J.E. Pyers and Senghas, "Language Promotes False Belief Understanding: Evidence from Learners of a New Sign Language," *Psychological Science*, 2000, 20, 7.
39. See Ted Remington's interview, "Metaphor and the Rhetorical Structuring of Consciousness," in this volume.

KIHLSTROM: I agree that a lot depends on how we define "consciousness." It's certainly not tantamount to perceiving, learning, or responding behaviorally to environmental stimuli, as all of those functions can go on unconsciously, as I have been at pains to argue in my work. About attention, I'm not so sure: attention and consciousness are intimately related, and the argument that consciousness and attention can be dissociated is, I think, not all that compelling.[40] But this is not the place to have that discussion. I think I define consciousness the same way Jaynes does. The phrase "consciousness of consciousness," which forms the title of his first chapter, implies that consciousness is something that we are *conscious of* — or not. It seems very likely to me that many nonhuman animals, and infant humans, have sensory experiences associated with vision, hearing, equilibrium, pain, hunger, and the like — what the philosophers call *qualia*. But at some point, at least in human development, these qualia get linked to the self as the one who's having the experience, so that the child realizes that *I'm* seeing something, *I'm* hearing something, *I'm* upside down, *I'm* hurt, *I'm* hungry — and, just as important, that somebody else *is not* seeing the same thing, *is not* upside down, *is not* hungry. When you realize that you're having experiences, and thinking thoughts, that others are not: that's when you've begun to acquire a theory of mind, and that's when you're conscious of consciousness.

KUIJSTEN: I agree with most of what you're saying there in terms of how consciousness is defined, other than to say many of these sensations and perceptions are often experienced nonconsciously. To put it another way, even after developing a sense of self, or the realization that we are the experiencer of our experiences, only a small fraction of those experiences are held in consciousness at any given moment.

Attention is another one of these somewhat slippery terms. I think of it as *focused perception*. So, if I take a break from working and sit in my backyard, I can, nonconsciously, direct my attention to all of the various birds, while thinking (consciously) about the tasks necessary to complete the book where this discussion will appear. In the Jaynesian sense, my visual perception and focused attention are happening nonconsciously, while my consciousness is occupied in that moment with planning, deliberating, etc. The birds, in turn, nonconsciously direct their attention toward me, or perhaps some seed that I've placed on the ground. Or a dog can,

---

40. C. Koch and N. Tsuchiya, "Attention and Consciousness: Two Distinct Brain Processes," *Trends in Cognitive Sciences*, 2007, 11, 1.

nonconsciously, direct its attention to searching for a ball. Jaynes suggests that the conscious analog to sensory attention is *concentration*.[41]

I'd like to go back for a moment to some of the points you raised earlier. You touched on a few different critiques of Jaynes's theory that I've seen come up before, so I'd like to take this opportunity to attempt to clarify them, or at the very least offer a different perspective to consider.

After the publication of his book, Jaynes further clarified his theory by breaking it down into four separate hypotheses that can each stand or fall on their own: (1) that consciousness (as he defines it) is based on language, (2) that prior to the development of consciousness, humans had a bicameral mentality, (3) dating the transition from bicameral mentality to Jaynesian consciousness to roughly 1500-1200 BCE in places like Egypt, Greece, and Mesopotamia (the transition occurred at other times in other places), and (4) Jaynes's neurological model for bicameral mentality — what he thinks may have been taking place in the brain.[42] I think that framing Jaynes's theory as these four, separate hypotheses makes it easier to discuss and understand. I'll come back to this in a moment.

Let me first say something about your comment on Jaynes's use of the split-brain research. I don't want to overstate or misrepresent your view on this in any way, but I've heard variations of the suggestion before that either Jaynes made too much of the split-brain research or that the split-brain research had undue influence on his theory because of its popularity at the time, etc. — so it's that more general theme that I'd like to address.

I have a different view on this for two reasons. First, while I certainly agree that some of the right/left brain hemisphere differences were misunderstood or taken to extremes in the popular press and elsewhere, in my view many of the fascinating, legitimate findings that came out of the split-brain experiments remain valid to this day, including those most relevant to Jaynes's bicameral mind and neurological model hypotheses.

Let me provide some examples. In split-brain patients, after the surgery, experiments suggest that (1) the brain hemispheres can operate more independently than they typically seem to in non-split-brain individuals, (2) two distinct "selves," or "spheres of consciousness" seem to be present, one per hemisphere, (3) actions or responses initiated by the right or non-dominant hemisphere (for language) often feel alien to the person, and (4) our conscious sense of self seems to be associated with the left hemisphere,

---

41. See Jaynes, *The Origin*, pgs. 447-452 of the Afterword.

42. J. Jaynes, "Four Hypotheses on the Origin of Mind," *Proceedings of the 9th International Wittgenstein Symposium*, 1985, 135-142; reprinted in *The Julian Jaynes Collection*. See also the Afterword.

likely because of the left hemisphere's dominance for language.[43] (This last point seems to apply to both split-brain and non-split-brain individuals.) I recognize that there is a great deal of ongoing debate with regard to each of these points, but, when viewed as a whole, I find the overall body of evidence supporting these claims to be persuasive.[44]

So while perhaps the right/left brain hemisphere differences were overblown by the public, the backlash against the overreach has actually had the effect of overshadowing some of the stunning findings of this research. So the pendulum has now swung the other way: the dominant theme is that "right/left brain hemisphere differences were exaggerated" and the important discoveries of the split-brain experiments to a certain extent have been ignored — at least by those not still actively investigating the topic.

Perhaps there is something of a recency bias at play here as well.[45] Because the majority of the experiments were done decades ago (severe epilepsy now more often treated with the more effective pharmaceuticals that have since been developed), the findings are perhaps perceived by some as somehow being less valid or less important. Or perhaps the findings are simply too strange or counterintuitive for many to seriously entertain. But of course the evaluation of hypotheses should be based on evidence, regardless of when they were proposed or how they make us feel. Whatever the reason, many of the key findings from the split-brain research have never been fully explored, and I was pleased to see that the philosopher Elizabeth Schechter, specializing in the philosophy of neuropsychology, recently provided a new, comprehensive discussion of the subject.[46]

KIHLSTROM: I actually don't have a quarrel with the role of hemispheric specialization in bicameral mentality. I'm skeptical about the right-hemisphere theory of hypnosis, but as I said before, I don't think that's a problem for Jaynes's theory. I do think that the theory of mind offers an alternative, non-physiological framework for thinking about bicameral mentality. But of all the ways to bifurcate the brain, left vs right is the only one that will easily account for the auditory hallucinations that are central to Jaynes's theory. Maybe I'm picking a point, but what concerns me more is Jaynes's assertion, which is all too common, that a psychological phenomenon

---

43. For the sake of simplicity, my discussion here assumes a person that is right-handed.

44. Cases of hemispherectomy provide further supporting evidence, showing that the brain hemispheres can operate independently. See A.M. Battro, *Half a Brain is Enough: The Story of Nico* (Cambridge University Press, 2001).

45. A cognitive bias that favors recent ideas or events over those that are older or that are not being actively promoted.

46. E. Schechter, *Self-Consciousness and "Split" Brains: The Minds' I* (Oxford University Press, 2018).

"demands" a physiological explanation. It doesn't. As psychologists, we assume that the brain does it, somehow, but no psychological theory is required to specify a physiological mechanism, and the findings of neuroscience don't constrain psychological theory. Psychological theories stand or fall on their own, at their own level of explanation. Many psychologists, neuroscientists, and philosophers of science don't understand this, so I'm very sensitive to it and take every opportunity to make the point.

KUIJSTEN: Understood. So that was my first point — that in my view, many of the findings of the split-brain experiments, including those relevant to Jaynes's hypotheses, are still valid. My second point is that we have to be clear that Jaynes only uses the insights that came out of the split-brain experiments to support his second and fourth hypotheses: bicameral mentality and the neurological model for bicameral mentality. The split-brain research isn't directly relevant to his ideas on the origin of consciousness. However, I think there's a temptation people have to think that, if bicameral mentality involved the hemispheres operating more independently than they do today, then the shift to consciousness must have required changes to the physical structure of the corpus callosum, thus facilitating greater hemispheric integration.

However, Jaynes's argument is that consciousness, as he narrowly defines it, developed as a consequence of both writing and, more importantly, the development of metaphorical language that facilitated the creation of a metaphorical "mind-space" where we could visualize an analog 'I' and a metaphor 'me' engaging in virtual action, spatialize our lives on a timeline, etc. I suspect there was something of a see-saw effect, where as the various features of consciousness were cultivated via metaphorical language over generations, the right or non-dominant hemisphere language areas — the source of the auditory hallucinations — were correspondingly suppressed (for the many individuals who still hear voices, this process is still ongoing today).

Jaynes argues that this was all happening culturally. And yes, brain plasticity operates on the individual level, but if the majority of individuals in a culture are learning to use new technologies, in this case writing and more complex language — using metaphors of physical space to, for the first time, create an inner mental space — then conceivably the new skills would result in "software" changes to the brain that could spread throughout the culture. The new skills could then be taught to each successive generation.

So to sum up my second point: Jaynes only uses the insights from the split-brain experiments as evidence to support his hypotheses of bicameral mentality and his neurological model, and these hypotheses should each be evaluated separately from his hypotheses about the origin of consciousness based on language or dating the transition from bicameral mentality to consciousness.

KIHLSTROM: I agree that the split-brain experiments provide a good biological model for the sorts of things that Jaynes is talking about. And there's no question that consciousness requires some reference to the self — Jaynes's "narratizing I," if you will. All introspections take the form of "*I* think", or "*I* feel", or "*I* want." And there's no doubt but that the breakdown of the bicameral mind was facilitated by language because that's such an important modality for the transmission of knowledge within and across cultures — knowledge like "My thoughts are my own, and yours are yours."

So I accept two and a half of Jaynes's four hypotheses: I accept his reading of ancient texts, and his conclusion that ancient humans were bicameral seems very plausible to me. And, based on the same philological evidence, I think he's right that the breakdown in bicameral mentality occurred in historical time. I agree that the division of the brain into two hemispheres provides a neurological model of bicameral mentality, a way to think about the bicameral mind, but I don't agree that it provides a neurological explanation for either bicameral mentality or its breakdown, because bicameral mentality doesn't need a neurological *explanation*; psychological facts require only psychological explanations. And I worry about the idea that consciousness requires language: Invoking the Darwinian principle of evolutionary continuity across species, we have to consider the possibility that other species have consciousness too — and no other species has anything like human language.

KUIJSTEN: The relationship between language and consciousness is certainly a complex subject that could benefit from further study and empirical evidence. Your next point about theories in psychology not requiring — or "demanding" — a neurological explanation is certainly well taken. I completely agree — psychological theories certainly don't require that their underlying neurological mechanisms be known or understood — and from your comments I suspect there is something of a larger, ongoing debate here. Yet, on the other hand, if a plausible neurological explanation for a psychological observation presents itself, then it certainly also makes sense to offer a conjecture or a hypothesis as to what is going on in the brain, does it not?

In this specific case, I think it was a good thing that Jaynes did speculate about the possible underlying neurological mechanism for bicameral mentality — his neurological model — because (1) his initial speculations helped inform future investigations and (2) the evidence from neuroscience now suggests that he was in fact correct.

Beginning in 1999, brain imaging studies began to show the right/left temporal lobe interaction of the language areas during auditory verbal hallucinations that Jaynes predicted.[47] Of course the brain is complex and difficult to research, and not every study has demonstrated the same result. But a growing number have, to the point where it is now emerging as the most widely accepted view of the neurological mechanism of auditory verbal hallucinations.[48]

So while we can indeed divide the brain in different ways, such as the older, "reptilian" brain vs. the prefrontal cortex, etc., it now seems clear that Jaynes's neurological model was in fact accurate — it's the non-dominant (usually right) language areas that are responsible for auditory verbal hallucinations, which then travel across the corpus callosum and are "perceived" by the dominant (usually left) hemisphere language areas. In other words, the voices or behavioral commands aren't being generated in the limbic system, for example — even if that is where the initial "fight or flight" impulse is generated.

So to reiterate, bicameral mentality is a psychological hypothesis that may or may not be correct, independent of whether or not the neurological model for bicameral mentality is correct or incorrect. I think that this has been a major point of confusion for many people — because the two hypotheses are so closely related, there is a tendency to equate the two. In any case, I think that identifying the right or non-dominant temporal lobe language areas as the probable locus of auditory verbal hallucinations (and the "voices of the gods") — Jaynes's fourth hypothesis — along with recognizing that we likely operated under a more hemispherically disunified, nonconscious mentality based on auditory hallucinations in the past — Jaynes's second hypothesis — were two of Jaynes's greatest insights

47. B. Lennox, et al., "Spatial and Temporal Mapping of Neural Activity Associated with Auditory Hallucinations," *Lancet*, 1999, 353, 644.
48. L. Zmigrod, et al., "The Neural Mechanisms of Hallucinations: A Quantitative Meta-Analysis of Neuroimaging Studies," *Neuroscience & Biobehavioral Reviews*, 2016, 69, 113-123.

(his other two hypotheses are equally important). So, at least from my perspective, I don't think we should wave off these two hypotheses — or the supportive evidence from split-brain research — as in any way outdated or misguided.

KIHLSTROM: Don't get me wrong: I have no stake in the disconnection hypothesis either way. The role of the two hemispheres in consciousness is a very interesting topic for research, and I think that investigators would make more progress if they paid more attention to Jaynes.[49] I think about the origins of consciousness in terms of an alternative framework, the theory of mind, which is compatible with Jaynes's philological findings, and his ideas about the origins of consciousness, but doesn't involve any physiologizing. I like to think that Jaynes might have considered the theory of mind as a framework had it been available to him. Perhaps I'm overreacting to what Jaynes wrote, but all too many psychologists, neuroscientists, and philosophers think that the only legitimate explanations of psychological phenomena are at the biological level of analysis. So when I see someone write that a psychological finding "demands" a physiological explanation, I feel compelled to object.

KUIJSTEN: That does clarify why that aspect of Jaynes's argument stood out to you. And I agree that it is unfortunate that researchers studying the split-brain have thus far not connected their work to Jaynes. I also would like to emphasize that we can observe much of what Jaynes describes in action today. Children appear to develop Jaynesian consciousness as they learn language, and we can watch this process unfold. For example, what the developmental psychologist Philip Zelazo refers to as "reflective consciousness 2" (*refC2*) in his "levels of consciousness" model of children's conscious development equates roughly with some of the features of Jaynesian consciousness.[50] Many more people today experience behaviorally-oriented, often commanding auditory verbal hallucinations than was previously known, and there doesn't seem to be a persuasive explanation as to why this occurs, other than Jaynes's bicameral mind hypothesis. We now have the brain imaging studies that show that

49. R.W. Sperry, E. Zaidel, and D. Zaidel, "Self Recognition and Social Awareness in the Deconnected Minor Hemisphere," *Neuropsychologia*, 1979, 17, 2; E.H.F. de Haan, et al., "Split-Brain: What We Know Now and Why This Is Important for Understanding Consciousness," *Neuropsychology Review*, 2020, 30; T. Bayne and E. Schechter, "Consciousness after Split-Brain Surgery: The Recent Challenge to the Classical Picture," *Neuropsychologia*, 2021, 160.

50. P.D. Zelazo, H.H. Gao, and R. Todd, "The Development of Consciousness," in P.D. Zelazo (ed.), *The Cambridge Handbook of Consciousness* (Cambridge University Press, 2007).

there is in fact a left/right temporal lobe ("bicameral") interaction that takes place during this experience.

Finally, with regard to consciousness and bicameral mentality, I think that the evidence suggests that two separate systems are involved. In other words, I don't think that bicameral hallucinations were first experienced as external and then slowly became recognized as one's own internal thoughts. The reason that auditory hallucinations are experienced as "alien" seems to be that they originate in the non-dominant hemisphere. On the other hand, inner speech seems to involve activity in the pre-frontal cortex — by some accounts specifically the left inferior frontal gyrus.[51] We have to keep in mind that some people still experience both thoughts that they attribute to themselves and auditory hallucinations that they experience as "external" or "alien." So to use the computer metaphor, whereas most people replaced one operating system with another, some individuals are still running both in parallel.

So I wanted to take a moment to offer those perspectives — as I've seen some of these objections or general themes raised before, I think it's important to at least attempt to address them. There is still a great deal of confusion as to these more nuanced aspects of Jaynes's theory, and it's challenging to try to move the theory forward without first clarifying some of these issues.

So first your thoughts on that — if there's anything that you'd like to add or respond to, or anything you think I'm getting wrong on this — and then, any final thoughts on Jaynes's theory or anything else that we've covered? You have the last word.

KIHLSTROM: I appreciate your clarifications. I think that Zelazo's ideas about the development of consciousness are quite interesting. Antonio Damasio has offered similar notions.[52] I'd only note that other things seem to develop as children develop consciousness, like the theory of mind. And I really doubt that language is critical for the development of consciousness. If Jaynes is right (and I think he is), we had language before we had consciousness in his sense. And just because chimpanzees don't typically pass the false-belief test of theory of mind, doesn't mean that they don't have a theory of the chimpanzee mind. Based on evolutionary theory,

51. A. Morin and B. Hamper, "Self-Reflection and the Inner Voice: Activation of the Left Inferior Frontal Gyrus During Perceptual and Conceptual Self-Referential Thinking," *The Open Neuroimaging Journal*, 2012, 6, 78-89.

52. A. Damasio, "How the Brain Creates the Mind," *Scientific American*, 1999, 281, 6; A. Damasio, *Self Comes to Mind: Constructing the Conscious Brain* (Pantheon, 2010).

they've got to have something like human consciousness — the notion that "I think" and "I feel" — even though they don't have language.

I agree that the split-brain model, and hemispheric specialization in general, offered Jaynes an excellent heuristic model for what he was talking about. I also agree about the role of the self in consciousness, and about the role of language in consolidating the theory of mind in individuals and propagating it through cultures. I still disagree about the role of language in the "origins" of consciousness, because I assume that there is some level of consciousness, in Jaynes's sense of "consciousness of consciousness," in nonhuman animals who lack the human capacity for language.

Otherwise, I'm sticking to my story: Jaynes offered important insights into the history and cultural evolution of consciousness, based on his reading of ancient literature. But just as his theory doesn't stand or fall on its ability to explain hypnosis, it also doesn't stand or fall on any neurobiological facts. It stands or falls at the psychological and sociocultural levels of analysis — basically, on the philology. I don't read Greek, but my reading of the *Iliad* and the *Odyssey* in English translation (first Fitzgerald, later Fagles) comports with his. And I think that the framework offered by the theory of mind and metacognition offers a new perspective on the cultural evolution of consciousness that is fully compatible with Jaynes's insights. There's a point in life when individuals realize that their thoughts, feelings, and desires are the product of their own minds — which of course was always the case; and there's a time in history when that discovery was embraced by an entire culture.

KUIJSTEN: You've been extremely generous with your time — thank you again for discussing these topics and for sharing some of your very relevant research. I'd like to also thank you for your willingness to have more of a back and forth discussion. I think that's an important part of the process, and I enjoyed hearing your different perspectives on some of these issues — it helps with understanding where there are opportunities to extend Jaynes's theory into new areas, as well as to understand where some of the obstacles are in terms of the acceptance of Jaynes's theory.

KIHLSTROM: You're welcome, and thank you for asking me to participate in this project. I taught about Jaynes for almost 40 years, in one way or another, but never had a chance to get my thoughts in print, or to discuss them with someone who has a deep knowledge of Jaynes's theory.

HYPOTHESIS III

Dating the Transition from
Bicameral Mentality to Consciousness

16

Consciousness, Cave Art, and Dreams

Marcel Kuijsten

Interviewed by Brendan Leahy

BRENDAN LEAHY: Jaynes's third hypothesis is dating the transition from bicameral mentality to consciousness to roughly 1500 to 1200 BCE in the cultures around the Mediterranean. Can you talk about some of the evidence that Jaynes provides with regard to the dating for this transition?

MARCEL KUIJSTEN: Yes, there are a number of lines of evidence. Jaynes looked at the development of the words in ancient Greek that eventually came to mean "mind," such as the word *noos*. And initially, each of these words referred either to physical processes like "vision" or "to see," or they referred to parts of the body like the heart or the lungs. It was not until later that the meaning of these words evolved to mean things like "conscious mind." And so the thinking is that if the ancient Greeks did not have words for consciousness, they likely did not have the experience of consciousness.

Another line of evidence that Jaynes pursues is a linguistic analysis of ancient texts that are of a sufficient length and a reliable translation, such as the *Iliad*. And in the older layers of the *Iliad* — scholars believe that there were later additions — we see no evidence of introspection. The *Iliad* is very action-oriented, and in the moments that would normally call for introspection — for example, having to make a difficult decision — a god appears and commands their behavior. By contrast, the *Odyssey*, which reflects a more recent mentality, is full of introspection and deception.[1] We

---

1. See the interview with Boban Dedović, "The Evolution of Mental Language in the *Iliad* and the *Odyssey*," in this volume.

see a similar evolution of the language of introspection in other ancient texts as well, such as the Old Testament.[2]

Since the publication of Jaynes's book, other scholars have documented a similar evolution of words that came to mean "conscious mind" from more basic physical or bodily referents in other cultures. For example, Michael Carr has documented this in ancient China and Todd Gibson has documented this in ancient Tibet.[3]

LEAHY: In *Reflections on the Dawn of Consciousness,* you describe the case of a child with autism that supports Jaynes's third hypothesis. Can you describe that case?

KUIJSTEN: Yes, there is a well known case of a girl with autism named Nadia, who was described by the British psychologist Nicholas Humphrey. And Humphrey describes how Nadia, who had not acquired language by the age of three or four, made beautiful drawings of horses and other animals that were strikingly similar to what we see in early cave art.[4]

One of the popular views on consciousness — and it's really just speculation — is that the emergence of cave art should be viewed as an indication of the development of consciousness. In other words, because humans were drawing these interesting cave paintings about 50,000 years ago, this tells us that they had developed the modern mind.

Well, the case of Nadia essentially debunked that view, because here we have a four-year-old girl who had no language ability and did not possess many of what we would consider to be the features of consciousness, but she was drawing these beautiful horses and things that were very similar to cave art paintings. Interestingly, a few years later, after she did start to acquire some vocabulary, her artistic ability diminished.

So it may actually be the case that cave art is evidence that humans at that time *did not* have sophisticated language, and certainly not anything close to the modern mind. Jaynes explains that what these images likely represent are a type of rendering from photographic memory, called *eidetic imagery*. They likely had visual hallucinations of the animals that they were

2. See the interviews with James Cohn, "The Bible as a Written Record of the Dawn of Consciousness" and Brian McVeigh, "Evidence for Bicameral Mentality in the Bible," in this volume.
3. Michael Carr, "Sidelights on *Xin* 'Heart, Mind' in the *Shijing*," *Proceedings of the 31st CISHAAN*, Tokyo and Kyoto, 1983, 824-825, summarized in M. Carr, "The *Shi* 'Corpse/Personator' Ceremony In Early China," in M. Kuijsten (ed.) *Reflections on the Dawn of Consciousness* (Julian Jaynes Society, 2006); Todd Gibson, "Souls, Gods, Kings, and Mountains" in M. Kuijsten (ed.) *Gods, Voices, and the Bicameral Mind* (Julian Jaynes Society, 2016).
4. Nicholas Humphrey, "Cave Art, Autism, and the Evolution of the Human Mind," *Cambridge Archaeological Journal*, 1998, 8, 2, 165-191.

hunting, and they rendered these images from photographic memory onto the cave walls.[5]

It's interesting to note that the animals are beautifully drawn, but any drawings of people are nearly always just stick figures. Another reason why it's unlikely that this was any kind of artistic expression in the modern sense is that new drawings were placed right over the old ones, with no regard for what was there previously. They were also placed deep in caves, and not where others could observe them. So there are a number of different reasons to believe that the people who were drawing the cave paintings did not have modern consciousness as we know it, and the case of Nadia makes that point very clear.

LEAHY: How do dreams factor into Jaynes's theory, with respect to dating the development of consciousness?

KUIJSTEN: Dreams are a fascinating area of Jaynes's theory. Jaynes wrote a chapter on dreams, which was initially going to be included in his first book, but then was held for the second book that was never completed. I looked at the readings on dreams that were assigned by Jaynes to his students on his course syllabus, and I was able to get a fairly good idea of what his ideas were on dreams. Later I discovered a lecture by Jaynes on dreams, and this confirmed my earlier conclusions.[6]

Dreams turn out to be a fascinating way to gauge the development of consciousness in an individual or in a culture. Like most people, I thought that dreams had been consistent throughout recorded history — that there was essentially no difference between dreams in ancient societies and modern societies — but this turns out not to be the case. There are actually major differences in dreams both in ancient cultures and preliterate societies, when contrasted with modern culture.

In our modern, conscious dreams, we see ourselves engaging in all kinds of different activities, and these activities take place in other places. Jaynes uses the terms *vicarial* and *translocative* to underscore the fact that in modern dreams, we observe ourselves taking various actions, and those actions take place in other locations — in other words, you are not dreaming that you are asleep in your bed.

---

5. Julian Jaynes, "Paleolithic Cave Paintings As Eidetic Images," *Behavioral and Brain Sciences*, 1979, 2, 605-607; reprinted in M. Kuijsten (ed.), *The Julian Jaynes Collection* (Julian Jaynes Society, 2012). See also, David Lewis-Williams, *The Mind in the Cave: Consciousness and the Origins of Art* (Thames & Hudson, 2002).

6. Julian Jaynes, "The Dream of Agamemnon," in M. Kuijsten (ed.), *The Julian Jaynes Collection* (Julian Jaynes Society, 2012).

By contrast, in ancient dreams — in the oldest records of dreams that we have — the individual is lying in bed, and they are visited by a god, or perhaps a deceased relative. The god or spirit, who often stands at the head of the bed for some reason, then issues a command or guidance. So these visitation dreams, as they are called — we might call them bicameral dreams — very much parallel the waking bicameral experience of hearing voices from a god directing one's behavior.[7]

We can think of modern dreams as consciousness operating during sleep. Because people in ancient bicameral civilizations did not possess the modern, subjective consciousness that we have today, they did not see themselves acting vicariously and in other locations in their dreams.

Visitation dreams have been well documented in preliterate societies as well. They are sometimes called "divine dreams," or "prophetic dreams." Members of preliterate societies often view dreams as a form of divination, or as means of contacting spirits or dead ancestors in order to understand their requests or commands. Thus, waking bicameral hallucinations and visitation — or bicameral — dreams are like two sides of the same coin. And for reasons that are not entirely clear, bicameral dreams seem to have been more of a point of emphasis in Mesopotamia and Egypt than in other cultures, at least from what we know from the texts that have come down to us.

Perhaps even more interesting, this same transition has been observed in children. There is a certain age when children first start to see themselves as actors in their dreams, and their dreams start to take place in other locations, rather than taking place in their bed.[8] This very much supports the idea that children learn consciousness in the Jaynesian sense as they learn language, and these changes to their psychology are reflected in their dreams.

Far from being unchanged throughout history, dreams provide another window into the transition between bicameral mentality and consciousness. Records of ancient dreams can be used as a tool, along with other lines of evidence, to try to better determine exactly when the transition — or the stages of transition — from bicameral mentality to consciousness took place in a given culture.

---

7. See, for example, Robert Atwan, "The Interpretation of Dreams, The Origin of Consciousness, and the Birth of Tragedy," in *Gods, Voices, and the Bicameral Mind*; E.R. Dodds, *The Greeks and the Irrational* (University of Chicago Press, 1983), Ch. 4; W.V. Harris, *Dreams and Experience in Classical Antiquity* (Harvard University Press, 2009).

8. David Foulkes, *Children's Dreaming and the Development of Consciousness* (Harvard University Press, 1999).

This presents a real problem for the biological view of consciousness. If it were true that consciousness is biologically innate, based solely on the evolution of the brain, and dates back perhaps 50,000 or 100,000 years, then it becomes quite difficult to account for this more recent transition that we see in dreams. But looking at it from the perspective of Jaynes's theory, and a more recent date for the development of consciousness, this makes perfect sense.

LEAHY: Do you think that there is something to the idea of interpreting our dreams?

KUIJSTEN: While I have not done this myself, I do know people that are adamant about keeping a dream journal, and looking for insights in their dreams. I think that it could be a valuable practice, and perhaps another way to get at some of the insights that are in our nonconscious minds. A great deal of problem solving takes place nonconsciously, often during sleep. So whether the solution comes in a dream, or as a flash of insight the next day, the problem was solved outside of consciousness, and I think that's a very important point for people to understand.

Jaynes talks about the content of our dreams in a manner that is very much in line with the thinking of sleep psychologists. He describes dreams as generally being a combination of issues that we're concerned about, recent experiences that we've had, along with sensory elements from our environment — whether we're in a warm or cold room, for example — and these types of things.

It's interesting to note that, in dreams, our consciousness works all of these different elements into some form of narrative, similar to our waking experience of narratization. So our minds are constantly constructing narratives, both when we're awake and when we're asleep. And why this is the case, I don't think anyone really knows. But the primary thing that Jaynes was interested in terms of dreams was noting the major transformation that dreams underwent as we learned consciousness.

LEAHY: Will there be another transition in the future? What are your thoughts on where our consciousness might be headed?

KUIJSTEN: This is a popular question. After Jaynes's lectures, he was often asked, "If consciousness is a relatively recent historical development, and if it's learned and it's not biologically innate, then what is the future of consciousness? Where is it going from here?" Because Jaynesian consciousness is a recent development — perhaps only 3,000 years old — we are to some degree still in the midst of this transition, in that we still see many vestiges of bicameral mentality all around us.

So what is the next step, where is consciousness going from here? Of course no one knows the answer to that, but Jaynes would say that he preferred to be an optimist. He suggested that there is the potential to develop better ways of teaching consciousness to children, for example. Because consciousness, we have to remember, is something that is taught to each successive generation. This idea is somewhat counterintuitive to us, because the process now is more or less invisible. But in the cases of children who are raised in deprived environments, this point becomes very clear: they don't develop the features of Jaynesian consciousness because they don't have the language development necessary to facilitate that.[9]

So perhaps in the future we will develop better ways of teaching the different features of consciousness that Jaynes outlines. I also think that there are things that we can do even as adults to exert greater control over our inner dialogue. We can see this in, for example, modern cognitive behavioral therapy and in various meditative practices that aid people in gaining greater conscious control over their thoughts and behavior — and teaching them to respond less automatically or in less conditioned, habitual ways.

Jaynes suggests that there is the potential to expand consciousness and to develop methods to, for example, gain greater control over our ability to break bad habits.[10] Perhaps in the future, some of the things that currently we are able to achieve with hypnosis, we will be able to do completely on our own. We could simply make a decision to change some habit or behavior, and have the conscious control, or perhaps mental discipline, to follow through. Currently, much of our behavior is habitual and based on nonconscious processes.

Now one could also make the case that as new technology handles more of our tasks and solves more of our problems, that we are thinking less and less and that we run the risk of slowly becoming less conscious. If that's the case, then we may end up in a state that is not necessarily bicameral but that is less conscious than the state we are in now. One can easily find evidence to support either scenario.

---

9. See my interview, "Consciousness and Language," in this volume.

10. Julian Jaynes, "The Consequences of Consciousness: Emory University Discussion," in M. Kuijsten (ed.), *The Julian Jaynes Collection* (Julian Jaynes Society, 2012); see also the interview with Laurence Sugarman, "Authorizing Clinical Hypnosis: From Bicameral Mentality to Autonomy," in this volume.

For example, in ancient Greece, the *aoidoi*, or bards, memorized and recited the entire *Iliad*. Once writing became widespread, that type of memorization was eroded and I think that it would be very difficult for someone to do that today. Anyone that has taken an acting class can tell you how difficult it is to memorize lines. Perhaps the widespread use of calculators has diminished the ability to do math in one's head for many people. So the more that computers and emerging technologies like artificial intelligence and autonomous vehicles do our thinking and actions for us, the more I think at least the potential is there for these technologies to have a negative effect on some of the features of consciousness that Jaynes describes.

It's an interesting side note that current technology has always been used as a metaphor for how the brain works. In the ancient past, the workings of the brain were compared to aqueducts and plumbing. Later the brain was compared to the workings of a machine. In the nineteenth century, it was not uncommon to compare the operations of the brain to the telegraph system. In recent decades, we often talk of the brain as though it were a computer. With the advent of quantum computing, we already see lectures with titles like "Is the brain a quantum computer?" As a result of computer networking and the internet, in recent years there has been more talk of potentially "networking" brains, or linking the brain to external sources of knowledge. Perhaps there is some potential there in the distant future, but I think that these kinds of things are still a very long way off. Metaphors of technology help to frame the way we think about the brain, but it's important to keep in mind that they are just metaphors, and that they are inexact. Metaphors can often be helpful in framing the way we think about things, but they can also be limiting.[11]

When we talk about the future of consciousness, we're generally speaking on a population level, not an individual level. But there are things one can do to enhance our capacity for consciousness right now — there's no need to wait for future technology. One can explore a wide variety of different approaches, including meditation, visualization, and self-hypnosis, just to name a few. Affordable neurofeedback devices are now available that can assist with practicing meditation. There are also various approaches to things like building mental discipline. A key aspect of developing consciousness is learning to increase the gap between stimulus and response — to be able to pause, deliberate, and choose one's actions consciously, rather than reacting automatically. This concept can be applied to nearly every area of one's life.

---

11. Anna Vlasits, "Tech Metaphors Are Holding Back Brain Research," *Wired*, June 22, 2017.

17

The Bible as a Written Record
of the Dawn of Consciousness

Rabbi James Cohn

Interviewed by Brendan Leahy

James Cohn (1952-2018), served as a Rabbi for more than forty years, most recently at Temple Israel, a Reform Jewish congregation in Charleston, West Virginia. He received his M.A. in Hebrew and Cognate Languages and Literatures from Hebrew Union College. He was a talented speaker and writer with a deep understanding of both Biblical history and Julian Jaynes's theory. He authored of *The Minds of the Bible: Speculations on the Cultural Evolution of Human Consciousness*, which is both highly readable and a major contribution to the advancement of our understanding of Jaynes's theory. Rabbi Cohn first spoke on Jaynes's theory at the 2008 Julian Jaynes Conference on Consciousness in Prince Edward Island. In the fall of 2012, he taught a course at Marshall University titled "The Brain, the Self, the Voice of God," that centered on Jaynes's theory and used *The Julian Jaynes Collection* as the course text. In 2013, Rabbi Cohn co-chaired (with Marcel Kuijsten) and helped fund the Julian Jaynes Society Conference on Consciousness and Bicameral Studies — the largest conference ever held on Jaynes's theory.

BRENDAN LEAHY: I'm curious to hear how you came across Julian Jaynes's theory and how your understanding has shifted, like you said it percolated over the course of — I don't know how long?

JAMES COHN: I first read Jaynes's *The Origin of Consciousness* in 1982. At that time I was out of Rabbinical school. I had been serving as a Rabbi, pulpit Rabbi as I am now, and I was intrigued by his juxtaposition of two events chronicled in human literature. One of them is well known, and that's the disappearance of the experience of encountering God in sight and sound as a completely external being apprehended through vision and hearing. The early books of the Bible rely strongly on an immediate direct experience of God through sound and sight, principally through sound. That tends to fade as one moves through the books of the Bible from the deep past until the more recent past.

That was not new. What Jaynes did was to ask the question, "Do we see at the same time, and over the same period, and in an accelerating way as these visions and auditory experiences decelerate, an increased language describing an interior dialogue with the self?" That these two things are not coincidental, that they might be related. And what Jaynes was proposing, which struck me as innovative and explanatory in its power, is that there are simply two ways that culture can frame human experience; they're both in terms of dialogue.

And the dialogue is between two entities. The one, the early one, is between God and me. If I have a question, if I have a dilemma, I go to God, I ask the question, and an answer, a decision is communicated to me, and I carry it out. The other is an internal dialogue with myself. And it struck me when reading Jaynes, that I should pay more attention to this internal dialogue and the way I experience it, and particularly the way I talk about it. It began to strike me that expressions like "I'm so mad at myself," are on some level nonsensical. Statements like "I just don't know what I should do and I'm having an argument with myself over this," or when we say "part of me thinks I should do this, but part of me thinks I should do that."

These expressions create an assumption of some duality that comes together in a single human being that all of us experience. All of us can relate to those statements, even though they are self-contradictory. Who are these two people who are having this dialogue, this argument, this agony over decision-making. So I began to pay attention to that in my own conversations with others and in my own internal experience with this dialogue, particularly my wrestling over decision-making.

It seemed reasonable to me that these were simply two dimensions of the same process. One in which culture externalizes volition, so that God makes a decision, and then I implement it. And one that teaches children to internalize volition, so that we teach introspective consciousness to our children. This means that as children learn language, only then do they acquire the language of "I" and "myself," and after awhile they internalize it. I've been able to notice this process better in my grandchildren than in my children — when you're a parent it's hard to pay attention to this stuff because you're busy putting out one fire after another in terms of parenting.

But as I've watched my grandchildren grow — one experience I had was when Miriam, my granddaughter who is 5 years old, said, "You know I was going to pet Ellen, the cat, and then I remembered she doesn't like to be petted while she's eating and I told myself 'Don't pet her while she's eating!'" Now she had already internalized this experience of having a conversation with herself, she could relate it to me as a conversation she had, and I was able to understand it and relate to it. Of course — great! That's wonderful! You're learning how to be a person in the world. But in another culture, she might have felt some indecision, and then experienced a voice that said, "Don't pet the cat. The cat doesn't like to be petted when it's eating."

Now, Jaynes's conjecture, and I agree with him on this, is that both of those are internal experiences. So according to this supposition, Miriam is not hearing the voice of God, but if the culture structures her experience that way, she will actually experience it as a voice. So the idea is that our earliest ancestors didn't have that dialogue with the self, and that there's this transition period where the voices of the gods go silent, and the dialogue becomes constant. And I think that's correct. I think that's a reasonable explanation based on my going back to texts, looking at words and their meaning, and asking myself if I could subtract that introspective dialogue and still have the text present the way that it does. And I think that is mostly possible if you arrange the books, not in the order in which they appear in the canon — the accepted sequence — but in the order they were likely written.

Let me elaborate on that point. Sometimes someone will say to me, "You know, I've decided to read the Bible from start to finish," and what they do of course is begin with Genesis. Appropriately, because that's the first book, and the book about creation. The problem is, Genesis is not necessarily the oldest book in the Bible in terms of its creation. If you came across a stack of books with all of the title and copyright pages ripped out, you would have the task of trying to identify the sequence of dates of authorship. A book about creation, you would naturally put that earlier than a book about Julius Caesar. The problem is that the book about creation might have been written by Carl Sagan, and the book about Julius Caesar by William Shakespeare. So when you're looking at one book, you're seeing a point of view which is decades old, and when you're looking at another book, you're looking at a point of view that's half a millennium old. But you've got them switched out, and you don't know that because of the subject matter. This is where we have to rely upon good scholarly research, not only in terms of translation but the conjecture about the probable date of composition. And so, if we look at the books in that sequence, the probable date of composition, then I think we can see what Jaynes is describing.

LEAHY: How would you personally order the Old Testament books then, based upon your understanding?

COHN: Everything I'm about to say was known and accepted even in the scholarly community a century and a half ago. This is well before Jaynes and is the substratum of his argument. You look at a book like Amos, the book of the prophet Amos, that prophecy comes into being as one of the very earliest books of the Bible, one of the first to be written. The Torah particularly, the books of Exodus through Deuteronomy, come into being a couple of centuries later, but they're about the exodus from Egypt, which is — read back into history — five centuries before Amos. So if you read the book of Exodus, you're reading a story whose narrative is set five centuries before Amos, but is written a couple of centuries after Amos, but it's retrojected because the people who are writing it have read the book of Amos; people writing the book of Exodus have read Amos' prophecy. So as they write the book of Exodus, they might describe Moses's prophecy this way: "there has never been a prophet like Moses, whom the Lord knew face to face." What that accomplishes, after the prophets of Israel and Judah have started their prophecy, is to say: "any future prophecy is going to be acceptable only as long as it's consistent with Moses's prophecy."

That means that all existing books have to be read within the scope of a new book that is presented as having been written centuries earlier. Some of the prophetic books that happened after the time of the exodus were actually written before the story of the exodus. Some of the prophetic

books written afterwards, some of them are positioned to an earlier period in order to give more authenticity or weight to the books. So if you
look at a book like Ecclesiastes, which is attributed by tradition to King
Solomon, which would put it at about 3,000 years ago, we know that it's
one of the most recent books of the Bible, perhaps a couple of centuries
before the Common Era. There are 800 years between the time that tradition ascribes it to, and the time that it came into being. The book itself
doesn't make that claim, but Jewish and Christian evolving traditions do.
The books supposedly written by Moses were written down many centuries after the time of Moses, but they are put in his mouth as immediate
contemporary experiences that were written down and preserved. That's
how the Pentateuch, the first five books of the Torah, present themselves.

So the challenge for me is to go back and order those books according
to that scholarship, and see if the experience of an immediate and direct
communication with God, if that reporting is reduced at the same time
that experiences of internal dialogue with the self are accelerating, and I
think it is. In fact, I would argue it's pretty difficult to find a word that
accurately responds to our word "myself" anywhere in the early books
of the Hebrew Scriptures, and possibly nowhere at all. Translators will
sometimes freely translate a sentence like, "The fool says in his heart," as
"The fool says to himself." I think we need to look carefully at the word
"heart" (*leb* in Hebrew) which can mean "heart" or "mind," but can also
mean "being," and it might not be an internal dialogue in the way that we
experience it today. It's an assumption.

LEAHY: You're very good at explaining this.

COHN: Some people have said to me, "It's hard to work my way through
Jaynes, and it's much easier to hear you do it." This is the beauty of having
a good disciple. The disciple owes the original idea to you but might be
able to articulate it in a way that a lot of people can understand. And this
is why all great thinkers need translators, to translate the concepts (which
are rendered in plain English) in their work, into another plain English
that might be approachable in a different way. That's what I've tried to do
in my book *The Minds of the Bible*.[1]

LEAHY: Jaynes also discusses the problems inherent in translating ancient
texts, especially with regards to psychological terms. Could you further

---

1. James Cohn, *The Minds of the Bible: Speculations on the Cultural Evolution of Human Consciousness*
(Julian Jaynes Society, 2013).

explain what is problematic about translating ancient texts in regards to contemporary paradigms, vernacular, language, etc.?

COHN: When we encounter any text or any person involved in a process of translating, we're trying to take that person or that text's words and give meaning to them that we understand. So in this conversation there's a translation process, and we have all experienced the difficulties in translation in having a conversation with someone speaking the same language who's in the same culture, it might even be someone we have an intimate relationship with. Translation is a challenge in any connection between people.

It becomes hugely difficult if you're looking at cultures that are different in time and place. The Hebrew Scriptures developed over a period of 3,000 to 2,000 years ago. The translations that people use might be fairly contemporary, and so most people who have an encounter with a translation are relating not to the original text, but to decisions translators made about the meaning. Honest decisions, well thought out decisions, but not necessarily accurate. So the challenge is: how do we know whether our reading of a text in Biblical Hebrew is accurate in twenty-first century English in a way that any of us could understand?

There are two basic approaches to translation. One is to try to render the meaning as literally as possible. The other is called "dynamic," and that is an attempt to give meaning for meaning translation. So it might use contemporary idioms to try to communicate something which is expressed in an ancient Hebrew idiom which doesn't make any sense to us. Sometimes the words have different theological importance. So, for example in the seventh chapter of Isaiah, there's a passage that says "Behold an *almah*" — that's the Hebrew word — "will conceive and bear a child and you will call him Immanuel" — which means "God is with us." The Hebrew word *almah* in the Hebrew Scriptures, generally called the Old Testament, usually means "young woman." But it's translated into *parthenos*, which means "virgin" in the Septuagint, which is a Greek version of the Hebrew Scriptures.

Now, this makes all the difference in the world. If it's a prediction that a virgin will conceive and bear a child, then it's miraculous. If it's a prediction that a young woman will conceive and bear a child, it's not miraculous. And so the theological divergence there is well known and profound. These types of translation issues are also highly problematic when we're trying to understand the psychology of ancient cultures.

LEAHY: How are hallucinations perceived throughout history, and how did this inform Western religions and spirituality?

COHN: There's no word for hallucination in Hebrew Scriptures. There are words for "experiences" that involve visual or auditory components, but those are generally rendered by words that have the root meaning, for example of "vision." So, we would read about the vision of one of the prophets. On their simplest level, these words refer to literal, physical vision, the same word that we would use today to say "I'm going to the eye doctor to get my vision checked." They then become expanded to include other kinds of experiences. In our own day, the word "vision" typically is associated with some idealized expectation of what the world is going to be. So if you go to an organization like Care USA and you look for their vision statement, it's a hope for a world characterized by tolerance, understanding, the meeting of peoples' basic needs, and so on.

The usage among the Biblical prophets is somewhere between those two. It's not literal vision, but it's also not an idealized hope for what the world will be. Usually, these words *chazon* or *mareh* mean an ecstatic experience in which the person experiences through their visual and auditory apparatus, their physical apparatus, some reality that is believed to be authentic and real. It's not considered a hallucination, it's a vision in the sense that something is communicated and experienced in a way that presents ultimate reality and truth.

The expression "vision quest" in some cultures might have some similarity here; some experience which goes beyond the common physical experience of vision, but is considered to be an encounter with some "other." The word "hallucination" is typically used to refer to an experience that is completely internal and not brought into being by an encounter with another person or another being. The word "vision" is used in the Hebrew Scriptures to apply to something that is a genuine encounter with some other, or some perception that is accurate of true reality. There was a gradual historical shift in our understanding from "visions" to "hallucinations."

LEAHY: I'm curious how your understanding of Jaynes has shifted from when you first read his book and were thinking about it, to later when you began speaking about it and having conversations with other Jaynesian scholars. Did that create a shift?

COHN: The big challenge, I think, is accepting the idea that it's possible to think, to calculate, and to plan without introspection. And once one recognizes that that's not only possible, but that we do it all the time, then it's not so outrageous, and it's no insult to the intelligence of our Biblical ancestors to suggest that they did all these things without introspection. And one of the exciting things in research related to the brain is to come to understand that much of our decision-making is made before the challenges to our experience even arise in consciousness.

I became aware of a phenomenon that we all experience which is: I'm driving here to the temple and I'm thinking about a sermon I'm going to be giving at the service once I get to the temple. I'm focusing on that, and I'm imagining it, and I'm playing it out forward and backward in my imagination, all while I'm making sound decisions in executing a plan and revising my plan if I need to because of a change in a traffic light or someone suddenly veering into my lane. I'm able to do all these things accurately and competently without them being the focus of my imagined mental landscape. These things can happen separately and independently.

As I began to apply these ideas, it became clear to me that Jaynes was on the right track. That doesn't mean that all of his conjectures ended up being conjectures that my exploration validated. I think, for example, when he talks about stresses, national and cultural stresses, that lead to changes in the mentality of a people, when he talks about the Exodus being that shift source for the Hebrew and Israelite peoples, I think he's wrong about that. I think that's not the experience to focus on because we don't have independent confirmation of the Exodus apart from scripture. There are a couple of possibilities that might seem to support it, but they're not clear.

What we do know as historical is the destruction of the ancient temple, in the sixth century before the Common Era, by the Babylonians, and the deportation of most of the people of Judah to Babylonia. That I think is the key, because that is the place where God's voice was experienced and heard, at that point in the culture of the Israelite people. And when that was taken away there was a crisis. In my view, that's a more important event with regard to how historical developments changed the evolution of mentalities than the Exodus.

LEAHY: Could you elaborate on how you reconciled Jaynes to your spiritual and religious identity?

COHN: My approach to the Bible has always been an approach that operates on the belief that the Bible is a human document produced by human minds, using human language, and that it describes our ancestors' way about thinking about God and the world rather than God's communication to us about how we should understand the world. That is called the "historical critical" view of scripture; "critical" in the sense of being based on whatever the best current scholarship is. So I've always been focused on that scholarly and evidence-based interpretation.

If I had started with a view of scripture as literal and infallible "Truth" with a capital "T," there's no way I would have been open to what Jaynes was saying, because Jaynes began with that same assumption that I've held all my life. That assumption opened the door for me to look at different ways of thinking about the text and different ways of translating it. Now, the thing that attracted me to Hebrew Union College, which is where I was ordained, was an interest in learning about ancient texts, the more ancient the better. I wanted to see what the people who wrote the earliest texts were thinking about. And the only way I have to do that is through their words — it's all we have. Daniel Dennett calls this "software archaeology."[2] In the same way that we try to figure out what a broken vase looked like before it became a part of a rubbish heap, we have to look at scripture and try to disentangle the ways in which it came into being.

The thing about scripture that is different from the archaeological excavation of a vase is that scripture has been in continuous use for the past two to three thousand years, depending upon which scripture you're looking at. These are the stories we are taught in childhood: we learn about Joseph and his brothers, we learn about Abraham and Issac, and because we experience them as narratives about people struggling with their lives, we tend to see them as approachable characters who thought and lived pretty much as we do — allowing for the historical changes that have happened, but pretty much people like you and me. It's what Jan Sleutels calls the "Flintstone Fallacy."[3] It's a mistake we would never make with the Flintstones, but we tend to think that way about the characters of the Bible, who seem much more contemporary to us than say, the characters in Chaucer, who seem very far away from us, although they're much more recent in time.

The English translations of the Bible that we use go back to the seventeenth century — the very earliest are from the sixteenth century, after

---

2. Daniel Dennett, "Julian Jaynes's Software Archeology," *Canadian Psychology*, 1986, 27, 2.
3. See the interview with Jan Sleutels, "Julian Jaynes and Contemporary Philosophy of Mind," in this volume.

Chaucer, and they're written in language that's much more approachable to us. So, if we open up an English translation of the Bible, particularly if it's a fairly recent contemporary translation, it's going to seem to describe characters who are pretty much like us, only historical. But it might be that that's not the case, and what's contemporary is not the way they experienced the world, but the way that contemporary translators translate the texts, because their assumption is that words then mean the same as words now.

But there are difficulties — I'll give you an example. In the third chapter of the book of Genesis, there's a statement that the serpent was a creature who was the most *arum* of all the creatures. The word *arum* is translated in various ways. Depending on which translation you read, it might be "clever," it might be "subtle," it might be "crafty," it might be "deceptive," it might be "wily." So what I try to do is look at a single translation, for example the King James Bible, and see how that word is translated in other appearances and instances. It's used several times in the book of Proverbs, but it's translated three different ways, just in the book of Proverbs. Sometimes it's translated as "wisdom," sometimes it's translated as "prudence," and sometimes it's translated as "subtlety" — all of which are different from "crafty." "Crafty" has a kind of negative quality to it, so when we describe the serpent as "crafty," we're already putting a spin on the character of the serpent. Then if we look at the word "crafty" itself in English, it has a historical evolution. The earliest appearances in English of the word "crafty" are not negative; to be "crafty" means to be a good craftsperson. It is only later that it comes to have the negative connotations of being deceptive.

Most religious traditions view the serpent negatively — in the three monotheistic religions. And therefore the tendency in translating is to look at that word and give it a negative spin. The thing is if we do that, we're missing lots of connections, not the least of which is that there's a play on words in the proceeding sentence. There's a reference to Adam and Eve being naked and unashamed, and the Hebrew word for "naked" is *erom*, which is a play on *arum*. So to be "naked" is very close to being "crafty" or "prudent," and later in chapter three when God says, "who told you that you were naked?", there is also a play on words: "who told you that you were wise? who told you that you were prudent?" — which is what would happen if you were eating from the tree of knowledge of good and evil. So the language is important and the way we choose to cast it makes a difference both in the ways that we encounter the text but also in how we filter it through the lens of our own culture.

I think the most crucial distinction to be made in approaches to the Bible is whether or not one understands the Bible to be a communication from God, or a human expression of what the people who wrote it believed and understood about God. Those are part and parcel of different worldviews; you either see the world as a world in which God communicates through a perfectly revealed, perfectly communicated text to human beings, or whether you believe there's no proof that such a document exists. And I fall into that latter category, which means that although I have a particular kinship and affection with Hebrew Scriptures, in principal I don't presume that it's any more or less accurate in describing reality or God than any other scripture; it's just my peoples' story, so it's compelling to me in a different way — it's our narrative.

That difference I think is the major dividing difference in how one approaches scripture. If one approaches it as a human document, it's not such a huge leap to look at Jaynes's conjecture and say, "this is interesting." That's not necessarily to say it's proven. There's no way to prove every aspect of it because there's no way to know what the contents of consciousness were on the part of the person writing the text. But we should, from our own experience, be able to recognize that there are enough difficulties in communicating from one person to another in our own culture to recognize that perhaps our understanding of ancient cultures is at least as subject to the same possibility of error and differences in thinking — if not much more so.

If I had to pick the most important statement that Jaynes made in terms of my own resonance to his understanding, it's this: Jaynes said (and I'm paraphrasing), "Give me a desert island, 200 actors, and a newborn baby, and let me write the script, and I can raise that child to experience their internal conversation as a dialogue with the self or as a conversation with God, depending on how I write the script, and how the actors read their lines."[4] That coalesced everything for me, and it is I think the best essential starting point: if the culture supports an idea, is it possible to frame reality that way so that newly born children will be acculturated to understand their reality that way? And if that's the case, to me that's sufficient.

4. Julian Jaynes, "McMaster-Bauer Symposium on Consciousness: Response to Discussants," *Canadian Psychology*, 1986, 27, 2; reprinted in M. Kuijsten (ed.), *The Julian Jaynes Collection* (Julian Jaynes Society, 2012).

Let me mention something that I think is a great illustration. In Bob Newhart's sketch comedy there's a driving instructor. The driving instructor is sitting in the passenger seat and talking to the student driver, and says, "Ok, I want you to turn here. Oh! Sorry, that was my fault, I meant at the street." The reason that's funny is because the contents of the driving instructor's consciousness were not the same as the contents of the student's consciousness. If that's funny because we can understand how such an error can be made, then it's not too great a leap to think that perhaps we could be erroneous in our understanding of what someone said 2,500 years ago, and what they meant by it.

There's also a joke about the mother who looks at the four-year-old who has put the left shoe on the right foot and the right shoe on the left foot, and says, "Oh honey, your shoes are on the wrong feet." And the four-year-old says, "But these are the only feet I have…" You can tell that joke to a three-year-old, and you might not get much traction with it. But if you tell it to a five or six-year-old, they get it immediately, it's hilarious to them. They understand the use of metaphor, they understand how misunderstanding can happen, they are able to narratize into a mental mind space, they're able to narratize into a conceptual mind space: what the child was thinking when the mother was speaking, what the mother was thinking when she was speaking, how the language got corrupted in translation, and get the joke. I'm not sure that joke would come across if you told it in 1000 BCE Israel.

LEAHY: Do you think religions will have to evolve to survive in the contemporary spiritual realm?

COHN: I define religion as human beings' complete response to reality: the person's mental/intellectual response — the person's psychic response — the person's emotional response. Reality is something that we encounter through whatever tools our culture provides to our disposal. Science is a tool that tells us things about reality. Our own experience of our mental life is something that tells us about reality. Some people regard scripture as something that tells us about reality. Religion is the way that I, as an individual, or we as a community, respond in all of the dimensions of our life to what that truth is. As the perception of the truth changes, then our response has to also change. That doesn't mean that God changes — that doesn't mean that reality changes — but it does mean that my response is going to change, based on the closer I can get, albeit imperfect, to truth.

LEAHY: Did any members of your congregation attend the conference that you co-chaired on Julian Jaynes's theory?

COHN: Yes, there were members of the Temple Israel and there were other people who were not temple members, not Jewish, who live in Charleston or in West Virginia, who came. And of course people came from all over — all over the U.S. and from seven or eight different countries. It was remarkable to see how wide the appeal was of Jaynes's understanding of the development of introspection. And I mean diverse in terms of culture, nationality, disciplines — it was a great opportunity to experience fertility of thinking. And it was fun!

LEAHY: Do you have an idea as to why his theories appeal to so many people, while others have difficulty with it?

COHN: I think the biggest roadblock for people encountering Jaynes's thinking is his employment of the word "consciousness." That's not a settled word in the academic community, it's not settled in psychology, it's not settled in neurology. Some people understand consciousness to mean, on its lowest level, simple irritability, so that if you poke a one-celled organism and it shies away, that would be considered "consciousness." Some people identify consciousness with certain types of brain function. If Jaynes had not used the word "consciousness" and had focused instead on our experience of introspection, I think it's possible that many of the people who don't engage with his ideas would be able to overcome their aversion. The word "consciousness" is problematic.

On the plus side, recent research in brain studies seems to bear out much of what Jaynes was saying in terms of the interaction of left and right hemispheres — the importance of having two hemispheres, which Jaynes suggested is not unrelated to the dialogue with the self. For example, Michael Gazzaniga's related work on split-brain patients, who have their corpus callosum severed, surgically or through accident — particularly those who had already reached maturity before that surgical procedure was performed. Also relevant is our understanding of autism spectrum disorder, our understanding of remarkable people like Kim Peak — "Rain Man" — and especially our understanding that interior subjective introspection is not required for extremely accurate, sophisticated judgments, decisions, and calculations. In other words, our understanding that it is possible for people to think and solve problems — often very complex problems — without introspective subjectivity.

We should also remember that Jaynes's theory is not an all or nothing proposition. One can accept some of the specific applications that Jaynes or his proponents advance while rejecting others. For me, the great "aha" moment was simply to recognize that he was on to something. I don't know of any other explanation that charts together the rise of introspective language, a dialogue with the self, and the disappearance of a heard voice of God. I don't know of any other explanation that satisfies the need the way that Jaynes does. If one comes along, I'll be happy to consider it.

I'd like to put the onus on those who say that our Biblical ancestors did have a mentality similar to ours. The question isn't, "Why does Jaynes insist that they didn't have a mentality that was familiar to us?" The question should be, "Why is it necessary for us to assume that they did?" We should come to understand that our mentality, our way of interpreting and giving meaning to our experience, is shaped not only by our genes and our neurons, but also by our culture and our language. If one doesn't have the words to describe a subjective interior existence, it's very difficult to experience it. This is part of what modern philosophy is all about — a recognition that our way of thinking is significantly affected by the words and the syntax that are available to us.

Further Reading

Rabbi James Cohn, *The Minds of the Bible: Speculations on the Cultural Evolution of Human Consciousness* (Julian Jaynes Society, 2013).

18

Evidence for Bicameral Mentality in the Bible

Brian J. McVeigh

Interviewed by Marcel Kuijsten

MARCEL KUIJSTEN: You've recently published a book titled *The Psychology of the Bible: Explaining Divine Voices and Visions.*[1] To start with, could you give us a summary of your new book and some of your main arguments?

BRIAN McVEIGH: This book really is inspired by my interest in how history and psychology interact. And I think there's no better record than the Bible, because it deals with so many things that really aren't adequately explained in the literature, especially in psychology. I look at things like prophecy, the role of idolatry, the meaning of angels, and the Ark of the Covenant. I try to address any of the main topics or themes that people usually think of when they hear the word "Bible," and of course I look at things from a Jaynesian perspective.

One of the criticisms I've heard about Jaynes is that "Well, it's an interesting theory but it's just speculation — you can't really scientifically prove or illuminate any of his claims." And of course I completely disagree. I think that you just have to come up with good hypotheses, you have to use good research tools, and you can show that either Jaynes has something to offer us or that Jaynes was wrong. And that's what I try to do in this book about the Bible. I rely on linguistic analysis and I reinterpret certain quotations — certain parts of the Bible — to show how they make sense from

1. Brian J. McVeigh, *The Psychology of the Bible: Explaining Divine Voices and Visions* (Imprint Academic, 2020).

a Jaynesian perspective. I also look at, for example, the changing definition of God — I ask the question, "Why has the definition of God changed so much within the Old Testament itself?" I also rely on systems and communication theory to look at consciousness as a problem of communication. Those are some of the key aspects of the book.

KUIJSTEN: That sounds very interesting. We know Jaynes writes about the Old Testament in his book, and he looked at it as a way of documenting the transition from bicameral mentality to consciousness, but why did you choose to do this project and why did you want to use the Bible specifically to test Jaynes's theory?

McVEIGH: So if the claims of Jaynes hold any weight, they should be indicated in ancient texts. And I think they are, of course. But the Bible is a bit different, in a sense, because the Bible offers us a more or less continuous record from different periods that trace out the bicameral period, or close to the end of the bicameral period — the semi-bicameral period, we might say, where we have a lot of vestiges of bicameral mentality — the emergence of consciousness, and then what we might call full-blown consciousness. So there's really no other ancient religious texts that show the transition in such a step-by-step manner. The Bible is a very valuable piece of evidence in trying to understand Jaynes.

And of course the good thing about the Bible — whether you're a believer or not — is that everyone is familiar with it, at least to a degree. It's divided into the Old Testament and New Testament, and divided into books, chapters, and verses. If anyone wants to question a claim that I make or that Jaynes makes, or they want to do their own research, it's relatively easy. Of course there's the problem of learning ancient Hebrew and Greek, but nevertheless the Bible offers us a window into a transition of mentality.

KUIJSTEN: What were some of the challenges that you had with this project?

McVEIGH: Well, for the sake of convenience, I would put them into three categories. The first one is the dating of the books, because of course Jaynes's arguments don't make much sense unless you can follow a certain trajectory. Before I say anything about dating, there is a very important point that should be made: we have to make a clear distinction between when a book was written versus what period the book refers to. For example, a good number of books in the Old Testament were compiled in the fifth or sixth century BCE, however they often refer to events that happened centuries earlier. We have to keep that in mind. In terms of the dating, there's a lot that can be said. I don't get into it too much in my book — there are a lot of debates about it — but I rely on what's called the "Documentary Hypothesis," which views the Old Testament as coming in four different layers, and that seems to work. That's the first issue.

The second issue concerns which Bible do we use. Right now, in English at least, there may be anywhere between 15 to 20 different Bibles.

KUIJSTEN: Wow!

McVEIGH: Yes, and this is very problematic for a number of reasons. But I asked the advice of Rabbi James Cohn on this issue — who you know — before he unfortunately passed away. He advised me that, at least with regards to the Old Testament, for quotations and things of that nature, I should rely on the publication by the Jewish Publication Society, which is just called the Jewish Bible, the Tanakh.

With the New Testament I rely on different books, but overall what I try to do is get to what we might call more of a literal translation of the text, rather than relying on some Bibles which try to update the language and try to make the language accommodate modern sensibilities. I'm more interested in revealing just how different — how alien — the mentality of the ancient Israelites was. That's the second issue.

There's a third issue with regard to methodology that concerns interpretation. To give you one example of how problematic it can be, I took 14 Bibles and then I looked at eight or nine key terms across those texts. And for example, the word "angel" in one Bible shows up 231 times, while in another Bible it doesn't show up at all — which is very surprising, because we assume that we know what all of these words mean.

Another key term that we take for granted is "soul." In one Bible it shows up 458 times, and in another Bible it shows up 45 times. That's just two examples, and while those are a bit extreme, there are other examples as well that show us the incredible variation when it comes to translating what these terms mean.

There's something else related to interpretation that I should mention that is related to this. We hear words like "heaven," "hell," "evil," "sin," "soul," all the time, and we assume that these terms were used in the Old Testament, and of course we can find some of those words, but often they meant something completely different. Because people forget: the Bible is not a work of theology — the Bible was a recording of religious experiences that people had. And of course a lot of it is didactic, but the Bible is not trying to explain or theorize on certain things, such as "heaven," "hell," "sin," "evil." I just mention these examples to illustrate what a challenge it is to come to terms with a book that to my mind — especially the earlier books of the Old Testament — reveals a very different mentality.

KUIJSTEN: It sounds like you did a tremendous amount of research and dealt with a number of different issues that many people aren't aware of. Jaynes also discusses the difficulty of translating ancient texts — not only ancient Hebrew, but also Sumerian, ancient Egyptian, and ancient Greek — and how quite often there is a great deal of modern interpretation and modern psychology that gets put into these translations, and what an enormous problem that is. It will be necessary to go back and re-translate these ancient texts more literally and through the lens of Jaynes's theory.

So it's important that you underscore the problem of the translations. Rabbi Cohn addressed this problem as well — he gave a lecture on this topic, and we have that available for people to watch.[2] Literal translations will be critical to getting a more accurate understanding of the time period that Jaynes discusses, and the degree to which many of the ancient texts have been artificially modernized is a big problem.

In your book you describe something you call the "Bicameral Civilizational Inventory Hypothesis" — can you explain that?

McVEIGH: Yes, that's a mouthful, so I abbreviate it to "BCI Hypothesis," and really it's a challenge to researchers who are interested in Jaynes to find civilizations before about 1000 BCE that lacked the traits of bicameral mentality, and in my book I list about 17 or 18 of these key traits — based on Jaynes — that I think describe a typical bicameral civilization. So it's a hypothesis — it's meant to show how Jaynes's ideas are either right or wrong.

KUIJSTEN: What are some of the traits that factor into your inventory?

McVEIGH: Well, for example, hearing voices — that's an obvious one I suppose. Also treating statues as idols — as if they're alive. Ancestor worship — treating dead ancestors as though they still play an important role in their lives. And by the way, when you study ancient religions, even in the Near East — for example in Egypt — ancestor worship played a key role.

---

2. James Cohn, "A Jaynesian Philology: The Bible as a Written Record of the Dawn of Consciousness," Julian Jaynes Society, 2013 (https://www.youtube.com/watch?v=P-7I55QWnxM).

People often forget that — ancestor worship is typically associated with the civilizations of East Asia. Something else I would look at: I would also search to see if there are any of what I call "philosophical works" before 1000 BCE. What I mean by "philosophical works" are texts that deal with existential issues or question the existence of gods — you simply don't find that before 1000 BCE. You find people complaining to the gods and begging from the gods, but no one actually questions the existence of the gods. So those are just a few of the traits that I would look at.

KUIJSTEN: That's fascinating. I think it also speaks to some of the confusion people have who are unfamiliar with Jaynes, or new to Jaynes, about the differences between ancient religion and modern religion. It's very easy for people to again impose our modern concepts of religion onto these ancient cultures, when actually it was a very different experience for them — having the gods always present and, as you said, not having any question as to their existence, versus this much more philosophical type of religion that we have today. Something you talk about in the book is the concept of "super-religiosity." Would you like to say something about that?

McVEIGH: I know that the term "super-religiosity" is a little bit baroque, but the idea is to stress that there was a significant rupture in the history of humankind — again around 1000 BCE depending on where you happen to look. Before 1000 BCE, you have super-religiosity — which more or less means the same thing as a bicameral civilization — and then after 1000 BCE, you have the emergence of the kind of religious beliefs and religious thoughts that we're more comfortable with and that make more sense to us — where people start to question the existence of gods.

KUIJSTEN: Another thing you talk about is the concept of the "mind as a machine for social communication." Can you explain that idea and how it relates to consciousness in the Jaynesian sense?

McVEIGH: A key aspect of consciousness that Jaynes talks about is the idea of volition — who is making the decision. And of course in bicameral civilizations the idea is that your gods or spirits or dead ancestors were making decisions for you — not all decisions but key decisions. The way I view a decision, it basically comes down to problems of communication, command, and control — in military jargon "the three C's."

You can't really make an informed decision unless those three C's are working properly. The idea here is that this communication-command-control process occurs not just between people — not just within social organizations — it also occurs within the individual mind. And the idea is that the bicameral mentality was good enough for a certain level of social complexity, but once that complexity started to strain the structures of society, a new mentality was needed — a new system of communication was needed. The individual psyche would have to scale up to meet the social complexity.

That sounds somewhat abstract, but really what we're talking about is the challenge that any society faces when it comes to making not just the correct decision on how to do something, but also how to make that decision quickly — we're talking about speed. We're very used to speed in modern times of course, but we have to remember that in the ancient world — especially among preconscious people — things did not move so quickly. The idea is that as societies transitioned from bicameral mentality to consciousness, they were able to exchange information faster, they were able to convey and express their sentiments with better nuance, they were able to overall meet social demands as societies became more complex. Basically the idea here is to view the mind as a piece of machinery that had to be upgraded because of social complexity.

KUIJSTEN: You describe how communication seems to be breaking down in certain instances. Can you share some of those examples?

McVEIGH: Yes. When you turn to the Bible, there are examples of the breakdown of communication — many examples where you have patterns of very odd communication.

For example, mistaken identity is a theme in certain books of the Old Testament, and there are many cases where it's not clear if a person is communicating with God, or the same person may think he or she is communicating with an angel, or maybe someone in their family. Another example is inconsistency between persons when it comes to communicating with Yahweh. For example, in the Book of Numbers there's a scene where Moses, Aaron, and Miriam all claim to be speaking for Yahweh, and yet in the text it's not clear. And one final example is inconsistency within the person when it comes to lines of communication. You'll have someone who will hear God tell him or her to do one thing, and then the next moment God tells them to do something else, contradicting the first command.

In any case, you can see that as bicameral mentality was breaking down, the lines of communication were getting tangled. And I think the fact that they recorded these stories of inconsistent communication must have meant something. Those are some examples to make my claim more concrete.

KUIJSTEN: It's interesting that you've been able to document the changing nature of the voices and the kind of confusion that results. We can also compare and contrast that with people who hear voices today. Something that has always been fascinating to me is the somewhat artificial break that's been created between hearing voices in the ancient world and modern voice hearing. Those two phenomena have always been treated so differently, and while perhaps there's been a few others, Jaynes was really the first to connect the dots between the psychology of these ancient cultures and modern psychology.

On the one hand, most psychiatrists and psychologists are focused on their patients and mental illness in the modern world, while on the other, most classicists apparently are not particularly interested in psychology. If one reads books about ancient civilizations, they document these fascinating phenomena involving all of the rituals with idols and hearing the commands of the gods, but the authors are generally not thinking about these things in terms of their psychology, much less connecting the dots with modern voice hearing.

You also talk about music as being something that is important in the Old Testament, and I think that's something that not everyone is familiar with. Would you like to talk about that?

McVEIGH: Music of course plays a role in all societies, ancient and modern. I have an entire chapter devoted to music, and what I try to do is make linkages between prose, music, poetry, and the right hemisphere, because of course if we do accept a Jaynesian neurology, the right hemisphere is going to play an important role. It's very important to point out that one-third of the Old Testament is written in poetry — that's a lot of poetry. Something must be going on there. We won't get too technical here today, but music and poetry are very much related.

So music-poetry, in fact I call it the music-poetry modality, is significant, and we can ask the question, "When does music-poetry start to become important for people in a society?" We find this anytime we have intense emotions — that's one part of it. The other part is anytime there's a transition or there's a change. Whether it's at the group level or the individual level, we want to hear music or music somehow triggers or facilitates change. So anytime there's a celebration or anytime there's some intense negative emotions, or mourning or grief, we're going to see music-poetry play a big role, as well as if we're leaving or entering a new social status.

We see this in modern times with movies and television programs — try to think of a movie that does not begin and end with music. The idea is that they're trying to draw us in somehow by playing on our emotions. This is a key aspect of the human condition. You'll especially see music when you have an event, such as some sort of supernatural visitation, and in the Bible of course there are many instances where you have perhaps prophets — not necessarily just prophets, but what we can vaguely call a "spiritual specialist" — relying on music in order to trigger a visit from Yahweh or some sort of a hallucination.

KUIJSTEN: That's very interesting — all of these things that in our modern world we more or less take for granted. Also interesting are the neurological aspects to all of this. Jaynes describes the involvement of the right temporal lobe in the bicameral voices. This same area, when stimulated — whether artificially or in cases of temporal lobe epilepsy — often elicits a form of hyper-religiosity. The right temporal region has also been shown to be associated with processing music and poetry.[3] So to have all three of these functions located in the right temporal lobe is both fascinating and also strong supporting evidence for Jaynes's theory — this association really only makes sense in terms of bicameral mentality.

Another thing that you discuss in your book is the revolutionary politics of the early Israelites. Can you explain what you meant by that?

McVEIGH: Sure. Probably it should be reworded "revolutionary theopolitics," or maybe even a "revolutionary theology" of the ancient Israelites, because of course back then there was no difference at all between what we would call politics and religion — that's a very modern idea. To answer your question, I'll start with a little bit of context. At that time, in the neighborhood of the ancient Israelites, maybe eleventh or twelfth century BCE — there's a lot of debate on where the early Israelites came from and who they were, and I don't want to get into that too much. The reason why I say that is because I know that I'm going to offer a very simplistic explanation — the details are more complicated for this, and I do deal with these details in my book.

---

3. Carole Brooks Platt, "Presence, Poetry and the Collaborative Right Hemisphere," *Journal of Consciousness Studies*, 2007, 14, 3; Julie Kane, "Poetry as Right-Hemispheric Language," *Journal of Consciousness Studies*, 2004, 11, 5.

But the context — the theopolitical context at the time — was that most people in that area of the world were living in urbanized areas, you might call them city-states, and these city-states typically had a patron god, and under the god was the king who took orders from the god, and under the king was the priesthood, and under the priesthood were the commoners — peasants and everyone else, and many of these people of course worked outside the walls of the city in the hinterlands.

But the ancient Israelites preferred to be ruled by tribal chieftains, what are called Judges in the Bible. They did not like kings — they were anti-monarchical. Basically the way they saw it, Yahweh was their king — God should be their king.

Now of course we know that eventually, around 1000 BCE, the Israelites did establish a kingdom. But even after the kingdom was established, they still had this powerful idea that no king should directly rule them — and their theology was revolutionary, it was radical at the time. Their idea is that the individual should have a direct line of communication to Yahweh, that there should not be any intermediate bureaucratic layers of priests, kings, and monarchs. And this is something that weaves its way in and out of Judaism, and eventually it would become a key issue in the Judeo-Christian tradition centuries later.

So to sum up, the idea is that even though they did establish a kingship eventually, the ancient Israelites were very suspicious of monarchies and they wanted Yahweh to be their king. In fact, before they established a kingship, Yahweh more or less was their king.

KUIJSTEN: Looking at these concepts through the lens of Jaynes's theory, they take on a completely different meaning. You also talk about Yahweh and how important he is in all of this, and how, in terms of the transition from bicameral mentality to consciousness, the nature of Yahweh changes over time. Can you explain that?

McVEIGH: In the earliest books of the Old Testament, Yahweh comes across as almost just another god. He was anthropomorphic, in many passages — he was someone who communicated to people face-to-face.

Of course eventually — it would take centuries — but probably by the fifth or sixth century BCE, we saw the beginning of strict monotheism. And part of that strict monotheism was the idea that God was not a part of nature — that God was above and beyond nature, that he had created nature. That is another radical idea that came about at this time — because up until that time, most people believed that the gods were somehow a part of nature, or worked within nature. It's an interesting question: why was Yahweh elevated to this sort of "super-God," if you will, above other gods?

So the whole story of Yahweh is much more complicated than most people assume. Yahweh probably came together from a confluence of different local gods — warrior gods, for example. There are many passages in the Old Testament where Yahweh is actually quite violent against the enemies of the ancient Israelites.

I'm mentioning this to show how complicated the evolution of Yahweh was, but the key point here is the transition that Yahweh went through. Yahweh started out as a bicameral god who spoke directly to people. Over time, he would only speak with religious leaders like Moses. Then eventually, Yahweh in a sense became removed from the world. And by the time you get up to around the fourth or fifth century BCE, Yahweh doesn't want to talk to anyone anymore — people stopped having direct revelations, at least they were not supposed to be speaking directly to Yahweh.

KUIJSTEN: Viewing the idea of Yahweh as another way of documenting the transition from bicameral mentality to consciousness is very interesting. This reminds me of a PBS documentary called *From Jesus to Christ: The First Christians*. It provides a lot of background regarding the period where all of this was taking place, and could be thought of as almost a companion piece to this interview. There is a discussion of paganism being the dominant practice during this time, and the idea of there being hundreds of gods. The theologian Holland Hendrix talks about these multitudes of gods, saying, "It [was] like going to a supermarket and being able to sort of shop for God." All of these different gods played different roles and served different functions in people's lives. They describe how the early Jews, with their ideas of monotheism, emerged as a distinct minority from that.

In your book you also discuss "objects of hallucinatory focus." What do you mean by that?

McVEIGH: So concrete examples of objects of hallucinatory focus might be statues, altars, idols, and in the case of the ancient Israelites, the Ark of the Covenant, perhaps even the Tabernacle. In bicameral times, when people wanted to communicate with one of their gods, they probably often had to have their hallucinations triggered, and that was the role of statues and idols.

Now of course among the ancient Israelites, eventually they would develop prohibitions against idols — but they still had some, what we might strictly call idols, such as the Ark of the Covenant. So even though the ancient Israelites trimmed down the number of objects of hallucinatory focus, they did keep a few around, and many times objects of hallucinatory focus were used for divination.

For example, something else that pops up a lot in the Old Testament are what are called *urim* and *thummim*. We're not really clear what they were — some sort of pebbles or stones that were used for divination. Related to the *urim* and *thummim* was the *ephod*, which sometimes seems to be an ornate robe that perhaps the high priest might wear. Other times it seems to be some sort of image.

So among the Israelites, even though they were told many times by the prophets and by Yahweh not to use images or things to worship Yahweh, nevertheless you can find some exceptions. To me, these are good examples of vestiges of bicameral mentality, these material objects being used to trigger hallucinations.

KUIJSTEN: So in your view that's why idols were so important then to the ancient Israelites — they were using them to elicit hallucinations as bicameral mentality began to break down?

McVEIGH: Yes, and it gets somewhat complicated, because as I said, eventually they had strong prohibitions against most idols. However they did allow a few of what we might in a general sense call idols to still be used.

Anytime you read in the Bible, "thou shall not do this, thou shall not do that," you always find many exceptions, and this is definitely true with idols. They have many old Hebrew words for idols — it's almost as if they were obsessed with idols. And if you don't look at the Old Testament carefully, you can get the impression that they took this prohibition of not using idols seriously. But my sense is because they were always talking about idols, and always telling people not to use idols — in fact you could be put to death if you were found using an idol — that must mean the truth is that they were in fact using the idols quite a bit.

KUIJSTEN: You also talk about the concept of "ritual purity" and why that was important to the ancient Israelites. Could you say a few words about that?

McVEIGH: In all societies — ancient and modern — we have a notion of "purity" that we metaphorically connect with being good, with being bad, with being outside the community, or polluted. This is not limited to the ancient Israelites, but because they wrote about it so much, we have good records on it. I think what happened with the ancient Israelites — it seems that as bicameral mentality started to break down, they were no longer supposed to use idols to meet their spiritual needs. The priesthood wanted to remind people that Yahweh is omnipresent — that he is everywhere: "he's nowhere but he's everywhere." He's not in the idols, as was the case in other religions, and yet he is supposed to be this super force that somehow permeates the universe.

So how do you remind people that Yahweh is everywhere? Well, you do that by coming up with a very extensive code of protocols, behaviors, and practices — what we call rituals — in all domains of life. And of course if you're familiar with the Jewish tradition, we can still see many of these rituals that have played such an important role. And to my mind, this is just one way to reinforce Yahweh's authorization: use rituals to remind people that God is watching you.

KUIJSTEN: One of the things Jaynes discusses is the importance of writing, and how writing played a key role in the breakdown of bicameral mentality. Can you explain how the written word was important in terms of this early Jewish spirituality?

MCVEIGH: Yes. Again, written holy texts of course have played and still do play an important role in all religious traditions, but the ancient Israelites really emphasized them. I think the written word started to play the same role as rituals — they needed some sort of authorization that was controlled by a small elite, and that's what the written word was for the ancient Israelites. It codified their beliefs.

It gets somewhat complicated, because what happens is that once you start to write something down, you have more control over it. And the more they wrote down their beliefs, the more bicameral mentality was weakened. Because now you could pick up the Ten Commandments and you could pick up other scrolls and you could move them around. It's a bit of a paradox: on one hand Yahweh's voice is being eroded because of the written text, but at the same time Yahweh's rulership — his authorization — is becoming stronger because they're writing more and more — they are codifying their beliefs to a greater degree.

KUIJSTEN: And it's amazing the tremendous influence that those writings have had, and still have in the world today. Some of the things that I think we take for granted are concepts like angels and demons — we tend to think of them as being part of religion and part of the human experience since the very beginning. But these things had a specific origin. It's something Jaynes touches on, but that you also delve into — the role of angels in the Bible as new messengers to the gods. Can you tell us something about this?

McVEIGH: The more bicameral mentality was weakened, the more societies needed replacements to trigger hallucinations and the more they needed intermediary beings to communicate between themselves and the high gods — in this case Yahweh — and that's the role that angels played.

Now what's interesting is that when we think of angels, many of us think of Christmas cards, where angels are depicted with long, blonde, flowing hair, they are always white, wearing white robes and having wings. But if you look at the Old Testament, that's not the way angels are depicted. Angels are often just ordinary people that appear out of nowhere, as if someone is having a visual hallucination.

The word "angel" comes from the Greek *angelos*, which means "messenger," and in the old Hebrew (רְאָלַמ) it means the same thing: "someone who is conveying a message from God." And in many books in the Old Testament, it's unclear at times whether a passage is saying that God himself is speaking to someone, or God's angel is speaking to someone. But the point being that there was a very close relationship between what an angel does and with what God does — namely, communicating with mortals.

KUIJSTEN: Yes, that is another important piece of evidence in documenting the transition from bicameral mentality to consciousness. First there was no need for messengers, and then over time they play a more and more important role as the psychology changes and the gods retreat.

One of the things that I think we all associate as being tremendously important in the Old Testament are the prophets themselves, and how prophecy arose during this time period — during this transition. Can you talk about the prophets, the importance of prophecy, and how that provides evidence for Jaynes's theory?

McVEIGH: Sure. In my book I dedicate two chapters to the prophets because they were such an important part of Judaic spirituality. A lot has been written about prophets and it gets somewhat complicated. Some scholars make a distinction between the classical prophets versus what we might call "spiritual specialists" — people who may be engaged in prophecy but were not recognized as prophets. And actually, "prophet" is a word that is used to describe not just the classical prophets, but also any great religious leader in Judaic tradition — so it gets very complicated.

But for our purposes, it's important to keep in mind what's taking place when a prophet would prophesize. He — and it almost always was a "he," there are few exceptions of a "she," but it almost always is a "he" — was not engaging in bicameral behavior, but in a vestige of bicameral behavior. Jaynes discusses this, and he's actually not entirely certain what the neurology was. He suggests that when prophets were prophesying, perhaps the speech was being generated by the left hemisphere, however the right hemisphere was controlling the speech, or perhaps controlling the behavior associated with the speech. While it's still unclear exactly what was going on, clearly something was going on, because century after century we see this particular type of religious phenomenon.

In fact, prophets were not something that was found only in the ancient Judaic tradition — you also find the prophets in the ancient Near East, however their role was slightly different. It's not clear, at least to me, whether these prophets were "possessed" by a god. However, that seems to be the case with the Judaic prophets — that they were "possessed" by Yahweh, so to speak. So prophecy in the case of the Judaic prophets can be viewed as a form of spirit possession.

But it seems that in the centuries before the Israelites came on the scene, we can still find something like prophecy. These prophets were a bit different, because with the Jewish prophets, they would take on anybody. They were very strong personalities, very individualistic. They would take on the monarchs, they would take on foreign nations, they would criticize other prophets, and needless to say, they played a very important role in the history of Jewish spirituality. We have to stop and ask ourselves, "If this was considered unusual behavior back then, why was it allowed to carry on for century after century?" And again, that's one of these things where I think scholars and researchers are so used to these things that they forget how strange and unusual these ancient practices were.

KUIJSTEN: Indeed. It's quite difficult for us to step back and look at these things from an intellectual distance — something that Jaynes was quite good at. It's also interesting to observe these cultural differences — where we see an emphasis on prophecy in some places, oracles in others, and divination in other cultures. One of the things Jaynes looks at in documenting the evidence for the birth of consciousness is linguistics, and you also look at the role of language in your book. Can you tell us a little bit about that?

McVEIGH: In an effort to be as objective as possible, I came up with what I call the "Embryonic Psycholexicon Hypothesis." It's a bit of a mouthful, but "embryonic" just means incipient, or early, and "psycholexicon" just means mental language. My hypothesis is that before about 1000 BCE, when you look at those languages, their mental language is either going to be non-existent or very limited. Words that are obviously metaphoric to us are going to be concrete, action-oriented, behavioristic, and often related to internal organs, such as the heart. We still have that vestige in almost all languages. In ancient Hebrew it was called *leb* (בל). They also talked about the liver and the stomach, and they related these experiences to what we would call psychology.

Another aspect to the Embryonic Psycholexicon Hypothesis is that because mental language was so sparse, what took the place of mental language was religious language. One is going to find many more references to gods, spirits, ancestors, and things of that nature. And what I try to do, not just in this book but in earlier writings, is to show how as mental language increases, religious vocabulary decreases. So there is a relationship between them. That's difficult to show, I'll admit, but in any case, I just mention that because it's part of the Embryonic Psycholexicon.

It's very difficult to find words in the Old Testament that are clearly psychological. On page 157 of my book I list several words: *nephesh*, *ruwach*, and *nĕshamah*, and I try to show how difficult it is to determine what these terms meant. These words are often translated as "mind," or something to do with psychology, but when you look at the context — when you look at the actual translation — it's not clear that that's what they mean at all. Again, I just use that as an example to show how challenging it is to come up with a clear vocabulary of mental words.

KUIJSTEN: This is such important evidence and it's fantastic that you've been doing this research. People can certainly delve more into that when they have a copy of your book. I just have a few more questions for you. One of the things Jaynes discusses extensively are vestiges of the bicameral mind. Even today, in our modern world, we are surrounded by vestiges of bicameral mentality, and I think people who read Julian Jaynes's book and really understand his theory come to see much of the world in a very different way. You focus on the important transition that took place between the Old Testament and the New Testament — similar to how Jaynes contrasts the *Iliad* and the *Odyssey* or Amos and Ecclesiastes — and you document the emergence of vestiges of bicameral mentality in the New Testament. Can you tell us about some of these vestiges?

McVeigh: The two main vestiges that seem directly related to the neurology of the bicameral mind are demonic possession and glossolalia. With demonic possession — and this is somewhat questionable because we're not always sure what's going on from the text — for example, is a person actually trancing, or is a person just claiming that they have bad luck in that they're possessed by a spirit? That's a general problem when you study spirit possession — determining if it's trance-related. But it seems to me that in many cases in the New Testament, actual trance is taking place. As a matter of fact, there aren't that many references to demonic possession in the New Testament. On the other hand, when you look at the Old Testament, I don't think there are any clear cut references to demonic possession. The same thing holds true with glossolalia — so these seem to be newer types of psychological phenomena.

Kuijsten: There is important evidence for this transition and it's great that you are bringing so much of this to light. You also discuss the personage of Jesus and how the concept of Jesus factors into this change in ancient mentality. Can you explain what you mean by that?

McVeigh: Sure. By around the fourth or fifth century BCE, people were not supposed to be experiencing voices from Yahweh, and if they did, they had a word for it: *bat kol* (בת קול), which means something like "heavenly voice" or "small voice." So something was going on there. So how does this relate to Jesus? Well, of course people still wanted a connection with God, and one way to connect with God — if it was not going to be through direct revelation — then it would have to be through other people, especially charismatic people such as Jesus.

At that time, there were any number of wandering holy men and reformist rabbis, claiming to be masters, walking around and trying to gather followers. And why Jesus became so important is difficult to understand, but what is important is to focus on what his role was. Because I think anyone could have become a Jesus at that time if they were in the right place at the right time, given what was going on politically and psychologically. It gets very complicated, because Jesus was very much entangled in politics — supposedly being a messiah — so there are many directions that you could go in when you try to analyze the role of Jesus.

But to my mind, Jesus was at that time God's last and ultimate form of self-revelation for believers. You have to remember that for the first two or three centuries of the Common Era, there was really no clear distinction between early Christianity and Rabbinic Judaism — they were really the same thing. It wasn't until later that they started to diverge. And so the idea is that, as I said, Jesus was someone who people took a liking to, because he was God. In a way he represents something of a return to an earlier bicameral period, where you can communicate with God face-to-face, and not only that, he would perform miracles for you.

There are a lot of things that I think we tend to forget about the transition from Judaism to Christianity — for the people who became Christians. One reason for that is we have to understand that Christianity was really a confluence of three different intellectual streams. One stream comes from Judaism — with the belief in a transcendent but personal God, which is an unusual way to look at God: both transcendent and personal. The second confluence came from a sophisticated Greek philosophizing about "divine emanations" — which is a bit mystical. And the third confluence came from the mystery religions that were migrating around the Greco-Roman world at that time — these cults. And from those cults was introduced into Christianity the idea of the self-sacrificing God, who we would eat and drink his blood — which of course does not sound like Jewish spirituality at all. You can see how different these three very different elements were, that came together to form Christianity. I just mention that because while there was some continuity from the Old Testament into the New Testament, there are also some radical ruptures.

KUIJSTEN: It is interesting to view Jesus as another lens through which to look at this transition from the old, bicameral ways, to having a more modern, internal volition.

McVEIGH: Yes, Jesus really fit the time, because he said that "the Kingdom of Heaven is within you." In other words, the Kingdom of Heaven is something psychological — that's how we would express it in modern terms.

KUIJSTEN: This has been very illuminating, thank you for sharing all of your research and knowledge on this topic. I would encourage everyone to read your book, *The Psychology of the Bible*.

McVEIGH: Thank you, it was my pleasure.

19

Evidence for Bicameral
Mentality in Ancient Tibet

Todd Gibson

Interviewed by Marcel Kuijsten and Brian J. McVeigh

Todd Gibson was born in Colorado, and began his working life in natural resources management. He has advanced degrees in Tibetan Studies, and has spent many years in Asia. He currently lives in Thailand. His articles on ancient Tibet and Julian Jaynes's theory, "Souls, Gods, Kings, and Mountains: Julian Jaynes's Theory of the Bicameral Mind in Tibet, Part One," and "Listening for Ancient Voices: Julian Jaynes's Theory of the Bicameral Mind in Tibet, Part Two," appear in *Gods, Voices, and the Bicameral Mind: The Theories of Julian Jaynes*.

MARCEL KUIJSTEN: How did you first become interested in studying Tibetology?

TODD GIBSON: I worked in Forestry as a young man, and had the good luck to be sent to Nepal for a two-year stint there; my interest in the Himalayan region and Inner Asia in general started then. When it became difficult to find forestry work, I went to graduate school at Indiana University to begin a new career in that area. Tibet and Inner Asia are much better understood than formerly, but there is still plenty of unexplored territory for scholars.

KUIJSTEN: When did you first discover Julian Jaynes's theory?

GIBSON: I first heard about it through John Leo's review of Jaynes in *Time* many decades ago (1977, actually), and was immediately fascinated.[1] I bought and read the book as quickly as I could find it.

KUIJSTEN: When did you decide to reexamine early Tibetan culture and linguistics through the lens of Jaynes's theory, to see if you could find evidence for the transition from bicameral mentality to consciousness?

GIBSON: Jaynes's theory was always at the back of my mind, but I didn't connect the two interests until much later, when I was in graduate school. It began to occur to me that the theory could shed a lot of light on little-understood aspects of Tibetan religion and culture.

KUIJSTEN: Let's go through some of your findings. Jaynes documented words in ancient Greek — such as *noos* — that changed in meaning from physical, bodily meanings — such as "vision" or "perception" — to meanings related to "mind" or "consciousness." He argues that these linguistic transitions can be seen as evidence of corresponding psychological changes. Can you describe your similar findings in Tibetan linguistics?

GIBSON: It's really quite difficult to simplify the arguments I present in my paper. Tibet borrowed most of its mentational language from Buddhism, but here and there one finds evidence of how the language dealt with mentational issues before Buddhism arrived. To my mind, the most interesting example is the transformation of the word *tuk* (Tib. *thugs*), which early on referred simply to a rather undefined force that had to be properly handled at death, but which later developed into a term of conscious mentation, so that these days it is often translated simply as "mind."

KUIJSTEN: You suggest that the ancient Tibetan term *ku la* (Tib. *sku bla*) has been misinterpreted and that a more accurate translation would be something like "a king's bicameral voice." Can you elaborate on that?

GIBSON: *Ku la* is a difficult and controversial term, but *la* refers to some sort of vital spirit, and *ku* has to do with its embodiment. The *ku la* was crucial to the functioning of the early kings, and thus the kingdom, and in my work I explain how the concept of a guiding voice fits well with the function of the *ku la*. The term as I see it does not only refer to the bicameral voice itself, but also the object which was its "trigger," which seems early on to have been a mountain, but also might have been an image.

---

1. John Leo, "The Lost Voices of the Gods," *Time*, March 14, 1977.

KUIJSTEN: Can you talk about the role of oracles and shamans in early Tibet?

GIBSON: Little is actually known about the function, or even the existence, of "oracles" and "shamans" in earliest Tibet, and, as Jaynes has emphasized, we have to be very careful about assumptions about the mental processes and religious beliefs of ancient humanity. The popular idea that "shamanism" is mankind's oldest religion is really based more on speculation and even wishful thinking than on empirical evidence; Jaynes touches on this issue several times in his writings. However, religious specialists to whom we can reasonably apply these names, and whom Jaynes would rightly see as comparable to the Greek oracles he discusses in some detail, played a major role in Tibetan religion up until the twentieth century and the destruction of their traditional culture.

KUIJSTEN: Can you discuss the role of spirit guides and other forms of bicameral guiding voices in Tibetan culture?

GIBSON: The most dramatic example of this would be the State Oracle of Tibet, who was relied on by the government of the Dalai Lama in difficult situations, and who made his pronouncements in a state of possession trance. There were other less prominent oracles and visionaries at all levels of Tibetan society, including within Buddhist institutions. At the personal level, there is artistic, literary, and anthropological evidence for guiding voices, sometimes physically located on the shoulder of an individual. There is some literature, for example, which talks about the *drala*, a non-material entity whose name, depending on the spelling used, can either mean "enemy god" or "sound spirit." And in Tibet, as in so many other places in humanity's religious history, there has been a persistent belief in the power of some images to speak.

KUIJSTEN: Can you compare your findings in Tibet to Michael Carr's work on the evidence for bicameral mentality in early China? Are there similarities?

GIBSON: Michael Carr's work was very influential to my approach, particularly his valuable treatment of "personation" of the dead in ancient China.[2] Like the ancient Chinese, Tibetan funeral culture "summons" the spirit of

---

2. Michael Carr, "The *Shi* 'Corpse/Personator' Ceremony in Early China," in M. Kuijsten (ed.), *Reflections on the Dawn of Consciousness* (Julian Jaynes Society, 2006).

the deceased into a concrete talisman, although what happens after that is very different between the two cultures.

KUIJSTEN: Do you think the transition from bicameral mentality to consciousness occurred in Tibet around the same time that it did in the civilizations around the Eastern Mediterranean?

GIBSON: Not at all. My current opinion is that Tibet's geographical situation and cultural history resulted in a much more gradual transition than that proposed by Jaynes for the Near East and Greece, and that as a result what Jaynes might have called residual elements of bicameral mentality persisted much longer.

KUIJSTEN: Can you describe some of the connections you've observed between Jaynes's theory and the Buddhist tradition?

GIBSON: This is another very interesting area which I am currently preparing a publication on.[3] First, I discuss the legend of the Buddha's awakening as an almost perfect mythological encapsulation of the transition from bicameral mentality to consciousness. In this context, it might be mentioned that the Buddha appeared roughly during the so-called "Axial Age," when the problems brought about by a new consciousness appeared all across Eurasia.[4] I then discuss the directions that the Buddhist tradition took after his passing, and the tension and balance — which still characterize Buddhism — between the "rational," objective aspects of the religion (which might be called "left-hemisphere dominant") and the more "religious" aspects, which preserve some elements of bicameral mentality, or at least right-hemisphere inspiration.

BRIAN MCVEIGH: Is there any evidence that *thangka*, or iconographic paintings and mandalas, were originally used to elicit audiovisual hallucinations?

GIBSON: This is a very large question. Of course, much Buddhist art serves simply as a focus for devotion and religious aspiration. In Vajrayana Buddhism, though, visualization of deities plays an important part, and art serves to aid in that process. In some very early Mahayana literature, there were practices in which a meditator would simply practice absorption until a deity appeared, and its authenticity was shown by such things as light rays and voiced pronouncements. Images used for these practices may have

---

3. Todd Gibson, "Buddhism and Bicamerality" (Julian Jaynes Society, 2021).
4. Karl Jaspers, *The Origin and the Goal of History* (Routledge, 1953/2011).

been a later development; in terms of Jaynes's theory this might be because additional support became necessary.

McVEIGH: It seems that concepts in Tibetan Buddhism can have very philosophically sophisticated meanings. But I wonder if certain notions were updated from earlier concepts rooted in an earlier mentality. For example, *yidam* is translated as "meditational deity" or "tutelary deity." I wonder if it was originally an individual's personal deity similar to what was seen in ancient Mesopotamia. Do you have any thoughts on this?

GIBSON: It's difficult to say. The practice of meditation on *yidams* may have had its origin in the process mentioned above, but other than that, historical data are scanty. In any case, a more literal translation of the word *yidam* might be "fixing the mind." They might well be considered tutelary deities, but they are usually taken from the Buddhist or Bonpo pantheons.

McVEIGH: Could you describe any practices in modern Tibetan Buddhism that might be called examples of bicameral vestigiality?

GIBSON: The whole idea of direct communication with and even embodiment of deities, which could be seen as related to bicameral mentality, is at the heart of Vajrayana Buddhism. The possessed oracles I mentioned in my article as being widespread in traditional Tibet are not a part of "orthodox" doctrinal Buddhism, but were well accepted at the popular level as being compatible with it.

McVEIGH: We always have to be cautious when trying to discern truths about the nature of human psychology from religious traditions, ancient or modern, but I wonder if you have any opinions on what insights about the workings of mind we can glean from Tibetan Buddhism. Related to this question is whether practices such as visualization meditation might have beneficial or even therapeutic uses. Any comments?

GIBSON: The question is, again, a very large one. H.H. the Dalai Lama used to have regular conferences with psychologists and psychiatrists and other scientists at his home in India, and much of the resulting discussion has been published in the form of several books. There is also a large popular literature of varied quality that introduces Tibetan meditation practices that reduce stress, etc.

MᴄVᴇɪɢʜ: I read an account of how Mikyö Dorje (1507–1554), head of the Kagyu School, questioned a painting of the god Mañjuśrī and received answers in the form of revelations. Do you have any sense of how common such practices were?

Gɪʙsᴏɴ: I briefly addressed the phenomenon of talking images in Tibet in my article [see Further Reading, below]. Such people as Mikyö Dorje were never really common in Tibet, and seem to have gradually become less and less so; this is in accord with the decline in bicameral abilities that Jaynes documents elsewhere. That it seems to have been more gradual in Tibet may be due to both environmental as well as social factors. For example, the terrain reduced Tibetans' interactions with different peoples, and an interest in the persistence of bicameral behaviors seems to have been more emphasized in Tibet than in some of the cultures that Jaynes describes.

Further Reading

Todd Gibson, "Buddhism and Bicamerality" (Julian Jaynes Society, 2021).

Todd Gibson, "Souls, Gods, Kings, and Mountains: Julian Jaynes's Theory of the Bicameral Mind in Tibet, Part One" and "Listening for Ancient Voices: Julian Jaynes's Theory of the Bicameral Mind in Tibet, Part Two," in M. Kuijsten (ed.), *Gods, Voices, and the Bicameral Mind* (Julian Jaynes Society, 2016).

20

The Evolution of Mental Language in the *Iliad* and the *Odyssey*

Boban Dedović

Interviewed by Marcel Kuijsten

Boban Dedović is an interdisciplinary Croatian-American researcher working in the fields of linguistics, psychology, and ancient studies. His training and exposure in ancient languages includes Classical Latin, Homeric Greek, Old Babylonian, and Middle Egyptian. As an undergraduate, he studied Religions of Antiquity (B.A.) and Psychology (B.S.) at the University of Maryland, College Park. His senior seminar work won the University's competitive Library Award for Research in 2019 and 2020, which implemented methods of scientific inquiry when analyzing ancient mythology. He earned his master's degree in the Humanities from the University of Chicago. His thesis analyzed psychological activity in the Middle Egyptian *Story of Sinuhe*. Dedović also worked in the field of software development for over ten years, starting and growing several funded technology companies as a founder, founding partner, or principal. He founded and serves as the Executive Director of the OMNIKA Foundation, which is a Nevada based nonprofit focused on making available the world's mythological stories. He is also a Vice President and Chief Technology Officer of the Nevada Center on Foreign Relations.

MARCEL KUIJSTEN: Let's start with you giving us a sense of the program that you're in right now at the University of Chicago, what it's like, what you've been learning, and how that informed the study that you recently released.

BOBAN DEDOVIĆ: Sure. Right now I'm at the University of Chicago. It's a special graduate program that allows you to basically build your own curriculum. It is a basic thesis track and I'm only studying ancient languages. I've moved into the intermediate level for both Middle Egyptian and old Babylonian. The people at the Oriental Institute in the Department of Near Eastern Languages and Civilizations are some of the brightest people that I've ever met. My thesis, which will hopefully be done by the end of the year, has to do with mental language — not surprisingly — in the *Story of Sinuhe*. It's a Middle Egyptian tale about a man displaced from his home and living among Asiatic people. So that's what I'm working on right now. I'm just trying to learn as much as I can around people that are much smarter than me on these topics.

KUIJSTEN: So we're going to be talking a lot about the *Iliad* and the *Odyssey* today, and much of the material that Julian Jaynes covers in Book Two, Chapter Five, "The Intellectual Consciousness of Greece." It's probably one of the more difficult chapters in Jaynes's book, so I'm glad that we're going to be discussing it today. To start with, can you tell us about the authorship of the *Iliad* and the *Odyssey*?

DEDOVIĆ: Sure, and based on what we discussed before, the paper is very technical, and it has a lot of information about the background and everything, but for the purpose of this discussion we agreed it was important to try to keep things on a layman's or a general level, just so it's approachable by a wide audience. So, for that reason most of my answers here are going to be simplifications, and if anyone is looking for anything more specific it's likely in the paper. Having said that, basically these are just very long pieces of epic poetry in an archaic Greek script. They were said to be written down around 750 BCE — before the classical period in Greece. Traditionally, people assumed that they were composed by a single man named Homer, one in his youth and one in his older age.

But in the 1920s and '30s, a classicist from Harvard named Milman Parry did some work with Yugoslavian folk tales — which ironically enough is my native language, Serbo-Croatian — and he discovered patterns of poetry and meter. He then took what he found and applied it to his analysis of Greek text. In his analyses he concluded that this was poetry that was passed down orally over generations. So, to answer your question directly, while many people still believe that the *Iliad* and the *Odyssey* were composed by a single man named Homer, there is little convincing evidence for that conclusion.

Instead, the accepted view is that the works were part of an oral tradition, performed orally and passed down through groups of people. Then, with the invention of writing, they came to be written down. And likely there was some restoration and changes and so forth that may have happened at that time. So, rather than a single author, the texts are really a part of a cultural tradition, and I think that it's more appropriate to call it the "Homeric Tradition" instead of "Homer" as a single man.

KUIJSTEN: That's an important point for people to understand. What is the time frame that we are talking about in terms of the *Iliad* versus the *Odyssey*? Jaynes discusses evidence for why he felt there was a later date for the *Odyssey*, having to do with some historical facts regarding Odysseus, among other things. What is the evidence for the *Iliad* being of an older origin than the *Odyssey* — and what are the time periods that these works reflect?

DEDOVIĆ: So again, they were written down roughly around 750 BCE. But that does not necessarily mean that they were created at that time, because the stories reference material culture and other topics that happened much farther in the past. So we can immediately move past the actual date they were written down. The second point is that most scholars already accept that the *Iliad* reflects an older time period than the *Odyssey*. But the real matter of debate is how much older? Is it older than one person's lifetime — which would be the case if Homer had been the author.

Jaynes speculates that the *Iliad* and the *Odyssey* were culturally created about one hundred years apart. I was very interested in this question and I reviewed all of the evidence regarding the dating, which is summarized in my introduction. I think it's reasonably safe to say that you have up to a couple of hundred years of difference, and I'll point to two examples that make that very clear.

The first example is that some of the material culture that's referenced, for example certain kinds of helmets, spears, or weaponry — some of them are very old, dating to perhaps 1400–1200 BCE, whereas some of them are more recent. It's also interesting how much bronze and iron are referenced, because in the *Iliad* you do have mention of both bronze and iron, but the weapons are not made from one of the substances. And if weapons are not made from these substances, if they were only used as implements, it means that soldiers and sovereigns don't trust in that material, similar to how someone today would not want to go into a building made out of a weak metal; they would need it to be tested.

That's for starters, but I think the more important thing to consider is that contextually these are very different stories, and things happen in one of the stories — psychologically speaking — that don't happen in the other. For example, I'm not aware of any passages in the *Iliad* that have to do with someone keeping a secret, while on the other hand, Odysseus is quite a prolific liar. Many scholars have written about these differences. Across the board we see estimates of events of the *Iliad* taking place around 1200 BCE — and one less conservative scholar even suggested that the *Iliad*'s origins are about 1700-1500 BCE — the actual contextual date.

KUIJSTEN: Thank you for clarifying that. One of the critiques from some time ago of Jaynes's theory, looking at the *Iliad*, was that there are a few passages that suggest introspection. However Jaynes countered that the *Iliad* consists of both older and more recent layers, and these layers reflect different time periods. So there may have been much later additions to what has now been passed down to us as the *Iliad*. Can you speak on the topic of the older and more recent layers, and how it's thought that these later additions came about?

DEDOVIĆ: Sure. I appreciate the question, because it's a thorny one, and one that I think to this day still needs more attention. The first thing that's very clear and well accepted among scholars is that the additions are done book by book. Each work has twenty-four books. While it's debatable, Book One of the *Iliad* is said to be more recent. Most of Book Two of the *Iliad* is literally a catalog of ships and the people there. Anyone reading that — any modern person like us — will say, "My, this is kind of bizarre, it's just page after page of the names of ships and the soldiers therein." So we can say that perhaps this book is older because it reflects a convention that is no longer used.

Another way to determine the differences is by conducting a statistical analysis of the words. There's a study I cite that was done by Martindale and Tuffin from the University of Maine, and they tested all of the books of the *Iliad* and the *Odyssey*; they did a statistical test called "discriminant validity."[1] Essentially, they compared how different the words were and beyond what threshold the writing style was different based on the words.

---

1. C. Martindale and P. Tuffin, "If Homer is the Poet of the *Iliad*, Then He May Not Be The Poet of the *Odyssey*," *Literary and Linguistic Computing*, 1996, 11, 3.

And their analyses picked out exactly which books were believed to be older editions based on the use of certain words that are archaic.

For example, if I asked you which text is from the 1700s versus the 2000s, you might say the text that uses the word "forsooth" is the one from the 1700s, because we no longer use that word. Methods like these make it evident that the *Iliad* has been kind of chopped up. Of course with an oral background based in ancient history, it can be difficult to prove any argument conclusively.

With respect to Jaynes's notions of introspection, people make statements such as: "Well, here's an example of introspection," and so forth. Creation, modification, and addition dates aside, one example isn't that significant, because you have to treat the books as a whole. These books have so many lines in them and so many words that you can come up with any argument you'd like and you can find textual examples to support it.

That's a part of the reason why I did my study the way I did: I think one needs to look at the two works as the absolute whole and on a holistic basis before they can be compared. I'm not too intrigued if someone comes up with ad hoc disagreements with respect to introspection, by just selecting random quotes, because anyone can do that and I don't think that really says very much. The more interesting analysis is of the works as a whole.

KUIJSTEN: In regards to the later additions to the *Iliad*, were these changes introduced by scribes? Do we know when these later additions occurred?

DEDOVIĆ: Yes, so it was written down about 750 BCE, and from there you still had about 150 years roughly of the archaic period, moving into the classical age that most people are familiar with. A lot of the changes may have occurred over the period of oral transmission and when it came to be written down. And of course a lot of calamities happened around the classical period. But it's really between the fifth and fourth centuries BCE where they come to be written down and many of the copies end up in the Alexandria Library in Egypt. From there, whenever scribes made copies, sometimes conventions changed and I'm sure a number of other minor changes happened. One would have to do a comparative analysis of all the various manuscripts in order to see the differences.

But there are certainly large chunks of books that are very late additions. In fact, I would argue that the *Iliad* is an epic, and it takes place over the last two weeks of the Trojan War, but the *Odyssey* is not really an epic — it's more like a collection of stories, and many of these stories don't rely on referencing the earlier ones. They flow well enough, but they can each more or less stand on their own as a story or mini-epic. This was popular at the time, and that's why there is another work called the *Little Iliad*, which was also popular, but that most people aren't familiar with. I don't know if that answers your question?

KUIJSTEN: Yes, it does, and Jaynes relates how some of the stories that came to make up the *Odyssey* may have initially described different heroes, but they were later patched together and attributed to Odysseus. So delving now into more specifics — as I mentioned at the beginning, we're going to be covering a lot of the material that Jaynes describes in his chapter, "The Intellectual Consciousness of Greece," and then getting more specifically into your paper, "'Minds' in 'Homer.'"[2] In "The Intellectual Consciousness of Greece," Jaynes introduces what he calls the "preconscious hypostases." I think this is one of the more difficult parts of Jaynes's book to understand, perhaps second to his discussion of metaphor. Can you explain what the Homeric preconscious hypostases are — for the average person that has read Jaynes but perhaps needs a refresher on this topic?

DEDOVIĆ: Sure, I'll do my best. The preconscious hypostases are a handful of words; and, in my research I focus on seven or eight of them. They're words in ancient Greek that are translated by modern translators either as "soul" or "mind," but they evolved from meanings that had more physical referents, such as "heart," "lungs," "stomach," "chest," or "breast." Before proceeding, it's important to note that the way these words were used and how these uses changed over time is very important. That is, when meanings of words change so drastically with respect to thinking, it means that something culturally important is going on. Mainly, the words went from being physical objects or sensations and they began to be used in more abstract ways. This transition is something that Jaynes's theory on the relatively recent origin of consciousness predicted.

The first word that I look at is *thymos*. It's usually described as being in the chest area, and the related terms have to do with fire, smoke, or violent commotion. It came to Latin as *fumus*, and in English we have the word "fumes," or "fuming" — that comes from the word *thymos*. And *thymos* in the ancient Greek is like the seat of courage, or of will, and it's very often where the conflict of indecision takes place.

---

2. Boban Dedović, "'Minds' in 'Homer': A Quantitative Psycholinguistic Comparison of the *Iliad* and *Odyssey*," *PsyArXiv Preprints*, 2021.

Next we have a second important word called *phrenes*. Jaynes associated *phrenes* with the respiratory system and breathing — *phrenes* is also a word that's also localized in the chest. But it's also an organ of grief. I think a simple way to visualize this is to watch somebody crying — watch somebody who is devastated by some sort of tragic state of affairs, and you'll see as they're crying there's a lot of breathing happening, and there's a visible effect on the person. So in the *Iliad* it might say "grief was cast into her *phrenes*" — that's how it's described.

From there you have the words that came to be associated with our word "heart," such as *ker, cardia,* and *kradie*. These usually just represent the heart, or your actual, physical beating heart. Later they are sometimes translated as "mind."

Next we have a somewhat ambiguous word *etor*, which Jaynes believes means "stomach," but I won't go into detail on *etor* because it's not as common.

The word that is often translated as "soul" is the Greek *psykhe* — or Anglicized that would be "*psyche*" — it's the root word for our word "psychology." And initially this was just a thing that every person has, and even animals have one, and at death it leaves your body. *Thymos* does the same thing.

Many death scenes in the *Iliad* are described by a very formulaic pattern: the weapon is described where the entrance wound is, where the exit wound out of the person's body was, what's spilled out — such as intestines — what color it was, and then it says either the *psykhe* or the *thymos* left his limbs and darkness covered the eyes. Many times, they don't say people died in the *Iliad*, they say "darkness covered his eyes," or "the black of night covered his eyes." We may say, then, that it's similar to how we use the word "soul" in English — it's more abstract, and there's no anatomical location.

But the last word is the most important and it's the most interesting. It's the word often pronounced as "noos"; spelled *noos* or *nous*. It's believed to come from *noein* which means "to see." Some scholars believe it originally came from **snu*,[3] which means "to sniff." In my native language, which is Serbo-Croatian, the word for nose is literally "*nos*." And this is the closest thing to our contemporary notion of "mind." It usually has no anatomical location, and is very rarely seen as in the chest, but it's something to be learned, it's something you discover. So, if I want to find out what Marcel is doing, in the *Iliad* it's not "I have to find out what Marcel is doing," it's "I have to know the contents of his *noos*."

---

3. The asterisk indicates a reconstructed or hypothetical form of a word that is not attested in written artifacts.

I started my paper with the line when Achilles is on the beach. It's one of the most modern lines in Book One — line 360 and onward I believe. While Achilles is crying, his mother Thetis says, "What grief has been cast into your *phrenes*? Speak, conceal not in *noos*, in order that we both may know." This is interesting because *noos* has become a container space where you can hide things — which is very interesting for the subject at hand. But basically it's translated as someone's plan, will, or intention. However, most of the time in the *Iliad*, it just means something like "recognition," "field of vision," or literally what's in front of you — being able to perceive or recognize something.

I said all that to make this point: you can't call these mental organs, because not all of them do exclusively mental action, but you have to give it a name, so Jaynes picked *hypostases*. And in Greek, *hypostasis* just means "underlying object" or "underlying essence" — it can be material or immaterial.

So that's what this word means — it's a placeholder for the words that are associated with mental language in archaic Greek culture. And Jaynes believed that all of these different words started out as many words and then they slowly became what we use today, which is basically just "soul," "mind," "heart" and sometimes "stomach" or "belly." That's a condensed simplification of some very complex terms. As Greek culture produced more evidence of writing about philosophy, the use of these words became more abstract. By the fourth and third centuries BCE, the Greeks themselves were confused about how the *Iliad* and the *Odyssey* used these same words. Ironically, here we are several thousand years later and we're still wrestling over the meanings of these words.

KUIJSTEN: Yes, that's a great explanation. I think the idea that we want to emphasize again is that in dating the transition from bicameral mentality to consciousness, we see the transformation of these words going from bodily, physical references to mental, psychological references, and that's a method of dating the timing of this transition. In the chapter in Jaynes's book, he talks about four phases that the preconscious hypostases go through in this transition from the physical to the psychological.

The first phase is the *objective*, then the *internal*, the *subjective*, and then the *synthetic*. Can you explain the "container metaphor of mind" and how, over time, the preconscious hypostases transform from external to internal? I think this is a key aspect of Jaynes's discussion of the development of consciousness from the time period referred to in the *Iliad*, as contrasted with the time period of the *Odyssey*.

DEDOVIĆ: Sure, so when we talk about "mind" from a contemporary stand-point, we're normally using some type of a "container metaphor." For example, when we say "what's on your mind?" — we can imagine a box with something on top of it. Or "keep that in the back of your mind," or "it crossed my mind." These are typically archery and container metaphors. So what the container metaphor space can do — grammatically and contextually — is what makes it unique. We moderns use this container space as an instrument, as in "put your *mind* into it," or "you are out of your *mind*." Different ways of applying physical properties to the word mind therefore describes different psychological states. These are murky waters and much more research needs to be done in the area of grammar versus context. I am working on this now at the University of Chicago within the Middle Egyptian language.

And what Jaynes believed was that these Greek words started out as external sensations. So for example, if it was windy and branches were moving — the visual aspect of seeing branches moving when it's windy — that might have been called *phren* or something similar. Whereas if you see waves crashing, perhaps the word for that was *thym* — a raging ocean.

But then in the second phase, the *internal* phase, these words for external observations started being applied to internal sensations. So "the ocean is raging" — this word "raging" — well, "I'm raging." And that rage is a thing that's put into me and I feel it in my chest. Of course it implies the heart beating and all of the physiological things that happen in situations of increased stress for people in general. In this second phase, these sensations are actually described as happening in the body.

The second to third phase transition is very important, because these sensations — which may be adjectives like raging chest, raging body — start being transformed and being used as nouns: nouns that can actually function as container spaces and nouns that accept things to be held in them. You can have something "in your *thymos*." You can have something going on "in your *phrenes*." There's one passage where, when a man was ripped apart, they found "his throbbing *ker* enclosed within his *phrenes*" — which lends support for the idea that the respiratory system is related to the word *phrenes*.

In the second phase, you have the words *thymos* and *phrenes*, etc., being used as container spaces, and at that point interesting things start happening, such as indecision. This marks the third phase. For example, in Book 1 of the *Iliad* (around line 185), during the argument between Achilles and

Agamemnon, Achilles is divided — or literally one of his *hypostases* (like *thymos* or *etor*) is in two parts regarding whether to pull out his sword.

Now this is interesting, because it suggests that a decision-making situation is taking place. Here you now have certain properties that these abstract words can have: they are divisible, they can be cut into parts, they can accept other things — for example, you can have grief, or you can have vigor in your *thymos* or grief in your *phrenes*. This third phase thus showcases words like *thymos* being used in a contextually contemporary sense (e.g., "I am of two minds about it").

The fourth and final phase is what Jaynes called the *synthetic* phase. This is when you start observing complex actions of verbs, and complex things actually taking place in the container space. What is interesting about this phase is the word *noos*. Unlike *thymos* and others, *noos* generally does not have any activity going on "inside" it. That is, there are almost no passages between both works where someone is deciding "in his *noos.*" This is important, because it departs massively from the way we use the word "mind" today, wherein "mind" is the location that most people believe that their own thinking takes place.

Decision-making is usually described as motion, but there's one kind of dubious passage in the *Odyssey* where Odysseus is talking to bright-eyed Athena, who is a goddess or deity, and he's lying to her. And as he's lying to her, one translation suggests that Odysseus "keeps the truth ever-revolving in his *noos.*"

So you have a verb indicating motion with a very abstract noun such as "truth" — actually "revolving" in his *noos* — and these kinds of descriptions get us to just about where we are today with how people talk when they speak about very complex cognition. That's the last phase — you have these seven or eight *hypostases* — or "mind words" — fusing together, and the result is a container space which many consider to be the seat of rationality. It's also where many moderns believe thinking happens, in the English language, at least. Also, you can keep your recognitions there, you can do a lot of things, and in doing so you can make use of every physical property, via words, when you are describing mental action.

KUIJSTEN: That's a great explanation. I think it makes these concepts much more understandable, and it's important to understand this background material before we get into the specifics of your study. One last question before we get to your article — Jaynes spent a lot of time talking about the evolution of mind words in ancient Greece and he had a lot of very revolutionary ideas on this subject. Did you find in your research that Jaynes was frequently cited by other scholars, specifically on this subject?

DEDOVIĆ: I read through what I consider to be a lot of material — even somewhat fringe material that wasn't directly related, because I'm very susceptible to rabbit holes. But I only saw Jaynes cited a handful of times. And almost always it was in the form of a footnote, or it was a statement that was somewhat pejorative or dismissive. And what's interesting to me about that is that when I go on to read the rest of their paper, it's very clear that they likely did not read all of Jaynes's book and I don't think they understood the distinct hypostases as Jaynes describes them.

In fact, in the case of one scholar — who is very prominent in this field — I contacted him, he responded, and we had a number of discussions. And this is an individual who had made one of these comments. We went through the material together, we analyzed and unpacked it, and in the end he seemed to be much more receptive to Jaynes's findings. Why other scholars don't give Jaynes credit I don't really know. Maybe it's certain parts of Jaynes's theory that they don't want to assign credit for. But I do worry that a lot of his ideas are misappropriated — they're very much misappropriated. He's not getting credit where credit is due, because he did much of his work before some of the foundational things on language and metaphor came out. I certainly think it's important to make sure that the public understands where some of these ideas originally came from, and Jaynes was the first to write about a lot of them, especially with respect to this very topic.

KUIJSTEN: That's important and I've noticed this in psychology as well. While his work is increasingly cited — by more than 8,000 publications by last count[4] — it is also the case that some articles that clearly build on his ideas fail to mention his theory. One psychologist in particular has repackaged many of Jaynes's original insights and presented them as his own — and when asked about the connection to Jaynes he typically offers some kind of very vague critique. It is unfortunate that Jaynes hasn't received the credit that he deserves, at least in some cases. Let's talk more specifically about your article "'Minds' in 'Homer.'" Can you tell us what you set out to investigate, what dataset you used, and describe your methodology?

DEDOVIĆ: Sure. I wanted to know whether one work, the *Iliad* or the *Odyssey,* had more mental language than the other. I read nearly all of the

---

4. See Jaynes's Google Scholar profile: https://scholar.google.com/citations?user=je9ezUIAAAAJ.

arguments regarding this topic, and everyone finds passages of interest and support, and what you have is essentially 100 years of this type of debate.

I wanted to answer this question holistically and I wanted to treat it via concerned scientific inquiry, by taking a statistical approach. My data set was based on convenience sampling, which means as quickly as I could acquire the largest possible sample size. I made a very important early decision to do what's called a *within-subjects design*. This means that I didn't simply use every translation of the *Iliad* and the *Odyssey*, instead I only used single translators who had translated both works.

So the entire sample size of 17 translators each contains two works translated by the same person. I did this because when you run the statistical tests, it gives you more of a term called *statistical power* — that is, it gives you a very high level of statistical precision when you're comparing works done by the same person. The methodology I took was very straightforward: I compiled all of these works, then I removed all of the footnotes, title pages, and anything that was not part of the translation. This process of preparing the data took several years.

Once I finished this sanitation process, I analyzed the word frequencies in a freely available digital linguistic analysis tool called Voyant. It's a little cumbersome to use at first, but it's free and it does its job — it can process large numbers of words and do math quickly. From there I did some additional statistical tests, in order to see if there were correlations between certain factors, and to see what would explain the results that I observed.

The method was primarily comparing those two works, the *Iliad* and the *Odyssey*. I also compiled a "mental language glossary," because you first have to answer "what is mental language and how do you measure it?"

What I did was this: I took all of the translations — all 34 of them — and I created one long list of all of the most common words. I went down that list and I picked the top 40,000 words, which represented about 95% of all of the words — so words that were common. Then I went through several specific steps to filter them using an algorithm.

For example, the verb "to divide" — sometimes it's mental language and sometimes it's not. I can't go through all of the instances manually in all of the 34 works because it's a common word. So I came up with a method that's fully explained in the article, with examples: if a particular word is used and within five words there is an occurrence of one of these other words, then keep it — if not, then don't.

This is why passages such as "they divided their share of spoils among the hungry men" is not included but something like "they were counsels divided of mind" is retained. So I conducted algorithmic filtering, and when the word list reached a reasonable size, I did a good amount of manual filtering as well. So that was the methodology. And the goal was to be very transparent — to tell people, "Here is what I have, these are the tests I did, this is how I came up with them, and this is why I think it's a robust way of measuring what I'm conceptually defining."

I report many tables of data, so I make everything available for people to see, and I want to encourage other people to also take a look at it and perhaps see if they can find other interesting ways to analyze the data. No one had ever done this study with this sample size — it's a very large sample size compared to what has been done previously.

KUIJSTEN: It sounds like you put a tremendous amount of time and effort into this. This is the kind of research that's necessary if we're going to advance Jaynes's theory and gain a better understanding of many of the concepts that he put forth in his book. So it's wonderful that you're doing this type of research. Tell us about your conclusions — what did you find as a result of this research?

DEDOVIĆ: Sure. So, first and foremost, I believe that the *Odyssey* has more mental language than in the *Iliad* — roughly about 8–12% more — comparing all of the 17 English translators as well the Greek, because I ran all of these analyses for the Greek translations as well.

So a few things — we should start with what are called the important "Homeric questions." These are, number one: are the *Iliad* and *Odyssey* composed by one author or multiple authors? My study suggests that the two are different enough with respect to mental language that the composer's psychology is not the same. The second question has to do with the dating, and in my view these results suggest that the *Iliad* is much older than the *Odyssey*.

And from that, you move into some other conclusions which are more far-reaching as to how the problem can be approached. I should say that most people have tried to take these words and put them into a neat framework; and it never really worked out. Jaynes's model, however, did apply. You have fewer *hypostases* in the *Odyssey* for these "mind words," and you start to see consolidation. Not just consolidation, but you begin to see certain ones being used more than others — statistically much more. And the words that are used more frequently are of course things like "heart," "mind," and "soul," because this is closer to what we use today, and we are intellectual descendants of that culture. So in summary, the *Odyssey* represents how we use "mind words" today more closely than the *Iliad* does, across several important metrics.

Because Jaynes's model applies, and because there are these significant differences between the two texts, it seems to me quite necessary for future investigators to stop using the term "Homeric psychology," and to start considering distinctions between "Iliadic psychology" and "Odyssean psychology." I no longer think that these two works are compatible, and I think that any discussion that does not parse the two is not going to be productive. Other scholars — including another person I consulted with for this paper named Joseph Russo, who has written a great deal about this topic — have come to this conclusion as well: that these works need to be treated with distinction, psychologically speaking. I think that's a very important point and represents a step forward for classical studies.

My last main conclusion, which I address at the beginning of my paper using a very "winged word"[5] — I say that it's "repugnant" to assume that the mentality of people has always been the same. I use this strong word intentionally, not to disrespect any field, but I use it because the assumption of the similarity of historical peoples' mentalities does not get challenged often enough.

In the final part I suggest that more work needs to be done on defining what "mental language" is. There needs to be a standardized register — which I've done some work on — and people from different fields need to participate in this. There needs to be a word for avoiding "presentism" for psychological contexts in the translation of ancient texts. We cannot simply assume that someone's mentality is the same as ours, and very few people are thinking about this problem. So in conclusion, I believe this is very important and more people need to work on it.

KUIJSTEN: Yes, I certainly agree. Again, it's great that you're doing this research and presenting these ideas. I think the term that you use to describe the problem of making assumptions about others' mentality is "mento-centrism" — derived from "ethnocentrism"?

---

5. An expression that has its origin in the *Iliad,* implying that words are like arrows traveling toward their intended target. For example, in the *Iliad* and *Odyssey,* words are said to be "winged" when two characters are debating one another, or tensions are otherwise high.

DEDOVIĆ: I'm not a fan of inventing words — I don't think it's my station to do that. But in sociology the word that's used is "ethnocentrism," or judging another culture by your own standards. It's injurious if you practice it and it's useful if you're aware of that potential pitfall, because it informs your approach to the problem. But there is no equivalent word for the field of psychology, so in brackets I suggest the term "mento-centrism," which is assuming or judging the mental state and psychological makeup of another person based on your own — or simply projecting your own psychology into historical documents. But yes, almost no one is talking about this, especially in ancient studies.

KUIJSTEN: It's shocking that Jaynes put forth all these very important ideas more than four decades ago, and yet we're still laboring under this problem of what some historians call the "presentist fallacy," or the imposition of modern culture, psychology, and beliefs onto the study of ancient civilizations. We have the same problem of translation in other texts, such as the Old Testament, and that's something that we touched on in Brian McVeigh's interview about the evidence for bicameral mentality and the transition to consciousness in the Old and New Testaments.[6]

It's also something that Rabbi James Cohn discusses in his lecture [from the Julian Jaynes Society conference]. He identifies many of these mistranslations — for example the translation of non-psychological words as psychological words, and how the translators have often imposed a modern psychology into their translations.[7] It's going to require a wide scale retranslation of ancient texts in a more literal fashion, and I think this is an important step that you've taken.

Is there anything that you encountered in your research that you think contradicts Jaynes's theory in any way? Or are there details that you can further refine from what Jaynes put forth in his book?

DEDOVIĆ: Sure, and let's start by acknowledging that Jaynes isn't here in this discussion to defend himself against anything I might say. Furthermore, he didn't have the option of using Voyant — my linguistic analysis tool — as well as many of the other resources that I had at my disposal. I think it's important to make sure to ground any of my feedback with respect to the time Jaynes lived in and the tools that he had available to him. There are a number of small, nitpicky things — for example, his counts of

---

6. See Brian McVeigh's interview, "Evidence for Bicameral Mentality in the Bible," in this volume.
7. James Cohn, "A Jaynesian Philology: The Bible as a Written Record of the Dawn of Consciousness," Julian Jaynes Society, 2013 (https://www.youtube.com/watch?v=P-7I55QWnxM).

the amount that certain words increased from the *Iliad* to the *Odyssey*. I think that he arrived at that number perhaps from a sampling method of several books — which is a smart way to do it if you don't have a computer to count them all for you. Things like that, with some of the minor details here and there.

But in terms of the big conceptual things, for example the whole notion that these words start with descriptions of things that happen in the outside world, and then they are used to describe parts of the body anatomically, then they are adopted as a container metaphor as language evolves, and then they consolidated into fewer words over time — this and the other big, important things — I think he got those right. Darwin made many mistakes in *The Origin of Species*, but it doesn't matter, because what he got right was the most important idea: that living organisms generally change over time with respect to the impact of their environment.

KUIJSTEN: Of course we recommend that everyone read your paper, "'Minds' in 'Homer',", and that's available for people to read online. Are there any other things that you recommend people read who are interested in learning more about the evolution of mental and metaphorical language from the *Iliad* to the *Odyssey*?

DEDOVIĆ: If you are looking for statistical analyses, I would recommend the work of Shirley Sullivan at the University of British Columbia — I list several of her works in my bibliography. She produces appendices which have very informative data tables — which were the inspiration for how I organized my own tables. On the lighter side, or the more readable side, Andreas Zanker published a book called *Metaphor in Homer: Time, Speech, and Thought* that I highly recommend.[8] There's a researcher in Germany named Fabian Horn who is doing a lot of work on specific metaphors used to think — like the verb "to construct," which is often used in phrases related to thinking. He's done interesting work on metaphors for thinking, for example "building in the deep."[9] They all lean on Lakoff and Johnson's conceptual metaphor theory.[10] Those are good places to start.

Of course, the *Iliad* and the *Odyssey* are available for free online, and any library should also have them. Those are great resources. Finally, I would encourage people, if they can, to study ancient languages such as classical

8. Andreas Zanker, *Metaphor in Homer: Time, Speech, and Thought* (Cambridge University Press, 2019).
9. Fabian Horn, "'Building in the Deep': Notes on a Metaphor for Mental Activity and the Metaphorical Concept of Mind in Early Greek Epic," *Greece and Rome*, 2016, 2, 63.
10. George Lakoff and Mark Johnson, *Metaphors We Live By* (University Of Chicago Press, 1980).

Latin or Greek — there are benefits to doing that. I know it's not fun or easy to go through a couple years' worth of grammar and reading classes, but you do get a completely different perspective. If you are reading someone else's translation, unfortunately you're often at a disadvantage by not knowing exactly how some terms were translated.

KUIJSTEN: Thank you for those resources. Before we wrap up, did you want to share some details about what you're currently working on at the University of Chicago and what you expect to publish in the near future?

DEDOVIĆ: Sure, I'm happy to share my progress. I came to the University of Chicago because it is a world-leading institution for learning ancient languages like Middle Egyptian and Old Babylonian (Akkadian). These languages are quite difficult to learn, so having access to the people at the Oriental Institute makes things much easier. I'm currently working on two different research projects and there are some preliminary observations that I can share.

First, I'm analyzing the language of intentionality and volition in ancient Mesopotamian law codes. I was lucky enough to take a Mesopotamian Law class taught by Professor Martha Roth. Professor Roth is a leading authority on that topic and was responsible for completion of Chicago's Assyrian dictionary. In that class, Professor Roth was kind enough to share some of her "in progress" translations of legal texts — in both Sumerian and Akkadian. I observed that personal agency is expressed less in older texts but more so in more recent ones. I'm working on the *Code of Hammurabi* and assessing how often and with what words agency is expressed. There's a curious formulaic pattern with the word *libbum*, which is "heart" in Akkadian. It is mostly present in statutes related to a woman's "choice" to remarry under certain marital circumstances. I hope to release my literature review and notes on this topic later this year.

In the course of doing this work, I was also inspired by Chicago's efforts to digitize and make available research from the Oriental Institute. I decided to digitize the *Law Code of Hammurabi* by making a single-page website that includes the cuneiform signs and all textual parts of the English translation. One can see the signs, phonetic values, application of Akkadian grammar, and an English translation for each statute. To my knowledge, a tool like this did not previously exist. It is now available at eHammurabi.com, thanks to help from the OMNIKA Foundation. I plan to write up and share the technical aspects so that other people can do the same for other texts — that will be more focused on computer science, which is my professional background.

Second, I'm finishing my graduate thesis on the Middle Egyptian *Story of Sinuhe*. I am very lucky to be working with Professor Janet H. Johnson as my advisor — she's a world-class Egyptologist and an incredible teacher. In my thesis, I attempt to understand the relationship between "mind" and "heart" in the *Story of Sinuhe*, and how behavior is initiated.

My preliminary conclusions are incredibly interesting. The word translated as "mind" is almost always the word for "heart" (*ib*). I think that I've discovered a grammatical pattern whereby one can distinguish between emotional affect, volition, and bodily or physiological excitation. I'm leaning heavily on integrating the latest research on the heart from the field of cardiology. I'm communicating with Dr. Stephen Porges — he's done some amazing work on explaining the heart-brain relationship that I'm investigating. I think one of the most debated lines from *Sinuhe* can probably be understood best as describing what's known as the "fight-or-flight" response. If accurate, this may impact how future investigators understand the story.

Finally, I have an overwhelming amount of evidence to believe that the language of thinking differs on the basis of language family. That is, English is a Proto-Indo-European language — like Latin and Greek — but Middle Egyptian is an Afro-Asiatic language. I'm observing that the metaphor used to describe thinking can be best explained by the differences in language family origins. To be sure, the grammatical characteristics of "mind" and "heart" in *Sinuhe* are unlike anything I have observed in archaic Greek or classical Latin. I'm hoping to release my thesis by the end of the year.[11] However, my conclusions depart from some important investigators, so as a result I need to spend more time justifying my differences of opinion. I've also developed some new humanities-friendly techniques for people to analyze mental language on a traditional scientific basis. It will likely require quite a bit of methodological explanation.

KUIJSTEN: That sounds very interesting indeed — we'll look forward to that. There is so much work still to do in accurately translating these ancient texts — avoiding any modern psychological impositions — and it's great that you are shedding new light on these issues. Thank you again for taking the time to share your interesting research.

DEDOVIĆ: Thanks again for having me.

---

11. Boban Dedović, "'Heart', 'Mind', and Behavioral Causation in the Songs of Sinuhe," 2021.

HYPOTHESIS IV

Jaynes's Neurological Model
for Bicameral Mentality

21

New Evidence for
Jaynes's Neurological Model

Marcel Kuijsten

Interviewed by Brendan Leahy

BRENDAN LEAHY: Can you explain Jaynes's fourth hypothesis, his neurological model for the bicameral mind?

MARCEL KUIJSTEN: Yes, it was Jaynes's conjecture as to the neurology of bicameral mentality. I say conjecture because the technology simply was not available in the late 1970s to test this hypothesis.

So in right handed people, our language ability resides in two areas of the left temporal lobe called Wernicke's area and Broca's area. In left handed people, the dominant hemisphere for language can be reversed, or language can be more evenly distributed between the two hemispheres. But for sake of simplicity, for this discussion we'll assume that we're talking about a right-handed person. The hemisphere for language, in this case the left hemisphere, is often referred to as the "dominant" hemisphere, with the right hemisphere referred to as the "non-dominant" hemisphere. This terminology can be somewhat confusing, but it is simply referring to the hemisphere's dominance for language.

Jaynes reasoned that if we're processing language and speech comprehension in our left hemisphere language areas, then auditory hallucinations were likely being generated from the temporal lobe areas of the non-dominant right hemisphere. This makes intuitive sense, as these are the only other plausible speech areas in the brain. Jaynes suggested the stored up, admonitory knowledge and experience of the right hemisphere was being communicated across the corpus callosum via language, and then "heard" by the language areas of the left hemisphere.

And again, Jaynes came to that idea based on deduction: if we have most of our language ability associated with the left temporal lobe, then what are the right temporal lobe areas doing? Another line of evidence is the fact that the kind of things that the bicameral voices were doing — seeing the big picture, recognizing patterns, etc. — were also the kind of things that we generally associate with right hemisphere activity. Psychological tests, particularly on split-brain patients, have shown us that the right hemisphere is better at seeing patterns and working with geometric shapes, and these types of things, whereas the left hemisphere is more logical, methodical, and concerned with detail. So the kind of things that people experience in bicameral hallucinations were the kind of things that you would associate with the right hemisphere.

Finally, there were also some neurological studies, done by Wilder Penfield, that involved stimulating the right hemisphere with a mild electric current — when someone was having brain surgery, for example, and the brain was exposed. What Penfield found was that when the temporal lobe areas of the right hemisphere were stimulated, it often eliciting hallucinations.[1] So Jaynes arrived at his neurological model for bicameral mentality by looking at these various lines of evidence.

LEAHY: Is there new evidence that supports Jaynes's neurological model?

KUIJSTEN: Yes, actually there has been quite a bit of new evidence, so this has been an exciting area of support for Jaynes's theory. In 1999, Belinda Lennox and her colleagues in the UK did one of the first fMRI (functional magnetic resonance imaging) studies on a person while they were experiencing auditory verbal hallucinations.[2] A young man was placed in the MRI scanner with a joystick button that he would press at the moment that an auditory verbal hallucination began, at which point they would scan his brain. And what they found was more or less exactly what Jaynes had predicted: the hallucination started in the right temporal lobe language areas, traveled across the corpus callosum, and was "perceived" by the left hemisphere language areas. So they documented a right/left temporal lobe — or "bicameral" — interaction during auditory verbal hallucinations.

---

1. Wilder Penfield, "Wilder Penfield and Phanor Perot, "The Brain's Record of Auditory and Visual Experience: A Final Summary and Discussion," *Brain*, 1963, 86, 595-702.
2. Belinda Lennox, et al., "Spatial and Temporal Mapping of Neural Activity Associated with Auditory Hallucinations," *Lancet*, 1999, 353, 644.

The significance of this groundbreaking study for Jaynes's theory was immediately recognized. The professor of medicine Robert Olin commented on this study in the prestigious journal *Lancet*, saying "Neuroimaging techniques of today have illuminated and confirmed the importance of Jaynes' hypothesis."[3] In the *Journal of Psychiatry and Neuroscience*, the psychiatrist Leo Sher wrote that "contemporary neuroimaging data have been used to revive and support ... [Jaynes's] controversial hypothesis."[4]

In the years since, there have been many more studies confirming this finding: that auditory verbal hallucinations are initiated by the language areas of the right (or non-dominant) hemisphere, travel across the corpus callosum, and are perceived by the language areas of the left (or dominant) hemisphere. And one of the things that is interesting to me about these findings is the idea that the fact that the voices are coming from the right hemisphere is perhaps what gives them their "alien" quality — the perception that they are coming from outside of oneself or from someone other than oneself.[5] So, in essence, our sense of self seems to be associated with our hemisphere that is dominant for language.

This conclusion is also supported by experiments with split-brain patients.[6] In a discussion of Julian Jaynes's theory, the neuropsychiatrist Andrea Cavanna also notes this idea:

> Recent functional neuroimaging findings seem to confirm the hypothesis that the right middle temporal gyrus represents the source of auditory hallucinations in at least some schizophrenic patients. Arguably, this lateralization pattern could well be the reason why these inner voices lack the characteristic of being self-generated.[7]

I'd like to take a moment to run through some of the subsequent studies, along with some quotes, because I think it's important that people understand the fact that Jaynes's fourth hypothesis, his neurological model for bicameral mentality, has essentially been confirmed by modern neuroscientific studies.

---

3. Robert Olin, "Auditory Hallucinations and the Bicameral Mind," *Lancet*, 1999, 354, 9173.
4. Leo Sher, "Neuroimaging, Auditory Hallucinations, and the Bicameral Mind," *Journal of Psychiatry and Neuroscience*, 2000, 25, 3.
5. Henry A. Nasrallah, "The Unintegrated Right Cerebral Hemispheric Consciousness as Alien Intruder: A Possible Mechanism for Schneiderian Delusions in Schizophrenia?" *Comprehensive Psychiatry*, 1985, 26, 3.
6. Michael S. Gazzaniga, "Forty-five Years of Split-brain Research and Still Going Strong," *Nature Reviews Neuroscience*, 2005, 6.
7. Andrea Cavanna, et al., "The 'Bicameral Mind' 30 years on: A Critical Reappraisal of Julian Jaynes' Hypothesis," *Functional Neurology*, 2007, 22, 1.

LEAHY: Yes, please do.

KUIJSTEN: In 2002, the Canadian psychiatrist Lahcen Ait Bentaleb and his colleagues used functional magnetic resonance imaging (fMRI) to investigate the brain activity of a woman who hallucinated continuously, except when she heard loud, external speech. They reported that "AVHs [auditory verbal hallucinations] were associated with increased metabolic activity in the left primary auditory cortex and the right middle temporal gyrus. Our results suggest a possible interaction between these areas during AVHs."[8] The "possible interaction" between the language areas of the right and left hemispheres during auditory verbal hallucinations that the authors propose is exactly what Jaynes predicted in his neurological model for bicameral mentality.

In 2007, the French psychiatrist Renaud Jardri and his colleagues published a study in *Molecular Psychiatry* titled "Activation of Bilateral Auditory Cortex during Verbal Hallucinations in a Child with Schizophrenia." They used fMRI to study the "neural substrates of verbal auditory hallucinations in a child suffering from very early onset schizophrenia." The analysis performed "shows bilateral activation of the superior temporal gyri" during auditory hallucinations.[9] What that means is that, during auditory hallucinations, there was activation of the language areas of the temporal lobe in both the right and left hemispheres ("bilateral"). Again, this is exactly what Jaynes predicted more than 40 years ago.

In an article published in 2007 in *Schizophrenia Research*, the psychiatrist Iris Sommer and her colleagues in the Netherlands reported that "the majority of schizophrenia patients showed prominent activity in the right-sided homologues of the classical language areas during AVH [auditory verbal hallucinations] (i.e. in the right inferior frontal gyrus, right superior temporal and supramarginal gyrus), while normal language is generally produced in the left hemisphere in right-handed subjects."[10] What they are saying here is that, during auditory verbal hallucinations, the language areas of the right or non-dominant hemisphere become active. So again, this corresponds precisely with Jaynes's predictions.

---

8. Lahcen Ait Bentaleb, et al., "Cerebral Activity Associated with Auditory Verbal Hallucinations: A Functional Magnetic Resonance Imaging Case Study," *Journal of Psychiatry & Neuroscience*, 2002, 27, 2.
9. Renaud Jardri, et al., "Activation of Bilateral Auditory Cortex during Verbal Hallucinations in a Child with Schizophrenia," *Molecular Psychiatry*, 2007, 12, 319.
10. I.E.C. Sommer, et al., "Can fMRI-guidance Improve the Efficacy of rTMS Treatment for Auditory Verbal Hallucinations?" *Schizophrenia Research*, 2007, 93, 1.

In another study published in 2008, Sommer and her colleagues measured cerebral activation using fMRI in 24 psychotic patients. They report that "group analysis for AVH revealed activation in the right homologue of Broca's area, bilateral insula, bilateral supramarginal gyri and right superior temporal gyrus." They go on to speculate that "the association between AVH and activity in right hemisphere language areas could explain the low linguistic complexity and derogatory content, characteristic for AVH in psychotic patients."[11] In 2009, Iris Sommer and René Kahn edited a book of articles on this subject titled *Language Lateralization and Psychosis.*[12]

In an article titled "Functional MRI of Verbal Self-Monitoring in Schizophrenia" published in *Schizophrenia Bulletin*, psychologist Veena Kumari and her colleagues in the UK conclude that positive schizophrenic symptoms (hallucinations and persecution) show "exaggerated activation of the right superior-middle temporal gyrus."[13]

Also noteworthy, Dr. Yair Lampl in the Department of Neurology at Tel Aviv University and his colleagues published an article in late 2005 that studied auditory hallucinations in stroke patients. According to Lampl, auditory hallucinations occur only rarely after a stroke. So of the 641 stroke patients in the study, only four experienced auditory hallucinations. What is interesting about this study in terms of Jaynes's neurological model is that all of the cases of auditory hallucinations "occurred after an ischemic lesion of the right temporal lobe."[14]

More recently, Judith Ford and her colleagues at the University of California, San Francisco noted in the *Oxford Research Encyclopedia of Neuroscience* that "AVHs [auditory verbal hallucinations] were associated with activation in bilateral language and motor regions."[15]

This is just a small sampling of the many recent studies that provide compelling evidence in support of Jaynes's neurological model. I describe more of these studies in *Reflections on the Dawn of Consciousness* and on the Julian Jaynes Society website.[16] The studies have been published in

11. I.E.C. Sommer, et al., "Auditory Verbal Hallucinations Predominantly Activate the *Right* Inferior Frontal Area," *Brain*, 2008, 131, 12.
12. Iris Sommer and René Kahn (eds.), *Language Lateralization and Psychosis* (Cambridge University Press, 2009).
13. Veena Kumari, et al., "Functional MRI of Verbal Self-monitoring in Schizophrenia: Performance and Illness-Specific Effects," *Schizophrenia Bulletin*, 2010, 36, 4.
14. Yair Lampl, et al., "Auditory Hallucinations in Acute Stroke," *Behavioral Neurology*, 2005, 16, 4.
15. Judith M. Ford, et al., "Neurobiology of Auditory Hallucinations," *Oxford Research Encyclopedia of Neuroscience*, November 2019.
16. Marcel Kuijsten (ed.), *Reflections on the Dawn of Consciousness* (Julian Jaynes Society, 2006); Marcel

peer-reviewed journals by different researchers working in different labs around the world. And while their research provides strong evidence in support of Jaynes's neurological model, it's important to note that these scientists did not have the goal of providing evidence for Jaynes's fourth hypothesis, and in some cases may not even be aware of Julian Jaynes or his theory.

I should point out that, as most people are aware, studying the brain is quite complicated, and there are other studies that show different results. Yet because of the number of studies showing results similar to those that I have outlined, a consensus on this issue is beginning to emerge. A recent meta-analysis — a study that looks at data from a number of previous studies — concluded that "AVH [auditory verbal hallucination]-related activity was ... observed in Broca's area and its right hemisphere homologue."[17]

LEAHY: That's very interesting to hear that there are now so many new studies that support Jaynes's predictions.

KUIJSTEN: Yes, these are exciting new developments, because in the case of Jaynes's neurological model, we don't have to speculate about what may or may not have taken place in ancient history. Using various types of modern brain imaging technology, we can see the bicameral mentality in real time in those who still hear voices today. I think that Jaynes's speculation about what might be taking place in the brain during auditory hallucinations perhaps served to inspire some of these early investigations,[18] and that research in turn now shows that very likely he was in fact correct. This in turn supports his second hypothesis, that prior to the development of consciousness, humans had a bicameral mentality.

LEAHY: Are there other lines of evidence that support Jaynes's neurological model?

KUIJSTEN: Absolutely. There are actually several other lines of evidence. There are studies that look at the subject of language lateralization and auditory verbal hallucinations, for example. And what many of these studies find is that the more language is distributed between the two

Kuijsten, "Neuroscience Confirms Julian Jaynes's Neurological Model," https://www.julianjaynes.org/blog/featured/neuroscience-confirms-julian-jaynes-neurological-model/

17. Leor Zmigrod, et al., "The Neural Mechanisms of Hallucinations: A Quantitative Meta-Analysis of Neuroimaging Studies," *Neuroscience & Biobehavioral Reviews*, 2016, 69.

18. Iris E.C. Sommer, "Language Lateralization in Schizophrenia" (Doctoral dissertation, Department of Psychiatry, University Medical Center Utrecht, 2004), p. 5.

hemispheres, rather than being concentrated in one (usually the left in right-handed people) — what they call "reduced language lateralization" — the more likely it is that a person will hear voices.[19]

This term "reduced lateralization" can initially seem a bit counterintuitive for people. The more language is *lateralized*, the more it is concentrated in one hemisphere (typically the left). So "reduced language lateralization" means that language processing is *less* concentrated in one hemisphere — in other words, more evenly distributed between the two hemispheres.

So from the perspective of Jaynes's theory, this is quite interesting. It suggests that the more a person processes language in both hemispheres ("reduced lateralization"), the more likely they are to also experience auditory verbal hallucinations. Put another way, greater language activity in the language areas of the non-dominant hemisphere can lead to the experience of auditory hallucinations. Again, this is what we would expect to see based on Jaynes's neurological model.

Furthermore, there have been a number of studies reporting both auditory and visual hallucinations in individuals suffering from temporal lobe epilepsy. Some of these studies show activation of the right or bilateral language areas during auditory hallucinations.[20] One study notes that "psychotic syndromes in epilepsy are most common but not exclusively associated with temporal lobe epilepsy."[21] While results are not always clear cut, abnormal brain activity in the temporal lobes can in some cases trigger hallucinations, which I suggest provides another line of supporting evidence for Jaynes's neurological model.

It's important to emphasize that when we're talking about something as complex as the human brain, just looking at one study or another is not going to provide conclusive evidence. But what we now have is a pattern of evidence across a large number of different studies conducted by many different researchers, using a variety of different technologies, and approaching the problem in a number of completely different ways — all converging to support the same hypothesis: that auditory verbal hallucinations, at least in many cases, involve the language areas of both hemispheres. I've

19. I.E.C Sommer and René Kahn (eds.), *Language Lateralization and Psychosis* (Cambridge University Press, 2009).
20. Andreas Hug, et al., "Voices Behind the Left Shoulder: Two Patients with Right-sided Temporal Lobe Epilepsy," *Journal of the Neurological Sciences*, 2011, 305, 1-2.
21. Siddhartha Nadkarni, et al., "Psychosis in Epilepsy Patients," *Epilepsia*, 2007, 48, s9.

provided references to many of the studies on these topics on the Julian Jaynes Society website, so those interested can learn more there.[22]

LEAHY: That is very compelling. Jaynes also mentioned evidence from the split-brain experiments. Is that research still relevant?

KUIJSTEN: Yes, absolutely — psychological experiments conducted with "split-brain" patients — who have had their corpus callosum severed (the primary connection between the two brain hemispheres) are still quite relevant and they provide further evidence for Jaynes's neurological model. These experiments suggest that the two hemispheres can in some ways operate independently, express different preferences, that our sense of self is associated with our primary hemisphere for language,[23] and that the actions of the right hemisphere can often feel "alien" to the person.

For example, the person's right hand (controlled by the left hemisphere) might hold up a newspaper to read, while the left hand (controlled by the right hemisphere) knocks it away. These experiments also show that the right hemisphere can understand language and, in some cases, even generate speech. It's even been suggested that, after the split-brain surgery, what we find are two independent "spheres of consciousness," one per hemisphere.

There are others that argue against these interpretations — this is still an area of intense philosophical debate. But, generally speaking, I have not found the arguments against the view that, after surgery, under experimental conditions we see two separate spheres of consciousness, one per hemisphere, to be convincing. Those interested in this fascinating area of research can read the material for themselves and draw their own conclusions.[24]

So how does this research support Jaynes's neurological model? Well, it shows that the brain hemispheres, when disconnected, can operate more or less independently. And if that's the case, we can then extrapolate that the brain hemispheres could also have operated more independently during the bicameral period, even with the corpus callosum intact and biologically identical to what it is today — and with the voices of the

22. Marcel Kuijsten, "Neuroscience Confirms Julian Jaynes's Neurological Model," https://www.julian-jaynes.org/blog/featured/neuroscience-confirms-julian-jaynes-neurological-model/.
23. Typically the left hemisphere in right-handed people.
24. See Elizabeth Schechter, *Self-Consciousness and "Split" Brains: The Minds' I* (Oxford University Press, 2018) for a recent discussion of the split-brain experiments and their philosophical implications.

non-dominant hemisphere, originating in the non-primary language areas, having an "alien"or "external" quality to them.

Somewhat related to this are cases of hemispherectomy — where an individual has one brain hemisphere completely removed. This is sometimes done with children, usually in cases of some type of brain disease. If the procedure is done early enough, the child's brain can adapt and the person can go on to function in a remarkably normal way.[25] And in terms of Jaynes's theory, what we learn from these cases is that one brain hemisphere is entirely sufficient for the development of "a person" or a "self." It follows then that conceivably, two hemispheres, if unintegrated, could result in two "selves" — or a "bicameral mind."

This brings me to my next point, having to do with what's called "brain plasticity." What we've learned over the past several decades from these hemispherectomy cases, as well as many other different types of studies, is that the same brain, biologically speaking, can operate in different ways based on what is happening culturally and environmentally. So in other words, if part of the brain is removed or damaged, other areas of the brain can to some degree take over the functions of the removed or damaged areas. Similarly, if we learn new skills, the way that we use our brains can change. So with regard to Jaynes's theory, the evidence suggests that as we learned language, the brain began to operate differently, without the need for any significant biological changes.

I say "significant"because it does get a bit complicated, in that based on what you learn and what type of activities you engage in, we do see minute changes to brain structure. But the point here is that we don't need to look to biological evolution over many thousands of years to see changes in how the brain functions. In other words, we don't require biological changes to the structure of the corpus callosum to facilitate a greater integration of the brain hemispheres — language can serve that function.[26]

Brain plasticity is something that is now very well documented. Once thought to be relatively fixed by a certain age, we now know that neurogenesis — the growth of new neurons — as well as other changes to the brain take place throughout the lifespan. We also know that even things

25. Antonio M. Battro, *Half a Brain Is Enough: The Story of Nico* (Cambridge University Press, 2000).
26. Jack Gandour, et al., "Temporal Integration of Speech Prosody is Shaped by Language Experience: An fMRI Study," *Brain and Language*, 2003, 84, 3; Xinhu Jin, et al., "Functional Integration Between the Two Brain Hemispheres: Evidence From the Homotopic Functional Connectivity Under Resting State," *Frontiers in Neuroscience*, 2020, 14.

like learning a second language or learning to play a musical instrument change how the brain works.

Changes to the brain based on environmental factors, such as the development of sophisticated language, can then spread through a population and be taught to successive generations. So to use the computer metaphor, the transition from bicameral mentality to the consciousness was a "software" change, not a "hardware" change — there was no need for evolutionary based, macro biological changes to brain structure. There's been a tremendous amount of confusion on this point.

But getting back to the split-brain research, I should also mention that recently, based on both Jaynes's neurological model and the mounting evidence from studies like the ones I previously mentioned, two neurosurgeons recommended this same split-brain surgical procedure for patients with auditory hallucinations that are of a severe or debilitating nature and don't respond to medication. They suggested that severing the corpus callosum could stop the hallucinations from traveling from the right to the left temporal lobe:

> The theory of a bicameral mind evolved the psychology and neuropsychiatric concepts of some disorders including the one for schizophrenia. ... Jaynes' theories were further confirmed by ... other authors. ... According to all these findings and theories, it is postulated that anterior corpus callosotomy would be beneficial in controlling the auditory and visual hallucinations in those with schizophrenia refractory to the highest medical therapy.[27]

So to sum up, over the past four decades, we've gone from Jaynes's neurological model for bicameral mentality being largely ignored, to possibly informing some of the early fMRI investigations into the origin of auditory hallucinations, to largely being vindicated by these studies, to now forming the basis for potential surgical interventions. There are less drastic, non-surgical and non-pharmaceutical treatments for auditory hallucinations now being tested as well. One of these that has shown some preliminary positive results is transcranial magnetic stimulation (TMS), which uses magnetic fields applied outside of the skull to stimulate a focused area of the brain.[28]

---

27. Mousa Taghipour and Fariborz Ghaffarpasand, "Corpus Callosotomy for Drug-Resistant Schizophrenia; Novel Treatment Based on Pathophysiology," *World Neurosurgery*, 2018, 116.
28. See the interview with Iris Sommer and Sanne Brederoo, "Auditory Hallucinations and the Right Hemisphere," in this volume.

22

Auditory Hallucinations
and the Right Hemisphere

Iris E.C. Sommer & Sanne Brederoo

Interviewed by Brendan Leahy & Marcel Kuijsten

Iris Sommer is a Dutch psychiatrist who is professor of cognitive aspects of neurological and psychiatric disorders at the Departments of Neuroscience of University Medical Center Groningen. She previously served as Professor of Psychiatry at the University Medical Center Utrecht beginning in 2011.

Sanne Brederoo works as a researcher and healthcare psychologist in psychiatry in the Netherlands. Among the topics that her research focuses on are hallucinations and brain lateralization.

BRENDAN LEAHY: Could you please start by introducing yourself?

IRIS SOMMER: I'm a Professor of Psychiatry and I'm also a psychiatrist. I have a very nice job combining clinical work with scientific work — I think it's very nice doing them both together. My group has concentrated on the pathophysiology of auditory verbal hallucinations, or hearing voices.

LEAHY: Could you tell us about your research into auditory verbal hallucinations, and your findings regarding language lateralization and hearing voices?

SOMMER: Yes, I first wrote my Ph.D. thesis — which was finished in 2004 — about language lateralization in patients who have psychosis. We found that normal language — so both language production and language perception — was lateralized to a lower degree.[1] So in most healthy individuals, language functions are strongly lateralized to the left hemisphere. The left hemisphere is dominant for things like writing, reading, speaking, and listening to language. What you see in patients with psychosis — some of them are diagnosed with schizophrenia — is that those language functions are more bilateral. So, the right hemisphere is more involved — it is active more during language production and also during language perception. In most patients, the left hemisphere is still dominant, but the role of the right hemisphere is increased compared to healthy individuals.

After my Ph.D. thesis, I had the opportunity to form a small research group focused on auditory verbal hallucinations — or hearing voices — and we investigated that phenomenon both in patients who are suffering from psychosis, and in healthy individuals who function well in society, but still experienced hallucinations on a frequent basis.

We did some phenomenological research and we also used fMRI and other functional imaging techniques to look at the neurobiological backgrounds. In a study that was published in *Brain* in 2008, we describe which brain areas are active during the experience of auditory hallucinations. In that study, we had 24 patients with a diagnosis of schizophrenia, who were actually experiencing auditory verbal hallucinations in the MRI scanner, and we looked at which brain areas were involved.[2]

The area that we found was most active was the inferior frontal area in the right hemisphere. The inferior frontal area is well known for its important role in language production, but usually it's the left hemisphere, which is known as Broca's area — that is the area that has long been understood to be the language production area. But during the experience of auditory verbal hallucinations, we found the most extensive activity in the right hemisphere homologue of Broca's area. There were also other areas involved, and another very important area was the language perception area, and that was mainly active in the left hemisphere. So those are the most important active areas. They are probably both language-related areas, and we thought it was important to note that the speech production area was more active in the right hemisphere, rather than the left hemisphere, which is what would have been expected.

---

1. Iris E.C. Sommer, *Language Lateralization in Schizophrenia* (Doctoral dissertation, University of Utrecht, 2004).
2. I.E. Sommer, et al., "Auditory Verbal Hallucinations Predominantly Activate the *Right* Inferior Frontal Area," *Brain*, 2008, 131, 3169-77.

Now in the same 24 individuals, we also asked them to produce words while they were in the MRI scanner. So we presented them with a letter every six seconds, and we asked them to produce words from these letters — so that was a clear language production task. What we saw was that it was more Broca's area in the left hemisphere which was activated. So these people did have left hemisphere dominance for normal language tasks, but nonetheless during the experience of auditory hallucinations, we saw that language production areas were more activated in the right hemisphere. So the contribution of the right hemisphere areas may be an important factor in the experience of auditory verbal hallucinations.

LEAHY: Can you tell us something about the content of auditory verbal hallucinations?

SOMMER: Yes, we also looked at the content of auditory verbal hallucinations, and we studied that both in healthy individuals and in patients suffering from psychosis.[3] And especially in the patients, we have found that the hallucinations had a very similar content. They are typically short phrases — sometimes only one or a few words — that are said repeatedly. So people hear the same short sentence over and over again.

Also there's a lot of "street language" in the content of the hallucinations — so they hear a lot of swear words. Even very religious people — who said that they don't normally swear at all — still heard swear words. So it seems that the language of their hallucinations is different from the language that they would typically use. Abusive content is also very frequent in the hallucinations. Especially in the patient group, the hallucinations frequently have a very negative emotional content — so they are very nasty to listen to. They call the patients names and they give them terrible commands to harm themselves, so they are very nasty to hear.

Also, the hallucinations are very different from their normal verbal thoughts. We all have a little voice speaking to ourselves, and we're aware of that — but the hallucinated voices are different from that. The first thing is that people often really "hear" them, as if they come through their ears. And the other thing is that the content is really quite different — it's not the usual way that you tend to speak to yourself.

Our findings about the content of hallucinations goes well with the fact that we saw the most extensive activity in the right language production

3. Frank Larøi, Iris E. Sommer, Jan Dirk Blom, et al., "The Characteristic Features of Auditory Verbal Hallucinations in Clinical and Nonclinical Groups: State-of-the-Art Overview and Future Directions," *Schizophrenia Bulletin*, 2012, 38, 4.

area of the right hemisphere. That would also suggest that language that is heard during auditory hallucination comes from a different source than our usual speech and verbal thoughts.

LEAHY: You mentioned that the voices often command the person to do harm to themselves, and I've read about voices commanding the person to commit suicide. Do the voices lack an interest in self-preservation?

SOMMER: Well I don't think that the voices have a completely distinct personality of their own — I think that they are just a product for our mind. In my view they are comparable to dreams. So our mind is perfectly capable of creating a reality of its own that is really not based on any stimuli from the outside world. And we also tend to have nightmares, and in our nightmares our greatest fears become real. Well, they are not really "real," but they are real for the period that we are dreaming. And I think that hallucinations are quite similar to that.

So what I see in patients is that their voices talk about their greatest fears. For example, women with children may hear voices that threaten their children, or that tell them that they are a very poor mother — which is often their greatest fear. Or some men, who may have concerns about their sexual functioning, may have voices that tell them that they are gay — even though they're not, but perhaps they have a fear about it. Other people's voices tell them that they have committed all kinds of crimes, and even that they have harmed their loved ones. So often our greatest fears are what is expressed by these voices, which is similar to nightmares.

I have some ideas about how that might work. I think that hallucinations are related to memory. So just like dreams, I think that hallucinations are a kind of potpourri created from elements from our memory. And strong emotional elements — like our greatest fears, but also love — have such a strong component, because it's very important to remember them. So they come up first. These connections are so strong, so these highly emotional contents come bubbling up from our memories first. So that would be my explanation. It's still very speculative, but that would be my idea as to why these voices are often so negative.

I should also say that not all people have negative hallucinations. We have interviewed some 150 healthy individuals, who experience hallucinations on a very frequent basis — so for example, they hear voices once a week, or sometimes even several times a day — yet they function well, and they are not bothered by these voices. The very important difference between those people and the patients who do suffer from their voices is that the emotional content of their voices is neutral, or sometimes even positive. They sometimes hear comforting words from the voices, or neutral words, or very practical warnings. So it's not the "nightmare" kind of hallucination, but more the "normal dream" kind of hallucination. So that exists too, but of course those people don't come into hospitals, and so most psychiatrists don't speak to those people very often — but that variant also exists.

LEAHY: What do you think accounts for the fact that, historically speaking, hallucinations were more accepted, whereas now they are often viewed as a sign of mental illness?

SOMMER: Hallucinations have become associated with mental illness in Western societies, but there are many other cultures where hallucinations are still accepted. Even in our Western society, hearing voices is still accepted by some groups — for example, in the Catholic Church, in Muslim culture, and in the Vodou religion. Hallucinations are also accepted by people that are drawn to the paranormal, so for example, there are many healers and mediums for whom it's perfectly acceptable to hear voices, and they're actually viewed as being gifted. So in some areas, they are still accepted, but yes, in mainstream Western psychiatry hearing voices has been pathologized.

LEAHY: Can you speak about some of the treatments or therapies that you've developed for individuals that are troubled by their auditory hallucinations?

SOMMER: Yes, for the past six years we have studied auditory verbal hallucinations quite intensively, and we've developed quite a bit of knowledge about what is going on in the brain, and why people experience hallucinations. So the very critical step that we're taking now is how to treat them. Many people are not bothered by their voices, but there are others — such as those patients here at our clinic — who are very troubled by their voices.

We do have antipsychotic medication, and that works quite well for the majority, but there is still a significant minority — some 25 to 30 percent — of patients that are diagnosed with schizophrenia who do not respond, or who respond insufficiently to antipsychotic medication. These patients still experience these very nasty voices, for years without end. So we want to develop alternative therapies that can help those patients as well. That's what we're working on right now, and I really hope that we will succeed.

* * *

MARCEL KUIJSTEN: Thank you for taking the time to answer some follow-up questions on Professor Sommer's interview.

SANNE BREDEROO: I'm happy to. Like Professor Iris Sommer, I'm both a researcher and a clinician, which I find to be a pleasant combination. My daily contact with people who experience auditory verbal hallucinations strongly motivates me to better understand the working mechanisms of voice hearing, which I believe will ultimately lead to better treatment of those who suffer from bothersome voices. However, hearing voices is more common than people generally think, and not all voice hearers experience distress from them.

KUIJSTEN: Can you describe some of the recent research from Professor Sommer's lab that supports the hypothesis that activity in the language areas of the non-dominant hemisphere (typically the right hemisphere in right-handed individuals) is responsible for the generation of auditory verbal hallucinations?

BREDEROO: Recent work from Iris Sommer's lab and others has focused on characterizing connectivity patterns between brain areas in people who experience hallucinations. Some of these studies show that brain networks related to hallucinations are characterized by altered connections between regions typically implicated in hearing, language, emotion, and executive control.[4] Moreover, it was reported that language areas in the right hemisphere show increased connectivity in patients with a schizophrenia-spectrum disorder, of whom the large majority experienced hallucinations.[5] Recently, converging evidence for the right hemisphere hypothesis of hallucinations came from a study from Iris Sommer's lab performing linguistic typology of auditory verbal hallucinations. The study showed that different subtypes of auditory verbal hallucinations exist, with one such subtype being characterized by short utterances that lack linguistic or syntactical complexity.[6] The type of "speech" of such auditory verbal hallucinations is

---

4. Haiyang Geng, et al., "Abnormal Dynamic Resting-state Brain Network Organization in Auditory Verbal Hallucination," *Brain Structure and Function*, 2020, 225, 2315–2330.

5. Edwin van Dellen, et al., "Functional Brain Networks in the Schizophrenia Spectrum and Bipolar Disorder with Psychosis," *NPJ Schizophrenia*, 2020, 6, 2.

6. Currently in press. See also: J.N. de Boer, et al., "A Linguistic Comparison Between Auditory Verbal

much in line with what we understand to be the language capacity of the non-dominant hemisphere.

KUIJSTEN: Have possible factors that lead some people to have non-dominant hemisphere language activity, resulting in auditory verbal hallucinations, been identified? Are these areas of the brain normally inhibited in non-voice hearers?

BREDEROO: Yes, the idea would be that also in non-voice hearers, the hemisphere that is not dominant for language (often the right hemisphere) could produce some — very simplistic — language. However, in these people, the language-dominant hemisphere inhibits such activation through strong connections between the two hemispheres. As a result, these people do not experience auditory hallucinations. In individuals in whom the non-dominant language hemisphere gets free rein because it is not properly inhibited, the experience of auditory verbal hallucinations can arise. This implies that having a less strongly lateralized brain for language (i.e., both hemispheres deal more equally with language-related processes and therefore do not inhibit each other as much) produces a higher chance of hearing voices. This is in line with what we know about patients with schizophrenia, who often show weaker lateralization than people without this disorder.[7] The search for factors implicated in lateralization strength is ongoing.

KUIJSTEN: So if language is distributed more evenly in both hemispheres, people are more likely to experience auditory hallucinations. This is very interesting, and it certainly extends the evidence for the involvement of the right hemisphere language areas in auditory hallucinations.

According to Jaynes, during the what he calls the bicameral period, auditory hallucinations served the purpose of directing people's behavior in non-habitual situations. People are often surprised to learn that some people today continue to experience hallucinations that direct their behavior. How prevalent are "command hallucinations," as they are called, or hallucinations concerned with directing a person's behavior?

Hallucinations in Patients with a Psychotic Disorder and in Nonpsychotic Individuals: Not Just What the Voices Say, But How They Say It," *Brain and Language*, 2016, 162, 10-18.
7. I.E. Sommer, N.F. Ramsey, and R.S. Kahn, "Language Lateralization in Schizophrenia, an fMRI Study," *Schizophrenia Research*, 2001, 52, 1-2; Iris Sommer and René S. Kahn (eds.), *Language Lateralization and Psychosis* (Cambridge University Press, 2009).

BREDEROO: Among psychiatric patients who hear voices, about half of them have heard command voices (although this is based on several studies, producing quite a large range of 18%-89%).[8] With our lab we recently published a large-scale study about the phenomenology of hallucinations in the general population, and found that 8.3% of a little over 10,000 participants reported to have heard a command voice at least once during their lifetime.[9]

KUIJSTEN: It's very interesting that command hallucinations are found among the general population, and not just in those diagnosed with psychiatric disorders. Can you describe some of the other similarities and differences between auditory hallucinations in clinical versus non-clinical populations?

BREDEROO: Yes, there are some known differences in auditory hallucinations between clinical and non-clinical populations. One is that the content of hallucinations on average is less negative in non-clinical voice hearers, although it is not the case that non-clinical voice hearers only hear positive hallucinations. It has also been reported that non-clinical voices lead to less experienced distress than voices in people who are diagnosed with a psychiatric disorder. There are no clear differences in terms of phenomenological aspects of the voices such as volume, the number of voices, or gender of the voices. Personification of the voices is known to occur in both clinical and non-clinical voice hearers.[10]

KUIJSTEN: The findings of relatively wide-spread auditory hallucinations among the general population is particularly interesting, as is the personification of the voices. It has been discovered that auditory hallucinations are also common among the hearing impaired, although this has not been studied extensively. Can you describe your research on auditory hallucinations in the hearing impaired?

---

8. F. Shawyer, et al., "Command Hallucinations and Violence: Implications for Detention and Treatment," *Psychiatry, Psychology, and Law*, 2003, 10.

9. Currently in press. See also: Mascha M.J. Linszen, et al., "Phenomenology of Hallucinations in the General Population: A Large Online Survey," in M.M.J. Linszen, *Understanding Hallucinations Outside the Context of Psychotic Disorders* (Doctoral dissertation, University of Groningen, 2021).

10. Kirstin Daalman and Kelly M. Diederen, "A Final Common Pathway to Hearing Voices: Examining Differences and Similarities in Clinical and Non-Clinical Individuals," *Psychosis*, 2013, 5, 3; Wei Lin Toh, et al., "Characteristics of Non-Clinical Hallucinations: A Mixed-Methods Analysis of Auditory, Visual, Tactile and Olfactory Hallucinations in a Primary Voice-Hearing Cohort," *Psychiatry Research*, 2020, 289; Kirstin Daalman, et al., "The Same or Different? A Phenomenological Comparison of Auditory Verbal Hallucinations in Healthy and Psychotic Individuals," *Journal of Clinical Psychiatry*, 2011, 72, 3.

BREDEROO: It has long been thought that auditory hallucinations occurring in the context of hearing impairment are relatively simple in nature, for example presenting as tinnitus, or in the form of music. To the contrary, in recent studies from our lab we show that hearing-impairment can be associated with quite complex hallucinations, and hearing voices is relatively common. We also found that spontaneous activity of language-related brain areas is associated with voice hearing in the hearing-impaired, and that hearing impairment should be considered a risk factor for the development of hallucinations.[11]

KUIJSTEN: Can you update us on the treatments being developed in Professor Sommer's lab for persistent auditory hallucinations?

BREDEROO: A line of research that Iris Sommer and her lab colleagues have been pursuing is the effect of safe and non-invasive brain stimulation over certain brain areas in the hope of diminishing brain activation that could lead to auditory hallucinations. Results so far are mixed, so it's difficult to draw any strong conclusions at this moment.[12] Other non-pharmaceutical therapies that are carried out are, for example, based on coping and cognitive behavioral therapy. A specific example is competitive memory training, in which resilience against abusive content of auditory hallucinations is created by strengthening positive feelings about oneself, and evaluating the perceived status of the voices.[13]

KUIJSTEN: What are some of the things that you hope to investigate in the future?

BREDEROO: The past decades have taught us a lot about voice hearing and the phenomenology and working mechanisms of voices, which had been investigated predominantly in light of psychosis. Recently, more attention has been given to non-clinical hallucinations, which I think is an

11. Theresa M. Marschall, et al., "Spontaneous Brain Activity Underlying Auditory Hallucinations in the Hearing-Impaired," *Cortex*, 2021, 136, 1-13; M.M.J. Linszen, et al., "Auditory Hallucinations in Adults with Hearing Impairment: A Large Prevalence Study," *Psychological Medicine*, 2019, 49, 1.
12. Sanne Koops, et al., "Predicting Response to rTMS for Auditory Hallucinations: Younger Patients and Females Do Better," *Schizophrenia Research*, 2018, 195; Elias Wagner, et al., "Repetitive Transcranial Magnetic Stimulation (rTMS) for Schizophrenia Patients Treated with Clozapine," *The World Journal of Biological Psychiatry*, 2021, 22, 1; Sanne Koops, et al., "Treating Auditory Hallucinations with Transcranial Direct Current Stimulation in a Double-Blind, Randomized Trial," *Schizophrenia Research*, 2018, 201, 329-336.
13. Mark van der Gaag, et al., "Initial Evaluation of the Effects of Competitive Memory Training (COMET) on Depression in Schizophrenia-Spectrum Patients with Persistent Auditory Verbal Hallucinations: A Randomized Controlled Trial," *British Journal of Clinical Psychology*, 2012, 51, 2.

important avenue to explore further. I am also interested in investigating auditory hallucinations in other disorders, such as dissociative identity disorder, personality disorders, and neurodegenerative disorders. Of particular interest to me remain the differential roles of the two cerebral hemispheres in the occurrence and characterization of hallucinations. Finally, I'm interested in elucidating the influence of sleep on hallucinations.[14]

KUIJSTEN: Thank you again. It's been fascinating to hear about your research and how much more has been learned about the nature of auditory hallucinations in recent years. We will be following your future research with interest.

BREDEROO: My pleasure.

---

14. Sanne G. Brederoo, et al., "Fragmented Sleep Relates To Hallucinations Across Perceptual Modalities in the General Population," *Scientific Reports*, 2021, 7735.

Epilogue

JULIAN JAYNES'S THEORY provides convincing explanations to many of the mysteries of both ancient history and our modern world, as I hope the preceding interviews made clear. Furthermore, Jaynes's theory provides the foundational groundwork of four testable hypotheses on the origin of the modern mind. Presenting the evidence for each of Jaynes's four hypotheses individually helps clarify misunderstandings and facilitates a better understanding of the overall theory.

As the interviews in this volume have illustrated, a tremendous number of new studies have emerged over the past four decades that both inform and extend our understanding of Jaynes's four hypotheses. On the other hand, much more work remains to be done.

Jaynes did not claim to have all of the answers or to have investigated every possible detail. He understood that many of the details of his theory would have to be elucidated by future scholars. His four testable hypotheses provide practically limitless opportunities for future investigations. Potential topics include:

Hypothesis I: Consciousness Based on Language
- metaphorical language in the development of consciousness
- individual and cultural differences in consciousness
- elaborating and expanding the features of consciousness
- differences between linguistic and non-linguistic thought
- the mentality of non-linguistic individuals
- children's development of consciousness through language
- nonconscious learning and cognition
- consciousness and self-control
- consciousness and cognitive behavioral therapy
- individual differences in inner dialogue
- individual differences in mental imagery
- mental imagery in sports performance

- changes to dreams as children develop consciousness
- strategies for expanding and developing the features of consciousness
- consciousness and the self
- consciousness and meditation
- consciousness and neurofeedback
- consciousness and lucid dreams
- consciousness and the conception of time
- consciousness and the development of deceit
- changes to consciousness in the Middle Ages
- connections between Buddhism and Jaynes's conception of consciousness
- reinterpreting art history from a Jaynesian perspective

Hypothesis II: Bicameral Mentality

- biographical studies of well known voice hearers throughout history
- analysis of ancient texts for evidence of bicameral mentality
- archaeological evidence for bicameral mentality in different cultures (idols, monumental mortuary architecture, etc.)
- anthropological evidence for bicameral mentality in different cultures (prophecy, oracles, divination, "spirit possession," glossolalia, etc.)
- vestiges of bicameral mentality in different cultures, especially in recently contacted preliterate societies
- bicameral mentality in isolated populations, such as Fiji and Easter Island
- cross-cultural studies of hearing voices
- the prevalence and content of command hallucinations
- the nature and prevalence of voice hearing in non-clinical populations
- voice hearing in children, and the degree to which imaginary companions involve actual hallucinations
- religion as a vestige of bicameral mentality
- hypnosis as a vestige of bicameral mentality
- nostalgia for bicameral mentality in various aspects of culture
- vestiges of bicameral mentality in cults
- placebo effects and bicameral mentality
- the role of visual hallucinations in bicameral mentality
- applying Jaynes's idea of authorization to better understand politics and political movements

Hypothesis III: Dating the Development of Consciousness

- literal retranslations of ancient texts that avoid misleading, modern impositions
- analysis of the evolution of mind-related words in ancient languages
- analysis of the occurrence of mental language in texts over time
- cultural changes as a result of the transition to consciousness
- changes to dreams (from visitation/bicameral to modern/conscious) as cultures develop consciousness
- evidence for the transition from bicameral mentality to consciousness in different cultures (Egypt, Mesopotamia, China, etc.)
- the transition of law from bicameral to conscious
- Jesus as a reformer who tried to accommodate the change from a bicameral to a conscious type of spirituality

Hypothesis IV: Jaynes's Neurological Model

- brain areas that are active during auditory verbal hallucinations
- language lateralization and voice hearing
- non-pharmaceutical alternatives to the treatment of auditory hallucinations, such as transcranial magnetic stimulation
- potential surgical interventions for severe, debilitating auditory hallucinations that do not respond to medication, such as severing the corpus callosum
- neurological substrates of hyper-religiosity and their relationship to hallucinations
- mental duality in split-brain individuals

Important studies have already been done in many of these areas, many of which have already been mentioned. Other topics remain largely unexplored. Paradigm shifting ideas often take generations to be fully understood and appreciated, and it is my hope that future generations will come to a fuller understanding and appreciation of Julian Jaynes's momentous insights, and build upon his important and foundational work.

Appendix:
Additional Discussion

Additional discussion with Marcel Kuijsten from Chapter 1, "Julian Jaynes, the Bicameral Mind, and the Origin of Consciousness":

HENRIK PALMGREN: How does Jaynes explain certain things that were accomplished in history — if we look at, for example, architecture and the building of cities. An obvious example is the building of the pyramids at Giza. They are believed to have been built around 2500 BCE — something like that — which would place it before the time of the development of our modern consciousness. The pyramids are very sophisticated — did we have some type of skill then that we do not have now? Did Jaynes tackle these types of issues?

MARCEL KUIJSTEN: It's a great question, and there are a number of different aspects to this. I will give you a short answer and then a longer answer that addresses the broader context of this question.

The short answer is that bicameral hallucinations likely provided much of the planning, problem solving, and direction that would now take place in our introspectable mind-space. In other words, imagine that the thoughts or insights that you introspect upon are instead perceived as an auditory or visual hallucination from a god — either while awake or in a dream. There are cases of people who, even today, experience extremely vivid visual hallucinations and even visual command hallucinations.[1] So we can imagine not only auditory hallucinations of commands and instructions but also visual hallucinations of something that might even look like building blueprints.

In a lecture given some years after the publication of his book, Jaynes relates a number of different bicameral — or "visitation" — dreams. One of these is the story of Gudea's dream. Gudea was a ruler in the city of

---

1. Oliver Sacks, *Hallucinations* (Alfred A. Knopf, 2012); D.H. ffytche, et al., "Visual Command Hallucinations in a Patient with Pure Alexia," *Journal of Neurology, Neurosurgery and Psychiatry*, 2004, 75.

Lagash in southern Mesopotamia around 2100 BCE. Cuneiform tablets tell us that Gudea experiences a series of visitation dreams, and in the first dream he is commanded to build a temple. And in the following visitation dreams, Gudea receives the precise building instructions for the temple and its furnishings.[2]

The classicist H.W.F. Saggs notes that Gudea's dream is "one of the best known instances of divine instructions for the building of a temple."[3] Saggs also relates a similar story where the Babylonian king Nabu-na'id "received instructions through a dream about the rebuilding of the temple of the god Sin at Harran."[4] According to Saggs,

> the restoration of a temple or the building of a new temple was an undertaking requiring the most complicated rituals, as well as the most precise investigations to ensure that the god's will was properly understood and carried out.[5]

So we have specific historical examples of how bicameral voices and visions were instrumental in the building of things like ziggurats, temples, and pyramids.[6] Visitation dreams instructing temple and monastery construction continue well into the conscious era. For example, around the year 1080 in France, the monk Gunzo was visited by Saint Peter, who provides "the measurements and the methods of construction for [the monastery] Cluny III ... [and] admonishes Gunzo to memorize them."[7] In another example, Saint Benedict instructed two monks in a dream on how to build the monastery of Terracina, and "showed them exactly where each section of the monastery was to stand."[8]

But I think the larger question is, "Can people plan and build things without Jaynesian consciousness?" And this gets back to our common sense intuitions about consciousness, that often mislead us into thinking that consciousness is necessary for much more than it is. We have to step back and remind ourselves that, based on what constitutes Jaynesian

---

2. Julian Jaynes, "The Dream of Agamemnon," in M. Kuijsten, *The Julian Jaynes Collection* (Julian Jaynes Society, 2012).

3. H.W.F. Saggs, *The Greatness that Was Babylon* (New American Library, 1962), p. 346.

4. Ibid., p. 347.

5. Ibid., p. 346.

6. See also A. Leo Oppenheim, *The Interpretation of Dreams in the Ancient Near East* (American Philosophical Society, 1956); William V. Harris, *Dreams and Experience in Classical Antiquity* (Harvard University Press, 2009).

7. See Carolyn M. Carty, "The Role of Gunzo's Dream in the Building of Cluny III," *Gesta*, 1988, 27.

8. *Saint Gregory the Great, Dialogues*, p. 90, quoted in Carty, "The Role of Gunzo's Dream." See also, Carolyn M. Carty, "The Role of Medieval Dream Images in Authenticating Ecclesiastical Construction," *Zeitschrift für Kunstgeschichte*, 1999, 62.

consciousness, even things like architecture and construction can be accomplished without the use of introspection — it's another type of problem solving that could have been done nonconsciously.

Something that can help us to think about this is to look at the animal kingdom. Animals accomplish all kinds of amazing things nonconsciously. We can look at things like determining the location of and the building of nests, hives, and mounds — which are often quite elaborate. Some ant species are excellent fungus farmers. Crows demonstrate impressive problem-solving skills. Many different species migrate, engage in cooperative hunting, and elaborate mate selection processes are seen even in insects.

These are just a few brief examples, but it helps to remind ourselves that animals and even insects accomplish many different amazing things without consciousness — things that often seem to involve what we would call "planning." In non-human animals we attribute these things to "instincts," yet when it comes to similar activities in humans, we are quick to attribute just about everything to consciousness. We simply assume that the kind of "planning" necessary to build a structure *must* require consciousness.

This is likely not the case, but as conscious beings, it is extremely difficult for us to imagine. Traditionally there has been a somewhat arbitrary distinction between human and nonhuman animals in this regard, but over the past several decades the field of evolutionary psychology has demonstrated that much of what we think we "decide" consciously often has a nonconscious, instinctual, or genetically hard-wired component. Evidence suggests that our inner dialogue may simply rationalize many of our nonconsciously driven behaviors after the fact, all the while giving us the illusion of making conscious choices. Even many of our beliefs may be based less on sound reasoning than the matching of ideas to our genetically-based temperaments — which is perhaps why seemingly unrelated groups of beliefs tend to cluster in individuals.[9]

Also worth mentioning here is the evidence we see from prodigies and savants.[10] For example, there are cases of individuals who have the ability to solve complex mathematical problems instantly and nonconsciously. Or consider the case of Stephen Wiltshire, a British artist who has autism. Wiltshire is able to nonconsciously recreate city skylines entirely from memory. These and other interesting cases tell us that we at least have the

---

9. See Steven Pinker, *The Blank Slate: The Modern Denial of Human Nature* (Viking, 2002).

10. D.H. Feldman and M.J. Morelock, "Prodigies and Savants," in R.J. Sternberg and S.B. Kaufman (eds.), *The Cambridge Handbook of Intelligence* (Cambridge University Press, 2011).

potential to carry out complex tasks and solve many different types of difficult problems nonconsciously.

In order to get a better understanding of these things, the first step is to continue to determine exactly what kinds of things Jaynesian consciousness is necessary for and what can be accomplished without it, all the while being aware of our natural inclination to conclude that consciousness is necessary for just about everything.[11] Although it's highly counterintuitive, I think we will continue to discover that consciousness in the Jaynesian sense — an analog 'I' narratizing in a mind-space — is simply not essential to many activities and behaviors. At the same time, it is absolutely essential for other things. So, using the foundation that Jaynes provides, we must continue to develop a better understanding of exactly where this line is, so to speak. On this point, I like to encourage people to re-read Jaynes's first two chapters several times in order to fully understand his arguments.

Finally, it is also important to understand that consciousness is not an all-or-nothing proposition, but rather a package of features. These different features likely develop gradually over time, and in somewhat different ways in different cultures. The transition from bicameral mentality to consciousness probably took place over many generations. So some of the features of consciousness that Jaynes outlines may have been present before others, and may have been present in some individuals before others — just as we see variability in the features of consciousness between individuals and cultures to this day.

Just as today there are individuals who excel in various areas, that indeed have talents that far exceed the average person — whether it be in business, academics, medicine, music, art, athletics, or what have you — it seems reasonable to assume that there were also individuals in the past who possessed higher than average intelligence, skills, or abilities. Perhaps there were also individuals who began to develop certain features of consciousness earlier than the population as a whole, especially in cultures where literacy was not widespread.

In Egypt, evidence suggests that we start to see a gradual transition towards consciousness at a slightly earlier date than in some of the other civilizations around the Mediterranean, but also one that took place over a much longer period of time — when compared to what we see in ancient Greece, for example. To gain a better understanding of exactly when the transition from bicameral mentality to consciousness took place in different

---

11. See Tor Nørretranders, *The User Illusion: Cutting Consciousness Down to Size* (Penguin Books, 1991).

cultures will require years of research by many different scholars. Much of this is lost to history, but there is still much more that can be learned.

What is so interesting about the pyramids, in terms of Jaynes's theory, is that the whole purpose behind them was to create temples for the gods. In Egypt, each king in death becomes the god Osiris, likely because it is the king's voice that his subjects continued to hallucinate. The pyramids and other similar structures likely also served as large, visual hallucinatory aids for the surrounding population. So the driving force behind the construction of the pyramids really only makes sense if we look at it through the lens of Jaynes's theory.

I think this point is easily overlooked because to some degree we take these things for granted. But it's the fact that in death, each king becomes a god, and it's the continued hearing of the voices of the gods issuing commands that was very likely the driving force behind the process of pyramid and temple construction, not only in Egypt but in other parts of the world. And we see evidence, as I mentioned, that the gods were in fact directing their construction, along with the other major decisions of the populace.

All of these things have been well documented, but are truly a mystery outside of Jaynes's theory. They simply do not make any sense from the perspective of our modern psychology. But if we step back and look at them objectively from the perspective of Jaynes's bicameral mind theory — then suddenly all of this starts to make sense. In other words, I think that the reason why the pyramids were constructed in the first place has never been adequately explained, unless we look at this from this perspective. Without Jaynes's theory, we are just left with rather unconvincing speculation. This speculation was largely accepted, because before Jaynes's theory, there simply were no other competing ideas.

PALMGREN: That's quite interesting. Do you then consider the development of consciousness to be an advantage or a hindrance? In one sense, it seems like we were already very sophisticated, in terms of the kinds of things that we could accomplish. Perhaps there were even things that we could accomplish then that we can no longer accomplish now. It seems that at that time we were closer to nature and closer to the natural world, and now we are becoming further and further removed from nature.

KUIJSTEN: It is an interesting question, and one that has come up before. I think the broader context to your question is something of a motif that I've heard in different contexts, which is the idea of a lost "Golden Age."

PALMGREN: Yes.

KUIJSTEN: We can see this theme in the Book of Genesis, in the story of The Fall and the Garden of Eden. There is this recurring theme in different cultures that there was a Golden Age in the past that has been lost, and that we should in some sense strive to recapture. Jaynes suggests — and I agree — that some aspects of this recurring theme are actually a parable for the breakdown of the bicameral mind.

PALMGREN: That's right.

KUIJSTEN: What Jaynes means by that is that there is this similar theme that we see in many ancient texts that has to do with this "lost age" where we were in direct contact with the gods. People tend to think of the ancient civilizations in terms of our modern-day concept of religion, but in reality it was very different. The gods were always there, they were very present, and they were telling people what to do, more similar to — as a friend of mine once put it — a high school football coach than to our modern concept of a very distant, remote God.

So the gods were right there with them, often in the form of idols: they dressed them, they bathed them, and they performed ceremonies with them. And the idols did not *represent* the gods — the way we might think of it today — the idols *were* the gods. This is clearly a very different type of psychology than we have today, and a concept that is very hard for us to relate to. The idol was the god, and every one of another thousand idols of that god were also the same god. It was not a "representation" of the god, in the way we might perhaps think of a symbol as being representative of some larger idea. For them, this idol actually was the god, and it was issuing direct commands. And this was the way things operated for thousands of years.

But as things slowly began to change, and the features of consciousness developed and the bicameral voices were suppressed, there was subsequently a great deal of anguish and despair. This is similar to how someone today might feel if a close friend suddenly stopped talking to them, without explanation. For many people, the natural inclination is to think, "What did I do wrong, why is this person upset with me?" And we see the same kind of thing in many ancient stories: "Why are the gods angry with us? Why have they abandoned us?"

As the voices fell silent, there is a sense of a fall from grace and a feeling of abandonment, and I think much of this idea of a loss that took place in ancient history can be attributed to the breakdown of the bicameral mind.

But to get back to your original question: "Was the development of consciousness a net positive or a net negative?" I think that what we have gained outweighs what we have lost. If we look at this transition objectively, the development of modern, subjective consciousness is what enabled what Jaynes calls the "cognitive explosion" — the sudden birth in ancient Greece of things like philosophy, science, mathematics, theater, and history. Of course there will always be some sense of a trade-off, as with consciousness came some negatives as well, such as the beginnings of many of our modern mental illnesses, which are often exacerbated by our internal dialogue, as we see in things like anxiety and depression.

PALMGREN: I'd like to talk about drugs, entheogens, and various hallucinogenic substances that seem to have played a major role in terms of different cultures trying to get in contact with gods and spirits, as well as inspiring creativity. What is your take on the use of drugs and entheogens and the importance of that for the development of consciousness?

KUIJSTEN: It's interesting that Jaynes did not delve into this subject more in his book. There is an article on this topic in *The Jaynesian* (the newsletter of the Julian Jaynes Society) by the psychiatrist Rick Strassman. Professor Strassman details his extensive research of the hallucinogen DMT (N,N-Dimethyltryptamine). I think that the use of hallucinogenic substances — either in our ancient past or modern use — is yet another way that we see people trying to regain what they perceive as this lost connection to the gods, or the guiding bicameral voices. As the breakdown of the bicameral mind occurred, many different practices emerged to try to discern the will of the gods. We see the proliferation of things like divination, omens, oracles, and prayer — as well as the use of hallucinogenic substances — all as attempts to elicit the direct communication with the gods that had been lost. And we see this attempt to reconnect with the lost bicameral voices in different cultures throughout history and around the world.

Of course we're speaking about this metaphorically — what is being attempted is to stimulate right temporal lobe or other brain activity, triggering a hallucinatory experience, or to use other means to make decisions in the absence of the bicameral hallucinations. I want to be clear that we are not talking about "gods" in a literal sense, but rather that that was how the voices were interpreted.

Another important point to note is that the onset of hallucinations via these substances underscores the fact that hallucinations can be elicited in a wide variety of ways. Hallucinations can be brought on in normal people by sleep deprivation, sensory deprivation, social isolation, intense stress, and any number of other ways. To me this provides additional evidence for Jaynes's theory by showing that hallucinations are not a rare aberration that only occur in a small number of people with some type of brain pathology, but that they are actually fairly widespread and found on a spectrum throughout societies. So in other words, many people who are not considered psychotic — people who are considered normal and have not been diagnosed with any type of mental illness — experience auditory hallucinations to one extent or another, sometimes on a daily basis. This fact was largely unknown until recently — because people tend not to talk openly about it — and this supports the idea that hallucinations played an important role in our psychology during the previous bicameral period.

PALMGREN: So are hallucinations then perhaps a vital form of human functioning? Do they help one to realize unconscious or suppressed ideas?

KUIJSTEN: In our modern culture, where we learn consciousness in childhood, I think that experiencing hallucinations is generally more harmful than helpful. But the experience occurs on a very wide spectrum, so on one extreme you have people with hallucinations that are so persistent and intrusive that they need to seek medical help, while on the other extreme you have people that only rarely have the experience and do not find it at all distressing. And then there are others, who we might say are somewhere in the middle of the spectrum, who hear voices more frequently, but in fact have developed a positive relationship with their voices, almost like an imaginary companion or a helpful guide.

For a long time, the stigma of mental illness caused people to not want to share their experiences, so it's only in the past few decades that we have begun to learn more about just how diverse these experiences are. And to your point, yes, in some cases, the voices can be a source of inspiration or creativity, as they were for many of the inspired poets, for example. There is a long standing association of creativity and "madness," that I think comes from the idea of bicameral hallucinations as a source of inspiration.

An example of this that Jaynes discusses is William Blake.[12] Blake relates that he was not so much composing his poetry as transcribing it — he felt that angels were dictating his poems to him and he was simply

---

12. Julian Jaynes, "The Ghost of a Flea: Visions of William Blake," in M. Kuijsten (ed.), *Reflections on the Dawn of Consciousness* (Julian Jaynes Society, 2006).

transcribing them. A neurological explanation of this might be that he was tapping into the nonconscious creativity of his right hemisphere via bicameral hallucinations.

So perhaps we can say that one should look for ways to tap into the latent creativity of the right hemisphere, that, given the structure and routine of our modern daily life, we may not always be fully utilizing. We see this in moments of inspiration and what people call "intuition." I think are both examples of nonconscious brain processing, and perhaps we should look for ways to enhance the process of bringing these insights into conscious awareness — whether it be through hypnosis, meditation, or, as you mentioned previously, some type of hallucinogenic substance. I don't know very much about hallucinogens, other than to say that they have seen something of a renewed interest in recent years, especially in therapeutic settings.[13]

There is still much more to learn about the content of the voices and the variety of these experiences in both clinical and non-clinical populations. I think this underscores the fact that as a species, we still have not completely made the transition from bicameral mentality to subjective consciousness — many people still experience bicameral hallucinations in one form or another.

PALMGREN: I've heard that it's optimal for us to look at problems or find solutions using both of our hemispheres more in balance — to look at things with our entire brain, so to speak — or when there is better communication between the two hemispheres. Or that perhaps in some cases, for various reasons we are more predisposed to using one hemisphere more than the other. What are your thoughts on that?

KUIJSTEN: Yes, there has been a great deal of talk in popular psychology about the different areas of specialization in each of the two hemispheres, and things like how perhaps we should be "using our right hemisphere more" or that our current educational system predisposes us to be more "left brained." Like with any serious topic that becomes popularized, a degree of flakiness was added that confused the subject — I think that it's fairly widely agreed upon now that in many cases those ideas were taken too far. In reality, we are using both of our hemispheres all of the time.

That being said, there are distinct differences between the two hemispheres, and at its core, there are some solid ideas there. I think there are

---

13. Michael Pollan, *How to Change Your Mind: What the New Science of Psychedelics Teaches Us About Consciousness, Dying, Addiction, Depression, and Transcendence* (Penguin Press, 2018).

things that we can do to enhance our creativity and indeed our conscious thought. After all, if subjective consciousness is something that we learn, then it should be something that we can work to enhance. So one of the things we can be aware of is what I call "consciousness diminishing activities." We need a certain amount of quiet, uninterrupted time in order to think and have creative new ideas and insights. So we have to be careful that we are not getting too caught up in our routines, taking on too many obligations, or always busy with one thing or another.

Also, a lot of what we talk about as "escapism" can be consciousness diminishing. If we step back and think about it, that is actually the goal. We want to "turn off" for a bit and quiet our inner dialogue. So while a little bit of escapism is a good thing — we all need time to relax and recharge — it becomes a problem when it's used to chronically avoid thinking about difficult problems or life challenges that one may be dealing with. So whether it be chronically playing video games, drugs and alcohol, endless television watching — even music can be consciousness diminishing. Don't misunderstand, I think that listening to music is generally a good thing — I'm a musician myself. What I am referring to specifically is chronic music listening in order to activate the right hemisphere and diminish conscious thought. This is something we often see in teenagers, for example, walking around with their headphones on. They can be going through a lot of challenges and difficulties and having to make important life decisions, and rather than have to deal with all of that, music becomes a means of escape.

I think that Jaynes would have delved into this more in his second book, *The Consequences of Consciousness*, had he completed that, but we can see some of his thoughts on this in the Afterword that he wrote in 1990. So if we think about it, much of what we consider to be various mental illnesses are in fact what we might call "problems of consciousness." Whether we're talking about depression, anxiety, or obsessive thoughts, these are all examples of our internal dialogue gone awry. So people then try to diminish their internal dialogue through some of these behaviors that I just mentioned.

PALMGREN: Right.

KUIJSTEN: On the other hand, I think there are things we can do to increase our conscious thought, to make sure that we are taking a deliberative, active role in the decisions that we are making, and that we are not just floating along, stuck in our routines, and acting primarily unthinkingly based on habit, or leaving all of our decisions up to others. So, for example, taking the time for things like critical thinking, self reflection, future planning, and certain types of meditation could all be consciousness enhancing activities. Things like martial arts and physical fitness can also help build mental discipline. Then there are things we can do in terms of engaging our right hemisphere, and perhaps enhance our ability to come up with creative solutions to problems. So we might learn or practice a musical instrument, draw, paint, or write, for example.

PALMGREN: So would you say that we are at risk of reducing our ability for consciousness based on the fact that we are now drowning in all kinds of media, and social media, for example? In the same sense that if you don't use a muscle, it will eventually begin to atrophy, if we don't use and train our brain, will consciousness begin to diminish? Is that a possibility?

KUIJSTEN: Yes, I definitely think so. This is the question of, "if consciousness is something that we learned, where is consciousness going from here?" And I think it's an open question. As technology starts to do more and more for us, we start to lose some of our mental abilities. So, for example, before the widespread use of calculators, people did more math in their head. Spell checkers allow us to think less about the correct spelling of words. Or if we think about the ancient Greeks, and the bards that memorized and sang epics like the *Iliad* prior to the development of writing. While they certainly used various memorization techniques and improvisations, I think it's clear that their memory was superior to what we typically see today, because most of us no longer use that skill. So the more our modern technology does our thinking for us, the more I think at least the potential is there for us to think less and less for ourselves.

On the other hand, in some ways technology can free us from routine tasks and give us more time for critical thinking and problem solving. But the potential is there, over the next 100 years or so, for us to see a diminishment of consciousness — perhaps similar to what occurred during the Dark Ages[14] — or perhaps it will go the other way, through better educational practices and things of that nature. It's difficult to say.

People sometimes ask if it would be possible for us to completely revert back to bicameral mentality, but I think something like that could happen only under conditions of a complete societal collapse. I think that would require almost a post-apocalyptic situation, perhaps due to a severe pandemic, a global environmental disaster, or a nuclear war — where there

---

14. Morris Berman, *Coming to Our Senses* (Simon & Schuster, 1998).

is no longer any type of formal education, a complete loss of literacy, and people are forced back into more of a purely survival mode. That kind of scenario could make the basis for a good science fiction novel.

PALMGREN: Right. [laughs]

KUIJSTEN: But yes, I think the potential is there, and we should look for ways to enhance consciousness both throughout our lifetime as well as look for better ways to teach consciousness to each successive generation.

Incidentally — just as a side note — Jaynes's theory has been the inspiration for a number of different fiction and science fiction writers, including Neal Stephenson, Robert Sawyer, Philip Pullman, Terence Hawkins, and Philip K. Dick. More recently, Jaynes's theory was incorporated into the plot of the HBO series *Westworld*, which exposed many new people to Jaynes's ideas.

PALMGREN: Do you know of Michael Persinger at Laurentian University? He developed something called the "god helmet." Have you heard about that?

KUIJSTEN: Yes, and I'm glad you brought that up. Michael Persinger has had a long standing interest in Jaynes's theory and he wrote a wonderful Foreword to *Reflections on the Dawn of Consciousness*. His research is highly relevant to Jaynes's theory. As you mentioned, he has developed something called the "god helmet," which is a helmet that stimulates the right temporal lobe with weak electromagnetic fields. He found that during this process, people often experience what he calls a "sensed presence." And this presence is interpreted within the context of the individual's belief system — so it could be viewed as a ghost, or God, or a deceased relative, etc. But the person has the feeling of someone else being present.

So, yes, Michael Persinger's work is very much related, and there has been work by others on the experience of a sensed presence as well. The psychologist Peter Suedfeld and the wilderness explorer John Geiger published an article titled, "The Sensed Presence as a Coping Resource in Extreme Environments," that details the experience of a sensed presence by extreme environment explorers, often when in life or death situations.[15] The presence is often experienced as quite real, to the extent that even food is offered, and it helps guide them back to safety. John Geiger popularized this experience, that has been described by many different people, in a

---

15. P. Suedfeld and J. Geiger, "The Sensed Presence As A Coping Resource in Extreme Environments," in J.H. Ellens (ed.), *Miracles: God, Science, and Psychology in the Paranormal: Parapsychological Perspectives* (Praeger Publishers, 2008).

book called *The Third Man Factor*.[16] Over the years I've come across many of these accounts, by people escaping the twin towers on 9/11, for example. And so again, in the context of Jaynes's theory, this sensed presence is likely a vestige of what during the bicameral period would have been an individual's personal god and bicameral guiding voice.

So the right temporal lobe is implicated in auditory hallucinations, it's implicated in the feeling of a sensed presence, and then — something that we have not touched on — it's also implicated in religious experience. Without the bicameral mind theory, this is difficult to explain. On this third point, there are cases of people with temporal lobe epilepsy, who generally are relatively normal before the onset of the illness — perhaps they have some vague ideas about religion or they go to church on occasion but it's not particularly important to them — and then they have all of this excitation in the right temporal lobe and they suddenly become what we might call religious zealots: they walk around prophesying and proselytizing, writing large tomes of what they consider to be divine inspiration, dressing in robes, and all of these kinds of behaviors.[17]

The only theory that I am aware of that would explain why auditory hallucinations, the feeling of a sensed presence, and hyper religiosity are all associated with the right temporal lobe would be Jaynes's bicameral mind theory. We just don't see other, competing theories that can offer any kind of explanation for this observation.

PALMGREN: So the similarities and differences that are seen in the experience of a sensed presence are due to the fact that the experience is being interpreted through the lens of one's culture and life experience?

KUIJSTEN: Yes, that's exactly right. The biological basis for the experience is then interpreted through one's own upbringing and worldview. So, we also see cases of people being visited by what they consider to be a ghost or an angel. In our modern society, people often interpret bicameral and sensed presence experiences either in terms of their religious upbringing, or, in some cases, more from the perspective of science fiction, and things like alien abductions. So what today might be perceived as an alien abduction, several hundred years ago might have been perceived as perhaps an incubus or a demon. And we see the ancient bicameral experience interpreted in different ways as well. I mentioned Michael Carr's work on ancient China:

---

16. John Geiger, *The Third Man Factor: Surviving the Impossible* (Hachette Books, 2009).
17. See K. Dewhurst and A.W. Beard, "Sudden Religious Conversions in Temporal Lobe Epilepsy," *British Journal of Psychiatry*, 1970, 540, 497-507.

they had the same type of bicameral experience that Jaynes documents in places like Greece, but they interpreted them in different ways. In China, the concept of gods was not as prominent, and instead we see more of an emphasis on the visitation of dead ancestors.

PALMGREN: That's very interesting. How do you then view the world's religions? Are they based on what we might call a mass delusion, or is there a quality there that is essential to the human experience? Perhaps there is a sense of comfort for people in the idea that we have some kind of "companion" or parental figure that guides us through difficult experiences?

KUIJSTEN: I think that there is some truth to both of those interpretations. I think there is some validity to the idea that as a child grows up, they feel the comfort and protection of their parents, and then as they get older, that feeling is transferred to the idea of a protecting God. So there definitely is some validity to that view, but what I think many of the theories on the origin or the perpetuation of religion miss, or leave out, is that there definitely is a neurological component to all of this. There has been something of an explosion of books on this topic, all proposing various theories about the origin of religion. But I think for the most part they tend to miss that point, and they are often proposing purely sociological explanations. Yet the studies of temporal lobe epilepsy suggest that there is definitely a neurological component to religious beliefs. So then the question we have to ask ourselves is, "Why is this the case? Why would this have evolved?"

There had to be a reason. So some of these other explanations for the origin of religion — having to do with social cohesion and that type of thing — don't look at all of the evidence in its totality, the way that Jaynes's theory does. Jaynes's bicameral mind theory is perhaps the best explanation for the origin of religion in that, we had the phenomena of auditory hallucinations that evolved along with language, that not only conveyed experience from one hemisphere to the other but also served the purpose of reinforcing the hierarchical nature of these early civilizations.

As Jaynes explains, first there would be a chief or king issuing commands, and people hearing repetitions and improvisations of his commands as bicameral hallucinations, and then at some point, he would die, but his voice would still continue to be heard. And now "the king dead is a living god" — his commanding hallucinations continue to be heard after his death.[18] So I do not think that these early, hierarchical civilizations

---

18. Jaynes, *The Origin of Consciousness in the Breakdown of the Bicameral Mind*, p. 143.

would have functioned as effectively as they did without the feelings of authority and externality of the bicameral hallucinatory experience.

So in Jaynes's theory we have both a social and a neurological explanation for how religion, in the modern sense of the term, began. We have to keep in mind that ancient religion, during the bicameral period, was quite different. The gods at that time were very active and present in people's daily lives. And we see this in preliterate societies as well, where they are interacting with the spirit world on a daily basis. So the modern psychiatric view of auditory hallucinations as only being associated with mental illness completely misses the extremely important role that they played throughout human history.

Once the bicameral voices were suppressed and fell silent, we continued to long for this lost source of guidance. And this is how modern religions came about — as an attempt to study, preserve, and teach the guidance of the last known bicameral voices. Jaynes called our modern religions "the nostalgic anguish for the lost bicamerality of a subjectively conscious people."[19] And there are a variety of religious texts that convey this sense of trying to get back to this direct communication with God or the gods that we once had but that was lost.[20]

PALMGREN: I once read that a researcher studying primates — I don't recall the name — observed their reaction to thunder. Primates also have this hierarchical structure lead by an alpha male, and this researcher's interpretation of their behavioral response to the thunder was almost as though there was an alpha male in the sky, so to speak. So there was this idea that the origins of our notion of something "higher than ourselves" could go as far back as the animal kingdom. What are your thoughts on that?

KUIJSTEN: Yes, I think that the idea of thunder and lightning as possibly giving rise to our first notions of there being a God is a very common view, and this idea is mentioned by the philosopher David Stove in his chapter on the origin of religion in my first book. I think that is one aspect of it — there's no question. But if we start to look at the specifics of how all of our modern religions came about, they all have their origin in divine revelation — whether it's the prophets of the Old Testament, or Muhammad in the seventh century, or other figures such as Emanuel Swedenborg, who was a Swedish philosopher and scientist in the eighteenth century who

---

19. Ibid., p. 297.
20. See Psalm 42, for example.

began to hear voices and founded a minor religion, or Joseph Smith and the founding of Mormonism in the nineteenth century.

In each of these cases, the basis for the movement was the experience of divine revelation. And if we interpret this in the context of Jaynes's theory, then all divine revelation is based on auditory hallucination. This of course is a controversial idea that perhaps not everyone will be comfortable with — and it's not something that Jaynes delves into in great depth, because he wanted to keep the focus on his ideas on the origin of consciousness — but I think that it's something that we need to look at, if we really want to have a compelling theory on the origin of religion that takes into account all of the available data.

PALMGREN: That's very interesting. I think that Julian Jaynes's theory has helped us to come a long way in terms of solving the mystery of consciousness, but obviously there are still questions that remain. Over the years, a number of new technologies have emerged that give us greater insights into the workings of the brain. Are you optimistic that we will make further progress in term of solving the mystery of consciousness?

KUIJSTEN: I think that one of the exciting things about this topic is that we are going to be discussing and debating these ideas for many decades to come. And I think that Jaynes's theory is going to continue to be very relevant. Jaynes was far ahead of his time, and many of his ideas are still very much ahead of the thinking in the field of consciousness studies today. After a long period of time where it was not considered a viable topic for research, consciousness is a topic that has now become very popular again. I do think that the new brain imaging technologies have a lot to do with this renewed interest, because they enables us to see the brain in action.

There have been some interesting studies, for example, of people that are in a vegetative state, and it's difficult to determine whether that person is still able to think and perceive their environment, or whether they are essentially "brain dead." And using brain imaging, researchers devised a way to determine which patients were still conscious, by asking them to visualize certain actions — such as playing tennis or navigating their home — and looking for certain pattens of activity.

So I think that, yes, there will be many new interesting developments and insights in the decades ahead, and some of this will be driven by new technological advancements. But having said that, I think that the keys to gaining a better understanding of Jaynesian psychology are actually much more "low tech." What I would like to see more of are studies, such as those done by the developmental psychologist Philip Zelazo, that carefully look at how the various features of consciousness develop in children as they learn language.[21] We need a much better understanding of the role of language in consciousness and higher forms of thought, and particularly the importance of metaphorical language.[22] I think that an interdisciplinary investigation involving both linguists and developmental psychologists would be particularly interesting. And there has been some research on non-linguistic or minimally linguistic children, in terms of understanding the relationship between thought and language, but much more could be done here as well.[23]

Additional discussion with Brian McVeigh from Chapter 3, "Julian Jaynes and the Features of Consciousness":

MARCEL KUIJSTEN: I'd like to discuss some of the key findings from some of your other works, for readers who may not yet be familiar with them. Let's start with your book *A Psychohistory of Metaphors*. Jaynes describes how our interior mind-space is built up through metaphors of the physical world, and in *A Psychohistory of Metaphors* you explore similar themes such as the development of introspection, the relationship between metaphorical language and thought, and some of the implications of our newly learned consciousness. Can you discuss some of your findings?

BRIAN J. McVEIGH: This work attempts to show how wide-ranging the implications of Jaynes's thinking are from what we might call a philosophical perspective. It's a bit ambitious, but I look at how the building blocks of experience — space, time, introspection — share the same metaphors. When cognitive abilities evolve to keep up with social and technological changes, our understandings of location, history, and the interior life are altered. For example, think of how "new spaces" have been opened up by science, such as the astronomical and microscopic. These new spatial scales changed not just how we envision the natural world but, in a way that is

21. Philip Zelazo, et al., "The Development of Consciousness," in P. Zelazo, et al. (eds.), *The Cambridge Handbook on Consciousness* (Cambridge University Press, 2007).
22. See, for example, John Limber, "Language and Consciousness," in M. Kuijsten (ed.), *Reflections on the Dawn of Consciousness* (Julian Jaynes Society, 2006); José Luis Bermúdez, "The Limits of Thinking Without Words," in J. L. Bermúdez, *Thinking Without Words* (Oxford University Press, 2007); Daniel Dennett, *Kinds of Minds* (Basic Books, 1997); Peter Carruthers, *Language, Thought and Consciousness* (Cambridge University Press, 1998).
23. See Susan Curtiss and Harry A Whitaker, *Genie: A Psycholinguistic Study of a Modern-Day Wild Child* (Academic Press, 2014).

not always obvious, they have altered how our introspectable capabilities process visual and spatial modes of experience.

KUIJSTEN: In your book *The 'Other' Psychology of Julian Jaynes*, you discuss a "second" or "other" psychological tradition — one that explores a cultural-historical evolution of the psyche. Can you elaborate on this "other" psychological tradition and some of the implications of this tradition for Jaynes's theory?

McVEIGH: Let me begin to answer your question with an irony of intellectual history. Wilhelm Wundt (1832–1920) is considered to be the founder of modern, experimental psychology. But he devoted a considerable amount of his efforts to what might be called cultural psychology (*Völkerpsychologie*). Mainstream research psychology is presently dominated by laboratory-based, experimental investigations that view mind as something ensconced within the individual. But Wundt was fascinated by how forces external to the psyche shape its operations. Jaynes, of course, originally made a name for himself as a comparative psychologist working in a laboratory. However, he soon saw the limitations of this approach for understanding consciousness and found important answers in history, culture, and language. In this regard his theorizing fits neatly into what we can call the "second" or "other" psychological tradition that explores the cultural-historical evolution of psyche as proposed by Wundt, as well as others. Jaynes's value is in how he points out the blind spots of mainstream, establishment psychology.

The takeaway message here is that to understand certain psychological phenomena, an interdisciplinary approach is a must. In the book I use statistics to trace the development of ancient mental lexicons and look at the adaptive role of hallucinations. Hallucinations, by the way, are still with us, not just among those suffering from mental illness, but also among people who experience them in a more benign fashion, though such experiences can still be distressing. I also propose the Bicameral Civilization Inventory Hypothesis. This postulates that from around 3500 to 1000 BCE the archaeological and historical record reveals features of hallucinatory super-religiosity in every known civilization. This is a testable theory.

KUIJSTEN: You also published *Discussions with Julian Jaynes*, which consists of interviews that you conducted with Julian Jaynes, covering a broad range of topics. What would you say were some of the key takeaways from those interviews, or the things that most surprised you?

McVEIGH: Some of the key themes include the need to clarify the definition of consciousness and the pivotal role language studies can play in revealing the development of consciousness, the significance of religion for appreciating certain facets of psychology, and the fraudulence of Freudianism, and the centrality of evolution — though broadly understood to include cultural changes — for understanding the trajectory of consciousness.

What really struck me when looking back on those discussions was how mainstream psychology has marginalized consciousness as a serious research topic, though my talk with Jaynes was about three decades ago and much has changed since then. Nevertheless, even today not a few researchers shy away from consciousness since they have a difficult time formulating exactly what they mean by it. In any case, related to not taking consciousness seriously is how many sweep the social and historical aspects of psyche under the rug. And yet, beginning in the 1960s psychologists fell in love with "cognitive" — anything with "cognitive" in front of it was suddenly an important subject worthy of investigation. But "cognitive" doesn't explain anything. It's a bit vague, sort of in the same way that many use "consciousness" without defining it.

KUIJSTEN: After his lectures, Julian Jaynes was often asked about the relevance of his theory to mental health. He felt that his theory provides a historical context for people who hear voices, which often allows them to better make sense of and cope with their experience. The recognition of the historical role of hearing voices via Jaynes's bicameral mind theory helped to inspire the Hearing Voices Movement, which seeks to remove the stigma from hearing voices and reframe them as part of the normal spectrum of human experience.

Jaynes also suggests that his theory has implications for modern cognitive behavioral therapy — the idea that redirecting negative or self-destructive thoughts to more positive ones is essentially altering one's inner dialogue. Most mental illness is therefore in some sense either a consequence of consciousness — for example, an inner dialogue gone astray in the case of depression and anxiety — or, in the case of intrusive voices, a vestige of the bicameral mind. You transitioned from teaching anthropology to doing mental health counseling, and I understand you are working on a book that applies certain aspects of Jaynes's theory to psychotherapy?

McVEIGH: Yes, that's right. So this question relates to the practical applications of a Jaynesian perspective. Let me explain. In psychotherapy there's much attention given to what are called common factors that explain why treatment works across a range of different therapeutic interventions. I argue that understanding consciousness positions us better to understand how these common factors — I call them active ingredients of the mind — enable the brain to heal itself. Many mental health disorders occur when there's too much consciousness, as when consciousness spirals out of control, resulting in runaway rumination. Or if there's not enough consciousness, as when we lose perspective and can't step back and see matters objectively. I expand upon Jaynes's definition of consciousness by exploring the "features of conscious interiority" — or FOCI — and how each feature, or we might say function, can help or hinder the healing properties of the psyche. I've identified thirteen FOCI. There are many examples I could give of how FOCI can be harnessed for mental health purposes.

For instance, consider the use of mental imagery in therapy. This is grounded in mind space, a key feature of consciousness. It offers us an introspectable stage on which a patient can manipulate mental images, offering them the opportunity to "see" their problems from different perspectives. Another example concerns the feature of self-narratization. This permits patients to view their circumstances with more self-objectivity by placing themselves on an imaginary timeline. They may be able to rewrite a painful and traumatic past or envision a better future. I also explore the benefits of temporarily suspending FOCI, or what is called hypnosis, and self-regulating features of consciousness as in meditation. My approach is inspired by positive psychology — that our own introspectiveness undergirds the effectiveness of psychotherapeutic techniques and that therapeutically-directed consciousness can repair the mind.

KUIJSTEN: In a lecture titled "Imagination and the Dance of the Self," Julian Jaynes touched on the nature of the self as it relates to consciousness. You've also discussed the nature of the self in your book *The Propertied Self*. Can you comment on that?

McVEIGH: Yes. So this is a project that attempts to show how changes in mentality have relevance for understanding the psychology of economic history and politics. I'm interested in how the mass affluence of modern times has been driven by and shapes psychological processes. We usually separate psyche out from historical or economic forces, but I think they are really inextricable. I show how an interiorized consciousness legitimizes and promotes the "propertied self." Inspired by a Jaynesian perspective, this describes how we have increasingly privileged our inner life of feelings, thoughts, opinions — rather than externally-imposed social attributes such as economic class or religious affiliation — to justify the individual-centered acquisition of possessions. This leads to hyper-consumerism and the so-called hedonistic treadmill. In other words, the more we consume, the larger our "space" for consumerist desires becomes, and the more we want. The steady accumulation of wealth, especially since the industrial revolution, and its impact on mentality, have implications for political freedoms, understandings of self, identity politics, and public policy.

KUIJSTEN: Over the years Jaynes's theory has influenced a number of different novelists, artists, and musicians. Recently, Jaynes's theory was incorporated into the storyline of the first season of the HBO series *Westworld*. There's a scene in the third episode where Dr. Ford (played by Anthony Hopkins) and Bernard Lowe (played by Jeffery Wright) discuss the bicameral mind. You've written a short book on *Westworld* and its incorporation of Jaynes's theory — can you comment on that?

McVEIGH: Yes. Like all good science fiction, *Westworld* is really a commentary on how technology alters human nature and where we are going as a species. In the series, Dr. Ford is actually skeptical that bicameral mentality explains the history of human psychology. However, he believes that it can be used as a blueprint for building artificial consciousness. This was the intention of Arnold Weber, also played by Jeffrey Wright, who wanted the androids to "hear" their own programming as an inner monologue. Arnold's hope was that eventually his voice would become their consciousness. This attempt to build self-aware androids was abandoned. Dr. Ford, however, pointed out that vestiges of voice commands remain buried in the software. This allows the hosts to access Arnold's code which functions as an authoritative, directing voice.

Besides science fiction, *Westworld* can also be seen as a meditation on the philosophy of mind. For example, what is consciousness? Can it be reduced to computational algorithms, as the series suggests? The central idea here is artificial intelligence. But notice how the debate changes — or at least it does for me — when we use terms such as artificial experience or artificial emotions. It seems that many assume subjectively-felt, introspective consciousness is in essence a matter of rationality, logic, and intellectual power, all things within the orbit of AI. But rationality, logic, and intelligence do not define consciousness. Somehow the notion that machines will eventually be able to feel a very human experience seems less persuasive. In any case, that's my view.

KUIJSTEN: Is there anything else you'd like to say that we haven't covered?

McVEIGH: Well, I'd like to comment on what direction Jaynesian-inspired research should go. Often I get the impression that some assume that Jaynes offered a set of ideas that have settled a number of questions. His project is completed, concluded, finalized. But a perusal through his work shows that, as convincing as his arguments were, he merely offered us a blueprint or roadmap to follow up with more detailed research. In the same way that the theories of Darwin or Einstein offered us a set of general directions to investigate the natural world, Jaynes has given us an agenda for tackling a key problem of psychology — the origins and implications of conscious interiority. What is needed are focused, detailed investigations that propose hypotheses.

Science makes progress by relying on two, mutually supporting methods. The first is coming up with a grand hypothesis, often based on a speculative hunch. The second method is when carefully-designed experiments test some hypothesis or intensive, detailed, and long-term scholarship is pursued to provide empirical support to a theory. Ideally the first and second methods should work together. Darwin's and Einstein's theories were originally just that, abstract propositions. It wasn't until others put their ideas to the test that they really impacted the scientific community in a meaningful, practical way.

I would also like to say that Jaynes should be seen as offering us not just a set of interesting ideas but rather giving us an entirely new way of thinking. He has ushered in a paradigm shift. I state this because his theorizing has consequences for a long list of fields, such as the arts, developmental psychology, evolutionary theory, history, literature, linguistics, neuroscience, philosophy, psychotherapy, and religious studies. The three volumes that you yourself have put together contain writings not just by Jaynes himself, but also by researchers who have taken up the challenge of exploring and expanding upon Jaynesian psychology. Every time I flip through the pages of his *The Origin of Consciousness in the Breakdown of the Bicameral Mind* I learn something new and am inspired to look at a topic from a new angle. We are just beginning to recognize the importance of his contributions. Jaynes offers us a beginning, not a conclusion.

Acknowledgments

This project would not have been possible without the efforts and contributions of many others. I would like to extend my sincere thanks to Brendan Leahy for his efforts in conducting many of the interviews in the book, and for making those interviews available. I would also like to thank all of the interviewees for taking the time to share their important research, powerful insights, and enthusiasm for the subject matter. I would also like to acknowledge their individual efforts to explore, build upon, and promote Julian Jaynes's theory — each of the interviewees has contributed to our understanding of Jaynes's theory in unique and important ways. I would like to thank Philip Ardery, Jr., Boban Dedović, Christian Y. Dupont, John F. Kihlstrom, Brian J. McVeigh, Bruce W. Ollstein, Martin E.P. Seligman, and Laurence I. Sugarman for their helpful comments and suggestions on the introduction. Many thanks also to Philip Ardery, Jr., Helena Kuijsten, Brian J. McVeigh, and Patricia Eyzaguirre Petit for carefully reviewing the entire book. Finally, I would like to extend a heartfelt thanks to the members and donors of the Julian Jaynes Society, whose ongoing support helped to make this book possible.